Economic Analysis of Social Common Capital

Social common capital provides members of society with those services and institutional arrangements that are crucial in maintaining human and cultural life. The term *social common capital* comprises three categories: natural capital, social infrastructure, and institutional capital. Natural capital consists of all the natural environment and natural resources, including the earth's atmosphere. Social infrastructure consists of roads, bridges, public transportation systems, electricity, and other public utilities. Institutional capital includes hospitals, educational institutions, judicial and police systems, public administrative services, financial and monetary institutions, and cultural capital. This book attempts to modify and extend the theoretical premises of orthodox economic theory to make them broad enough to analyze the economic implications of social common capital. It further aims to find the institutional arrangements and policy measures that will bring about the optimal state of affairs in which the natural and institutional components are blended together harmoniously to realize the sustainable state suggested by John Stuart Mill.

Hirofumi Uzawa is Director of the Research Center of Social Common Capital at Doshisha University and Emeritus Professor of Economics at the University of Tokyo. He is a Fellow and former President of the Econometric Society and a former President of the Japan Association for Economics and Econometrics. He is a Member of the American Academy of Arts and Sciences, a Foreign Associate of the U.S. National Academy of Sciences, a Foreign Honorary Member of the American Economic Association, and a Member of the Japan Academy.

Professor Uzawa has also served for more than thirty years as Senior Advisor in the Research Institute of Capital Formation at the Development Bank of Japan.

Professor Uzawa has been one of the leading economic theorists for the past four decades. In recent decades, he has become particularly well known for applied research in the areas of the economics of pollution, environmental disruption, and global warming, the economics of education and medical care, and the theory of social common capital.

Professor Uzawa is the author of more than twenty books, including *Economic Theory and Global Warming* (Cambridge University Press, 2003). He is the recipient of the Matsunaga Prize (1969), the Yoshino Prize (1970), and the Mainichi Prize (1974). The government of Japan designated him a Person of Cultural Merit in 1983, and the Emperor of Japan conferred the Order of Culture upon him in 1997.

Economic Analysis of Social Common Capital

HIROFUMI UZAWA

CAMBRIDGE
UNIVERSITY PRESS

CAMBRIDGE UNIVERSITY PRESS
Cambridge, New York, Melbourne, Madrid, Cape Town, Singapore, São Paulo

Cambridge University Press
40 West 20th Street, New York, NY 10011-4211, USA

www.cambridge.org
Information on this title: www.cambridge.org/9780521847889

First published 2005

Printed in the United States of America

A catalog record for this publication is available from the British Library.

Library of Congress Cataloging in Publication Data

Uzawa, Hirofumi, 1928–

Economic analysis of social common capital / Hirofumi Uzawa.

p. cm.

Includes bibliographical references and index.

ISBN 0-521-84788-5 (hardcover : alk. paper)

1. Natural resources, Communal. 2. Sustainable development.
3. Environmental policy. I. Title.

HD1286.U95 2005
333.2 – dc22 2004022137

ISBN-13 978-0-521-84788-9 hardback
ISBN-10 0-521-84788-5 hardback

Contents

Figures

Preface

Social common capital provides members of a society with those services and institutional arrangements that are crucial in maintaining human and cultural life. It is generally classified in three categories: natural capital, social infrastructure, and institutional capital. These categories are neither exhaustive nor exclusive; they merely illustrate the nature of functions performed by social common capital and the social perspectives associated with them.

Natural capital consists of the natural environment and natural resources such as forests, rivers, lakes, wetlands, coastal seas, oceans, water, soil, and, above all, the earth's atmosphere. They all share the common feature of being regenerative, subject to intricate and subtle forces of the ecological and biological mechanisms. They provide all living organisms, particularly human beings, with the environment to sustain their lives and to regenerate themselves.

Social infrastructure is another important component of social common capital. It consists of roads, bridges, public transportation systems, water, electricity, other public utilities, and communication and postal services, among others. Social common capital also includes institutional capital such as hospitals and medical institutions, educational institutions, judicial and police systems, public administrative services, financial and monetary institutions, cultural capital, and others. They all provide members of a society with services that are crucial in maintaining human and cultural life, without being unduly influenced by the vicissitudes of life.

Social common capital in principle is not appropriated to individual members of the society but rather is held as common property resources to be managed by the commons in question, without, however, precluding private ownership arrangements. Nor is it to be controlled bureaucratically by the state. Thus, a problem of crucial importance in the theory of social common capital is to devise the institutional arrangements that result in the management of social common capital that is optimum from the social point of view. In this book, we introduce an analytical framework in which economic implications of social common capital are fully examined and we explore the conditions under which the intertemporal allocation of scarce resources, including both social common capital and private capital, is dynamically optimum or sustainable from the social point of view.

The dynamic models of social common capital introduced in this book may be regarded as the general equilibrium versions of those formulated in Uzawa (1974a,b,c; 1975; 1982; 1992b), in which, however, the phenomenon of externalities was not explicitly discussed. In the general model of social common capital introduced in this book, the phenomenon of externalities, both static and dynamic, is explicitly incorporated in the construct of the model and their implications for the processes of resource allocation, including both social common capital and privately managed scarce resources, are fully explored. The dynamically optimum or sustainable allocation of scarce resources occurs when the imputed prices associated with the accumulation and use of social common capital are used as signals in the allocative processes. Privately owned scarce resources and goods and services produced by private economic units are allocated through the mechanism of market institutions.

The present study, in conjunction with *Economic Theory and Global Warming*, recently published by Cambridge University Press, is an offshoot of my attempt to modify and extend the theoretical premises of orthodox economic theory to make them broad enough to analyze the economic implications of social common capital, and to find the institutional arrangements and policy measures that will bring about the optimal state of affairs in which the natural and institutional components are blended together harmoniously to realize the sustainable state in the sense introduced by John Stuart Mill in his classic *Principles of Political Economy* (1848), particularly in the chapter entitled "On Stationary States."

In this book and *Economic Theory and Global Warming*, I have endeavored to construct a theoretical framework that enables us to examine in detail the institutional and policy arrangements under which the utopian stationary state envisioned by John Stuart Mill may be realized. However, the problems posited here have turned out to be much more difficult than I originally anticipated. This book, therefore, presents the results of my endeavor, albeit in a very preliminary stage, in a form that may be accessible to colleagues and students interested in the economics of social common capital as well as in economic theory in general. Each chapter is presented in such a manner, occasionally at the risk of repetition, that it may be read without prior knowledge of other chapters. I wish that young economists with competent analytical skills and a deep concern for the welfare of future generations will follow the lead suggested and develop a comprehensive theory of social common capital.

I would like to acknowledge with gratitude the valuable comments and suggestions my colleagues have given me while I have been engaged in the study and research for this book. I particularly thank Kenneth J. Arrow, Kazumi Asako, Partha Dasgupta, Yuko Hosoda, Dale W. Jorgenson, Karl-Göran Mäler, Robert M. Solow, Keisuke Takegahara, David Throsby, and Katsuhisa Uchiyama. I would also like to thank the readers of the original manuscript, who made thoughtful and detailed comments and suggestions.

Generous support, financial or otherwise, from the Japanese Ministry of Education and Science, the Keiyu Medical Foundation, the Research Center of Social Common Capital at Doshisha University, the Development Bank of Japan, and the Beijer International Institute of Ecological Economics in the Royal Swedish Academy of Sciences is greatly appreciated.

Last, but not least, I would like to acknowledge with gratitude the patience and encouragement that my wife, Hiroko, and other members of my family have extended to me while I have been engaged in the study and research of economic theory in general and social common capital in particular during the past 40-some years.

Introduction
Social Common Capital

RERUM NOVARUM INVERTED: THE ABUSES OF SOCIALISM AND THE ILLUSIONS OF CAPITALISM

In his historic 1891 encyclical *Rerum Novarum*, Pope Leo XIII identified the most pressing problems of the times as "the abuses of capitalism and the illusions of socialism" (Leo XIII 1891). He called the attention of the world on "the misery and wretchedness pressing so unjustly on the majority of the working class" and condemned the abuses of liberal capitalism, particularly the greed of the capitalist class. At the same time, he vigorously criticized the illusions of socialism, primarily on the ground that private property is a natural right indispensable for the pursuit of individual freedom. Exactly 100 years after *Rerum Novarum*, the *New Rerum Novarum* was issued by Pope John Paul II on May 15, 1991, identifying the problems that plague the world today as "the abuses of socialism and the illusions of capitalism" (John Paul II 1991 and Uzawa 1991a, 1992c).

Contrary to the classic Marxist scenario of the transition of capitalism to socialism, the world is now faced with an entirely different problem of how to transform a socialist economy to a capitalist economy smoothly. For such a transformation to result in a stable, well-balanced society, however, we must be explicitly aware of the shortcomings of the decentralized market system as well as the deficiencies of the centralized planned economy.

The centralized planned economy has been plagued by the enormous power that has been exclusively possessed by the state and has been arbitrarily exercised. The degree of freedom bestowed upon the average citizen has been held at the minimum, whereas human dignity and professional ethics have not been properly respected. The experiences of socialist countries during the last several decades have clearly shown that the economic plans, both centralized and decentralized, that have been conceived of by the government bureaucracy, have been inevitably found untenable either because of technical deficiencies or in terms of incentive incompatibility. The living standard of the average person has fallen far short of the expectations, and the dreams and aspirations of the majority of the people have been left unfulfilled.

On the other hand, the decentralized market economy has suffered from the perpetual tendency toward an unequal income distribution, unless significant remedial measures are taken, and from the volatile fluctuations in price and demand conditions, under which productive ethics have been found extremely difficult to sustain. Profit motives often outrun moral, social, and natural constraints, whereas speculative motives tend to dominate productive ethics, even when proper regulatory measures are administered.

We must now search for an economic system in which stable, harmonious processes of economic development may be realized with the maximum degree of individual freedom and with due respect to human dignity and professional ethics, as eloquently prophesied by John Stuart Mill in his classic *Principles of Political Economy* in a chapter entitled "On Stationary States" (Mill 1848). The stationary state, as envisioned by Mill, is interpreted as the state of the economy in which all macroeconomic variables, such as gross domestic product, national income, consumption, investments, prices of all goods and services, wages, and real rates of interest, all remain stationary, whereas, within the society, individuals are actively engaged in economic, social, and cultural activities, new scientific discoveries are incessantly made, and new products are continuously introduced still with the natural environment being preserved at the sustainable state. [Regarding Mill's stationarity state, one may be referred to an excellent discussion by Daly (1977, 1999).]

We may term such an economic system as institutionalism, if we adopt the concept originally introduced by Thorstein Veblen in his classic *The Theory of Leisure Class*, (Veblen 1899) or *The Theory of Business Enterprise* (Veblen 1904). It has been recently reactivated as a theory of institutions by Williamson (1985) and others, in which institutions are defined by the rules of games that specify the incentives and mechanisms faced by the members of the society engaged in social activities. We would like to emphasize that it is not defined in terms of a certain unified principle, but rather the structural characteristics of an institutionalist economy, as symbolized by the network of various components of social common capital, are determined by the interplay of moral, social, cultural, and natural conditions inherent in the society, and they change as the processes of economic development evolve and social consciousness transforms itself correspondingly. Institutionalism explicitly denies the Marxist doctrine that the social relations of production and labor determine the basic tenure of moral, social, and cultural conditions of the society in concern. Adam Smith emphasized several times in his *Wealth of Nations* (Smith 1776) that the design of an economic system conceived of purely in terms of logical consistency inevitably contradicts the diverse, basic nature of human beings, and instead he chose to advocate the merits of a liberal economic system evolved through the democratic processes of social and political development. It is in this Smithian sense that we would like to address the problems of the economic and social implications of social common capital, as well as the analysis of institutional arrangements and policy measures that ensure the processes of consumption and accumulation of both social common capital and private capital that are either dynamically optimum or sustainable in terms of a certain well-defined, socially acceptable sense.

SOCIAL COMMON CAPITAL

Social common capital constitutes a vital element of any society in which we live. It is generally classified into three categories: natural capital, social infrastructure, and institutional capital. These categories are neither exhaustive nor exclusive, but they merely illustrate the nature of functions performed by social common capital and the social perspectives associated with them.

Natural capital consists of the natural environment and natural resources such as forests, rivers, lakes, wetlands, coastal seas, oceans, water, soil, and the earth's atmosphere. They all share the common feature of being regenerative, subject to intricate and subtle forces of the ecological and biological mechanisms. They provide all living organisms, particularly human beings, with the environment to sustain their lives and to regenerate themselves. However, the rapid processes of economic development and population growth in the past several decades, with the accompanying vast changes in social and natural conditions, have altered the delicate ecological balance of natural capital to such a significant extent that their effectiveness has been lost in many parts of the world.

The sustainable management of natural capital may be made possible when the institutional arrangements of the commons are introduced, as indicated by the historical and traditional experiences of the commons, with a particular reference to the fisheries and forestry commons, as discussed in detail by McCay and Acheson (1987) and Berkes (1989).

However, processes of industrialization themselves, together with the ensuing changes in cultural, social, and political conditions, have made the survival of the commons extremely difficult. Only a handful of the commons now remain as viable social institutions in which economic activities are effectively conducted with natural capital prudently sustained.

Social infrastructure is another important component of social common capital. It consists of roads; bridges; public mass transportation systems; water, electricity, and other public utilities; communication and postal services; and sewage, among others. Social common capital also includes institutional capital such as hospitals and medical institutions, educational institutions, judicial and police systems, public administrative services, financial and monetary institutions, and so on.

Cultural capital may also be regarded as an important component of social common capital, as extensively examined in particular by Throsby (2001). Cultural capital comprises those capital assets in society that yield goods and services of cultural value, including artworks, historic buildings, and so on, together with intangible assets such as language, traditions, and others.

A word of caution may be necessary regarding the concept of social capital, originally introduced by James Coleman, Robert Putnam, and others. The standard reference is Putnam (2000), and an extensive discussion is reported in Dasgupta and Serageldin (2000). Social capital refers to intangible social networks and relationships of trust that exist in communities. It means the connectivity of the social network each individual is embedded in, and facilitates the exchange of information and encourages reciprocal altruism. It is an interesting and fascinating concept, molded in the traditional framework of sociology and political science, though in good contrast with that of social common capital as envisioned in this book. [See also Arrow (2000) and Solow (2000).]

Social common capital is held by the society as common property resources to be managed by social institutions of various kinds that are entrusted on a fiduciary basis to maintain social common capital in good order and to distribute the services derived from it equitably. Social common capital is in principle not appropriated to individual members of the society, without, however, precluding the private ownership arrangements. Nor is it to be controlled bureaucratically by the state. Thus, a problem of crucial importance in the theory of social common capital is how to devise the institutional arrangements that result in the management of social common capital that is optimum from the social point of view.

DYNAMIC OPTIMALITY AND SUSTAINABILITY

The problem of dynamic optimality was originally discussed by Ramsey (1928) and Hotelling (1931). It was revived as the theory of optimum economic growth in the 1960s, particularly by Koopmans (1965), Cass (1965), and others, and mathematical techniques of Pontryagin's maximum method have been effectively applied, as summarily described in Uzawa (2003, Chapter 5) and again in Chapter 3 of this book.

The concept of sustainability is formally defined as the efficient pattern of intertemporal allocation of private capital and social common capital for which the imputed price of social common capital is assumed to remain at a stationary level. As the imputed price of social common capital expresses the subjective value of social common capital each generation inherits from the past, the concept of sustainabililty thus defined may be regarded as expressing in formal terms the concept of the stationary state as envisioned by John Stuart Mill. It is closely linked to the concept introduced by Pezzey (1992), in which the utility remains constant over time. On the other hand, it is not apparent to see the link with Page's concept of sustainability, which emphasizes maintaining life opportunity from generation to generation (Page 1997).

In reference to the context of environmental economics, Mäler (1974) and Dasgupta and Heal (1974) formulated the intertemporal general equilibrium model in which economic implications of the environment could be fully explored, and then developed a detailed analysis of the pattern of intertemporal allocations of scarce resources, including the accumulation and depletion of the environment, that are dynamically optimum from the social point of view. Since then, a large number of contributions have been made to the optimum theory of economic growth and environmental quality. The dynamic analysis of social common capital introduced in this book is largely within the framework of the optimum theory of environmental quality as introduced by Mäler, Dasgupta, Heal, and others.

EXTERNALITIES

One of the intricate problems inherent in social common capital concerns the phenomenon of externalities. Since the classic treatment of Pigou (1925) and Samuelson (1954), economists were always puzzled by the phenomenon of externalities, but it was put aside as peripheral and not worthy of serious consideration. Concern with environmental issues, however, has changed this habit of economic thinking, and a large number of contributions have appeared in which the issue of externalities occupies a central place from both theoretical and empirical points of view. The analytical treatment of externalities to be formulated in this book is adopted from that introduced in Uzawa (1974a,b,c; 1975; 1982; 1992a), in which two kinds of externalities, static on the one hand and dynamic on the other, are recognized with respect to the services derived from social common capital. Static externalities occur when the levels of marginal products or utilities of individual economic units are affected by the aggregate amount of services of social common capital used by all members of the society, assuming that the stock of social common capital is kept at a constant level. Dynamic externalities, on the other hand, are observed when the conditions of production and consumption for each individual economic unit change over time owing to the changes in the stock of social common capital, either accumulation or depreciation, that occur today. The analysis of dynamic optimality developed in Uzawa (1974a), however, was confined to a restrictive type of social common capital, and due attention was not paid to those categories of social common capital, such as natural capital, whose regenerative capability has been damaged to a significant extent largely because of the rapid processes of industrialization. In the formulation of a general dynamic model of social common capital recently developed in Uzawa (1998), an attempt was made to incorporate some of the more salient aspects of the disruption of natural capital and to elucidate their implications for the economic welfare of the society in concern. The introduction of the general models of social common capital in this book is preceded by the simple analysis of a specific type of social common capital – the natural environment.

The natural environment, or rather natural capital, has been subject to an extensive examination in the literature, particularly with respect to the fisheries and forestry commons. The analysis of the fisheries commons was initiated by Gordon (1954) and Scott (1955), and was later extended to the general treatment within the framework of modern capital theory by Schaefer (1957), Crutchfield and Zellner (1962), Clark and Munro (1975), and Tahvonen (1991), among others. The simple dynamic model of the natural environment introduced in Chapter 1 that has the case of the fisheries commons primarily in mind belongs to the lineage of their approach. It is an extension of the analysis developed by Uzawa (1992b), in which it is used to examine critically the theory of the tragedy of the commons, as advanced by Hardin (1968).

The model of the natural environment developed in Uzawa (1992b) may be applicable to the dynamics of the forestry commons as well. As with the fisheries commons, the dynamics of the forestry commons has been extensively analyzed in the literature. Indeed, it was made a central issue in economic theory by Wicksell (1901), who developed the core of modern capital theory with the analysis of forests as the prototype. The most recent contribution to forestry economics was made by Johansson and Löfgren (1985), and the basic premises of the dynamic model of natural capital introduced in this book may also be regarded as an application and extension of these contributions.

In this book, we address ourselves to formulating in analytical models some of the empirical findings concerning the economic, technological, and ecological structure of the commons, and then to formulating in terms of the theory of social common capital some of the more critical problems concerning the dilemma between economic development and environmental degradation.

The theory of social common capital provides us with the theoretical framework within which the role of institutional arrangements concerning social, cultural, and natural environments in the processes of resource allocation and income distribution may be effectively analyzed. Social common capital is generally composed of those scarce resources that are in principle neither privately appropriated nor subject to market transactions. Social common capital or the services derived from it play a crucial and indispensable role for each member of the society in concern to conduct at least the minimum level of human and dignified life. The management of social common capital thus is entrusted on a fiduciary basis to autonomous social institutions, to provide the environmental framework within which all human activities are conducted and the allocative mechanism through which market institutions work. The analysis of social common capital, as previously introduced by Uzawa (1974a, 1989, 1991a, b) and recently developed in Uzawa (1998), may be applied to discuss some of the difficulties arising out of the tragedy-of-the-commons phenomenon. Particularly, the institutional arrangements whereby the dynamically optimum or sustainable use of resources in the commons may ensue are examined in terms of the concept of imputed price of social common capital.

The society generally allocates a significant portion of scarce resources for the construction and maintenance of social common capital, particularly social infrastructure, and one of the central issues in the dynamic theory of social common capital is to find the criteria by which scarce resources are allocated between investment in social common capital on the one hand and production of goods and services that are transacted on the market on the other.

In this book, we formulate an analytical framework in which economic implications of social common capital of various kinds are examined and we explore the conditions under which the intertemporal allocation of social common capital and privately owned scarce resources is either dynamically optimum or sustainable from the social point of view. The dynamic models introduced in this book may be regarded as the general equilibrium versions of those formulated in Uzawa (1992b), in which the phenomenon of externalities is not explicitly discussed. In the dynamic models of social common capital introduced in this book, the phenomenon of externalities, both static and dynamic, is incorporated in the construct of the model, and its implications for the processes of resource allocation, including both social common capital and privately managed scarce resources, are fully explored. The dynamically optimum or sustainable allocation of scarce resources occurs when the imputed prices associated with the accumulation and use of social common capital are used as signals in the allocative processes. Privately owned scarce resources and goods and services produced by private economic units are allocated through the mechanism of market institutions.

In the dynamic analysis concerning the accumulation of social infrastructure, referred to above, the technological conditions are assumed to remain largely constant, independent of the accumulation of the stock of social infrastructure. Technological progress induced by the availability of social infrastructure and the accompanying increase in investment activities in the stock of privately owned scarce resources may be regarded as the central issue in the theory of social infrastructure, particularly within the context of developing nations, as examined in detail by Hirschman (1958) in terms of the concept of social overhead capital. Social overhead capital as defined by Hirschman comprises those basic services without which primary, secondary, and tertiary productive activities cannot function. In its wider sense, social overhead capital includes all public services, including law and order, education, public health, transportation, communications, and power and water supplies, as well as agricultural overhead capital such as irrigation and drainage systems. Thus the concept of social common capital as introduced in this book may be regarded as an extension of the concept of social overhead capital, in which natural resources are included in addition to social infrastructure and institutional and cultural capital.

The theory of social common capital as developed in this book may also be regarded as an extension of the two-sector models of capital accumulation originally introduced by Uzawa (1962, 1963, 1964). Similarly, the problems of designing an institutional framework in which the optimum allocation of both social common capital and privately owned scarce resources may be realized are crucial in any attempt to practically implement the theory of social common capital to be developed in this book.

When we include all components of social common capital in a particular nation, the social institutions entrusted on a fiduciary basis with their management constitute the public sector in the broadest sense of the word. The aggregate expenditures incurred by all these social institutions are nothing but the governmental expenditures, either on the current account or on the capital account. Thus, the problem we address may be interpreted as that of devising an institutional framework in which the ensuing governmental activities are dynamically optimum or sustainable from the social point of view.

SUMMARY OF THE CONTENTS

In Chapter 1, dynamic models are constructed to analyze the interrelationships between the natural environment and economic development, with explicit reference to the phenomenon of externalities, both static and dynamic. The institutional arrangements and behavioral criteria under which the processes of dynamically optimum economic development necessarily ensue are characterized.

Analysis of the static and dynamic implications of the externalities is carried out with reference to three specific types of natural resources – fisheries, forestry, and agriculture – in which the modern theory of optimum economic growth and the theory of social common capital may be effectively utilized.

In Chapter 2, the prototype model of social common capital is introduced with a particular type of social common capital – social infrastructure, such as highways, ports, and public transportation systems – in mind. We consider the general circumstances under which factors of production that are necessary for the professional provision of services of social common capital are either privately owned or are managed as if privately owned. Services of social common capital are subject to the phenomenon of congestion, resulting in the divergence between private and social costs. Therefore, to obtain efficient and equitable allocation of scarce resources, it becomes necessary to levy social common capital taxes on the use of services of social common capital. The prices charged for the use of services of social common capital exceed, by the tax rates, the prices paid for the provision of services of social common capital to social institutions in charge of social common capital. One of the crucial problems in the prototype model of social common capital introduced in Chapter 2 is to examine how the optimum tax rates for the services of various components of social common capital are determined. In describing the behavior of social institutions in charge of social common capital, we assume that the levels of services of social common capital provided by these institutions are optimum and the use of factors of production by them are efficient. When we use the term profit maximization, it is used in the sense that the efficient and optimum pattern of resource allocation in the provision of services of social common capital is sought strictly in accordance with professional disciplines and ethics.

In Chapter 3, we examine the problems of social common capital primarily from the viewpoint of the intergenerational distribution of utility. Our analysis is based on the concept of sustainability introduced in Uzawa (1991b, 2003), and we examine the conditions under which processes of the accumulation of social common capital over time are sustainable. The conceptual framework of the economic analysis of social common capital developed in Chapter 2 is extended to deal with the problems of the irreversibility of processes of the accumulation of social common capital owing to the Penrose effect.

In Chapter 4, we introduce a commons model of social common capital in which the interplay of several commons is examined in detail and the institutional framework whereby the sustainable pattern of resource allocation over time may be realized. The sustainable time-path of consumption and investment is characterized by the stationarity of the imputed prices associated with the given intertemporal preference ordering, whereas the efficiency of resource allocation in the short run is preserved at each time. When the natural environment is regarded as social common capital, there are two crucial properties that have to be explicitly incorporated in any dynamic model. The first property concerns the externalities, both static and dynamic, with respect to the use of the natural environment as a factor of production. The second property is related to the role of the natural environment as an important component of the living environment, significantly affecting the quality of human life.

In Chapter 5, we formulate a model of social common capital in which the energy use and recycling of residual waste are explicitly taken into consideration and the optimum arrangements concerning the pricing of energy and recycling of residual wastes are examined within the framework of the prototype model of social common capital introduced in Chapter 2. We consider a particular type of social institution that specializes in reprocessing the disposed residual wastes and converting them to raw materials to be used as inputs for the production processes of energy-producing firms.

Services of social common capital are subject to the phenomenon of congestion, resulting in the divergence between private and social costs. To obtain efficient allocation of scarce resources, it becomes necessary to levy taxes on the disposal of residual wastes and to pay subsidy payments for the reprocessing of disposed residual wastes. Subsidy payments are made to the social institutions specialized in the recycling of disposed residual wastes based on the imputed price of the disposed residual wastes, whereas members of the society are charged taxes for the disposal of residual wastes at exactly the same rate as the subsidy payments made to social institutions in charge of the recycling of residual wastes. One of the crucial problems is to see how the optimum tax and subsidy rates are determined for the recycling model of residual wastes, as is the case with the various components of social common capital discussed in other chapters of this book.

Agriculture concerns not only economic, industrial aspects, but also virtually every aspect of human life – cultural, social, and natural. It provides us with food and the raw materials such as wood, cotton, silk, and others that are indispensable to sustain our existence. It also has sustained, with few exceptions, the natural environment such as forests, lakes, wetlands, soil, subterranean water, and the atmosphere. In Chapter 6, we formulate an agrarian model of social common capital that captures some of the more salient aspects of the Sanrizuka Agricultural Commons and we examine the conditions for the sustainable development of social common capital and privately owned scarce resources. The Sanrizuka Agricultural Commons is a symbolic model of the agricultural commons that has been devised as the prototype of the "stationary state" advanced by John Stuart Mill in his *Principles of Political Economy* (Mill 1848) to solve the difficulties facing Japanese agriculture today.

In Chapter 7, we are primarily concerned with the economic analysis of global warming within the theoretical framework, as introduced in Uzawa (1991b, 2003). We are particularly concerned with the policy arrangements of a proportional carbon tax scheme under which the tax rate is made proportional either to the level of the per capita national income of the countries where greenhouse gases are emitted or to the sum of the national incomes of all countries in the world. In the first part of Chapter 7, we consider the case in which the oceans are the only reservoir of CO_2 on the earth; whereas, in the second part, the role of the terrestrial forests is explicitly taken into consideration in moderating processes of global warming by absorbing the atmospheric accumulation of CO_2 on the one hand and in affecting the level of the welfare of people in the society by providing a decent and cultured environment on the other.

Education and medical care probably are the two most important components of social common capital and, as such, require institutional arrangements substantially different from those for the standard economic activities that are generally pursued from the viewpoint of profit maximization and are subject to transactions on the market. Education is provided to help young people develop their human abilities, both innate and acquired, as fully as possible, whereas medical care is provided for those who are not able to perform ordinary human functions because of impaired health or injuries. Both activities play a crucial role in enabling every member of the society in concern to maintain his or her human dignity and to enjoy basic human rights as fully as possible. If either education or medical care is subject to market transactions based merely on profit motives or under the bureaucratic control by state authorities, their effectiveness may be seriously impaired and the resulting distribution of real income may tend to become unfair and unequal. Thus, education and medical care may be regarded as the two most basic components of social common capital and the economics of education and medical care may be better treated within the theoretical framework of social common capital developed in this book. In Chapters 8 and 9, we examine, respectively, the role of education and medical care as social common capital within the analytical framework introduced in Chapter 2.

As in other chapters, social institutions in charge of education or medical care are characterized by the properties that all factors of production necessary for the professional provision of education or medical care are either privately owned or managed as if privately owned. However, as the social institutions in charge of social common capital, educational and medical institutions are managed strictly in accordance with professional discipline and expertise concerning education and medical care. In describing the behavior of educational and medical institutions, we assume that the levels of education and medical care provided by these social institutions are optimum and the use of factors of productions by these institutions are efficient. When we talk about the maximization of net value, the term is used in the sense that the optimum and efficient pattern of resource allocation in the provision of education and medical care is sought, strictly in accordance with professional disciplines and ethics.

The main conclusion of both chapters is that to attain sustainable patterns of resource allocation, including both privately owned scarce means of production and social common capital concerned with the provision of education or medical care, subsidy payments, at rates equal to the marginal social benefits of the services of social common capital, are made to social institutions in charge of social common capital, as is the case with the various types of social common capital discussed in other chapters.

1

Fisheries, Forestry, and Agriculture in the Theory of the Commons

1. INTRODUCTION

In the past three decades, we have observed a significant change in the nature of environmental problems and the economic, social, and cultural implications that the degradation of the natural environment has brought about. During the 1960s and early 1970s, our primary environmental concern was with the disruption of the environment and the ensuing hazard to human health caused by the rapid processes of industrialization and urbanization, both of which were taking place at an unprecedented, rapid pace in many parts of the world. The environmental damages were mainly caused by the emission of chemical substances such as sulfur and nitrogen oxides that themselves are toxic and hazardous to human health. In recent years, however, we have become increasingly aware of the extensive degradation of the global environment, as exemplified by such phenomena as global warming, the extensive depletion of tropical rain forests with the accompanying loss of biodiversity, and pollution of the oceans. Global environmental problems are primarily caused either by the imprudent use and excess depletion of natural resources or by the emission of chemical agents, such as carbon dioxide in the case of global warming, that by themselves are neither harmful to human health nor hazardous to the natural environment but on a global scale, contribute to atmospheric instability and global disturbances.

As for the industrial pollution and similar environmental problems that were rampant and widespread in the 1960s, the causal relationships were fairly easy to recognize, from both a social and scientific point of view, and the remedial measures were not too difficult to take, from both an economic and a political point of view. However, one has to be aware of a significant number of major environmental problems in the 1960s, such as the case of Minamata disease, that left a state of extreme social injustice for the victims.

On the other hand, global environmental problems concern the degradation and destabilization of the natural environment covering an extensive area, with a large number of people involved. They not only affect the current generation living in developing as well as developed countries but also irreversibly involve all future generations, as exemplified by the phenomena of global warming, loss of biodiversity, and pollution of the oceans.

Global environmental problems are also noted for the intricate and subtle interrelationships that exist between human activities, both economic and cultural, and the ecological and biological processes in the natural environment. Traditional economic theory has not paid sufficient attention to the damages and threats to the natural environment, particularly with respect to the stability and resilience of regenerative processes, that are exerted by industrial, urban, and other human activities. Instead, it has treated the natural environment simply as the stock of natural capital, from which various natural resources are extracted to be used as factors of production for the productive processes in the economy.

However, in the economic analysis of fisheries, forestry, and other agricultural activities, a large number of studies have explicitly recognized the implications of economic activities for the stability and resilience of the natural environment, either in the fisheries or in forestry commons, and have analyzed the patterns of resource allocation that are dynamically optimum in terms of the intertemporal preference ordering prevailing within the society, as described in detail, for example, by Johansson and Löfgren (1985) and Clark (1990).

When we examine the interaction of economic activities with the natural environment, one of the more crucial issues concerns the organizational characteristics of the social institutions that manage the natural environment as well as their behavioral and financial criteria, which realize those patterns of the repletion and depletion of the natural environment and the levels of economic activities that are dynamically optimum from the social point of view. The dynamically optimum time-paths generally converge to the long-run stationary state at which the processes of economic activities are sustained at levels that are at the optimum balance vis-á-vis the natural environment, and the problem we face now concerns the organizational and institutional arrangements for sustainable economic development.

Such an organizational framework may be provided by the institutional arrangements of the commons, as has been shown in terms of a large number of historical, traditional, and contemporary commons documented, for example, in McCay and Acheson (1987) and Berkes (1989). The commons discussed by McCay and Acheson (1987) and Berkes (1989) refer to a variety of natural resources from fisheries, forests, and grazing grounds to irrigation and subterranean water systems. The processes of industrialization, however, together with the accompanying changes in economic, social, and cultural conditions prevailing in modern society, have made these commons untenable from both an economic and a social point of view, and the survival of the majority of the traditional commons has become extremely difficult.

In this chapter, we focus our attention on examining the role of the commons in the intertemporal processes of resource allocation, with respect to both the natural environment and privately owned property resources, and on analyzing the dynamic implications of the institutional arrangements of the commons for the sustainability of economic development.

In our analysis, we are primarily concerned with the phenomenon of externalities, both static and dynamic, that is generally observed with respect to the allocative processes in the commons. Static externalities occur when, with the stock of the natural environment kept constant, the schedules of marginal products for individual members of the commons, of both private means of production and natural resources extracted from the environment, are affected by the levels of economic activities carried out by other members of the commons. On the other hand, dynamic externalities concern the effect on the future schedules of the marginal products for individual members of the commons due to the repletion or depletion of the stock of the commons caused by economic activities carried out by members of the commons today.

We are interested in analyzing those institutional arrangements regarding the use of the natural resources extracted from the stock of the commons that may result in the intertemporal allocation of scarce resources in the commons as a whole that is dynamically optimum in terms of the intertemporal criterion prevailing in the society. The analysis is carried out with respect to three kinds of commons, which represent most familiar cases of historical and traditional commons and are relatively easily examined in terms of the analytical apparatuses developed in the recent literature described in Clark (1990) and elaborated by Uzawa (1992b, 1998, 2003). They are the fisheries, forestry, and agricultural commons, and in this chapter, each case is discussed in such a manner, occasionally at the risk of repetition, that it does not necessarily presuppose the analysis of other types of the commons.

2. THE TRAGEDY OF THE COMMONS

In recent years, we have become increasingly aware of the extensive degradation of the global environment, as signalized by phenomena such as global warming, acid rain, and ocean pollution. In industrialized nations, the rapid processes of industrialization during the past four decades have been accompanied by the emission into the atmosphere of enormous quantities of radiative forcing agents, such as carbon dioxide and chlorofluorocarbons, resulting in the destabilization of atmospheric equilibrium on a global scale. On the other hand, developing nations have witnessed high population increases and rapid processes of urbanization, bringing about an extensive depletion of terrestrial forests, particularly tropical rain forests, together with extensive soil erosion, desertification, and loss of biodiversity. A large number of the reports issued by the Intergovernmental Panel on Climate Change (IPCC 1991a,b; 1992; 1996a,b; 2000; 2001a,b; 2002), for example, warn us that if the degradation of the global environment were to continue at the current pace, the changes we would experience in the next thirty to fifty years are most likely much more extensive than the climatic changes that took place during the 10,000 years from the end of the last Ice Age to the time of the Industrial Revolution.

The impact of the climatic changes due to the degradation of the global environment will be most painfully felt by developing nations, because it is the agriculture and related sectors of the economy that are most sensitively affected by changes in the climatic and ecological environments.

Environmental issues such as outlined above may be regarded as the outcomes of imprudent management of natural and environmental resources, of which basic tenure was categorized by Hardin (1968) as the tragedy of the commons. Hardin advanced the theory that all common property resources, that is, natural or biological resources that are communally owned and managed, tend to be overexploited, necessarily bringing about their complete depletion and thus "ruins to all those involved." Citing a tract written by an obscure political economist, William Lloyd (1833), Hardin's argument was presented in terms of the medieval English commons. A pasture is used as the commons by a group of herdsmen, each of whom has an open access to the pasture. It is then rational for each herdsman to put as many of his animals as possible on the pasture because his marginal gain of putting an additional animal on the pasture is always greater than his marginal costs of overgrazing that are shared by all herdsmen in the group. Hence, there is a tendency for the total number of animals put on the pasture to increase without limit, even when it is evident that additional stocking will definitely worsen the conditions of the pasture. Hardin tried to derive a lesson that, when common property resources are involved, the rational behavior of each individual implies the irrationality for the whole group.

According to Godwin and Shepard (1979), Hardin's theory of the tragedy of the commons presents us with "the dominant framework within which social scientists portray environmental and resource issues," whereas to some others, such as Smith (1984), it fits the definition of comedy rather than that of tragedy. Whichever the case may be, however, it has reminded us of the enormous costs, both social and ecological, of the processes of postwar economic development and the accompanying degradation of the natural environment, and a large number of contributions since have been devoted to the theme of the tragedy of the commons, reflecting upon the dilemma between individual freedom and social control.

The tragedy-of-the-commons dispute was elaborated by numerous contributions to the search for the institutional arrangements whereby the tragedy of the commons might effectively be avoided.

Among them, there are two influential papers, each of an entirely opposite view: Scott Gordon's study of the commons in the marine fishing industry (Gordon 1954) and Ronald Coase's classic paper (Coase 1960).

One school of thought, as forcefully brought forth by Demsetz (1967) and Furubotn and Pejovich (1972), argues that the tragedy of the commons is necessarily caused by the absence of the private-property arrangements for the ownership and use of the commons and that the dilemma can be resolved only by privatization that internalizes costs and benefits, reduces uncertainty, eliminates free-riders, and results in the prudent management of the natural environment and a rational use of its resources. It is the modern version of Lloyd's original argument for privatization. The commons, in which property arrangements are communalized, prevent the market mechanism from working properly and efficiently. Adam Smith's "individual hand" can only work when the commons are privatized. This school of thought had captured the mind of many economists and political scientists in the seventies and early eighties, when the conservative "new neoclassical economic theory" was the Zeitgeist. It fails, however, to recognize a critical distinction between open access and common property. As pointed out by Bromley (1995), open-access resources are those that may be used by anyone who wishes to do so, whereas common-property resources are defined with reference to the institutional arrangements specifying the persons who may use them and the rules concerning the way they may be used and how the costs incurred in the maintenance may be shared. The concept of property rights is deeply intertwined with the social, cultural, and historical contexts of the society involved, and it varies to a significant extent that the premises leading to the tragedy of the commons have to be critically examined in view of the experiences of the numerous historical, traditional, and contemporary commons that have functioned well, from both economic and cultural points of view. A large number of such cases have been documented, particularly in McCay and Acheson (1987) and Berkes (1989).

Contrary to the arguments presented by Demsetz and others, more reasonable and sane views were forcefully put forward by Sen (1973), Dasgupta (1982b, 1993), Cornes and Sandler (1983), Bromley (1991), Ostrom (1992), Uzawa (1992b), Ostrom, Gardner, and Walker (1994), and Barrett (1994), among others.

3. THE FISHERIES COMMONS

The dynamic analysis of the commons discussed in the previous section may be illustrated by extensive studies made for the fisheries commons, such as Gordon (1954), Scott (1955), Schaefer (1957), Crutchfield and Zellner (1962), Clark (1973, 1990), Clark and Munro (1975), Tahvonen (1991), and Tahvonen and Kuuluvainen (1993), among others. One of the focuses of these studies concerns casting the dynamic analysis of the fisheries commons in the mold of capital theory, in which the analytic techniques of the calculus of variations are effectively applied, as described in detail in Clark (1990). In this section, we develop the dynamic analysis of the fisheries commons along the lines introduced by Schaefer, Crutchfield and Zellner, Clark and Munro, and others in the literature cited above. Particular attention is paid to the implications of the communal property rights arrangements on the pattern of resource allocation in the fisheries commons that is dynamically optimum.

A Simple Dynamic Model of the Fisheries Commons

We consider a fisheries commons with a well-demarcated fisheries ground in rivers, lakes, marine coastal areas, or open seas. The rights to engage in fisheries activities in the fisheries ground are exclusively assigned to the group of fishermen in the fisheries commons as common property resources. The fishermen in the commons are engaged in fisheries activities subject to certain rules and regulations concerning the way they may fish, whereas those outside the commons are, in principle, prohibited from fishing in the fisheries ground.

To begin with, we assume that only one kind of fish exists in the fisheries ground and the stock of fish at each time is simply measured in terms of the number of fish in the fisheries ground, eliminating the complications that would arise from considering the various kinds and the age distribution of fish.

We denote by V_t the number of fish at time t in the fisheries ground. The change in the stock of fish V_t, to be denoted by $\dot{V}_t = \frac{dV_t}{dt}$, is determined depending on various ecological and biological factors. It is primarily determined by the ability of fish to breed; the availability of algae, plankton, and prey fish; and the ecological and climatic conditions around the fisheries ground. It also depends on the number of fish caught by the fishermen in the commons. The change in the stock of fish at time t, $\dot{V}_t$, may be expressed in the following manner:

$$\dot{V}_t = \gamma(X_t, V_t),$$

where X_t is the number of fish caught by the fishermen in the commons during the unit time period at t.

We assume that the regenerating function $\gamma(X, V)$ is a decreasing function of total harvest X and the stock of fish population V:

$$\gamma_X(X, V) < 0, \quad \gamma_V(X, V) < 0 \quad \text{for all } X, V > 0.$$

We also assume that there exists a critical value $\overline{X}$ such that associated with each level of total harvest X less than $\overline{X}$, two critical levels of the fish population, $V_0(X)$ and $V^0(X)$, exist such that

$$\gamma(X, V_0(X)) = \gamma(X, V^0(X)) = 0, \quad V_0(X) < V^0(X)$$
$$\gamma(X, V) > 0 \quad \text{for all } V \text{ such that } V_0(X) < V < V^0(X).$$

The change in the stock of fish is depicted in Figure 1.1, where the abscissa measures the stock of fish V and the ordinate measures the change in the stock of fish $\dot{V}$. The curve A^0A^0 corresponds to the case in which no fish are caught by the fishermen in the commons, whereas the general case is depicted by the curve AA.

The change in the stock of fish when no fish are caught, $\gamma(0, V)$, represents the regenerative ability of the fish population in its natural habitat, reflecting the ecological and biological conditions prevailing in the fisheries ground of the commons. It is significantly influenced by the climatic conditions as well as by the toxic substances discharged by industrial and urban activities in the surrounding areas of the fisheries ground. If the fish population is smaller than the lower critical level $V_0(0)$, then fish are unable to regenerate sufficiently to sustain the current population, resulting in a decrease in the stock of fish, $\dot{V} < 0$, eventually becoming extinct. On the other hand, when the fish population is larger than the upper critical level, $V^0(0)$, the fisheries ground is too small to sustain the fish population, resulting in a steady decrease in the number of fish until the upper critical level $V^0(0)$ is reached.

As the total number of fish caught X is increased, the change-in-population curve AA shifts downward, as indicated by the curves in Figure 1.1. The standard case discussed in the literature referred to

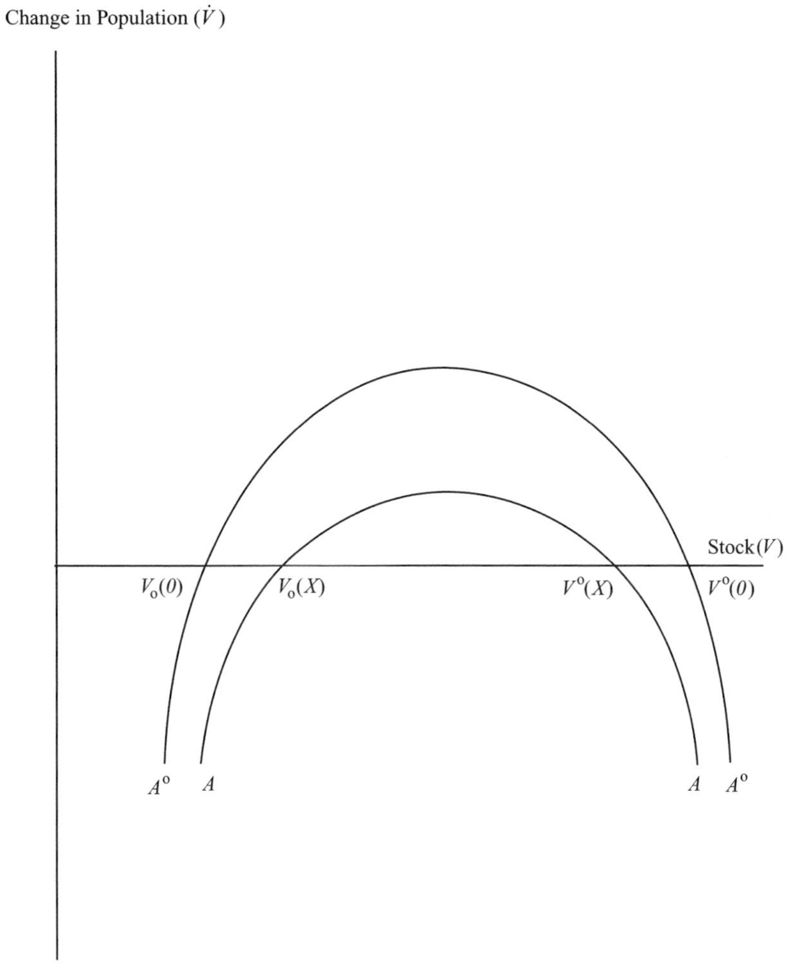

Figure 1.1. The change-in-population curves for the commons.

above specifies that

$$\gamma(X, V) = \gamma(0, V) - X. \tag{1}$$

It may be generally the case, however, that an increase in the number of the fish caught tends to affect the regenerating ability of the fish population more than proportionally to the decrease in the fish population directly caused by harvesting. In the following analysis, we assume that the change-in-population function $\gamma(X, V)$ is strictly concave with respect to (X, V). That is, it will be assumed that

(i) $\gamma_{XX}, \gamma_{VV} < 0, \quad \gamma_{XX}\,\gamma_{VV} - \gamma_{XV}^2 > 0 \quad \text{for all } (X, V) > 0.$

The following condition also will be assumed:

(ii) $\gamma_{XV} < 0 \quad \text{for all } (X, V) > 0.$

That is, the larger the stock of the fisheries ground V, the higher is the marginal decrease in the number of fish in the fisheries ground due to the marginal increase in fish harvesting γ_X.

It may be noted that the change-in-population function $\gamma(X, V)$ with the standard form (1) does not satisfy conditions (i) and (ii).

In what follows, we are interested in examining to what extent the conclusions for the standard case obtained in the literature referred to above may be generalized. We are particularly concerned with extending the basic proposition that the dynamically optimum pattern of resource allocation with respect to the fisheries commons asymptotically approaches the maximum sustainable level of the fish population. The latter concept, however, must be defined relative to the level of the total harvest being contemplated.

Of the two critical levels of the stock of the fisheries ground, $V_0(0)$ and $V^0(0)$, the more important role is played by the upper critical level $V^0(0)$ that is stable and corresponds to the maximum sustainable level of the fish population when no fish are caught. The concept of the maximum sustainable level of the fish population may be extended to the general situation in which a certain number of fish are caught by the fishermen in the commons. For each number of fish caught X, the upper critical level of the fish population $V^0(X)$ represents the maximum level of the stock of the fisheries commons that is sustainable when fish are caught by the number X in the unit time interval, provided that X does not exceed a certain critical level $\overline{X}$.

We have, by definition,

$$\gamma(X, V^0(X)) = 0,$$

which, by taking a differential, yields

$$\frac{dV^0(X)}{dX} = -\frac{\gamma_X}{\gamma_V} < 0$$

because we have assumed that $\gamma_X, \gamma_V < 0$. That is, the maximum sustainable level of the stock of the fisheries commons $V^0(X)$ is decreased as the total harvest of fish X is increased.

We denote by $X = X^0(V)$ the maximum level of total harvest that is sustainable when the stock of the fisheries commons is kept at V; that is,

$$\gamma(X^0(V), V) = 0.$$

Then, $X = X^0(V)$ is the inverse of the function $V^0(X)$ and

$$\frac{dX^0(V)}{dV} = -\frac{\gamma_V}{\gamma_X} < 0.$$

Static Externalities in the Fisheries Commons

The fisheries activities are noted for the extent to which they are subject to the phenomenon of externalities. Whereas the specifications concerning the regenerative processes of the fish population in the fisheries commons are related to what may be termed the dynamic externalities, those concerned with cost structure may be regarded as externalities of the static nature.

To examine the structure of static externalities with respect to fisheries activities conducted in a given fisheries commons, let us first look into technological conditions prevailing in the fisheries ground of the commons.

We postulate that the schedule of marginal products of labor for each individual fisherman is related to the number of fish caught by all other fishermen in the commons. Let individual fishermen in the commons be generically denoted by ν, and let the production function for each fisherman ν be expressed as

$$x^\nu = f^\nu(\ell^\nu, X, V),$$

where x^ν is the number of fish caught by fisherman ν, ℓ^ν the hours spent by fisherman ν for fisheries activities, X the total number of fish caught by all fishermen in the commons (all during the unit time period), and V the stock of fish in the fisheries ground. The total number of fish caught, X, is given by

$$X = \sum_\nu x^\nu. \qquad (2)$$

We assume that the production function $f^\nu(\ell^\nu, X, V)$ for each fisherman ν in the commons satisfies the following neoclassical conditions:

(i) $f^\nu(\ell^\nu, X, V) > 0, \quad f^\nu_{\ell^\nu}(\ell^\nu, X, V) \geqq 0, \quad f^\nu_{\ell^\nu\ell^\nu}(\ell^\nu, X, V) \leqq 0$ for all $(\ell^\nu, X, V) > 0$.

(ii) Marginal rates of substitution between the number of fish caught x^ν, the hours spent for fisheries activities ℓ^ν, the total number of fish caught X, and the stock of fish V in the fisheries ground are smooth and diminishing; that is, the production function $f^\nu(\ell^\nu, X, V)$ is concave with respect to (ℓ^ν, X, V).

(iii) An increase in the total number of fish caught X adversely affects fisheries activities in the commons in the sense that

$$f^\nu_X(\ell^\nu, X, V) < 0, \quad f^\nu_{\ell^\nu X}(\ell^\nu, X, V) < 0.$$

(iv) An increase in the stock of fish V in the fisheries ground has favorable effects upon fisheries activities in the sense that

$$f^\nu_V(\ell^\nu, X, V) > 0, \quad f^\nu_{\ell^\nu V}(\ell^\nu, X, V) > 0.$$

Perfectly Competitive Markets

We first consider the case in which the market for the fish from the commons is perfectly competitive and individual fishermen are engaged in fisheries activities without taking into account the number of fish caught by other fishermen in the commons. Then each fisherman ν decides the hours he or she works in fisheries, ℓ^ν, in such a manner that his or her net profit

$$\pi^\nu = px^\nu - w^\nu\ell^\nu$$

is maximized, where p is the market price of fish (measured in certain real terms) and w^ν is the maximum wage rate fisherman ν can earn while not working in the fisheries ground.

The maximum profit for each fisherman ν is obtained when the marginal product of his or her labor is equated to the marginal cost; that is,

$$f^\nu_{\ell^\nu}(\ell^\nu, X, V) = w^\nu, \tag{3}$$

for the given level of X. (The stock of fish in the fishing ground of the commons, V, is kept constant in the static analysis.)

The following analysis may be more easily carried out if we substitute the production function by the cost function. We solve (3) with respect to ℓ^{ν} for given x^{ν} to obtain the cost function

$$c^{\nu} = c^{\nu}(x^{\nu}, X, V) = w^{\nu}\ell^{\nu}(x^{\nu}, X, V),$$

for which the following conditions are satisfied:

(i)′ $c^{\nu}(x^{\nu}, X, V) > 0$ for all $(x^{\nu}, X, V) > 0$.
(ii)′ $c^{\nu}(x^{\nu}, X, V)$ is convex with respect to (x^{ν}, X, V).
(iii)′ $c^{\nu}_{X}(x^{\nu}, X, V) > 0, \quad c^{\nu}_{x^{\nu}X}(x^{\nu}, X, V) > 0$.
(iv)′ $c^{\nu}_{V}(x^{\nu}, X, V) < 0, \quad c^{\nu}_{x^{\nu}V}(x^{\nu}, X, V) < 0$.

The marginality conditions (3) are now written as

$$p = c^{\nu}_{x^{\nu}}(x^{\nu}, X, V). \tag{4}$$

By taking a differential of both sides of (4) and rearranging, we obtain

$$dx^{\nu} = -\frac{c^{\nu}_{X}}{c^{\nu}_{x^{\nu}}}dX - \frac{c^{\nu}_{V}}{c^{\nu}_{x^{\nu}}}dV + \frac{1}{c^{\nu}_{x^{\nu}}}dp.$$

Hence,

$$\frac{\partial x^{\nu}}{\partial X} < 0, \quad \frac{\partial x^{\nu}}{\partial V} > 0, \quad \frac{\partial x^{\nu}}{\partial p} > 0.$$

That is, the larger the total harvests of fish in the commons X, the smaller the optimum level of fish harvests x^{ν} for each fisherman ν; whereas the larger the total stock of the fisheries ground in the commons V, the larger the optimum level of fish harvests x^{ν} for each fisherman ν. The higher the price of fish p, the higher the optimum level of fish harvests x^{ν} for each fisherman ν.

To discuss the short-run determination of the individual levels of fisheries activities for perfectively competitive markets, let us assume that the stock of the fisheries commons V is kept at a constant level. Then, for the given level of market price p, the aggregate of fish harvests by individual fishermen at their profit-maximizing levels is given by

$$X_c = \sum_{\nu} x^{\nu}_{c},$$

where, for each fisherman ν, the level of harvest x^{ν}_{c} is determined by the cost minimization condition, (3) or (4), so that his or her net profit π^{ν} is maximized.

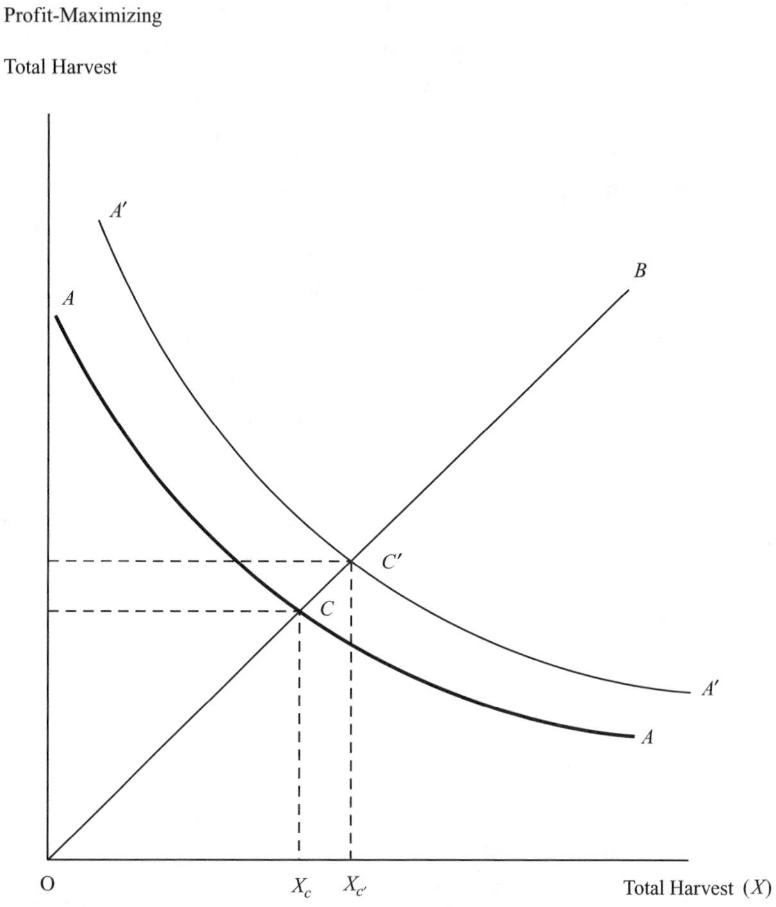

Figure 1.2. Determination of the profit-maximizing total harvest.

Thus the profit-maximizing level of the total harvest X_c is decreased as the given level of total harvest X is increased, as depicted in Figure 1.2, where the given level of total harvest X is measured along the abscissa, whereas the ordinate measures the profit-maximizing level of total harvest X_c. The intersection of the AA curve with the 45° line OB corresponds to the level of total harvest that is realized when the market price is at p and individual fishermen maximize their net profits without taking into account what others are doing. An increase in market price p will cause a shift upward of the AA curve, thus resulting in a larger level of total harvest X, whereas an increase in the stock of the commons V also shifts the AA curve upward, thus resulting again in a larger amount of total harvest, as is apparent from Figure 1.2.

It is apparent that, in view of the externalities postulated by (iii), the harvest plan under the competitive assumption thus obtained is not optimum from the point of view of the commons as a whole and it would be possible to find an alternative harvest plan that would result in a larger total profit

$$\Pi = \sum_{\nu} \pi^{\nu} = \sum_{\nu} [px^{\nu} - c^{\nu}(x^{\nu}, X, V)]. \tag{5}$$

To see this, let us suppose that the commons decides to levy "taxes" on the fishermen according to the number of fish they catch. We denote by θ the "tax" rate levied on individual fishermen by the number of fish they catch. The net profit of each fisherman ν is

$$\pi^{\nu} = px^{\nu} - c^{\nu}(x^{\nu}, X, V) - \theta x^{\nu}. \tag{6}$$

The modified net profit (6) is maximized when the following marginality conditions are satisfied:

$$p = c^{\nu}_{x^{\nu}}(x^{\nu}, X, V) + \theta. \tag{7}$$

The levels of individual harvests by fishermen satisfying the marginality conditions (7) are denoted by $x^{\nu}(\theta)$ to emphasize their dependency upon the "tax" rate θ. We also denote by $X(\theta)$ total harvests of fish; that is,

$$\sum_{\nu} x^{\nu}(\theta) = X(\theta). \tag{8}$$

By differentiating both sides of (7) and (8) with respect to θ, we obtain

$$c^{\nu}_{x^{\nu}x^{\nu}} \frac{dx^{\nu}(\theta)}{d\theta} + c^{\nu}_{x^{\nu}X} \frac{dX(\theta)}{d\theta} + 1 = 0 \tag{9}$$

$$\sum_{\nu} \frac{dx^{\nu}(\theta)}{d\theta} = \frac{dX(\theta)}{d\theta}. \tag{10}$$

By substituting (9) into (10), we obtain the following formula:

$$\frac{dX(\theta)}{d\theta} = -\frac{\sum_\nu \frac{1}{c^\nu_{x^\nu x^\nu}}}{1+\sum_\nu \frac{c^\nu_{x^\nu X}}{c^\nu_{x^\nu x^\nu}}} < 0. \tag{11}$$

Now let us denote by $\Pi(\theta)$ the total profit corresponding to "tax" rate θ; that is,

$$\Pi(\theta) = \sum_\nu [px^\nu(\theta) - c^\nu(x^\nu(\theta), X(\theta), V)]. \tag{12}$$

Differentiate (12) with respect to θ, and substitute (7) to obtain

$$\frac{d\Pi(\theta)}{d\theta} = (\mathrm{MSC} - \theta)\left[-\frac{dX(\theta)}{d\theta}\right], \tag{13}$$

where

$$\mathrm{MSC} = \sum_\nu c^\nu_X(x^\nu, X, V). \tag{14}$$

The MSC defined by (14) expresses the extent to which the marginal increase in total harvest X increases the marginal costs of all fishermen in the commons; it may be referred to as the *marginal social costs* of harvesting.

Because of relation (11), equation (13) implies

$$\frac{d\Pi(\theta)}{d\theta} \gtreqless 0, \quad \text{according to } \mathrm{MSC} \gtreqless \theta.$$

Hence, the total profits accrued to the fisheries commons $\Pi(\theta)$ attains the maximum when the "tax" rate θ is equated to the marginal social costs of harvesting:

$$\theta = \mathrm{MSC}. \tag{15}$$

Optimum Harvesting

Thus, we have shown that the "tax" rate evaluated at the marginal social costs brings the maximum profit to the commons. However, this is the maximum when a pricing scheme is used to regulate fisheries activities of fishermen in the commons, and it may be conceivably possible to come out with a larger total profit if some other means of allocating the fisheries resources among fishermen of the commons is adopted.

The maximum profits for the fisheries commons may be obtained by solving the following maximization problem:

Find the optimum harvest plan (x^{ν}) that maximizes the total profits (5) subject to the constraint (2).

This maximization problem is easily solved in terms of the Lagrangian form:

$$L = \sum_{\nu} [px^{\nu} - c^{\nu}(x^{\nu}, X, V)] + \theta \left[X - \sum_{\nu} x^{\nu} \right], \tag{16}$$

where the Lagrangian multiplier θ is associated with the constraint (2).

By differentiating the Lagrangian form (16) with respect to x^{ν} and X, we obtain, respectively, relations (7) and (15). Hence, the harvest plan obtained under the "tax" scheme based upon the marginal social cost pricing is identical with the optimum solution to the maximization problem above.

The properties concerning the cost functions $c^{\nu}(x^{\nu}, X, V)$ as obtained above, (iii)′ and (iv)′, enable us to derive the following conditions for the marginal social costs, MSC:

$$\frac{\partial \mathrm{MSC}}{\partial X} > 0, \qquad \frac{\partial \mathrm{MSC}}{\partial V} < 0.$$

That is, the larger the total harvests of fish in the commons X, the larger the marginal social costs MSC, whereas the larger the stock of the fisheries ground in the commons V, the smaller the marginal social costs MSC.

Monopolistic Markets

A similar analysis may be carried out for the case in which the fisheries commons in question is a monopolist in the market. If we denote by $p(X)$ the demand price for total harvest X, then the total net profit is given by

$$\Pi = \sum_{\nu} [p(X)x^{\nu} - c^{\nu}(x^{\nu}, X, V)], \tag{17}$$

where

$$\sum_{\nu} x^{\nu} = X. \tag{18}$$

The optimum harvest schedule is obtained by maximizing total net profit (17) subject to constraint (18). Such a harvest plan (x^ν) may be obtained in terms of Lagrangian form:

$$L = \sum_\nu [p(X)x^\nu - c^\nu(x^\nu, X, V)] + \theta\left[X - \sum_\nu x^\nu\right], \tag{19}$$

where the Lagrangian multiplier θ is associated with the constraint (18). (It may be noted that the Lagrangian multiplier θ for the monopolistic case takes a value different from that for the competitive case.)

By differentiating Lagrangian form (19) with respect to x^ν and X, and equating them to 0, we obtain

$$p(X) = c^\nu_{x^\nu}(x^\nu, X, V) + \theta \tag{20}$$

$$\theta = \sum_\nu c^\nu_X(x^\nu, X, V) + [-p'(X)X]. \tag{21}$$

The first term on the right-hand side of relation (21) is nothing but the marginal social costs for the competitive case, as defined previously. The second term, $[-p'(X)X]$, expresses the marginal loss in the total net profits of the commons due to the marginal decrease in the demand price caused by the marginal increase in total harvests X. The sum of these two terms may be regarded as the marginal social costs, MSC, for the monopolistic case:

$$\text{MSC} = \sum_\nu c^\nu_X(x^\nu, X, V) + [-p'(X)X].$$

The maximum total profit for the commons as a whole is obtained when the marginal social costs MSC thus defined are taken into account in the determination of the level of harvesting for each fisherman in the commons, so that, for each fisherman ν, the marginal private costs are equal to the market price p minus the MSC:

$$c^\nu_{x^\nu}(x^\nu, X, V) = p(X) - \theta,$$

$$\theta = \text{MSC} = \sum_\nu c^\nu_X(x^\nu, X, V) + [-p'(X)X].$$

In view of the principle of marginal social cost pricing, it is now possible to internalize the externalities associated with the use of fisheries resources in the commons ground. The analysis will be simplified if we introduce the concept of *consolidated cost function*.

The Consolidated Cost Function

Suppose the stock of the commons V and the total harvest X are given. We consider the harvest plan (x^ν) for the fishermen of the commons that minimizes the total cost

$$C = \sum_\nu c^\nu(x^\nu, X, V)$$

subject to

$$\sum_\nu x^\nu \geqq X. \tag{22}$$

Such a harvest plan (x^ν) is obtained in terms of the Lagrangian form:

$$L = \sum_\nu c^\nu(x^\nu, X, V) + \theta\left[X - \sum_\nu x^\nu\right], \tag{23}$$

where the Lagrangian multiplier θ is associated with the constraint (22). (It may be noted again that the Lagrangian multiplier θ for the present case takes a value different from that for the competitive or monopolistic case.)

By differentiating Lagrangian form (23) with respect to x^ν and equating it to 0, we obtain

$$\theta = c^\nu_{x^\nu}(x^\nu, X, V).$$

The minimized cost C becomes a function of (X, V), to be referred to as the consolidated cost function:

$$C = C(X, V).$$

The consolidated cost function $C(X, V)$ thus obtained is a convex function of (X, V). The marginal cost with respect to total cost X in terms of the consolidated cost function $C(X, V)$ is calculated as follows:

$$\begin{aligned} dC &= \sum_\nu c^\nu_{x^\nu} dx^\nu + \sum_\nu c^\nu_X dX \\ &= (\theta + \text{MSC}) dX, \end{aligned}$$

where MSC is the marginal social costs given by (14).

Hence, we have

$$C_X(X, V) = \theta + \text{MSC},$$

where θ is the marginal private costs.

The consolidated cost function $C(X, V)$ satisfies the following standard neoclassical conditions:

(i)″ $C(X, V) > 0$ for all $(X, V) > 0$.
(ii)″ $C(X, V)$ is a convex function of (X, V); that is,
$C_{XX} > 0, \quad C_{VV} > 0, \quad C_{XX}C_{VV} - C_{XV}^2 \geqq 0.$
(iii)″ $C_X(X, V) > 0, \quad C_{XV}(X, V) < 0.$
(iv)″ $C_V(X, V) < 0, \quad C_{VV}(X, V) < 0.$

In terms of the consolidated cost function $C(X, V)$ introduced above, the optimality conditions for the commons when the market is perfectly competitive are simply expressed as

$$p = C_X(X, V),$$

where $C_X(X, V)$ are the marginal costs in terms of the consolidated cost function $C(X, V)$.

When the market is monopolistic, the optimality conditions for the commons may be expressed by

$$\hat{p}(X) = C_X(X, V),$$

where $\hat{p}(X)$ is the marginal revenue function defined by

$$\hat{p}(X) = p(X) + p'(X)X.$$

We may assume that the marginal revenue function $\hat{p}(X)$ satisfies the following conditions:

$$\hat{p}(X) > 0, \quad \hat{p}'(X) < 0$$
$$0 < \hat{p}(X) < p(X) \quad \text{for all } X > 0.$$

Dynamically Optimum Harvest Plans

The gains accrued to the fishermen in the fisheries commons as expressed by total profits (5) are of the short-run nature. The fisheries ground provides the fishermen in the commons the pecuniary gains that may be obtained for the entire future as long as the stock of the fisheries ground remains sustainable; hence, the fishermen in the commons as a whole may be concerned with the harvest plan over time that gives them the maximum long-run profits.

We postulate that the fisheries commons seeks for the time-path of harvesting (x_t^ν) such that the discounted present value of future total net profits

$$\int_0^\infty \Pi_t e^{-\delta t} dt$$

is maximized, where total profits at each time t are given by

$$\Pi_t = p(X_t)X_t - C(X_t, V_t), \tag{24}$$

$C(X, V)$ is the consolidated cost function

$$C(X_t, V_t) = \sum_\nu c^\nu(x_t^\nu, X_t, V_t),$$

x_t^ν is the number of fish caught by fisherman ν, X_t is the total harvest, V_t is the stock of the fisheries commons at time t,

$$X_t = \sum_\nu x_t^\nu, \tag{25}$$

and

$$\dot{V}_t = \gamma(X_t, V_t) \tag{26}$$

with the given initial stock V_0.

Thus the problem of finding dynamically optimum time-paths of harvesting becomes a calculus-of-variations problem, and the techniques of the theory of optimum economic growth, as typically utilized by Ramsey (1928), Koopmans (1965), Cass (1965), and others, may be applied. In the context of fisheries commons, Clark and Munro (1975), Clark (1990), and Tahvonen (1991) in particular have developed the analysis of dynamically optimum time-paths of harvesting for dynamic models of fisheries commons. The dynamic model posited here is an extension of their analysis to the circumstances where the externalities concerning fisheries activities of individual fishermen in the commons are explicitly brought out and their implications for dynamically optimum harvest plans are effectively examined.

Our dynamic optimum problem may be solved in terms of the imputed price assigned to the stock of the fisheries commons at each time t, to be denoted by ψ_t. It expresses the extent to which the marginal increase in the stock of the commons at time t contributes to the long-run gain of the commons, which is defined as the discounted present value of all future marginal increases in total net profits due to the marginal increase in the stock of the commons V_t at time t.

The imputed real income at time t is defined by

$$H_t = [p(X_t)X_t - C(X_t, V_t)] + \psi_t \gamma(X_t, V_t),$$

where X_t is the total harvest at time t.

For the given time-path of harvest plan (X_t, V_t) to be dynamically optimum, the imputed real income H_t at each time t must be maximized. Hence,

$$\hat{p}(X_t) = C_X(X_t, V_t) + \psi_t[-\gamma_X(X_t, V_t)], \tag{27}$$

where $\hat{p}(X_t)$ is the marginal revenue at time t.

The second term on the right-hand side of equation (27), $\psi_t[-\gamma_X(X, V)]$, is the value of the marginal loss in the stock of the fisheries commons, $[-\gamma_X(X, V)]$, evaluated at imputed price ψ_t, expressing the *marginal environmental costs*, MEC:

$$\text{MEC} = \psi_t[-\gamma_X(X_t, V_t)]. \tag{28}$$

Equation (27) means that the amount equal to the marginal environmental costs, MEC, is levied on each individual fisherman so that the level of harvesting for each fisherman is determined in such a manner that the marginal private costs are equal to the market price subtracted by the marginal environmental costs, $p_t - \text{MEC}_t$.

We next pay our attention to the mechanism by which the time-path of imputed price, (ψ_t), is determined.

The imputed price ψ_t at time t may be expressed in analytical terms in the following manner:

$$\psi_t = \int_t^{\infty} [-C_V(X_\tau, V_\tau) + \psi_\tau \gamma_V(X_\tau, V_\tau)] e^{-\delta(\tau - t)} d\tau, \tag{29}$$

where $[-C_V(X_\tau, V_\tau)]$ represents the marginal increase in net profits at future time τ due to the marginal increase in the stock of the commons at time t, whereas $\psi_\tau \gamma_V(X_\tau, V_\tau)$ expresses the marginal increase in the imputed value of the stock of the commons at future time τ due to the marginal increase in the stock at time t.

By differentiating both sides of equation (29), we obtain

$$\dot{\psi}_t = \delta\psi_t - [-C_V(X_t, V_t) + \psi_t\gamma_V(X_t, V_t)]. \tag{30}$$

Because of the convexity assumptions concerning the relevant functions in the dynamic optimum problem, a time-path of harvesting (X_t, V_t) is optimum if, and only if, one finds a continuous, nonnegative time-path of imputed prices (ψ_t) such that equations (26) and (30) are satisfied together with the transversality conditions:

$$\lim_{t\to\infty} \psi_t V_t e^{-\delta t} = 0.$$

Perfectly Competitive Markets with Constant Prices

We first consider the case in which the market is perfectly competitive and the market price remains constant:

$$p_t = p \quad \text{for all } t.$$

For the sake of expository brevity, the relevant equations are reproduced with time suffix t being omitted:

$$\dot{V} = \gamma(X, V), \tag{31}$$

with the given initial condition V_0,

$$\frac{\dot{\psi}}{\psi} = \delta - \left[\frac{-C_V(X, V)}{\psi} + \gamma_V(X, V)\right], \tag{32}$$

where

$$p = C_X(X, V) + \psi[-\gamma_X(X, V)]. \tag{33}$$

The structure of solution paths to the pair of differential equations, (31) and (32), may be examined in terms of the phase diagram. Let us first consider the combinations of (V, ψ) for which the stock of the commons V remains stationary, $\dot{V} = 0$; that is,

$$\gamma(X, V) = 0. \tag{34}$$

Taking differentials of both sides of equations (33) and (34), we obtain

$$(C_{XX} - \psi\gamma_{XX})dX + (C_{XV} - \psi\gamma_{XV})dV - \gamma_X d\psi = 0 \tag{35}$$

$$\gamma_X dX + \gamma_V dV = 0. \tag{36}$$

By eliminating dX from the pair of equations (35) and (36), we obtain

$$\left[\frac{dV}{d\psi}\right]_{\dot{V}=0} = \frac{\gamma_X^2}{-\gamma_V(C_{XX} - \psi\gamma_{XX}) + \gamma_X(C_{XV} - \psi\gamma_{XV})}.$$

We have assumed that regenerating function $\gamma(X, V)$ and consolidated cost function $C(X, V)$ satisfy, respectively, conditions (i) and (ii), and (i)″–(iv)″. We may also assume that the stock of the commons V and total harvest X are in such a relation that the following condition is always satisfied:

$$\gamma_V(X, V) < 0.$$

Hence, we have

$$\left[\frac{dV}{d\psi}\right]_{\dot{V}=0} > 0. \tag{37}$$

The combinations of (V, ψ) for which imputed price ψ remains stationary, $\dot{\psi} = 0$, may be similarly examined. By taking differentials of both sides of the stationarity equation,

$$\frac{-C_V(X, V)}{\psi} + \gamma_V(X, V) = \delta,$$

we obtain

$$(-C_{VX} + \psi\gamma_{VX})dX - (C_{VV} - \psi\gamma_{VV})dV + C_V\frac{d\psi}{\psi} = 0,$$

which, together with equation (35), yields the following relation:

$$\left[\frac{dV}{d\psi}\right]_{\dot{\psi}=0} = \frac{C_V(C_{XX} - \psi\gamma_{XX}) - \psi\gamma_X(C_{VV} - \psi\gamma_{VV})}{(C_{XX} - \psi\gamma_{XX})(C_{VV} - \psi\gamma_{VV}) - (C_{XV} - \psi\gamma_{XV})^2}. \tag{38}$$

Because $C(X, V)$ is convex and $\gamma(X, V)$ is concave, both with respect to (X, V), and imputed price ψ is nonnegative, $C(X, V) - \psi\gamma(X, V)$ is a convex function of (X, V); hence, we have

$$(C_{XX} - \psi\gamma_{XX})(C_{VV} - \psi\gamma_{VV}) - (C_{XV} - \psi\gamma_{XV})^2 \geqq 0.$$

Hence, in view of conditions (i), (ii), and (i)″–(iv)″, relation (38) implies that

$$\left[\frac{dV}{d\psi}\right]_{\dot{\psi}=0} < 0. \tag{39}$$

The inequalities (37) and (39) enable us to draw the phase diagram for the pair of differential equations, (31) and (32), as depicted in

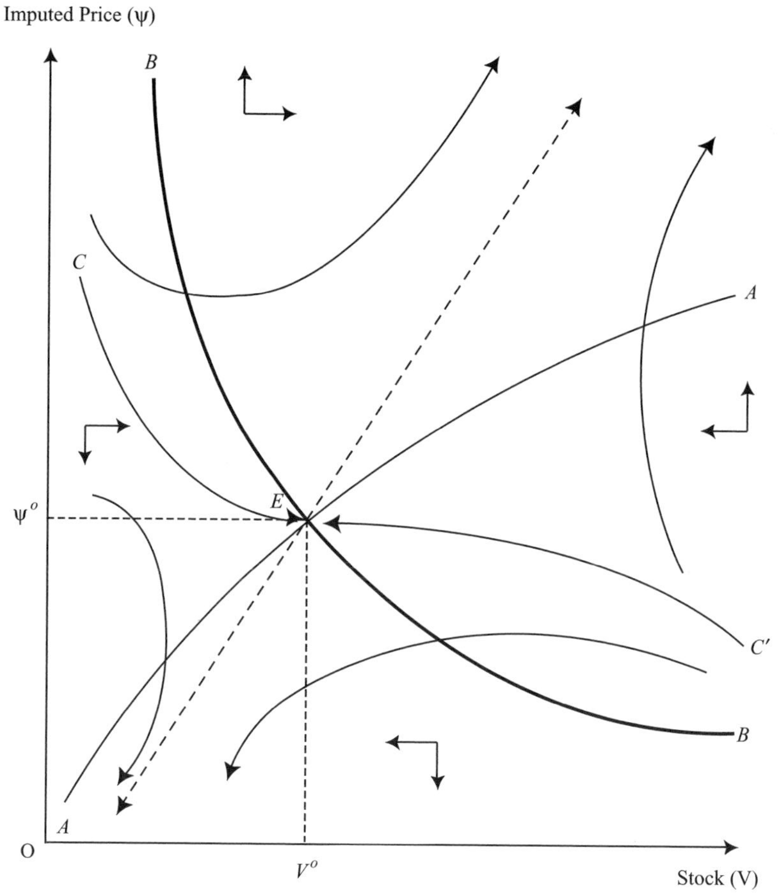

Figure 1.3. Phase diagram for the commons.

Figure 1.3. In Figure 1.3, the stock of the commons V is measured along the abscissa and the imputed price ψ along the ordinate. The combinations of (V, ψ) for which V remains stationary, $\dot{V} = 0$, is depicted by the upward sloping curve, AA, whereas those for which imputed price ψ remains stationary, $\dot{\psi} = 0$, are depicted by the downward sloping curve, BB.

It is apparent that solution paths (V, ψ) to the pair of differential equations, (31) and (32), are generically indicated by the arrowed curves. Hence, there always exists a pair of solution paths, CE and C′E, both of which converge to the stationary state E – the unique intersection of the AA and BB curves.

Let the stationary state E be expressed by (V^o, ψ^o). Then, for any given initial stock of the commons V_0, we determine the initial level of imputed price ψ_0 such that

$$\psi_0 = \psi^o(V_0),$$

where $\psi^0(V)$ represents the functional relationship associated with the stable solution paths, CE and C′E. The dynamically optimum time-path of harvesting may be obtained by choosing the imputed price ψ_t at each time t such that

$$\psi_t = \psi^0(V_t).$$

Structure of the Long-Run Stationary State: A Special Case

We have seen how the dynamically optimum time-path of harvesting may be obtained in terms of the imputed price of the stock of the commons. We now look more closely into the relationships between the stock of the fisheries commons, the total harvest, and the total net profits at the long-run stationary state to which the dynamically optimum time-path always converges. First, we consider a simple case in which the change-of-population function $\gamma(X, V)$ is of the following form:

$$\gamma(X, V) = \gamma(V) - X,$$

where V is the stock of fish in the fisheries ground of the commons and X is the total harvest at each time t. The $\gamma(V)$ function is the regenerating function, specifying the growth in the fish population when no fish are caught by the fishermen in the village. The regenerating function $\gamma(V)$ is assumed to satisfy the following conditions:

$$\gamma''(V) < 0 \quad \text{for all } V > 0$$
$$\gamma(\underline{V}) = \gamma(\overline{V}) = 0 \quad \text{for critical } \underline{V}, \ \overline{V} (\underline{V} < \overline{V}).$$

The regenerating function $\gamma(V)$ has a shape as illustrated in Figure 1.4, where the stock of the commons V is measured along the abscissa and the ordinate measures the change in the stock V, $\dot{V}$. There are two levels of the stock of the commons, V^m and V^a. The level of the stock V^m corresponds to the point M at which the $\gamma(V)$ curve attains

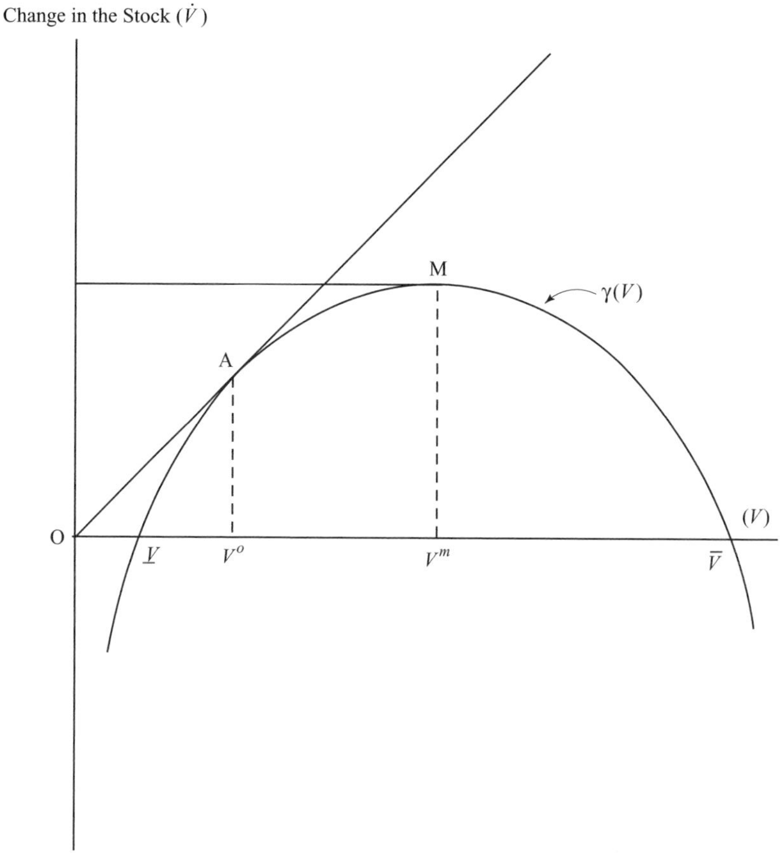

Figure 1.4. The change-in-population curves for the commons: a special case.

its maximum, whereas V^a corresponds to the point A at which the line OA is tangent to the $\gamma(V)$ curve. It is apparent that

$$\gamma'(V) \gtreqless 0, \text{ according to } V \lesseqgtr V^m$$

$$a'(V) \gtreqless 0, \text{ according to } V \lesseqgtr V^a,$$

where $a(V) = \dfrac{\gamma(V)}{V}$.

Thus, the marginal rate of change function $\gamma'(V)$ and the average rate of change function $a(V)$ are shaped as typically illustrated in Figure 1.5, where the stock of the commons V is measured along the

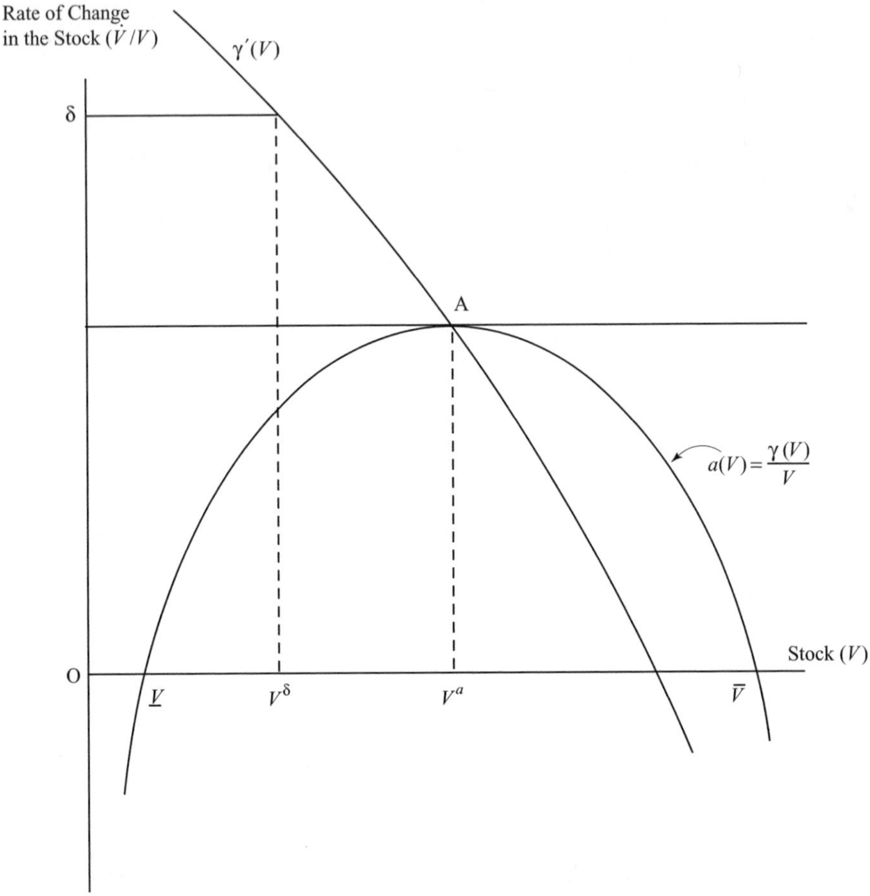

Figure 1.5. Average and marginal rates of change in the stock.

abscissa, but the ordinate now measures the relative rate of change in the stock, $\frac{\dot{V}}{V}$.

The Linear Homogeneous Case

We now assume that the consolidated cost function $C(X, V)$ is subject to constant returns to scale, so that we may write

$$C(X, V) = c(x)V, \quad x = \frac{X}{V},$$

where the cost-per-stock function $c(x)$ is assumed to satisfy the following conditions:

$$c(0) = 0; \quad c'(x) > 0, \; c''(x) > 0 \quad \text{for all } x > 0.$$

The basic differential equations, (31) and (32), that characterize the dynamically optimum time-path may be now expressed as follows:

$$\frac{\dot{V}}{V} = a(V) - x \tag{40}$$

$$\frac{\dot{\psi}}{\psi} = \delta - \gamma'(V) - \frac{\hat{c}(x)}{\psi}, \tag{41}$$

where

$$x = \frac{X}{V}, \quad a(V) = \frac{\gamma(V)}{V}, \quad \hat{c}(x) = c'(x)x - c(x).$$

The long-run stationary state is characterized by the values of V^{o}, x^{o}, and ψ^{o} that satisfy the following equations:

$$a(V) - x = 0 \tag{42}$$

$$\hat{c}(x) - [\delta - \gamma'(V)]\psi = 0 \tag{43}$$

$$c'(x) + \psi = p. \tag{44}$$

By taking differentials of both sides of equations (42)–(44), we obtain

$$\begin{pmatrix} -1 & a' & 0 \\ \hat{c}' & \gamma''\psi & -(\delta - \gamma') \\ c'' & 0 & 1 \end{pmatrix} \begin{pmatrix} dx \\ dV \\ d\psi \end{pmatrix} = \begin{pmatrix} 0 & 0 \\ 0 & \psi \\ 1 & 0 \end{pmatrix} \begin{pmatrix} dp \\ d\delta \end{pmatrix}. \tag{45}$$

The system of equations (45) may be solved to obtain

$$\begin{pmatrix} dx \\ dV \\ d\psi \end{pmatrix} = \frac{1}{\Delta} \begin{pmatrix} -a'(\delta - \gamma') & -a'\psi \\ -(\delta - \gamma') & -\psi \\ -a'\hat{c}' - \gamma''\psi & \psi a'c'' \end{pmatrix} \begin{pmatrix} dp \\ d\delta \end{pmatrix},$$

where

$$\Delta = -\gamma''\psi - a'[\hat{c}' + (\delta - \gamma')c''] > 0.$$

We assume that the following conditions are satisfied at the long-run stationary state:

$$a' = a'(x) < 0, \quad \gamma'(V) < \delta.$$

Then

$$\begin{pmatrix} dx \\ dV \\ d\psi \end{pmatrix} = \frac{1}{\Delta} \begin{pmatrix} + & + \\ - & - \\ + & - \end{pmatrix} \begin{pmatrix} dp \\ d\delta \end{pmatrix}.$$

A higher market price ($dp > 0$) entails a higher imputed price ($d\psi > 0$) and a lower long-run level of the stock of capital ($dV < 0$), together with a higher harvest/stock ratio ($dx > 0$).

Because of the relation

$$dX = \gamma'(V)dV, \quad \gamma'(V) < 0,$$

an increase in market price p implies an increase in the long-run level of the total harvest X^o. On the other hand, a higher rate of discount ($d\delta > 0$) entails a lower imputed price ($d\psi < 0$) and a lower long-run level of the stock of the commons ($dV < 0$) but a higher long-run level of the harvest/stock ratio ($dx > 0$).

The structure of the dynamically optimum time-path of the stock of the commons V may be more closely analyzed in terms of the basic differential equations (40) and (41), together with the short-run optimality condition (33), which, in the linear homogeneous case, may be written as

$$p = c'(x) + \psi. \tag{46}$$

To see how solution paths (V_t, ψ_t) to the basic differential equations (40) and (41) behave themselves, we express them in terms of the variables (V_t, x_t) rather than in terms of (V_t, ψ_t). Let us first take differentials of both sides of the short-run optimality condition (46) to obtain

$$d\psi = -c''(x)dx,$$

which may be substituted in (41) to obtain a differential equation with respect to x:

$$\dot{x} = \frac{p - c'(x)}{c''(x)} \left\{ \frac{\hat{c}(x)}{p - c'(x)} - [\delta - \gamma'(V)] \right\}. \tag{47}$$

The construction of the phase diagram for (V_t, x_t) is illustrated in Figure 1.6. The AA curve in the first quadrant depicts the average rate of change in the stock of the commons $a(V) = \frac{\gamma(V)}{V}$ that represents

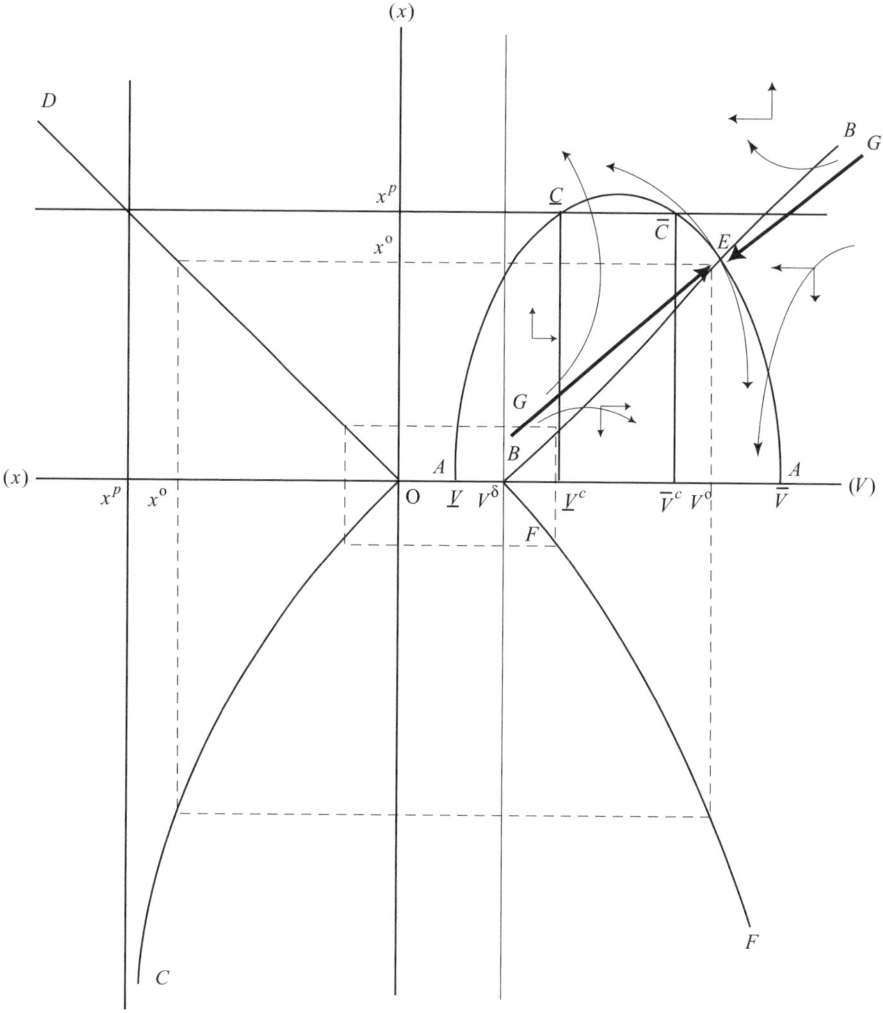

Figure 1.6. Construction of the phase diagram for the commons.

the combinations of (V, x) at which the stock of the commons V remains stationary $\dot{V} = 0$. When (V, x) lies above the AA curve, then the stock of the commons V tends to decrease: $\dot{V} < 0$; whereas, when it lies below the AA curve, V tends to increase: $\dot{V} > 0$.

On the other hand, the combinations of (V, x) at which the harvest/stock ratio x remains stationary may be characterized in terms of the CO and FF curves in Figure 1.6. In the third quadrant, the CO curve depicts the curve:

$$\left(x, \frac{\hat{c}(x)}{p - c'(x)}\right),$$

where x^p is the harvest/stock ratio at which $c'(x^p) = p$.

The FF curve in the fourth quadrant depicts the curve represented by $(V, \delta - \gamma'(V))$. By transposing the value of x via the 45° line OD in the second quadrant, we can draw the BB curve in the first quadrant that corresponds to the combinations of (V, x) at which the harvest/stock ratio x remains stationary: $\dot{x} = 0$. When (V, x) lies above the BB curve, x tends to increase: $\dot{x} > 0$; when it lies below the BB curve, x tends to decrease: $\dot{x} < 0$. Hence, solution paths (V, x) to the system of differential equations, (40) and (47), behave like the arrowed curves in the first quadrant in Figure 1.6.

It is apparent that there exist a pair of solution paths, GE and G′E, both of which converge to the stationary state $\mathrm{E} = (V^0, x^0)$. Let the curves, GE and G′E, be expressed in functional form:

$$x = x^{\mathrm{o}}(V).$$

Then, for each given level of the stock of the commons at time t, V_t, the optimum harvest/stock ratio x_t^{o} is given by

$$x_t^{\mathrm{o}} = x^{\mathrm{o}}(V_t),$$

and the optimum total harvest X_t^{o} may be accordingly obtained:

$$X_t^{\mathrm{o}} = x_t^{\mathrm{o}} V_t.$$

The imputed price ψ_t^0 is obtained by

$$\psi_t^0 = p - c'\left(x_t^0\right).$$

The effects of changes in the market price p and the rate of discount δ may be examined in terms of the diagram in the first quadrant in Figure 1.6. An increase in the market price p $(dp > 0)$ implies a shift in the CO curve upward, resulting in an upward shift in the BB curve. Hence, a higher market price p entails a lower long-run stationary level of the stock of the commons $(dV < 0)$ and a higher long-run harvest/stock ratio $(dx > 0)$, with a higher long-run total harvest $(dX > 0)$. Similarly, an increase in the rate of discount results in a shift downward of the FF curve in the fourth quadrant in Figure 1.6, resulting in an upward shift of the BB curve in the first quadrant. Hence, a higher rate of discount ($d\delta > 0$) entails a lower long-run level of the stock of the commons ($dV < 0$) and a higher long-run harvest/stock ratio ($dx > 0$), with a higher long-run total harvest ($dX > 0$).

Along the optimum trajectory, we have

$$\left(\frac{dx}{dV}\right)_{\text{opt.}} \sim \frac{\hat{c}(x) - [p - c'(x)][\delta - \gamma'(V)]}{\gamma(V) - x}, \tag{48}$$

where symbol $\sim$ indicates that both sides of the equation are proportional, with the coefficient of proportionality independent of the values of p and δ.

When the market price p or the rate of discount δ is increased, the right-hand side of equation (48) is decreased. Hence, an increase in the market price p or the rate of discount δ results in a shift upward of the optimum trajectory GE as is apparent from Figure 1.6. Thus an increase in the market price p or in the rate of discount δ implies an increase in the harvest/stock ratio, x_t^0, and an increase in the optimum total harvest, X_t^0, at each time t. Accordingly, as is shown above, the long-run level of the stock of the commons, V^0, is decreased.

Optimum versus Market Allocations of the Fisheries Resources

The analysis of dynamically optimum time-path of harvesting in the fisheries commons for the simple case may be applied to examine the intertemporal allocations of the fisheries resources under various institutional arrangements.

We first consider a case in which the market for fish is perfectly competitive, so that the number of fish caught by each individual fisherman is determined independently of the number of fish caught by other fishermen. Then, for the simple case discussed above, the harvest/stock ratio x_t at each time t is determined at the level x^p at which the marginal private cost is equal to market price p; that is,

$$p = c'(x^p), \quad x_t = \frac{X_t}{V_t} = x^p.$$

The long-run level of the stock of the commons then is specified by the condition that the average rate of change in the stock of the commons is equal to the competitive harvest/stock ratio, x^p. As illustrated in Figure 1.6, the long-run level of the stock of the commons is determined by the intersection of the AA curve in the first quadrant, depicting the schedule of the average rate of change $a(V)$, with the horizontal line at the height of x^p. In Figure 1.6, the case in which there exist two levels, $\underline{V}^c$ and $\overline{V}^c$, at which the average of change is equal to x^p is depicted; that is,

$$a(\underline{V}^c) = a(\overline{V}^c) = x^p, \quad \underline{V}^c < \overline{V}^c.$$

It is apparent that the higher level of the long-run stationary state $\overline{V}^c$ is stable, whereas the lower level $\underline{V}^c$ is unstable. When the initial stock of the commons V_0 is less than the lower long-run stationary level $\underline{V}^c$, then V_t tends to decrease, eventually converging to the state of extinction. On the other hand, when the initial stock V_0 is larger than the upper long-run stationary level $\overline{V}^c$, then V_t again tends to steadily decrease, converging to $\overline{V}^c$ as time t goes to infinity. When the initial level V_0 is between the two long-run stationary levels ($\underline{V}^c < V_0 < \overline{V}^c$), then V_t tends to increase steadily to approach $\overline{V}^c$.

There naturally exists the possibility that the AA curve does not intersect with the x^p line, implying that the stock of the commons V_t always is steadily decreasing to approach the state of extinction. Indeed, this is the situation referred to as the tragedy of the commons by Hardin (1968).

It is apparent from Figure 1.1 that the harvest/stock ratio x_t is always larger than the optimum ratio x_t^o, implying that the stable long-run level of the stock of the commons under the competitive market hypothesis $\overline{V}^c$ is always less than the optimum long-run level $\overline{V}^o$.

A similar analysis may be carried out for the situation in which the market for the harvest from the fisheries commons is monopolistic. One only has to substitute for the x^p line the harvest/stock ratio x_t^m obtained under the monopolistic market hypothesis; that is,

$$c'(x_t^m) = \hat{p}(X_t^m), \quad X_t^m = x_t^m V_t,$$

where $\hat{p}(X)$ is the marginal revenue function. Then we have

$$\frac{dx_t^m}{dV_t} = \frac{\hat{p}'(X_t^m)\, x_t^m}{c''(x_t^m)\, x_t^m - \hat{p}'(X_t^m) V_t} < 0.$$

Hence, we can show that the harvest/stock ratio under the monopolistic market hypothesis, x_t^m, may be expressed by a downward sloping curve of the stock V_t, and, when V_t is less than the long-run optimum level V^{o}, it always lies above the optimum trajectory GE. Accordingly, the long-run stationary level of the stock of the commons under the monopolistic market hypothesis is less than the long-run optimum level V^{o}.

In the analysis of the fisheries commons we have introduced above, two types of externalities are explicitly recognized. The first type of externalities concerns the effects upon each individual fisherman's cost schedule of the fisheries activities carried out by other fishermen in the village. The second type of externalities concerns the effects upon the schedules of marginal costs for fisheries activities carried out in the future owing to the decrease in the stock of the commons today.

Both types of externalities, static and dynamic, are internalized in terms of the imputed prices associated with fisheries activities to result in the time-path of harvesting in the fisheries commons that is dynamically optimum in the sense that the discounted present value of future total profits of the commons is maximized among all feasible time-paths.

4. THE FORESTRY COMMONS

Dynamic Analysis of the Forestry Commons

The analysis of the fisheries commons we have developed in the previous section may be readily applied to other types of the commons where natural resources are communally managed by a group of individuals. In this section, we take up the case of the forestry commons and see to what extent our analysis may be modified to examine the dynamic optimality of natural resources extracted from the forestry commons.

We consider a well-defined forestry area to which the property rights are held by a certain village community. The forestry may be used for slash-and-burn agriculture, fuels, the construction of residential buildings, or commercial purposes. As with the fisheries commons, the forestry area is open to any farmer belonging to the village community, but strictly prohibited to those outside the community. The community defines the rules, customs, and obligations concerning the use and management of the forestry resources.

As with the fisheries commons, the stock of the forestry commons is measured by the number of the trees in the forestry area, assuming that all trees are homogeneous. We thus avoid the complications that would arise if we were to consider the existence of various kinds of trees and differential age distribution of trees in the forest. This simplification imposes certain qualifications concerning the validity of institutional and empirical implications of our analysis, particularly regarding the problems related to global warming and biodiversity.

We denote by V_t the stock of the forestry commons at time t, measured in terms of the number of trees in the forest. There exist two types of factors in determining the rate at which the stock of the forest commons changes over time. The first factor concerns the ecological and biological processes by which trees in the forest grow, mature, and decay. The second factor concerns the economic, social, and cultural activities by which trees are cut down or reforested.

The ecological and biological processes by which the stock of the forest changes over time are expressed by the regenerating function $\gamma(V)$ that relates the change $\dot{V}$ in the stock of the forest to the stock V itself. The $\gamma(V)$ function is assumed to possess the shape, as typically illustrated by the change-of-population curve in Figure 1.4. That is, the function $\gamma(V)$ is a strictly concave function of the stock V, and there exist two critical levels of V, $\underline{V}$ and $\overline{V}$, at which the regenerative rate of growth in the stock of the forestry commons is 0:

$$\gamma''(V) < 0 \quad \text{for all } V > 0$$
$$\gamma(\underline{V}) = \gamma(\overline{V}) = 0, \quad \underline{V} < \overline{V}.$$

The upper critical level of the stock of the forest $\overline{V}$ is the long-run level of the stock that is stable; that is, if the forest is left at the natural state, then the stock of the forest V_t at time t tends to approach the upper critical level $\overline{V}$, provided V_t is not less than the lower level of the stock of the forest $\underline{V}$. If the stock of the forest V_t is less than the lower critical level $\underline{V}$, then the ecological environment of the forest is such that it is impossible for the forest to regenerate itself, resulting in a steady decrease in the stock of the forest V_t, converging eventually to the state of extinction.

The upper critical level $\overline{V}$ of the stock of the forest represents the ecologically sustainable maximum number of trees that are sustainable within the given forestry area, provided that no anthropogenic activities are carried out.

Unlike the case of the fisheries commons, the processes of extracting natural resources from the forestry commons are seldom subject to the phenomenon of static externalities. Let us focus our attention only on those activities involved with felling trees in the forest and selling them on the market. The number of trees each woodsman in the village community fells depends upon the hours he or she spends, assuming that the tools and equipments used by him or her remain constant throughout the following discussion; that is,

$$x^\nu = f^\nu(\ell^\nu, V),$$

where ν refers generically to individual woodsmen in the village and ℓ^ν is the hours a woodsman ν works in the forest, whereas V stands for the stock of the forest.

We assume that the production function $f^\nu(\ell^\nu, V)$ is a concave function of (ℓ^ν, V), satisfying the following conditions:

$$f^\nu(\ell^\nu, V) > 0, \quad f^\nu_{\ell^\nu}(\ell^\nu, V) > 0, \quad f^\nu_V(\ell^\nu, V) > 0$$
$$f^\nu_{\ell^\nu \ell^\nu},\ f^\nu_{VV} < 0, \quad f^\nu_{\ell^\nu \ell^\nu} f^\nu_{VV} - {f^\nu_{\ell^\nu V}}^2 \geqq 0 \quad \text{for all } (\ell^\nu, V) > 0.$$

The following analysis becomes simplified if we introduce the concept of consolidated cost function, as is the case with the fisheries commons. Let us denote by w^ν the wage rate woodsman ν would be paid if he or she would be engaged in other economic activities, then the net profit for woodsman ν is given by

$$\Pi^\nu = px^\nu - w^\nu \ell^\nu, \tag{49}$$

where ℓ^ν is the hours he or she works in the forest and p is the market price of the wood, to be measured in real terms as the wage rate w^ν. The maximum net profit for woodsman ν is obtained if the hours ℓ^ν he or she works in the forest are determined so that the marginal product of his or her labor is equal to the real wage rate:

$$pf^\nu_{\ell^\nu}(\ell^\nu, V) = w^\nu. \tag{50}$$

The marginal productivity condition (50) may be solved with respect to ℓ^ν to yield the following cost function:

$$c^\nu = w^\nu \ell^\nu = c^\nu(x^\nu, V). \tag{51}$$

The cost function (51) for each woodman ν satisfies the following conditions:

$$c^\nu(x^\nu, V) > 0, \quad c^\nu_{x^\nu}(x^\nu, V) > 0, \quad c^\nu_V(x^\nu, V) < 0$$
$$c^\nu_{x^\nu x^\nu}, c^\nu_{VV} > 0, c^\nu_{x^\nu x^\nu} c^\nu_{VV} - {c^\nu_{x^\nu V}}^2 \geqq 0 \quad \text{for all } (x^\nu, V) > 0.$$

The consolidated cost function $C = C(X, V)$ now is obtained by finding the harvest plan (x^ν) that minimizes the total cost

$$C = \sum_\nu c^\nu = \sum_\nu w^\nu \ell^\nu$$

subject to the constraint that

$$X = \sum_\nu x^\nu, \quad x^\nu = f^\nu(\ell^\nu, V).$$

It is apparent that the consolidated cost function $C(X, V)$ satisfies the following conditions:

$$C(X, V) > 0, \quad C_X(X, V) > 0, \quad C_V(X, V) < 0$$
$$C_{XV} < 0, \quad C_{XX}, C_{VV} > 0, \quad C_{XX}C_{VV} - {C_{XV}}^2 \geqq 0 \quad \text{for all} (X, V) > 0.$$

Because we postulate the absence of static externalities for the case of the forestry commons, there is no divergence between private and social costs, and, under the competitive market hypothesis, the harvest plan (x^ν) that is optimum from individual woodsman's point of view is also optimum from the viewpoint of the commons as a whole.

Reforestation Activities in the Forestry Commons

A substantial amount of labor is used in reforestation activities in the forestry commons. If we denote by Y the increase in the stock of the forest of the commons due to reforestation activities, then the change in the stock of the forest $\dot{V}$ is given by

$$\dot{V} = \gamma(V) + Y - X,$$

where X is the number of trees in the forest felled by deforestation activities.

The costs of reforestation activities of increasing the number of trees in the forest by Y may be expressed by the cost function of the form

$$B = B(Y, V),$$

where the dependency of the effect of reforestation on the stock V of the forest is explicitly brought out.

The cost function for reforestation, $B(Y, V)$, is assumed to satisfy the following conditions:

$$B(Y, V) > 0, \quad B_Y(Y, V) > 0, \quad B_V(Y, V) < 0$$
$$B_{YY}, B_{VV} > 0, \quad B_{YY}B_{VV} - B_{YV}{}^2 \geqq 0 \quad \text{for all } (Y, V) > 0.$$

Reforestation activities are purely external in the sense that the output is shared by all members of the forestry commons, not only the current generation but also all future generations. Hence, if things were done on an individually rational basis, no reforestation would take place. On the other hand, reforestation activities play a crucial role in maintaining the forest in the state that is optimum from both an ecological and an economic point of view. We first examine how much scarce resources must be devoted to reforestation activities to attain the time-path of harvesting and the stock of the forest that is dynamically optimum in terms of the pecuniary gains accrued to the forestry commons as a whole.

Let us denote, as previously, by V_t, X_t, and Y_t, respectively, the stock of the forest, the number of trees felled, and the number of trees reforested, all at time t. Then, the change in the stock of the forest, $\dot{V}_t$, is determined by

$$\dot{V}_t = \gamma(V_t) + Y_t - X_t, \quad V_0 = V^0, \tag{52}$$

where $\gamma(V)$ is the regenerating function, as previously introduced, and V^0 is the initial stock of the forest.

A time-path $(V_t^{\text{o}}, X_t^{\text{o}}, Y_t^{\text{o}})$ is dynamically optimum if it maximizes the discounted present value of future net profits accruing to the commons:

$$\Pi = \int_0^\infty \Pi_t e^{-\delta t} dt,$$

where δ is the rate of discount and

$$\Pi_t = pX_t - C(X_t, V_t) - B(Y_t, V_t)$$

among all feasible time-paths (V_t, X_t, Y_t) satisfying the basic dynamic equation (52).

The problem of the dynamic optimum thus formulated may again be solved in terms of the imputed price ψ_t of the stock of the forestry commons at each time t. The imputed net profit of the commons at time t is given by

$$H_t = [pX_t - C(X_t, V_t) - B(Y_t, V_t)] + \psi_t[\gamma(V_t) - X_t + Y_t].$$

The optimum levels of the depletion and reforestation of the forest at each time t, X_t^ν and Y_t^ν, are so determined as to maximize imputed profits H_t. Hence, we have

$$p = C_X(X_t, V_t) + \psi_t \tag{53}$$

$$B_Y(Y_t, V_t) = \psi_t. \tag{54}$$

On the other hand, the imputed price ψ_t satisfies the following Hamiltonian equation:

$$\dot{\psi}_t - \delta\psi_t = \frac{d}{dt}\left[\frac{\partial H_t}{\partial V_t}\right],$$

which may be worked out to yield

$$\dot{\psi}_t = [\delta - \gamma'(V_t)]\psi_t + [C_V(X_t, V_t) + B_V(Y_t, V_t)]. \tag{55}$$

The dynamically optimum time-path (V_t, X_t, Y_t) now is obtained if we find a continuous, positive time-path of imputed prices ψ_t such that the pair of differential equations, (52) and (55), together with conditions (53), (54), and the transversality condition

$$\lim_{t\to\infty} \psi_t V_t e^{-\delta t} = 0$$

are satisfied.

To examine the structure of the dynamically optimum time-path (V_t, X_t, Y_t) let us first look at the way the short-run optimization is determined. We take differentials of both sides of equations (53) and (54) to obtain

$$dX = -\left[\frac{C_{XV}}{C_{XX}}\right] dV + \frac{1}{C_{XX}} dp - \frac{1}{C_{XX}} d\psi \tag{56}$$

$$dY = -\left[\frac{B_{YV}}{B_{YY}}\right] dV + \frac{1}{B_{YY}} d\psi, \tag{57}$$

where time suffix t is omitted.

Because of the assumptions concerning cost functions $C(X, V)$ and $B(Y, V)$, equations (56) and (57) imply

$$\frac{\partial X}{\partial V} > 0, \quad \frac{\partial X}{\partial p} > 0, \quad \frac{\partial X}{\partial \psi} < 0, \quad \frac{\partial Y}{\partial V} < 0, \quad \frac{\partial Y}{\partial \psi} > 0.$$

We next see how the long-run stationary state $(V^{\text{o}}, X^{\text{o}}, Y^{\text{o}})$ is determined. The stationary conditions are

$$\gamma(V^{\text{o}}) - X^{\text{o}} + Y^{\text{o}} = 0 \tag{58}$$

$$[\delta - \gamma'(V^{\text{o}})][\psi^{\text{o}} + [C_V(X^{\text{o}}, V^{\text{o}}) + B_V(Y^{\text{o}}, V^{\text{o}})] = 0. \tag{59}$$

By taking differentials of both sides of two equations, (58) and (59), and by substituting (56) and (57), we obtain

$$\begin{pmatrix} \beta_{11} & \beta_{12} \\ \beta_{21} & \beta_{22} \end{pmatrix} \begin{pmatrix} dV^{\text{o}} \\ d\psi^{\text{o}} \end{pmatrix} = \begin{pmatrix} \dfrac{1}{C_{XX}} & 0 \\ -\dfrac{C_{XV}}{C_{XX}} & -\psi^{\text{o}} \end{pmatrix} \begin{pmatrix} dp \\ d\delta \end{pmatrix}, \tag{60}$$

where

$$\beta_{11} = \frac{C_{XV}}{C_{XX}} - \frac{B_{YV}}{B_{YY}} + \gamma' < 0$$

$$\beta_{12} = \frac{1}{C_{XX}} + \frac{1}{B_{YY}} > 0$$

$$\beta_{21} = \frac{C_{XX}C_{VV} - C_{XV}{}^2}{C_{XX}} + \frac{B_{YY}B_{VV} - B_{YV}{}^2}{B_{YY}} - \gamma'' > 0$$

$$\beta_{22} = -\frac{C_{XV}}{C_{XX}} - \frac{B_{YV}}{B_{YY}} + (\delta - \gamma') > 0.$$

The determinant Δ of the system of linear equations (60) is negative:

$$\Delta = \beta_{11}\beta_{22} - \beta_{12}\beta_{21} < 0,$$

and the long-run stationary state $(V^{\text{o}}, \psi^{\text{o}})$ is uniquely determined ℓ^{ν}.

The effects of changes in market price p and rate of discount δ on the long-run optimum level of the stock of the commons V^{o} may be calculated from the system of linear equations (60):

$$\frac{\partial V^{\text{o}}}{\partial p} = \frac{1}{\Delta}\left\{-\frac{C_{XV}}{C_{VV}} - \frac{B_{YV}}{B_{YY}} + (\delta - \gamma')\right\} < 0, \quad \frac{\partial V^{\text{o}}}{\partial \delta} = \frac{\beta_{12}\psi}{\Delta} < 0.$$

An increase in market price p generally tends to decrease the long-run optimum level of the stock of the forest, so does an increase in the rate of discount δ.

The calculation we have made proving the uniqueness of the long-run optimum levels of the stock of the forest and imputed price, V^o and ψ^o, is also used to examine the phase diagram of the system of dynamic equations (52) and (55).

First let us consider the combinations (V, ψ) at which the stock of the forest V remains stationary. It is apparent that

$$\left(\frac{d\psi}{dV}\right)_{\dot{V}=0} = \frac{-\beta_{11}}{\beta_{12}} > 0.$$

Hence, the $\dot{V} = 0$ curve may be expressed by the upward-sloping curve AA in Figure 1.3, where the stock of forestry commons V is measured along the abscissa, whereas the ordinate measures the imputed price of the forestry resources ψ. When (V, ψ) lies on the right-hand side of the AA curve, $\dot{V} < 0$; when it lies on the left-hand side of the AA curve, $\dot{V} > 0$.

Next, we consider the combinations of (V, ψ) at which the imputed price ψ remains stationary. We have

$$\left(\frac{d\psi}{dV}\right)_{\dot{\psi}=0} = \frac{-\beta_{22}}{\beta_{21}} < 0.$$

Hence, the $\dot{\psi} = 0$ curve may be depicted by the downward sloping curve BB in Figure 1.3. When (V, ψ) lies above the BB curve, $\dot{\psi} > 0$; when it lies below the BB curve, $\dot{\psi} < 0$. Thus, the solution paths (V_t, ψ_t) to the system of dynamic equations (52) and (55) behave as indicated by the arrowed curves in Figure 1.3.

Therefore, there exists a uniquely determined pair of solution paths, CE and C′E, both of which converge to the stationary state, $E = (V^o, \psi^o)$. They are the only solution paths to the system of basic dynamic equations, (52) and (55), for which the transversality condition is satisfied. The solution paths, CEC′, gives the optimal trajectory for the dynamic optimization problem of the forestry commons. Let us denote by $\psi = \psi^0(V)$ the function corresponding to the curve, CEC′. Then, if the imputed price of the forestry resources, ψ_t^0, is determined by

$$\psi_t^0 = \psi^0(V_t),$$

the associated time-path (V_t, X_t^0, Y_t^0) is the uniquely determined dynamically optimum time-path for the forestry commons in concern.

As indicated in Figure 1.3, the optimum imputed price $\psi = \psi^o(V)$ is a decreasing function of the stock of the forest V. The larger the stock of the forest V, the lower the optimum imputed price ψ^o.

The analysis we have carried out above may be applied to show that a higher market price ($dp > 0$) implies a shift upward in the AA curve accompanied by a slight upward shift in the BB curve, hence resulting in a decrease in the long-run optimum level V^o of the stock of the commons ($dV^o < 0$) and a higher long-run optimum level ψ^o of the imputed price of forestry resources ($d\psi^o > 0$).

A higher rate of discount ($d\delta > 0$) implies only a shift downward in the BB curve, resulting both in decreases in the long-run optimum level V^o of the stock of the commons ($dV^o < 0$) and in the long-run optimum ψ^o of the imputed price ($d\psi^o < 0$).

5. THE AGRICULTURAL COMMONS

Sustainability and the Agricultural Commons

Agriculture today in many parts of the world is not in a desirable state from either an economic or an environmental point of view. Agriculture has long ceased to provide honorable and gainful opportunities for those who have innate propensities for cultivation and the magnanimity to conform with the natural environment. Agriculture has ceased to be the core of human activities that effectively sustain the natural, ecological, and biological equilibrium in the forests, lakes, rivers, and woodlands. Instead, for agriculture to survive in a fiercely competitive economic world, particularly vis-á-vis the highly productive industry, occasionally it has become necessary for agriculture to adopt production technologies and processes that are highly destructive to the natural environment and hazardous to human health.

The decline of agriculture has accelerated during the more than fifty years since the end of the Second World War, primarily because of the prevalent political philosophy of neoclassical economic theory, which lies behind many international agreements and treaties concluded after the war. Neoclassical economic theory postulates that the allocative mechanism through market institutions is the only effective means by which socially desirable processes of economic development are realized. It is one of the more basic propositions in neoclassical economic theory that any obstacle to free trade or any governmental intervention to perfectly competitive market arrangements necessarily results in allocations of scarce resources that are neither efficient nor socially desirable. It implies, as a corollary, that only market forces may determine what will be the optimum pattern of industrial composition for each country and that there should not be any attempt to seek a notion of optimum allocations of scarce resources that contradicts the market allocation.

The political philosophy predominant in the postwar period has particularly harmful implications for agriculture, partly because of the significant difference in the overall productivity between industry and agriculture, in addition to the legal and institutional constraints imposed upon agricultural activities that still exist in many countries. In the manufacturing industry, productive activities are carried out by the organizational arrangements that best suit technological and market conditions. In agriculture, it is often the case that rather stringent constraints are imposed, legally or otherwise, particularly on the property rights regarding farmlands, and in many countries, it is virtually impossible to adopt the organizational framework needed to carry out productive activities in agriculture efficiently.

The best example may be that of Japanese agriculture, in which laws and regulations explicitly prohibit any organization other than farm households to have tenure on farmlands or to engage in agriculture. Japanese agriculture is subject to further constraints with respect to the sale of produce, the procurement of factors of production, the provision of daily necessities, and the availability of finances. These legal and administrative constraints have been imposed on the pretext of safeguarding farmers from the speculative and predatory activities of commercial interests, but they have in practice helped agriculture decline to the miserable situation it is in today.

This section concerns the problem of how to find the organizational framework that is best suited to the technological and market conditions of agriculture and to examine those time-paths of agricultural activities that are sustainable with respect to both the natural environment in which agricultural activities are carried out and the market economy in which the products of agricultural activities are sold and factors of production are procured.

The analytical framework is similar to those concerning the dynamic analysis of fisheries and forestry commons as described by Clark (1990), Tahvonen (1991), and others, as summarily stated in the previous sections. In the dynamic model of the agricultural commons, we explicitly recognize two types of static externalities. The first type of static externalities concerns the effects of social common capital of the commons, such as irrigation canals, drainage systems, and other common facilities, on the schedule of marginal products of various private factors of production for individual farmers. The second type of static externalities concerns the economies of scale observed in relation to the diversity of the crop, uncertainties due to climatic changes, damages by blight and insects, and the work schedule of rice planting, rice mowing, and so forth. The latter also may be observed in relation to the processing and sales activities of agricultural produce and the use of forestry resources.

Agricultural activities necessarily tend to depreciate the stock of the agricultural commons, thus resulting in the decrease in the stock of the commons in the future. The dynamic externalities due to the depreciation of the agricultural commons play a crucial role in the determination of the long-run stationary state at which the optimum balance between the levels of agricultural activities and the stock of the agricultural commons may be sustained.

A time-path of agricultural activities together with the stock of the commons is dynamically optimum when the resulting time-path of total net profits of the commons as a whole has the maximum discounted present value among all feasible time-paths of total net profits. It is generally shown that the dynamically optimum time-path always converges, as time goes to infinity, to the long-run stationary state at which the highest total net profits for the commons as a whole are obtained among all levels of agricultural activities that are sustainable with respect to the stock of the commons.

The relationships between dynamic optimality and sustainability as described above for the agricultural commons may be extended to the general case of social common capital, in which *dynamic optimality* is defined in terms of the intertemporal preference ordering prevailing within the society in question, whereas *sustainability* is defined in reference to the stock of social common capital, as will be discussed in detail in later chapters.

A Model of the Agricultural Commons

An *agricultural commons* consists of a village community of farmers and a well-defined acreage of land on which the village community as a whole possesses exclusive property rights, without, however, precluding the private ownership arrangements of land. The commons' land is primarily composed of arable land and forests, but it also includes land for irrigation and related infrastructure as well as land for residential and other purposes. The farmers in the village may possess private land, either arable or residential, of their own. However, in the analysis developed below, we focus our attention exclusively on the management and use of the land controlled by the agricultural commons. Our analysis, with slight modifications, will be applied to the general situation in which individual farmers in the village possess substantial private land holdings.

In the simple model of the agricultural commons discussed in this section, we assume that the outcome of agricultural activities is simply represented by the amount of a particular crop (produced annually or during the unit time period). We also postulate that labor is the only factor of production that is relevant for agricultural activities, assuming all other factors of production remain unchanged throughout the course of our discussion.

Let us denote generically by ν the farmers in the village commons; the amount of the crop produced by farmer ν, x^ν, is determined by the hours he works on the land ℓ^ν:

$$x^\nu = f^\nu(\ell^\nu),$$

where the production function $f^\nu(\ell^\nu)$ is assumed to satisfy the standard neoclassical conditions:

$$f^\nu(\ell^\nu) > 0, \quad f^{\nu\prime}(\ell^\nu) > 0, \quad f^{\nu\prime\prime}(\ell^\nu) < 0 \quad \text{for all } \ell^\nu > 0.$$

However, the productivity of agricultural activities crucially depends upon the expanse and quality of the land under the control of the commons, together with the irrigation system and other common facilities installed on the commons land. We postulate that the capacity of the commons land together with the infrastructure facilities, in the processes of agricultural production, is expressed by an index V. Then the production function for each farmer ν is of the form

$$x^\nu = f^\nu(\ell^\nu, X, V),$$

where x^ν is the quantity of crop produced by farmer ν, ℓ^ν is the number of hours spent on agricultural activities by farmer ν, X is the total quantity of crop produced in the commons:

$$X = \sum_\nu x^\nu,$$

and V is the stock of the commons.

The production function $f^\nu(\ell^\nu, X, V)$ for each farmer ν in the agricultural commons satisfies the following conditions:

(i) For any given $(X, V) > 0$, $f^\nu(\ell^\nu, X, V)$ satisfies the standard neoclassical conditions:

$$f^\nu(\ell^\nu, X, V) > 0, \quad f^\nu_{\ell^\nu}(\ell^\nu, X, V) > 0,$$
$$f^\nu_{\ell^\nu\ell^\nu}(\ell^\nu, X, V) < 0 \quad \text{for all } \ell^\nu > 0.$$

(ii) An increase in the total quantity of crop X favorably affects agricultural activities in the commons; that is,

$$f^\nu_X(\ell^\nu, X, V) > 0, \quad f^\nu_{\ell^\nu X}(\ell^\nu, X, V) > 0.$$

(iii) An increase in the stock of the commons V has favorable effects upon agricultural activities; that is,

$$f^\nu_V(\ell^\nu, X, V) > 0, \quad f^\nu_{\ell^\nu V}(\ell^\nu, X, V) > 0.$$

(iv) Marginal rates of substitution between the quantity x^ν of crop produced by farmer ν, the hours spent for agricultural activities ℓ^ν, the total quantity X of crop produced, and the stock of the commons V are smooth and diminishing; that is, the production function $f^\nu(\ell^\nu, X, V)$ is concave with respect to (ℓ^ν, X, V); in particular,

$$f^\nu_{\ell^\nu\ell^\nu}(\ell^\nu, X, V) < 0, \quad f^\nu_{XX}(\ell^\nu, X, V) < 0, \quad f^\nu_{\ell^\nu X}(\ell^\nu, X, V) < 0.$$

(v) Total quantity X of crop produced and the stock of the commons V are substitutes; that is,

$$f^\nu_{XV}(\ell^\nu, X, V) < 0.$$

The capacity of the commons is assumed to be depreciated by agricultural activities, with an increasing marginal effect with respect to the aggregate amount of the crop. Let us denote by $\mu(X, V)$ the rate of depreciation of the capacity of the commons V when the aggregate amount of the crop is X. We assume the following conditions:

(i)′ $\mu(X, V) > 0, \quad \mu_X(X, V) > 0, \quad \mu_V(X, V) > 0.$

(ii)′ $\mu(X, V)$ is a convex function of (X, V); that is,

$$\mu_{XX} > 0, \quad \mu_{VV} > 0, \quad \mu_{XX}\mu_{VV} - \mu_{XV}^2 \geqq 0.$$

(iii)′ For a fixed amount of total crop X, the marginal rate of depreciation of the stock of the commons V is decreasing as the stock of the commons V is increased:

$$\mu_{XV}(X, V) < 0.$$

The stock of the commons V may be increased by investing labor and other factors of production in the irrigation system and other infrastructure. To simplify the analysis, we postulate that the investment expenditures B associated with increasing the stock of the commons by the quantity Y is given by a well-defined functional form:

$$B = B(Y, V).$$

The investment expenditures B are measured in terms of the wage-units, assuming that the wage rate for standard labor is well defined and fixed. It may be assumed that investment activities concerning the stock of the common are subject to the Penrose effect, as was introduced in Uzawa (1968, 1969) and described in detail in Uzawa (2003); that is,

(i)″ $B(Y, V) > 0, \quad B_Y(Y, V) > 0, \quad B_V(Y, V) > 0.$

(ii)″ $B(Y, V)$ is a convex function of (Y, V):

$$B_{YY} > 0, \quad B_{VV} > 0, \quad B_{YY}B_{VV} - B_{YV}^2 \geqq 0.$$

The change in the stock of the commons V_t is described by the following dynamic equation:

$$\dot{V}_t = Y_t - \mu(X_t, V_t), \tag{61}$$

with the given initial stock of the commons V_0 and the total crop at time t, X_t, given by

$$X_t = \sum_{\nu} x_t^{\nu}, \quad x_t^{\nu} = f^{\nu}(\ell_t^{\nu}, X_t, V_t).$$

Total net profits accrued to the commons at each time t, Π_t, are given by

$$\Pi_t = pX_t - L_t - B_t,$$

where p is the market price of the crop measured in wage-units, which for the simple model of the agricultural commons, is assumed to remain constant throughout the course of our discussion; L_t is the total labor input at time t,

$$L_t = \sum_{\nu} \ell_t^{\nu};$$

and B_t is the investment expenditure at time t.

The agricultural commons, being a perpetual institution, is concerned with obtaining the maximum long-run net profits, the latter condition being expressed as follows:

The agricultural commons is interested in finding the time-path $(x_t^{\nu}, X_t, B_t, V_t)$ that maximizes the discounted present value of all future net profits,

$$\Pi = \int_0^{\infty} \Pi_t e^{-\delta t} dt,$$

among all feasible time-paths starting with the given initial stock of the commons V_0. The rate of discount δ is defined by the nominal rate of interest minus the expected rate of increase in the standard wage rate, and it is assumed to remain constant.

The problem thus defined is one of the calculus-of-variations problems and the standard techniques in terms of the concept of imputed price of the stock of the commons, as developed in relation to the analysis of fisheries and forestry commons in the previous sections. Because we have postulated that agricultural activities are subject to external economies, as formulated by conditions (iii) and (iv), we describe, at the risk of repetition, basic concepts required for our analysis and derivations of basic formulas and conclusions.

We first discuss the short-run allocation of agricultural resources of the commons and then proceed with the discussion of an intertemporal pattern of resource allocation that is dynamically optimum.

The Consolidated Cost Function

The dynamic analysis of the agricultural commons is simplified if we introduce the consolidated cost function, as with the fisheries commons. Let us consider an individual farmer ν and see how the individual cost schedule is derived under the conditions of the competitive market for the crop of the commons. The net profit for each farmer ν is given by

$$\pi^{\nu} = px^{\nu} - \ell^{\nu}, \quad x^{\nu} = f^{\nu}(\ell^{\nu}, X, V),$$

where X is the total crop of the commons:

$$X = \sum_{\nu} x^{\nu}.$$

For each farmer ν, the maximum profit is obtained if he or she chooses the amount of the crop x^{ν} so that the marginal product of his or her labor is equal to the wage/price ratio:

$$pf^{\nu}_{\ell^{\nu}}(\ell^{\nu}, X, V) = 1.$$

For given values of X and V, this marginality condition may be solved to obtain the cost function for each farmer ν:

$$\ell^{\nu} = c^{\nu}(x^{\nu}, X, V),$$

where market price p is parametrically changed. We may assume that the cost function thus derived, $c^{\nu}(x^{\nu}, X, V)$, is a convex function of (x^{ν}, X, V).

The consolidated cost function $C = C(X, V)$ is now given by

$$C(X, V) = \min \left\{ \sum_{\nu} c^{\nu}(x^{\nu}, X, V) \colon \sum_{\nu} x^{\nu} \geqq X \right\}.$$

Because each individual farmer's cost function $c^{\nu}(x^{\nu}, X, V)$ is convex with respect to (x^{ν}, X, V), the consolidated cost function $C(X, V)$ thus defined also is convex with respect to (X, V).

The assumptions made for individual production functions, particularly (i)–(iv), imply the following conditions for individual cost functions $c^\nu(x^\nu, X, V)$:

$$c^\nu(x^\nu, X, V) > 0 \quad \text{for all } (x^\nu, X, V) > 0,$$

and $c^\nu(x^\nu, X, V)$ is convex with respect to (x^ν, X, V); in particular,

$$\begin{aligned} &c^\nu_{x^\nu x^\nu} > 0, \quad c^\nu_{XX} > 0, \quad c^\nu_{VV} > 0 \\ &c^\nu_{x^\nu} > 0, \quad c^\nu_{X} < 0, \quad c^\nu_{V} < 0 \\ &c^\nu_{x^\nu X} < 0, \quad c^\nu_{x^\nu V} < 0, \quad c^\nu_{XV} < 0. \end{aligned}$$

Then, similar conditions are satisfied for the consolidated cost function $C(X, V)$:

(i)‴ $C(X, V) > 0$ for all $(X, V) > 0$.

(ii)‴ Consolidated cost function $C(X, V)$ is convex with respect to (X, V); that is,

$$C_{XX} > 0, \quad C_{VV} > 0, \quad C_{XX}C_{VV} - {C_{XV}}^2 \geqq 0.$$

(iii)‴ $C_X > 0, \quad C_V < 0.$

(iv)‴ $C_{XV} = C_{VX} < 0.$

The consolidated cost function $C(X, V)$ is normally obtained in terms of the Lagrangian method for constrained minimization problems. We consider the Lagrangian form:

$$L[(x^\nu), \lambda] = \sum_\nu c^\nu(x^\nu, X, V) + \lambda \left[X - \sum_\nu x^\nu \right],$$

where λ is the Lagrangian multiplier associated with the constraint:

$$\sum_\nu x^\nu \geqq X.$$

Then the optimum levels of agricultural activities (x^ν_{o}) are obtained if there exists a nonnegative Lagrangian multiplier λ_{o} such that $[(x^\nu_{\text{o}}), \lambda_{\text{o}}]$ is a saddlepoint of the Lagrangian form

$$L[(x^\nu), \lambda_{\text{o}}] \geqq L[(x^\nu_{\text{o}}), \lambda_{\text{o}}] \geqq L[(x^\nu_{\text{o}}), \lambda] \quad \text{for all } (x^\nu), \quad \lambda \geqq 0.$$

Hence, we have the following marginality conditions:

$$c^\nu_{x^\nu}(x^\nu_{\text{o}}, X_{\text{o}}, V) \leqq \lambda_{\text{o}}, \tag{62}$$

with equality whenever $x_o^\nu > 0$;

$$\sum_\nu x_o^\nu \geqq X_o, \tag{63}$$

with equality whenever $\lambda_o > 0$.

We would like to see how the marginal cost for each farmer is related to the marginal cost in terms of the consolidated cost function $C(X, V)$. Let us take a differential of the consolidated cost function

$$C = \sum_\nu c^\nu(x^\nu, X, V),$$

to obtain

$$dC = \sum_\nu [c_{x^\nu}^\nu dx^\nu + c_X^\nu dX + c_V^\nu dV]. \tag{64}$$

On the other hand, by taking a differential of both sides of (63), we obtain

$$\sum_\nu dx^\nu = dX. \tag{65}$$

By substituting (65) into (64) and noting the marginality conditions (62), we obtain

$$dC = \left[\lambda_o + \sum_\nu c_X^\nu\right] dX + \left[\sum_\nu c_V^\nu\right] dV.$$

Hence, we have

$$\frac{\partial C}{\partial X} = \lambda_o - \text{MSB}, \tag{66}$$

where

$$\text{MSB} = \sum_\nu [-c_X^\nu] \tag{67}$$

corresponds to the notion of the marginal social benefit associated with agricultural activities in the commons.

The external economies are observed with respect to agricultural activities in the commons, as expressed by conditions (iii) and (iv), and $[-c_V^\nu]$ denotes the extent of the marginal benefit accruing to each farmer ν owing to the marginal increase in the aggregate level of agricultural activities. Thus, the MSB given by (67) expresses the total benefits all the farmers in the commons may obtain owing to the marginal increase in the aggregate level of agricultural activities.

Formula (66) expresses that the marginal cost in terms of the consolidated cost function diverges from the private marginal cost λ_O by the marginal social benefit, MSB. It implies that to obtain the levels of agricultural activities of the farmers in the village commons that are optimum in the short run, it is necessary to make arrangements whereby each farmer in the commons receives a subsidy payment corresponding to the marginal social benefit, MSB, per unit of the crop being produced. This proposition will be examined in more detail.

We consider the static situation in which the stock of the commons, V, is given and fixed, and we determine the levels of agricultural activities in the village commons at which the total net profit for the commons as a whole is maximized. The problem for the commons is as follows:

Find the levels of agricultural activities, (x^ν), that maximize the total net profit

$$\Pi = \sum_\nu [px^\nu - c^\nu(x^\nu, X, V)]$$

subject to the constraint

$$X = \sum_\nu x^\nu, \tag{68}$$

where p is the market price (assuming a perfectly competitive market for the crop of the commons).

The maximization problem for the commons differs from the cost minimization problem we discussed above in relation to the definition of the consolidated cost function $C(X, V)$, where the aggregate level X of the crop of the commons is assumed to be given, together with the stock of the common V, whereas the aggregate level X now is a variable to be determined, together with individual levels of agricultural activities (x^ν).

Let us denote by λ the Lagrangian multiplier associated with constraint (68) and construct the Lagrangian form:

$$L((x^\nu), X; \lambda) = \sum_\nu \left\{ [px^\nu - c^\nu(x^\nu, X, V)] + \lambda \left[\sum_\nu x^\nu - X \right] \right\}.$$

Then the optimum levels of agricultural activities (x_o^ν) and the total output of the crop X_o are obtained as the solution to the following marginality conditions:

$$c_{x^\nu}^\nu(x_o^\nu, X_o, V) = p + \lambda \tag{69}$$

$$\sum_\nu x_o^\nu = X_o \tag{70}$$

$$\lambda = \sum_\nu [-c_{x^\nu}^\nu(x_o^\nu, X_o, V)] = \text{MSB}. \tag{71}$$

Marginality conditions (69)–(71) mean that the optimum level of the crop for each individual farmer is obtained if a subsidy payment in the amount equal to the marginal social benefit, MSB, is made per unit of the crop, so that the effective price for each farmer is the market price plus MSB.

In terms of the consolidated cost function $C(X, V)$, the optimum total crop in the short run is simply obtained by the condition:

$$C_X(X_o, V) = p.$$

Imputed Price and Dynamic Optimality

We now come back to the problem of the intertemporal allocation of agricultural resources in the commons that would result in the time-path of resource allocation in which the discounted present value of all future total net profits of the commons is maximized among all feasible time-paths of resource allocation in the commons.

Because our model of the agricultural commons is formulated in terms of the concepts and premises that are not readily found in the standard treatment of price theory, we put together some of the more relevant variables and conditions that we have introduced in the previous sections.

The stock of the commons V is assumed to serve as the capacity index, and the change of the stock over time is described by the basic dynamic equation:

$$\dot{V}_t = Y_t - \mu(X_t, V_t), \quad V_0 = V^0, \tag{72}$$

where Y_t is the increase in the stock of the commons V_t due to investment activities and $\mu(X_t, V_t)$ is the rate at which the stock of the common is depreciated owing to agricultural activities, to be summarized by the total output of the crop at time t, X_t.

The expenditures related to the investment activities to increase the stock of the common by the quantity Y_t is a function of Y_t and the stock of the common at time t, V_t:

$$B_t = B(Y_t, V_t),$$

where the expenditure function $B(Y, V)$ satisfies conditions (i)″ and (ii)″.

On the other hand, the deprecation function $\mu(Y, V)$ is assumed to satisfy conditions (i)′–(iii)′. The current expenditures related to agricultural activities are specified by the consolidated cost function $C(X, V)$, satisfying conditions (i)‴–(iv)‴.

The total net profit at time t, Π_t, is given by

$$\Pi_t = pX_t - B(Y_t, V_t) - C(X_t, V_t),$$

where market price p is assumed to remain constant.

A time-path of resource allocation (X_t, Y_t, V_t) is termed dynamically optimum if it maximizes the discounted present value of all future total net profits for the commons,

$$\Pi = \int_0^{\infty} \Pi_t e^{-\delta t} dt,$$

with a constant positive rate of discount δ, among all feasible time paths of resource allocation in the commons.

The dynamic optimum problem thus formulated may be solved in terms of the concept of imputed price, in a manner largely identical to that of the fisheries and forestry commons, described in detail in the previous sections. Because we are primarily interested in the institutional and behavioral implications of the various concepts and relationships that are introduced to solve the dynamic optimum problem for the agricultural commons, we describe the analysis of the optimum problem in detail, again at the risk of repetition.

We denote by ψ_t the imputed price of the stock of the commons at time t and define the imputed real income of the commons at time t by

$$H_t = \{pX_t - B(Y_t, V_t) - C(X_t, V_t)\} + \psi_t\{Y_t - \mu(X_t, V_t)\}. \qquad (73)$$

The optimum levels of total crop X_t and investment in the stock of the common Y_t at each time t are determined in such a manner that the imputed real income H_t is maximized for a given stock of the commons V_t and imputed price ψ_t. Therefore, by differentiating (73) with respect to Y_t and X_t respectively, we obtain

$$B_Y = \psi \tag{74}$$

$$C_X + \psi \mu_X = p, \tag{75}$$

where, for the sake of brevity, time suffix t is omitted.

Relation (74) simply means that the optimum level Y_t of investment in the stock of the commons is determined at the level at which the marginal cost of investment B_Y is equal to the imputed price ψ_t of the stock of the commons at time t.

On the other hand, a marginal increase in the total crop X_t entails not only the marginal increase in the current cost, in the magnitude of C_X, but also the marginal increase in the rate of depreciation of the stock of the commons, to be evaluated at $\psi_t \mu_X$. The left-hand side of relation (75) expresses the marginal social cost associated with agricultural activities in the commons, which, at the optimum in the short run, is equated with the market price p.

We may express the optimum condition (75) in terms of individual cost functions $c^\nu(x^\nu, X, V)$. By substituting (69)–(71) into (75), we obtain

$$c^\nu_{x^\nu} = p + \text{MSB} - \psi \mu_X. \tag{76}$$

Relation (76) means that for individual farmers' agricultural activities to result in the optimum allocation of resources in the commons in the short run, individual farmers must be given a subsidy payment in the amount of the marginal social benefit, MSB, to be levied as the marginal environmental tax in the amount of $\psi_t \mu_X$, both per unit of output.

We now look into the way the imputed price of the stock of the commons is determined. To do this, let us go back to the definition of the imputed price of the stock of the commons. The imputed price of the stock of the commons at time t, ψ_t, expresses the extent to which the commons as a whole enjoys the benefit due to the marginal increase in the stock of the commons at time t. It is represented by the discounted present value of all future marginal increases in the net profits of the commons. The marginal increase in the stock of the commons at time t first entails the marginal decreases in the consolidated costs, in the amount of $[-C_X]$, at all future times. Secondly, it entails the marginal increase in the investment expenditures, in the amount of B_V, at all future times. It may be recalled that it is assumed that $C_X < 0$ and $B_Y > 0$.

Because the marginal increase in the rate of depreciation is given by μ_V, the discounted present value of the marginal increases in future net profits due to the marginal increase in the stock of the commons at time t may be expressed as follows:

$$\psi_t = \int_t^{\infty} \{-B_V(\tau) - C_V(\tau)\} e^{-\int_t^{\tau} (\delta + \mu_V(v))dv} d\tau . \tag{77}$$

By differentiating both sides of (77), we obtain

$$\dot{\psi}_t = (\delta + \mu_V)\psi_t + (B_V + C_V), \tag{78}$$

where μ_V, B_V, C_V are measured at time t. The dynamically optimum time-path $(Y_t^{\text{o}}, X_t^{\text{o}}, V_t^{\text{o}})$ will be obtained if we find a positive, continuous function ψ_t that, together with $(Y_t^{\text{o}}, X_t^{\text{o}}, V_t^{\text{o}})$, satisfies the system of basic differential equations, (72) and (78), together with the transversality condition:

$$\lim_{t \to \infty} \psi_t V_t^{\text{o}} e^{-\delta t} = 0.$$

To see how the solutions to the system of differential equations, (72) and (78), behave, we examine how the optimum levels of investment and agricultural activities, Y_t and X_t, are related to changes in the stock of commons V_t and the imputed price ψ_t.

We take a differential of both sides of (74) and (75) and solve with respect to dY and dX to obtain

$$dY = -\frac{B_{YV}}{B_{YY}} dV + \frac{1}{B_{YY}} d\psi$$

$$dX = -\frac{C_{XV} + \psi \mu_{XV}}{C_{XX} + \psi \mu_{XX}} dV - \frac{\mu_X}{C_{XX} + \psi \mu_{XX}} d\psi.$$

We recall that we have made the following assumptions:

$$B > 0, \quad B_Y > 0, \quad B_V > 0, \quad B_{YY} > 0, \quad B_{YV} > 0, \quad B_{VV} > 0$$
$$C > 0, \quad C_X > 0, \quad C_{VV} < 0, \quad C_{XX} > 0, \quad C_{XV} < 0, \quad C_{VV} > 0$$
$$\mu > 0, \quad \mu_X > 0, \quad \mu_V < 0, \quad \mu_{XX} > 0, \quad \mu_{XV} < 0, \quad \mu_{VV} > 0.$$

Hence,

$$\begin{aligned} Y_V &= \frac{\partial Y}{\partial V} < 0, \quad Y_\psi = \frac{\partial Y}{\partial \psi} > 0 \\ X_V &= \frac{\partial X}{\partial V} > 0, \quad X_\psi = \frac{\partial X}{\partial \psi} < 0 \\ Y_\psi &= -\frac{1}{B_{YV}} Y_V, \quad X_\psi = \frac{\mu_X}{C_{XV} + \psi \mu_{XV}} X_V. \end{aligned} \tag{79}$$

We are now interested in the stationary state $(Y^{\mathrm{o}}, \psi^{\mathrm{o}})$ for the system of basic differential equations, (72) and (78), which is reproduced here without time suffix:

$$\begin{cases} \dot{V} = Y - \mu(X, V) \\ \dot{\psi} = (\delta + \mu_V) + (B_V + C_V). \end{cases} \tag{80}$$

The stationary state (Y^0, ψ^0) is characterized by the following system of equations:

$$\begin{cases} Y - \mu(X, V) = 0 \\ (\delta + \mu_V) + (B_V + C_V) = 0. \end{cases} \tag{81}$$

We take differentials of both sides of the system of equations (81) to obtain

$$\begin{pmatrix} \beta_{11} & \beta_{12} \\ \beta_{21} & \beta_{22} \end{pmatrix} \begin{pmatrix} dV \\ d\psi \end{pmatrix} = \begin{pmatrix} 0 \\ 0 \end{pmatrix},$$

where

$$\begin{aligned} \beta_{11} &= Y_V - \mu_X X_V - \mu_V < 0 \\ \beta_{12} &= Y_\psi - \mu_X X_\psi > 0 \\ \beta_{21} &= B_{YV} Y_V + (C_{XV} + \psi \mu_{XV}) X_V + (B_{VV} + C_{VV} + \psi \mu_{VV}) \\ \beta_{22} &= \delta + \mu_V + B_{YV} Y_\psi + (C_{XV} + \psi \mu_{XV}) X_\psi. \end{aligned}$$

In view of relations (79), we have

$$\beta_{11} + \beta_{22} = \delta > 0$$

$$\Delta = \beta_{11}\beta_{22} - \beta_{12}\beta_{21} = \beta_{11}\delta - \beta_{12}(B_{VV} + C_{VV} + \psi\mu_{VV})$$
$$+ \frac{1}{X}\left\{\mu_X + \frac{C_{XV} + \psi\mu_{XV}}{B_{YV}}\right\}^2 Y_\psi X_\psi - \mu_V(\mu_V - 2Y_V + \mu_X X_V) < 0.$$

Therefore, the stationary state (V^o, ψ^o) is uniquely determined, and the characteristic roots of the system of differential equations (80) are both real, one negative and another positive, with the negative root having a larger absolute value than the positive root. Thus, the phase diagram for the system of differential equations (80) may have a structure as illustrated in Figure 1.3, where the abscissa now measures the stock of the common and the imputed price is measured along the ordinate.

The combinations of (V, ψ) for which the stock of the common V remains stationary is depicted by an upward-sloping curve, AA. If (V, ψ) lies on the right-hand side of the AA curve, V tends to decrease $(\dot{V} < 0)$; if it lies on the left-hand side of the AA curve, V tends to increase $(\dot{V} > 0)$.

On the other hand, the combinations of (V, ψ) for which the imputed price ψ remains stationary are depicted by the BB curve, which intersects with the AA curve as illustrated in Figure 1.3. If (V, ψ) lies above the BB curve, ψ tends to increase $(\dot{\psi} > 0)$; if it lies below the BB curve, ψ tends to decrease $(\dot{\psi} < 0)$. Thus the solution paths to the system of differential equations (80) behave as indicated by the arrowed curves in Figure 1.3, and there always exists a pair of solution paths, CE and C′E, both of which converge to the stationary point, E $= (V^o, \psi^o)$. It is easily seen that the transversality condition is satisfied along these stationary solution paths.

The dynamically optimum allocation of resources in our agricultural commons is obtained if, at each time t, the imputed price ψ_t^o is assigned at the level

$$\psi_t^o = g(V_t),$$

where $g(V)$ is the functional form corresponding to the stationary solution paths, CE and C′E.

As the stock of the common V is increased, the imputed price associated with the dynamically optimum time-path tends to be decreased, as shown in Figure 1.3.

The effects of changes in the market price p and in the rate of discount δ are also easily examined in terms of the phase diagram in Figure 1.3.

6. CONCLUDING REMARKS

This chapter examines the phenomenon of static and dynamic externalities in terms of dynamic models concerning fisheries, forestry, and agricultural commons. The structure of the intertemporal processes of resource allocation that are dynamically optimum with respect to the given intertemporal preference ordering is analyzed within the framework of the Ramsey-Koopmans-Cass theory of optimum economic growth. Particular attention is paid to the role of the imputed price of the environment in the process of resource allocation, including the natural resources drawn from the given environment.

A number of propositions are established in which the implications of the static externalities are clarified for the patterns of intertemporal allocation of scarce resources that are dynamically optimum, and for the institutional arrangements whereby dynamically optimum patterns of intertemporal resource allocation necessarily ensue. However, we have not paid sufficient attention to the problems of actually designing feasible and efficient systems for the management of common property resources.

Particularly relevant to the problems of the optimum management of common property resources are the rules concerning individual members of the communities that have exclusive rights to the control of common property resources or to the use of natural resources to be derived from such common property resources.

We have also not paid enough attention to the role of the infrastructure, such as irrigation canals, drainage systems, and extension services, that is indispensable in carrying out agricultural activities. Infrastructure, or social common capital in general, plays a pivotal role in the processes of economic development. The structure of social common capital influences whether the resulting pattern of economic development is sustainable.

Finally, we have postulated throughout this chapter that the intertemporal preference ordering remains fixed regardless of changes in economic and other conditions, which is expressed by a Ramsey-Koopmans-Cass utility integral with a constant rate of utility discount. A detailed analysis of the implications of endogenous intertemporal preference orderings for either dynamically optimum economic growth or sustainable economic development awaits future study.

2

The Prototype Model of Social Common Capital

1. INTRODUCTION

In the prototype model of social common capital introduced in this chapter, we consider a particular type of social common capital – social infrastructure, such as highways, ports, and public transportation systems. We consider the general circumstances under which factors of production that are necessary for the professional provision of services of social common capital are either privately owned or managed as if private owned. Services of social common capital are subject to the phenomenon of congestion, resulting in the divergence between private and social costs. Therefore, to obtain efficient and equitable allocation of scarce resources, it becomes necessary to levy taxes on the use of services of social common capital. The prices charged for the use of services of social common capital exceed, by the tax rates, the prices paid to social institutions in charge of social common capital for the provision of services of social common capital. One of crucial problems in the economic analysis of social common capital is to examine how the optimum tax rates for the services of various components of social common capital are determined. The nature of services of social common capital varies to such a significant degree that it is extremely difficult to formulate a unifying theory concerning the determination of the optimum taxes on services of social common capital. In later chapters, we discuss the problem of the optimum taxation for a number of specific types of social common capital and examine the institutional and policy implications on the pattern of resource allocation. The prototype model of social common capital introduced in this chapter incorporates some of the more salient features of social common capital, and the analytical apparatuses and institutional and policy implications regarding the prototype model of social common capital may serve as guidelines for the analysis of the specific types of social common capital discussed in later chapters.

In the first part of this chapter, we examine the conditions for the social common capital taxes to ensue market equilibrium that is social optimum, or Pareto optimum if we use the more traditional terminology in neoclassical welfare economics. Under certain qualifying constraints concerning preference relations of individuals and production possibility sets of both private firms and social institutions in charge of social common capital, the ensuing market equilibrium is a social optimum if, and only if, social common capital taxes are levied with rates that are proportional to the prices of services of the various components of social common capital, with the coefficients of proportionality at certain specific values.

The concept of social optimality is primarily concerned with the efficiency aspect of resource allocation. Concerning the equity aspect of resource allocation and income distribution, the concept of Lindahl equilibrium that was introduced by Lindahl (1919) to examine the equity problems in the theory of public goods plays a crucial role in the analysis of social common capital as well. In the second part of this chapter, we examine the conditions for market equilibrium of the prototype model of social common capital to be a Lindahl equilibrium. We particularly show that the market equilibrium under the social common capital taxes with rates proportional to the prices of services of the various components of social common capital, with the coefficients of proportionality at certain specific values, is always a Lindahl equilibrium.

The analysis of social common capital introduced in this chapter is static in the sense that all fixed factors of production endowed within private firms and social institutions in charge of social common capital are kept at constant levels. In Chapter 3, a dynamic analysis of social common capital is developed whereby the sustainable processes of accumulation of factors of production endowed in both private firms and social institutions in charge of social common capital are analyzed and welfare implications for future generations are examined.

2. BASIC PREMISES OF THE PROTOTYPE MODEL OF SOCIAL COMMON CAPITAL

We consider a society, either a nation or a specific region. The society consists of a finite number of individuals and two types of institutions – private firms specialized in producing goods that are transacted on the market, on the one hand, and social institutions that are concerned with the provision of services of social common capital, on the other. In constructing the prototype model of social common capital, we have in mind particularly the case of social infrastructure such as highways, ports, and public transportation systems.

Basic Premises of the Model

The type of social common capital discussed in this chapter is characterized by the properties that all factors of production that are necessary for the professional provision of services of social common capital are either owned by private individuals, or if not, are managed as if privately owned. They are managed by social institutions in accordance with professional discipline and expertise.

Social common capital taxes are levied on the use of services of social common capital, with the tax rates to be administratively determined by the government and announced prior to the opening of the market. The prices charged for the use of services of social common capital exceed, by the tax rates, the prices paid to social institutions in charge of social common capital for the provision of services of social common capital. These two prices of services of social common capital are so determined that total amounts of services provided by all social institutions in charge of social common capital in the society are precisely equal to the total amounts of services required by all members of the society. One of the crucial roles of the government is to determine the tax rates on the use of services of social common capital in such a manner that the ensuing patterns of resource allocation and income distribution are optimum in a certain well-defined, socially acceptable sense. In the theory of social common capital, we are primarily concerned with defining the concept of optimality in an operational form and examining institutional and policy implications of the social common capital tax scheme that is optimum in the sense thus defined.

Individuals are generically denoted by $\nu = 1, \ldots, n$, and private firms by $\mu = 1, \ldots, m$, whereas social institutions in charge of social common capital are denoted by $\sigma = 1, \ldots, s$. Goods produced by private firms are generically denoted by $j = 1, \ldots, J$. We consider the situation in which there are several kinds of social common capital, to be generically denoted by $i = 1, \ldots, I$. However, in the description of the model, we occasionally make statements as if there is only one kind of social common capital. There are two types of factors of production: variable and fixed. Variable factors of production are generically denoted by $\eta = 1, \ldots, \mathrm{H}$, and fixed factors of production by $f = 1, \ldots, F$.

Typical variable factors of production are various kinds of labor, so we often refer to them as labor. Fixed factors of production are typically factories, machinery, tools, equipment, and others. They do not precisely coincide with the traditional concept of capital as the stock of material means by which industry is carried on, industrial equipment, raw materials, and means of subsistence. Fixed factors of production in the present context are those means of production that are made as fixed, specific components of private firms or social institutions in charge of social common capital, including intangible assets as well. In the following discussion, we occasionally refer to fixed factors of production as capital goods.

Static analysis of private firms or social institutions in charge of social common capital presupposes that the endowments of fixed factors of production are given as the result of past activities of capital investments carried out by the institutions in question. Dynamic analysis, on the other hand, concerns processes of the accumulation of fixed factors of production in private firms or social institutions in charge of social common capital and the ensuing implications for productive capacity in the future.

Production of Goods by Private Firms

Quantities of fixed factors of production accumulated in each private firm μ are expressed by a vector $K^\mu = (K_f^\mu)$, where K_f^μ is the quantity of factor of production f accumulated in firm μ. Quantities of goods produced by firm μ are denoted by a vector $x^\mu = (x_j^\mu)$, where x_j^μ is the quantity of goods j produced by firm μ, net of the quantities of goods used by firm μ itself. Amounts of labor employed by firm μ to carry out production activities are expressed by a vector $\ell^\mu = (\ell_\eta^\mu)$, where ℓ^μ_η is the amount of labor of type η employed by firm μ. To carry out production activities, private firms use services of social common capital. The amounts of services of social common capital used by firm μ are denoted by a vector $a^\mu = (a^\mu_i)$, where a^μ_i is the amount of services of type i used by firm μ.

Social Institutions in Charge of Social Common Capital

The manner in which social institutions in charge of social common capital provide their services with members of the society is similarly postulated.

Quantities of fixed factors of production accumulated in social institution σ are expressed by a vector $K^\sigma = (K^\sigma_f)$, where K^σ_f is the quantity of fixed factor of production f accumulated in social institution σ. It is assumed that $K^\sigma \geq 0$. Amounts of services of social common capital provided by social institutions are expressed by a vector $a^\sigma = (a^\sigma_i)$, where a^σ_i is the amount of services of type i provided by social institution σ, net of the amounts of services of social common capital used by social institution σ itself. Labor of various types employed by social institution σ for the provision of services of social common capital are expressed by a vector $\ell^\sigma = (\ell^\sigma_\eta)$, where ℓ^σ_η is the amount of labor of type η employed by social institution σ. We also denote by $x^\sigma = (x^\sigma_j)$ the vector of quantities of produced goods used by social institution σ for the provision of the services of social common capital.

Principal Agency of the Society

The principal agency of the society in question is the individuals who consume goods produced by private firms and use services provided by social institutions in charge of social common capital. The quantities of goods consumed by individual ν are denoted by a vector $c^\nu = (c^\nu_j)$, where c^ν_j is the quantity of good j consumed, whereas the amounts of services of social common capital used by individual ν are expressed by a vector $a^\nu = (a^\nu_i)$.

All variable factors of production, including various kinds of labor, are owned by the individuals. The amounts of labor of various types of each individual ν are denoted by a vector $\ell^\nu = (\ell^\nu_\eta)$, where ℓ^ν_η is the amount of labor of type η of individual ν. It is generally the case that for each individual ν, ℓ^ν_η are zero except for one type of labor η.

It is assumed that all variable factors of production are inelastically supplied to the market.

We also assume that both private firms and social institutions in charge of social common capital are owned by individuals. We denote by $s^{\nu\mu}$ and $s^{\nu\sigma}$, respectively, the shares of private firm μ and social institution σ owned by individual ν, where

$$s^{\nu\mu} \geqq 0, \quad \sum_{\nu} s^{\nu\mu} = 1; \quad s^{\nu\sigma} \geqq 0, \quad \sum_{\nu} s^{\nu\sigma} = 1.$$

3. SPECIFICATIONS OF THE PROTOTYPE MODEL OF SOCIAL COMMON CAPITAL

The economic welfare of each individual ν is expressed by a preference ordering that is represented by the utility function

$$u^{\nu} = u^{\nu}(c^{\nu}, a^{\nu}),$$

where $c^{\nu} = (c_j^{\nu})$ is the vector of goods consumed and $a^{\nu} = (a_i^{\nu})$ is the vector of amounts of services of social common capital used, both by individual ν.

Neoclassical Conditions for Utility Functions

We assume that, for each individual ν, the utility function $u^{\nu}(c^{\nu}, a^{\nu})$ satisfies the following neoclassical conditions:

(U1) $u^{\nu}(c^{\nu}, a^{\nu})$ is defined, positive, continuous, and continuously twice-differentiable with respect to (c^{ν}, a^{ν}) for all $(c^{\nu}, a^{\nu}) \geqq 0$.

(U2) Marginal utilities are positive both for the consumption of private goods c^{ν} and the use of services of social common capital a^{ν}; that is,

$$u_{c^{\nu}}^{\nu}(c^{\nu}, a^{\nu}) > 0, \quad u_{a^{\nu}}^{\nu}(c^{\nu}, a^{\nu}) > 0 \quad \text{for all } (c^{\nu}, a^{\nu}) \geqq 0.$$

(U3) Marginal rates of substitution between any pair of consumption goods and services of social common capital are diminishing, or more specifically, $u^{\nu}(c^{\nu}, a^{\nu})$ is strictly quasi-concave with respect to (c^{ν}, a^{ν}); that is, for any (c_0^{ν}, a_0^{ν}) and (c_1^{ν}, a_1^{ν}), such that $u^{\nu}(c_0^{\nu}, a_0^{\nu}) = u^{\nu}(c_1^{\nu}, a_1^{\nu})$ and $(c_0^{\nu}, a_0^{\nu}) \neq (c_1^{\nu}, a_1^{\nu})$,

$$u^{\nu}((1-t)c_0^{\nu} + t c_1^{\nu}, (1-t)a_0^{\nu} + t a_1^{\nu}) < (1-t)u^{\nu}(c_0^{\nu}, a_0^{\nu}) + t u^{\nu}(c_1^{\nu}, a_1^{\nu}) \quad \text{for all } 0 < t < 1.$$

(U4) $u^\nu(c^\nu, a^\nu)$ is homogeneous of order 1 with respect to (c^ν, a^ν); that is,

$$u^\nu(tc^\nu, ta^\nu) = tu^\nu(c^\nu, a^\nu) \quad \text{for all } t \geqq 0, (c^\nu, a^\nu) \geqq 0.$$

The linear homogeneity hypothesis (U4) implies the following Euler identity:

$$u^\nu(c^\nu, a^\nu) = u^\nu_{c^\nu}(c^\nu, a^\nu)\, c^\nu + u^\nu_{a^\nu}(c^\nu, a^\nu)\, a^\nu \quad \text{for all } (c^\nu, a^\nu) \geqq 0.$$

We will frequently make use of the Euler identity in the following discussion.

Effects of Congestion on Individuals

Services derived from social common capital exhibit the phenomenon of congestion in the sense that the effectiveness of services of social common capital for each member of the society depends upon the extent to which other members of the society are using the same services. The phenomenon of congestion may be expressed by the postulate that the effectiveness of services of social common capital for each member of the society is a decreasing function of the aggregate amount of services of social common capital used by all members of the society; that is, the utility function of each individual ν may be expressed as follows:

$$u^\nu = u^\nu(c^\nu, a^\nu, a),$$

where a is the total amount of services of social common capital used by all members of the society; that is,

$$a = \sum_\nu a^\nu + \sum_\mu a^\mu,$$

where a^ν and a^μ are the amounts of services of social common capital used, respectively, by individual ν and private firm μ.

We assume that the technological change induced by the phenomenon of congestion with respect to the use of social common capital is Harrod-neutral in the sense originally introduced in Uzawa (1961). That is, a function $\varphi^\nu(a)$ exists such that the utility function of individual ν may be expressed in the following manner:

$$u^\nu = u^\nu(c^\nu, \varphi^\nu(a)a^\nu).$$

The function $\varphi^\nu(a)$ expresses the extent to which the utility of individual ν is affected by the phenomenon of congestion with respect to the use of services of social common capital. It may be referred to as the *impact index of social common capital*, similar to the case of the economic analysis of global warming, as introduced in Uzawa (1991b, 1992a, 1993, 2003).

The phenomenon of congestion may be expressed by the conditions that, as the total use of services of social common capital a is increased, the effect of congestion is intensified, although with diminishing marginal effects. In terms of the impact index of social common capital $\varphi^\nu(a)$ for each individual ν, these conditions may be stated as follows:

$$\varphi^\nu(a) > 0, \quad \varphi^\nu_a(a) < 0, \quad \varphi^\nu_{aa}(a) < 0 \quad \text{for all } a > 0.$$

[As $\varphi^\nu_{aa}(a)$ is a matrix, $\varphi^\nu_{aa}(a) < 0$ means that matrix $\varphi^\nu_{aa}(a)$ is negative-definite.]

Impact Coefficients of Social Common Capital

The relative rates of the marginal change in the impact index due to the marginal increase in the use of social common capital are given by

$$\tau^\nu(a) = -\frac{\varphi^\nu_a(a)}{\varphi^\nu(a)},$$

which will play a crucial role in our analysis of social common capital. They may be referred to as the *impact coefficients of social common capital*.

As we consider the general circumstances under which there are several kinds of services of social common capital, the impact coefficients of social common capital $\tau^\nu(a)$ are expressed as a vector rather than a scalar, contrary to the case of global warming, as discussed in Uzawa (1991b, 1992a, 2003). That is,

$$\tau^\nu(a) = (\tau^\nu_i(a)), \quad a = (a_i),$$

where

$$\tau^\nu_i(a) = -\frac{\varphi^\nu_{a_i}(a)}{\varphi^\nu(a)} \quad (i = 1, \ldots, I).$$

It is apparent that impact coefficients $\tau^\nu(a)$ satisfy the following conditions:

$$\tau^\nu(a) > 0, \quad \tau^\nu_a(a) = \varphi^\nu_a(a)\varphi^\nu_a(a) - \frac{\varphi^\nu_{aa}(a)}{\varphi^\nu(a)} > 0.$$

[Note that $\varphi^\nu_a(a)\varphi^\nu_a(a)$ is a matrix of which (i,i') elements are $\varphi^\nu_{a_i}(a)\,\varphi^\nu_{a_{i'}}(a)$.]

In the following discussion, we assume that the impact coefficients $\tau^\nu(a)$ of social common capital are identical for all individuals; that is,

$$\tau^\nu(a) = \tau(a) \quad \text{for all } \nu.$$

The impact coefficient function $\tau(a)$ satisfies the following conditions:

$$\tau(a) > 0, \quad \tau_a(a) > 0 \quad \text{for all } a > 0.$$

As in the case of global warming, the impact index function $\varphi(a)$ of the following form is often postulated, originally introduced in Uzawa (1991b) and extensively utilized in Uzawa (2003):

$$\varphi(a) = (\hat{a} - a)^\beta, \quad 0 < a < \hat{a},$$

where $\hat{a}$ is the critical level of services of social common capital and β is the sensitivity parameter, $0 < \beta < 1$.

With respect to this impact index function $\varphi(a)$, the impact coefficient $\tau(a)$ is given by

$$\tau(a) = \frac{\beta}{\hat{a} - a}.$$

The Consumer Optimum

We assume that markets for produced goods are perfectly competitive; prices of goods are denoted by vector $p = (p_j)$. Considering the possibility of zero prices for some goods, we assume that price vectors p are nonzero, nonnegative: $p \geq 0$; that is, $p_j \geqq 0$ for all j, and $p_j > 0$ for at least one j. We denote by $\theta = (\theta_i)$ the vector of prices charged for the use of services of social common capital, where $\theta \geqq 0$, that is, $\theta_i \geqq 0$ for all i.

Each individual ν chooses the combination (c^ν, a^ν) of the vector of consumption of goods c^ν and the use of services of social common capital a^ν that maximizes individual ν's utility function

$$u^\nu = u^\nu(c^\nu, \varphi^\nu(a)a^\nu)$$

subject to the budget constraints

$$pc^{\nu} + \theta a^{\nu} = y^{\nu}, c^{\nu}, \ a^{\nu} \geqq 0, \tag{1}$$

where y^{ν} is individual ν's income. (In what follows, all relevant variables are generally nonnegative, so the reference to the nonnegativity is often omitted.)

The optimum combination (c^{ν}, a^{ν}) of vector of consumption c^{ν} and use of services of social common capital a^{ν} is characterized by the following marginality conditions:

$$u^{\nu}_{c^{\nu}}(c^{\nu}, \varphi^{\nu}(a)a^{\nu}) \leqq \lambda^{\nu} p \qquad (\text{mod. } c^{\nu})$$

$$u^{\nu}_{a^{\nu}}(c^{\nu}, \varphi^{\nu}(a)a^{\nu})\varphi^{\nu}(a) \leqq \lambda^{\nu}\theta \qquad (\text{mod. } a^{\nu}),$$

where $\lambda^{\nu} > 0$ is the Lagrange unknown associated with the budgetary constraint (1). Lagrange unknown λ^{ν} is nothing but the marginal utility of income y^{ν} of individual ν. [The notation (mod. c^{ν}) means that each component of the vector on the left-hand side of the referred inequality is less than or equal to the corresponding component of the vector on the right-hand side, and is actually equal to the latter when $c^{\nu}_j > 0$.]

To express the marginality relations in units of market prices, we divide both sides of these relations by λ^{ν} to obtain the following relations:

$$\alpha^{\nu} u^{\nu}_{c^{\nu}}(c^{\nu}, \varphi^{\nu}(a)\, a^{\nu}) \leqq p \qquad (\text{mod. } c^{\nu}) \tag{2}$$

$$\alpha^{\nu}\, u^{\nu}_{a^{\nu}}(c^{\nu}, \varphi^{\nu}(a)\, a^{\nu})\varphi^{\nu}(a) \leqq \theta \qquad (\text{mod. } a^{\nu}), \tag{3}$$

where $\alpha^{\nu} = \dfrac{1}{\lambda^{\nu}} > 0$ is the inverse of the marginal utility of individual ν's income.

Relation (2) expresses the familiar principle that the marginal utility of each good is exactly equal to the market price when the utility is measured in units of market prices. Relation (3) expresses the similar principle that the marginal utility of services of social common capital is equal to the price charged to the use of services of social common capital.

We derive a relation that will play a central role in our analysis of social common capital. By multiplying both sides of relations (2) and (3), respectively, by c^ν and a^ν, and adding them, we obtain

$$\alpha^\nu \left[u^\nu_{c^\nu}(c^\nu, \varphi^\nu(a)a^\nu)c^\nu + u^\nu_{a^\nu}(c^\nu, \varphi^\nu(a)a^\nu)\varphi^\nu(a)a^\nu\right] = pc^\nu + \theta a^\nu.$$

In view of the Euler identity for utility function $u^\nu(c^\nu, a^\nu)$ and budgetary constraint (1), we have

$$\alpha^\nu\, u^\nu(c^\nu, \varphi^\nu(a)a^\nu) = pc^\nu + \theta\, a^\nu = y^\nu. \tag{4}$$

Relation (4) means that, at the consumer optimum, the level of utility of individual ν, when expressed in units of market prices, is precisely equal to income y^ν of individual ν.

Production Possibility Sets of Private Firms

The conditions concerning the production of goods for each private firm μ are specified by the production possibility set T^μ that summarizes the technological possibilities and organizational arrangements for firm μ with the endowments of fixed factors of production available in firm μ given by a vector $K^\mu = (K^\mu_f)$, where $K^\mu \geq 0$.

In each private firm μ, the minimum quantities of factors of production that are required to produce goods by $x^\mu = (x^\mu_j)$ with the employment of labor by $\ell^\mu = (\ell^\mu_\eta)$ and the use of services of social common capital at the levels $a^\mu = (a^\mu_i)$ are specified by an F-dimensional vector-valued function:

$$f^\mu(x^\mu, \ell^\mu, a^\mu) = \left(f^\mu_f(x^\mu, \ell^\mu, a^\mu)\right).$$

We assume that marginal rates of substitution between any pair of the production of goods, the employment of labor, and the use of services of social common capital are smooth and diminishing, that there are always trade-offs among them, and that the conditions of constant returns to scale prevail. That is, we assume

(T$^\mu$1) $f^\mu(x^\mu, \ell^\mu, a^\mu)$ are defined, positive, continuous, and continuously twice-differentiable with respect to (x^μ, ℓ^μ, a^μ).

(T$^\mu$2) $f^\mu_{x^\mu}(x^\mu, \ell^\mu, a^\mu) > 0,\ f^\mu_{\ell^\mu}(x^\mu, \ell^\mu, a^\mu) \leqq 0,\ f^\mu_{a^\mu}(x^\mu, \ell^\mu, a^\mu) \leqq 0.$

(T$^\mu$3) $f^\mu(x^\mu, \ell^\mu, a^\mu)$ are strictly quasi-convex with respect to (x^μ, ℓ^μ, a^μ).

(T$^\mu$4) $f^\mu(x^\mu, \ell^\mu, a^\mu)$ are homogeneous of order 1 with respect to (x^μ, ℓ^μ, a^μ); that is,

$$f^\mu(tx^\mu, t\ell^\mu, ta^\mu) = t\, f^\mu(x^\mu, \ell^\mu, a^\mu) \quad \text{for all } t \geqq 0.$$

From the constant returns to scale conditions (T$^\mu$4), we have the Euler identity:

$$f^\mu(x^\mu, \ell^\mu, a^\mu) = f^\mu_{x^\mu}(x^\mu, \ell^\mu, a^\mu)x^\mu + f^\mu_{\ell^\mu}(x^\mu, \ell^\mu, a^\mu)\ell^\mu + f^\mu_{a^\mu}(x^\mu, \ell^\mu, a^\mu)a^\mu.$$

The production possibility set of each private firm μ, T^μ, is composed of all combinations (x^μ, ℓ^μ, a^μ) of vectors of production x^μ, employment of labor ℓ^μ, and use of services of social common capital a^μ that are possible with the organizational arrangements, technological conditions, and given endowments of factors of production K^μ in firm μ. Hence, it may be expressed as

$$T^\mu = \{(x^\mu, \ell^\mu, a^\mu)\colon (x^\mu, \ell^\mu, a^\mu) \geqq 0, \quad f^\mu(x^\mu, \ell^\mu, a^\mu) \leqq K^\mu\}.$$

Postulates (T$^\mu$1–T$^\mu$3) imply that the production possibility set T^μ is a closed, convex set of $J + \mathrm{H} + I$-dimensional vectors (x^μ, ℓ^μ, a^μ).

Effects of Congestion for Private Firms

Processes of production of private firms are also affected by the phenomenon of congestion regarding the use of services derived from social common capital. We assume that in each private firm μ, the minimum quantities of factors of production that are required to produce goods by x^μ with the employment of labor and services of social common capital, respectively, at the levels ℓ^μ and a^μ are specified by the following F-dimensional vector-valued function:

$$f^\mu(x^\mu, \ell^\mu, a^\mu, a) = \left(f^\mu_f(x^\mu, \ell^\mu, a^\mu, a)\right).$$

As with the case of the utility functions for individuals, we also assume that the technological change induced by the phenomenon of congestion with respect to the use of social common capital is Harrod-neutral. That is, the factor-requirement function of private firm μ may be expressed in the following manner:

$$f^\mu(x^\mu, \ell^\mu, \varphi^\mu(a)a^\mu) = \left(f^\mu_f(x^\mu, \ell^\mu, \varphi^\mu(a)a^\mu)\right),$$

where $\varphi^\mu(a)$ is the impact index with regard to the extent to which the effectiveness of services of social common capital in processes of production in private firm μ is impaired by congestion.

We assume that the impact index functions of social common capital $\varphi^\mu(a)$ for private firms μ possess properties similar to those for consumers. For each private firm μ, the impact index $\varphi^\mu(a)$ is positive, the marginal effect of congestion on the effectiveness of services of social common capital is negative, and the law of diminishing marginal rates of substitution always prevails; that is, $\varphi^\mu(a)$ satisfies the following conditions:

$$\varphi^\mu(a) > 0, \quad \varphi^\mu_a(a) < 0, \quad \varphi^\mu_{aa}(a) < 0 \quad \text{for all } a > 0.$$

The impact coefficients of social common capital for private firms are similarly defined; that is,

$$\tau^\mu(a) = -\frac{\varphi^\mu_a(a)}{\varphi^\mu(a)}.$$

We also assume that the impact coefficients $\tau^\mu(a)$ for private firms are identical to those for individuals; that is,

$$\tau^\mu(a) = \tau(a) \quad \text{for all } \mu.$$

The impact coefficient function $\tau(a)$ is assumed to satisfy the following conditions:

$$\tau(a) > 0, \quad \tau_a(a) > 0.$$

The production possibility set of each private firm μ, T^μ, may now be expressed as follows:

$$T^\mu = \{(x^\mu, \ell^\mu, a^\mu)\colon (x^\mu, \ell^\mu, a^\mu) \geqq 0,\ f^\mu(x^\mu, \ell^\mu, \varphi^\mu(a)\, a^\mu) \leqq K^\mu\}.$$

The Producer Optimum for Private Firms

As in the case of the consumer optimum, prices of goods on a perfectly competitive market are denoted by a price vector $p = (p_j)$, and prices charged for the use of services of social common capital are denoted by a vector $\theta = (\theta_i)$. Wage rates are denoted by a vector $w = (w_\eta)$.

Each private firm μ chooses the combination (x^μ, ℓ^μ, a^μ) of vector of production x^μ, employment of labor ℓ^μ, and use of services of social common capital a^μ that maximizes net profit

$$px^\mu - w\ell^\mu - \theta\, a^\mu$$

over $(x^\mu, \ell^\mu, a^\mu) \in T^\mu$.

Conditions ($T^\mu 1$–$T^\mu 3$) postulated above ensure that for any combination of prices p, wage rates w, and user charges for services of social common capital θ, the optimum combination (x^μ, ℓ^μ, a^μ) of vectors of production x^μ, employment of labor ℓ^μ, and use of services of social common capital a^μ always exists and is uniquely determined.

To see how the optimum levels of production, the employment of labor, and the use of services of social common capital are determined, let us denote the vector of imputed rental prices of fixed factors of production by $r^\mu = (r^\mu_f)$ $[r^\mu_f \geqq 0]$. Then the optimum conditions are

$$p \leqq r^\mu f^\mu_{x^\mu}(x^\mu, \ell^\mu, \varphi^\mu(a)\, a^\mu) \qquad (\text{mod. } x^\mu) \tag{5}$$

$$w \geqq r^\mu[-\, f^\mu_{\ell^\mu}(x^\mu, \ell^\mu, \varphi^\mu(a)\, a^\mu)] \qquad (\text{mod. } \ell^\mu) \tag{6}$$

$$\theta \geqq r^\mu \left[-\, f^\mu_{a^\mu}(x^\mu, \ell^\mu, \varphi^\mu(a)\, a^\mu)\varphi^\mu(a)\right] \qquad (\text{mod. } a^\mu) \tag{7}$$

$$f^\mu(x^\mu, \ell^\mu, \varphi^\mu(a) a^\mu) \leqq K^\mu \qquad (\text{mod. } r^\mu). \tag{8}$$

The first condition (5) means that

$$p_j \leqq \sum_f r^\mu_f f^\mu_{j x^\mu_f}(x^\mu, \ell^\mu, \varphi^\mu(a)\, a^\mu) \qquad (\text{with equality when } x^\mu_j > 0),$$

which expresses the familiar principle that the choice of production technologies and the levels of production are adjusted so as to equate marginal factor costs with output prices.

The second condition (6) means that the employment of labor is controlled so that the marginal gains due to the marginal increase in the employment of labor of type η are equal to the wage rate w_η when $\ell_\eta > 0$ and are not larger than w_η when $\ell_\eta = 0$.

The third condition (7) similarly means that the use of services of social common capital is controlled so that the marginal gains due to the marginal increase in the use of services of social common capital are equal to user charges θ_i when $a^\mu_i > 0$ and are not larger than θ_i when $a^\mu_i = 0$.

The fourth condition (8) means that the employment of factors of production does not exceed the endowments and the conditions of full employment are satisfied whenever imputed rental price r^μ_f is positive.

In what follows, for the sake of expository brevity, marginality conditions are occasionally assumed to be satisfied by equality.

The technologies are subject to constant returns to scale ($\mathrm{T}^{\mu}4$), and thus, in view of the Euler identity, conditions (5)–(8) imply that

$$\begin{aligned} px^{\mu} - w\ell^{\mu} - \theta a^{\mu} &= r^{\mu} \left[f^{\mu}_{x^{\mu}}(x^{\mu}, \ell^{\mu}, \varphi^{\mu}(a)a^{\mu})\, x^{\mu} \right. \\ &\quad + f^{\mu}_{\ell^{\mu}}(x^{\mu}, \ell^{\mu}, \varphi^{\mu}(a)a^{\mu})\ell^{\mu} \\ &\quad \left. + f^{\mu}_{\ell^{\mu}}(x^{\mu}, \ell^{\mu}, \varphi^{\mu}(a)a^{\mu})\, \varphi^{\mu}(a)a^{\mu} \right] \\ &= r^{\mu} f^{\mu}(x^{\mu}, \ell^{\mu}, \varphi^{\mu}(a)a^{\mu}). \end{aligned}$$

Hence,

$$px^{\mu} - w\ell^{\mu} - \theta a^{\mu} = r^{\mu} K^{\mu}. \tag{9}$$

That is, for each private firm μ, the net evaluation of output is equal to the sum of the imputed rental payments to all fixed factors of production of private firm μ. The meaning of relation (9) may be better brought out if we rewrite it as

$$px^{\mu} = w\ell^{\mu} + \theta a^{\mu} + r^{\mu} K^{\mu}.$$

That is, the value of output measured in market prices px^{μ} is equal to the sum of wages $w\ell^{\mu}$, user charges for services of social common capital θa^{μ}, and payments, in terms of imputed rental prices, made to fixed factors of production $r^{\mu} K^{\mu}$. Thus, the validity of the Menger-Wieser principle of imputation is assured with respect to the processes of production of private firms.

Production Possibility Sets for Social Institutions

As in the case of private firms, the conditions concerning the provision of services of social common capital by each social institution σ are specified by the production possibility set T^{σ} that summarizes the technological possibilities and organizational arrangements for social institution σ; the endowments of factors of production in social institution σ are given. The quantities of factors of production accumulated in social institution σ are expressed by a vector $K^{\sigma} = (K^{\sigma}_f)$, where it is assumed $K^{\sigma} \geq 0$.

In each social institution σ, the minimum quantities of factors of production required to provide services of social common capital by

a^σ with the employment of labor and the use of produced goods, respectively, by ℓ^σ and x^σ, are specified by an F-dimensional vector-valued function:

$$f^\sigma(a^\sigma, \ell^\sigma, x^\sigma) = \left(f^\sigma_f(a^\sigma, \ell^\sigma, x^\sigma)\right).$$

We assume that, for each social institution σ, marginal rates of substitution between any pair of the provision of services of social common capital, the employment of labor, and the use of produced goods are smooth and diminishing, that there are always trade-offs between any pair of them, and that the conditions of constant returns to scale prevail. Thus we assume

(T$^\sigma$1) $f^\sigma(a^\sigma, \ell^\sigma, x^\sigma)$ are defined, positive, continuous, and continuously twice-differentiable with respect to $(a^\sigma, \ell^\sigma, x^\sigma)$ for all $(a^\sigma, \ell^\sigma, x^\sigma) \geqq 0$.

(T$^\sigma$2) $f^\sigma_{a^\sigma}(a^\sigma, \ell^\sigma, x^\sigma) > 0,\ f^\sigma_{\ell^\sigma}(a^\sigma, \ell^\sigma, x^\sigma) < 0,\ f^\sigma_{x^\sigma}(a^\sigma, \ell^\sigma, x^\sigma) < 0$ for all $(a^\sigma, \ell^\sigma, x^\sigma) \geqq 0$.

(T$^\sigma$3) $f^\sigma(a^\sigma, \ell^\sigma, x^\sigma)$ are strictly quasi-convex with respect to $(a^\sigma, \ell^\sigma, x^\sigma)$ for all $(a^\sigma, \ell^\sigma, x^\sigma) \geqq 0$.

(T$^\sigma$4) $f^\sigma(a^\sigma, \ell^\sigma, x^\sigma)$ are homogeneous of order 1 with respect to $(a^\sigma, \ell^\sigma, x^\sigma)$; that is,

$$f^\sigma(t\,a^\sigma, t\,\ell^\sigma, t\,x^\sigma) = t\, f^\sigma(a^\sigma, \ell^\sigma, x^\sigma)$$
$$\text{for all } t \geqq 0,\ (a^\sigma, \ell^\sigma, x^\sigma) \geqq 0.$$

From the constant returns to scale conditions (T$^\sigma$4), we have the Euler identity:

$$\begin{aligned} f^\sigma(a^\sigma, \ell^\sigma, x^\sigma) = {} & f^\sigma_{a^\sigma}(a^\sigma, \ell^\sigma, x^\sigma)a^\sigma + f^\sigma_{\ell^\sigma}(a^\sigma, \ell^\sigma, x^\sigma)\ell^\sigma \\ & + f^\sigma_{x^\sigma}(a^\sigma, \ell^\sigma, x^\sigma)x^\sigma. \end{aligned}$$

For each social institution σ, the production possibility set T^σ is composed of all combinations $(a^\sigma, \ell^\sigma, x^\sigma)$ of provision of services of social common capital a^σ, employment of labor ℓ^σ, and use of produced goods x^σ that are possibly produced with the organizational arrangements, technological conditions, and given endowments of factors of production K^σ of social institution σ. Hence, it may be expressed as

$$T^\sigma = \{(a^\sigma, \ell^\sigma, x^\sigma)\colon (a^\sigma, \ell^\sigma, x^\sigma) \geqq 0,\ f^\sigma(a^\sigma, \ell^\sigma, x^\sigma) \leqq K^\sigma\}.$$

Postulates ($T^\sigma 1$–$T^\sigma 3$) imply that the production possibility set T^σ of social institution σ is a closed, convex set of $I + \mathrm{H} + J$-dimensional vectors $(a^\sigma, \ell^\sigma, x^\sigma)$.

The Producer Optimum for Social Institutions

As in the case of private firms, conditions of the producer optimum for social institutions in charge of social common capital may be obtained. We denote by $\pi = (\pi_i)$ the vector of prices paid for the provision of services of social common capital.

In describing the behavior of social institutions in charge of social common capital, we assume that the levels of services of social common capital provided by these institutions are optimum and the use of factors of production by them are efficient; that is, net profit, or rather net value, is maximized. When we use the term profit maximization, it is used in the sense that the efficient and optimum pattern of resource allocation in the provision of services of social common capital is sought, strictly in accordance with professional discipline and ethics.

We assume that each social institution σ chooses the optimum combination $(a^\sigma, \ell^\sigma, w^\sigma)$ of provision of services of social common capital a^σ, employment of labor ℓ^σ, and use of produced goods x^σ; that is, net value

$$\pi a^\sigma - w\ell^\sigma - px^\sigma$$

is maximized over $(a^\sigma, \ell^\sigma, x^\sigma) \in T^\sigma$.

Conditions ($T^\sigma 1$–$T^\sigma 3$) postulated for social institution σ ensure that, for any combination of prices paid for the provision of services of social common capital π, wage rates w, and prices of produced goods p that maximize net value, the optimum combination $(a^\sigma, \ell^\sigma, w^\sigma)$ of provision of services of social common capital b^σ, employment of labor ℓ^σ, and use of produced goods x^σ always exists and is uniquely determined.

The optimum combination $(a^\sigma, \ell^\sigma, w^\sigma)$ of provision of services of social common capital a^σ, employment of labor ℓ^σ, and use of produced goods x^σ may be characterized by the marginality conditions in exactly the same manner as for the case of private firms. We denote by $r^\sigma = (r^\sigma_f)$ $[r^\sigma_f \geqq 0]$ the vector of imputed rental prices of fixed factors of production of social institution σ. Then the optimum conditions are

$$\pi \leqq r^{\sigma} f^{\sigma}_{a^{\sigma}}(a^{\sigma}, \ell^{\sigma}, x^{\sigma}) \quad (\text{mod. } a^{\sigma}) \tag{10}$$

$$w \geqq r^{\sigma} [-f^{\sigma}_{\ell^{\sigma}}(a^{\sigma}, \ell^{\sigma}, x^{\sigma})] \quad (\text{mod. } \ell^{\sigma}) \tag{11}$$

$$p \geqq r^{\sigma} [-f^{\sigma}_{x^{\sigma}}(a^{\sigma}, \ell^{\sigma}, x^{\sigma})] \quad (\text{mod. } x^{\sigma}) \tag{12}$$

$$f^{\sigma}(a^{\sigma}, \ell^{\sigma}, x^{\sigma}) \leqq K^{\sigma} \quad (\text{mod. } r^{\sigma}). \tag{13}$$

Condition (10) expresses the principle that the choice of production technologies and levels of production are adjusted so as to equate marginal factor costs with output prices.

Condition (11) means that employment of labor ℓ^{σ} is adjusted so that the marginal gains due to the marginal increase in the employment of labor of type η are equal to wage rate w_{η} when $\ell^{\sigma}_{\eta} > 0$ and are not larger than w_{η} when $\ell^{\sigma}_{\eta} = 0$.

Condition (12) means that the use of produced goods is adjusted so that the marginal gains due to the marginal increase in the use of goods j are equal to price p_j when $x^{\sigma}_j > 0$ and are not larger than p_j when $x^{\sigma}_j = 0$.

Condition (13) means that the employments of fixed factors of production do not exceed the endowments and the conditions of full employment are satisfied whenever imputed rental price r^{σ}_f is positive.

We have assumed that the technologies are subject to constant returns to scale, (T$^{\sigma}$4), and thus, in view of the Euler identity, conditions (10)–(13) imply that

$$\pi a^{\sigma} - w\ell^{\sigma} - px^{\sigma} = r^{\sigma}\big[f^{\sigma}_{a^{\sigma}}(a^{\sigma}, \ell^{\sigma}, x^{\sigma})a^{\sigma} + f^{\sigma}_{\ell^{\sigma}}(a^{\sigma}, \ell^{\sigma}, x^{\sigma})\ell^{\sigma} + f^{\sigma}_{x^{\sigma}}(a^{\sigma}, \ell^{\sigma}, x^{\sigma})x^{\sigma}\big] = r^{\sigma} f^{\sigma}(a^{\sigma}, \ell^{\sigma}, x^{\sigma}).$$

Hence,

$$\pi a^{\sigma} - w\ell^{\sigma} - px^{\sigma} = r^{\sigma} K^{\sigma}. \tag{14}$$

That is, for each social institution σ, the net evaluation of services of social common capital provided by social institution σ is equal to the sum of the imputed rental payments to all fixed factors of production in social institution σ. As in the case for private firms, the meaning of relation (14) may be better brought out if we rewrite it as

$$\pi a^\sigma = w\ell^\sigma + px^\sigma + r^\sigma K^\sigma .$$

The value of services of social common capital provided by social institution σ, πa^σ, is equal to the sum of wages $w\ell^\sigma$, the payments for the use of produced goods px^σ, and the payments in terms of the imputed rental prices made to the fixed factors of production $r^\sigma K^\sigma$. The validity of the Menger-Wieser principle of imputation is also assured for the case of the provision of services of social common capital by social institutions.

4. ACTIVITY ANALYSIS OF PRODUCTION PROCESSES

Activity Analysis for Private Firms

The specifications of technological possibility sets as introduced in the previous sections contain certain ambiguities when more than one factor of production is involved. For each private firm μ, the quantities of factors of production required to produce goods by the vector $x^\mu = (x_j^\mu)$ with the employment of labor at $\ell^\mu = (\ell_\eta^\mu)$ and the use of services of social common capital at $a^\mu = (a_i^\mu)$ are determined by the choice of technologies and levels of productive activities; thus, the quantities of factors of production required for (x^μ, ℓ^μ, a^μ) are mutually dependent and the minimum quantity required for each type of factor of production may generally not be uniquely defined independently of the employment of other factors of production.

To explicitly examine the relationships between the choice of technologies and the employment of various factors of production, we may carry out the discussion better within the framework of the theory of activity analysis. For each private firm μ, let us denote the vector of activity levels by $\xi^\mu = (\xi_s^\mu), \xi_s^\mu \geqq 0$, where ξ_s^μ stands for the level of activity s. We assume that activities $\{s\}$ comprise all possible production activities carried out by the producers in the economy.

The vector of produced quantities of goods, the employment of labor, the use of services of social common capital, and the quantities of factors of production required when production activities are carried out at ξ^μ are, respectively, represented by the functional form

$$x^\mu(\xi^\mu), \quad \ell^\mu(\xi^\mu), \quad a^\mu(\xi^\mu), \quad K^\mu(\xi^\mu).$$

We assume that functions $x^\mu(\xi^\mu), \ell^\mu(\xi^\mu), a^\mu(\xi^\mu), K^\mu(\xi^\mu)$ satisfy the following conditions:

($T^\mu 1'$) Substitution between any pair of outputs and various factors of production are smooth; that is, $x^\mu(\xi^\mu), \ell^\mu(\xi^\mu), a^\mu(\xi^\mu), K^\mu(\xi^\mu)$ are defined, continuous, and continuously twice-differentiable for all $\xi^\mu \geqq 0$.

($T^\mu 2'$) Marginal rates of substitution are diminishing; that is, $x^\mu(\xi^\mu)$ is strictly quasi-concave with respect to $\xi^\mu \geqq 0$, whereas $\ell^\mu(\xi^\mu), a^\mu(\xi^\mu)$, and $K^\mu(\xi^\mu)$ are strictly quasi-convex with respect to $\xi^\mu \geqq 0$.

($T^\mu 3'$) Constant returns to scale prevail; that is, $x^\mu(\xi^\mu), \ell^\mu(\xi^\mu), a^\mu(\xi^\mu), K^\mu(\xi^\mu)$ are homogeneous of order 1 with respect to $\xi^\mu \geqq 0$.

The production possibility set T^μ of firm μ may now be defined by

$$T^\mu = \{(x^\mu, \ell^\mu, a^\mu)\colon 0 \leqq x^\mu \leqq x^\mu(\xi^\mu), \ell^\mu \geqq \ell^\mu(\xi^\mu), a^\mu \geqq a^\mu(\xi^\mu), K^\mu(\xi^\mu) \leqq K^\mu, \xi^\mu \geqq 0.\}.$$

The production possibility set T^μ of private firm μ thus defined is a nonempty set of (x^μ, ℓ^μ, a^μ) that describes the technologically possible combinations of vectors x^μ, ℓ^μ, and a^μ, respectively, specifying the produced quantities of goods, the employment of labor, and the use of services of social common capital by firm μ. Postulates ($T^\mu 1'$–$T^\mu 3'$) imply that the production possibility set T^μ is a closed, convex set in the space of $J + \mathrm{H} + I$-dimensional vectors (x^μ, ℓ^μ, a^μ).

The Producer Optimum for Private Firms

Suppose prices in a perfectly competitive market are given by price vector p, wage rates are given by w, and the use of services of social common capital are charged at θ. Then each private firm μ chooses the vectors of activity levels ξ^μ and the combination (x^μ, ℓ^μ, a^μ) of the produced quantities of goods, the employment of labor, and the use of services of social common capital that maximizes net profit

$$px^\mu - w\ell^\mu - \theta a^\mu$$

over $(x^\mu, \ell^\mu, a^\mu) \in T^\mu$.

Postulates ($T^\mu 1'$–$T^\mu 3'$) guarantee that, for any given prices of produced goods p, wage rates w, and user charges for the services of social common capital θ, the vector of the optimum activity levels ξ^μ always exists and is uniquely determined. The vector of the optimum activity levels ξ^μ may be characterized by the following marginality conditions, where $r^\mu = (r^\mu_f)$ denotes the vector of the imputed rental prices of factors of production:

(i) For each activity s, marginal net profit

$$px^\mu_{\xi^\mu_s}(\xi^\mu) - w\ell^\mu_{\xi^\mu_s}(\xi^\mu) - \theta a^\mu_{\xi^\mu_s}(\xi^\mu)$$

is less than or equal to marginal factor costs $r^\mu K^\mu_{\xi^\mu}(\xi^\mu)$,

$$px^\mu_{\xi^\mu_s}(\xi^\mu) - w\ell^\mu_{\xi^\mu_s}(\xi^\mu) - \theta a^\mu_{\xi^\mu_s}(\xi^\mu) \leqq r^\mu K^\mu_{\xi^\mu}(\xi^\mu),$$

with equality when activity s is operated at a positive level $\xi^\mu_s > 0$.

(ii) For each fixed factor of production f, the required employment $K^\mu_f(\xi^\mu)$ does not exceed the endowments K^μ_f,

$$K^\mu_f(\xi^\mu) \leqq K^\mu_f,$$

with equality when the imputed rental price r^μ_f of factor of production f is positive: $r^\mu_f > 0$.

From the optimum conditions together with the constant returns to scale hypothesis, we obtain

$$px^\mu - w\ell^\mu - \theta a^\mu = r^\mu K^\mu.$$

That is, the net evaluation of output is equal to the total sum of the rental payments to fixed factors of production.

For any given combination (x^μ, ℓ^μ, a^μ) of production vector x^μ, use of variable factors of production ℓ^μ, and use of services of social common capital a^μ, let us define the set of quantities of factors of production $T^\mu(x^\mu, \ell^\mu, a^\mu)$ by

$$T^\mu(x^\mu, \ell^\mu, a^\mu) = \{R^\mu : R^\mu \geqq K^\mu(\xi^\mu), x^\mu(\xi^\mu) \geqq x^\mu, \ell^\mu(\xi^\mu) \leqq \ell^\mu,$$
$$a^\mu(\xi^\mu) \leqq a^\mu, \text{ for some } \xi^\nu \geqq 0\}.$$

The set $T^\mu(x^\mu, \ell^\mu, a^\mu)$ thus defined is a closed convex set in the

F-dimensional vector space of the vectors of the quantities of fixed factors of production. When the number of factors of production is more than one ($F > 1$), the functions $f^\mu(x^\mu, \ell^\mu, a^\mu)$ specifying the minimum quantities of factors of production that are required to produce goods by x^μ with the employment of labor by ℓ^μ and the use of services of social common capital at a^μ as introduced above are generally not well defined.

However, all the analyses developed in this book remain valid for the general case formulated in terms of activity analysis. For the sake of expository simplicity and intuitive reasoning, our discussion will be carried out in terms of the functional approach.

The Case of Simple Linear Technologies

In the simplest case, the vector of activity levels $\xi^\mu = (\xi_s^\mu)$ may be identified with the vector of produced quantities of goods $x^\mu = (x_j^\mu)$ and all technological coefficients are assumed to be constant. Then the employment of labor $\ell^\mu(x^\mu)$, the use of services of social common capital $a^\mu(x^\mu)$, and the quantities of factors of production $K^\mu(x^\mu)$ required to produce x^μ are, respectively, expressed by

$$a^\mu(x^\mu) = \alpha^\mu x^\mu, \quad \ell^\mu(x^\mu) = \gamma^\mu x^\mu, \quad K^\mu(x^\mu) = \mathrm{A}^\mu x^\mu,$$

where $\alpha^\mu = (a_j^\mu)$ and $\gamma^\mu = (\gamma_j^\mu)$ are, respectively, the vectors of technological coefficients specifying the employment of labor and the use of services of social common capital required for the production of goods and $\mathrm{A}^\mu = (\alpha_{\ell j}^\mu)$ is the matrix of technological coefficients specifying the quantities of fixed factors of production required in the production of goods. Then the production possibility set T^μ of private firm μ may be given by

$$T^\mu = \{(x^\mu, \ell^\mu, a^\mu): x^\mu \geqq 0, \mathrm{A}^\mu x^\mu \leqq K^\mu, \ell^\mu \geqq \gamma^\mu x^\mu, a^\mu \geqq \alpha^\mu x^\mu\}.$$

In this simple linear case, the marginality conditions for the producer optimum are given by

$$p_j \leqq w\gamma_j^\mu + \theta\alpha_j^\mu + \sum_f r_f^\mu \alpha_{fj}^\mu$$

with equality when $x_j^\mu > 0$, and

$$\sum_j \alpha_{fj}^\mu x_j^\mu \leqq K_f^\mu$$

with equality when $r_f^\mu > 0$.

Activity Analysis for Social Institutions

In exactly the same manner as for private firms, the activity analysis approach for social institutions in charge of social common capital may be formulated. For each social institution σ, the quantities of fixed factors of production required to provide services of social common capital by the amounts a^σ with the employment of labor and the use of produced goods at the levels ℓ^σ and x^σ are determined by the choice of technologies and levels of production activities so that the quantities of fixed factors of production required for $(a^\sigma, \ell^\sigma, x^\sigma)$ are mutually dependent and the minimum quantity required for each type of fixed factor of production may generally not be uniquely defined, independently of the employment of other factors of production.

For each social institution σ, let us denote the vector of activity levels by $\xi^\sigma = (\xi_s^\sigma)$, $\xi_s^\sigma \geqq 0$, where ξ_s^σ stands for the level of activity s. The vector of provision of services of social common capital, the employment of labor, the use of produced goods, and the quantities of fixed factors of production required when productive activities are carried out at ξ^σ are, respectively, represented by the functional form

$$a^\sigma(\xi^\sigma), \quad \ell^\sigma(\xi^\sigma), \quad x^\sigma(\xi^\sigma), \quad K^\sigma(\xi^\sigma).$$

We assume that functions $a^\sigma(\xi^\sigma)$, $\ell^\sigma(\xi^\sigma)$, $x^\sigma(\xi^\sigma)$, and $K^\sigma(\xi^\sigma)$ satisfy the following conditions:

($T^\sigma 1'$) Substitution between the provision and the use of services of various components of social common capital are smooth; that is, $a^\sigma(\xi^\sigma)$, $\ell^\sigma(\xi^\sigma)$, $x^\sigma(\xi^\sigma)$, and $K^\sigma(\xi^\sigma)$ are defined, continuous, and continuously twice-differentiable, for all $\xi^\sigma \geqq 0$.

($T^\sigma 2'$) Marginal rates of substitution are diminishing; that is, $b^\sigma(\xi^\sigma)$ is strictly quasi-concave with respect to $\xi^\sigma \geqq 0$, whereas $\ell^\sigma(\xi^\sigma)$, $x^\sigma(\xi^\sigma)$, and $K^\sigma(\xi^\sigma)$ are strictly quasi-convex with respect to $\xi^\sigma \geqq 0$.

($T^{\sigma}3'$) Constant returns to scale prevail; that is, $a^{\sigma}(\xi^{\sigma})$, $\ell^{\sigma}(\xi^{\sigma})$, $x^{\sigma}(\xi^{\sigma})$, and $K^{\sigma}(\xi^{\sigma})$ are homogeneous of order 1 with respect to $\xi^{\sigma} \geqq 0$.

The production possibility set T^{σ} of social institution σ may now be defined by

$$T^{\sigma} = \{(a^{\sigma}, \ell^{\sigma}, x^{\sigma})\colon 0 \leqq a^{\sigma} \leqq a^{\sigma}(\xi^{\sigma}), \ell^{\sigma} \geqq \ell^{\sigma}(\xi^{\sigma}), x^{\sigma} \geqq x^{\sigma}(\xi^{\sigma}), K^{\sigma}(\xi^{\sigma}) \leqq K^{\sigma}, \xi^{\sigma} \geqq 0\}.$$

The production possibility set T^{σ} of social institution σ thus defined is a nonempty set of $(a^{\sigma}, \ell^{\sigma}, x^{\sigma})$ that describes the technologically possible combinations of a^{σ}, ℓ^{σ}, and x^{σ} specifying, respectively, the provision of services of social common capital, the employment of labor, and the use of produced goods by social institution σ.

Postulates ($T^{\sigma}1'$–$T^{\sigma}3'$) imply that the production possibility set T^{σ} is a closed, convex set in the space of $I + \mathrm{H} + J$-dimensional vectors $(a^{\sigma}, \ell^{\sigma}, x^{\sigma})$.

The Producer Optimum for Social Institutions

As with private firms, conditions for the producer optimum for social institutions in charge of social common capital may be similarly obtained.

Each social institution σ chooses the combination $(a^{\sigma}, \ell^{\sigma}, x^{\sigma})$ of provision of services of social common capital a^{σ}, employment of labor ℓ^{σ}, and use of produced goods x^{σ} that maximizes net value

$$\pi a^{\sigma} - w\ell^{\sigma} - px^{\sigma}$$

over $(a^{\sigma}, \ell^{\sigma}, x^{\sigma}) \in T^{\sigma}$, where π denotes the vector of prices paid for services of social common capital.

Postulates ($T^{\sigma}1'$–$T^{\sigma}3'$) ensure that, for any given prices for the provision of services of social common capital π, wage rates w, and prices of produced goods p, the vector of the optimum activity levels ξ^{μ} always exists and is uniquely determined. The vector of the optimum activity levels ξ^{μ} may be characterized by the following marginality conditions, where $r^{\sigma} = (r^{\sigma}_f)$ denotes the vector of the imputed rental prices of fixed factors of production of social institution σ:

(i)′ For each activity s, marginal net value

$$\pi a^{\sigma}_{\xi^{\sigma}_s}(\xi^{\sigma}) - w \ell^{\sigma}_{\xi^{\sigma}_s}(\xi^{\sigma}) - p x^{\sigma}_{\xi^{\sigma}_s}(\xi^{\sigma})$$

is less than or equal to marginal factor costs $r^{\sigma} K^{\sigma}_{\xi^{\sigma}_s}(\xi^{\sigma})$:

$$\pi a^{\sigma}_{\xi^{\sigma}_s}(\xi^{\sigma}) - w \ell^{\sigma}_{\xi^{\sigma}_s}(\xi^{\sigma}) - p x^{\sigma}_{\xi^{\sigma}_s}(\xi^{\sigma}) \leqq r^{\sigma} K^{\sigma}_{\xi^{\sigma}_s}(\xi^{\sigma}),$$

with equality when activity s is operated at a positive level $\xi^{\sigma}_s > 0$.

(ii)′ For each fixed factor of production f, the required employment $K^{\sigma}_f(\xi^{\sigma})$ does not exceed the endowments K^{σ}_f:

$$K^{\sigma}_f(\xi^{\sigma}) \leqq K^{\sigma}_f,$$

with equality when the rental price r^{σ}_f of fixed factor of production f is positive: $r^{\sigma}_f > 0$.

As with private firms, the optimum conditions and the constant returns to scale hypothesis imply

$$\pi a^{\sigma} - w\ell^{\sigma} - px^{\sigma} = r^{\sigma} K^{\sigma}.$$

That is, the net evaluation of output is equal to the sum of the imputed rental payments to the fixed factors of production.

The Case of Simple Linear Technologies

In the simplest case for social institutions in charge of social common capital, the vector of activity levels $\xi^{\sigma} = (\xi^{\sigma}_s)$ may be identified with the vector of the provision of services of social common capital $a^{\sigma} = (a^{\sigma}_i)$ and all technological coefficients are assumed to be constant. Then the employment of labor $\ell^{\sigma}(a^{\sigma})$, the quantities of produced goods $x^{\sigma}(a^{\sigma})$, and the quantities of fixed factors of production $K^{\sigma}(a^{\sigma})$ required to provide services of social common capital by a^{σ} are, respectively, represented by

$$\ell^{\sigma}(a^{\sigma}) = \gamma^{\sigma} a^{\sigma}, \quad x^{\sigma}(a^{\sigma}) = \chi^{\sigma} a^{\sigma}, \quad K^{\sigma}(a^{\sigma}) = \mathrm{A}^{\sigma} a^{\sigma},$$

where $\gamma^{\sigma} = (\gamma^{\sigma}_j)$ and $\chi^{\sigma} = (\chi^{\sigma}_i)$ are, respectively, the vectors of technological coefficients specifying the employment of labor and produced goods required for the provision of services of social common capital and $A^\sigma = (\alpha^\sigma_{fj})$ is the matrix of technological coefficients specifying the quantities of fixed factors of production required in the provision of services of social common capital. Then the production possibility set T^σ for social institution σ may be given by

$$T^\sigma = \{(a^\sigma, \ell^\sigma, x^\sigma): a^\sigma \geqq 0, A^\sigma a^\sigma \leqq K^\sigma, \ell^\sigma \geqq \gamma^\sigma a^\sigma, x^\sigma \geqq \chi^\sigma a^\sigma\}.$$

In this simple linear case, the marginality conditions for the producer optimum for social institution σ are given by

$$\pi_i \leqq w\gamma_i^\sigma + p\chi_i^\sigma + \sum_f r_f^\sigma \alpha_{fi}^\sigma$$

with equality when $a_i^\sigma > 0$, and

$$\sum_i \alpha_{fi}^\sigma a_i^\sigma \leqq K_f^\sigma$$

with equality when $r_f^\sigma > 0$.

5. SOCIAL COMMON CAPITAL AND MARKET EQUILIBRIUM

We first recapitulate the basic premises of the prototype model of social common capital as introduced in the previous sections.

The Basic Premises of the Model Recapitulated

The preference ordering of each individual ν is expressed by the utility function

$$u^\nu = u^\nu(c^\nu, \varphi^\nu(a)\, a^\nu),$$

where c^ν is the vector of goods consumed by individual ν, a^ν is the vector of the amounts of services of social common capital used by individual ν, $\varphi^\nu(a)$ is the impact index function indicating the effect on individual ν of congestion concerning the use of services of social common capital, and a is the total amount of services of social common capital used by all members of the society:

$$a = \sum_\nu a^\nu + \sum_\mu a^\mu.$$

Each individual ν chooses the combination (c^ν, a^ν) of the vector of consumption of goods and the use of services of social common capital in such a manner that the utility

$$u^\nu = u^\nu(c^\nu, \varphi^\nu(a)a^\nu)$$

is maximized subject to the budget constraint

$$pc^\nu + \theta a^\nu = y^\nu, \tag{15}$$

where y^ν is income of individual ν.

The consumer optimum is characterized by the following marginality conditions:

$$\alpha^\nu u^\nu_{c^\nu}(c^\nu, \varphi^\nu(a)\, a^\nu) \leqq p \quad (\text{mod. } c^\nu) \tag{16}$$

$$\alpha^\nu\, u^\nu_{a^\nu}(c^\nu, \varphi^\nu(a)\, a^\nu)\varphi^\nu(a) \leqq \theta \quad (\text{mod. } a^\nu). \tag{17}$$

The following basic identity holds:

$$\alpha^\nu\, u^\nu(c^\nu, \varphi^\nu(a)a^\nu) = pc^\nu + \theta a^\nu = y^\nu. \tag{18}$$

The conditions concerning the production of goods in each private firm μ are specified by the production possibility set T^μ:

$$T^\mu = \{(x^\mu, \ell^\mu, a^\mu)\colon (x^\mu, \ell^\mu, a^\mu) \geqq 0,\ f^\mu(x^\mu, \ell^\mu, \varphi^\mu(a)\, a^\mu) \leqq K^\mu\},$$

where $f^\mu(x^\mu, \ell^\mu, \varphi^\mu(a)\, a^\mu)$ is the F-dimensional vector-valued function specifying the minimum quantities of factors of production that are required to produce goods by x^μ with the employment of labor by ℓ^σ and the use of services of social common capital at the levels a^μ, $\varphi^\mu(a)$ is the impact index function expressing the effect of congestion concerning the use of services of social common capital, and K^μ is the vector of the endowments of fixed factors of production accumulated in private firm μ.

Each private firm μ chooses the combination (x^μ, ℓ^μ, a^μ) of vector of production x^μ, employment of labor ℓ^μ, and use of services of social common capital a^μ that maximizes net profit

$$px^\mu - w\ell^\mu - \theta a^\mu$$

over $(x^\mu, \ell^\mu, a^\mu) \in T^\mu$.

The producer optimum for private firm μ is characterized by the following marginality conditions:

$$p \leqq r^\mu f^\mu_{x^\mu}(x^\mu, \ell^\mu, \varphi^\mu(a)\, a^\mu) \quad (\text{mod. } x^\mu) \tag{19}$$

$$w \geqq r^\mu \left[-f^\mu_{\ell^\mu}(x^\mu, \ell^\mu, \varphi^\mu(a)\, a^\mu)\right] \quad (\text{mod. } \ell^\mu) \tag{20}$$

$$\theta \geqq r^{\mu}\left[-f^{\mu}_{a^{\mu}}(x^{\mu}, \ell^{\mu}, \varphi^{\mu}(a)\, a^{\mu})\varphi^{\mu}(a)\right] \quad (\text{mod. } a^{\mu}) \tag{21}$$

$$f^{\mu}(x^{\mu}, \ell^{\mu}, \varphi^{\mu}(a)a^{\mu}) \leqq K^{\mu} \quad (\text{mod. } r^{\mu}), \tag{22}$$

where r^{μ} $[r^{\mu} \geq 0]$ is the vector of imputed rental prices of fixed factors of production in private firm μ.

The following basic identity holds:

$$x^{\mu} - w\ell^{\mu} - \theta\, a^{\mu} = r^{\mu} K^{\mu}. \tag{23}$$

The conditions concerning the provision of services of social common capital by social institution σ are specified by the production possibility set

$$T^{\sigma} = \{(a^{\sigma}, \ell^{\sigma}, x^{\sigma})\colon (a^{\sigma}, \ell^{\sigma}, x^{\sigma}) \geqq 0,\ f^{\sigma}(a^{\sigma}, \ell^{\sigma}, x^{\sigma}) \leqq K^{\sigma}\}$$

where $f^{\sigma}(a^{\sigma}, \ell^{\sigma}, x^{\sigma})$ is the F-dimensional vector-valued function specifying the minimum quantities of factors of production in social institution σ that are required to provide services of social common capital by the amounts a^{σ} with the employment of labor and the use of produced goods, respectively, kept at the levels ℓ^{σ}, x^{σ}, and K^{σ} is the vector of endowments of factors of production accumulated in social institution σ.

Each social institution σ chooses the combination $(a^{\sigma}, \ell^{\sigma}, x^{\sigma})$ of provision of services of social common capital a^{σ}, employment of labor ℓ^{σ}, and use of produced goods x^{σ} that maximizes net value

$$\pi a^{\sigma} - w\ell^{\sigma} - px^{\sigma}$$

over $(a^{\sigma}, \ell^{\sigma}, x^{\sigma}) \in T^{\sigma}$.

The optimum conditions are

$$\pi \leqq r^{\sigma} f^{\sigma}_{a^{\sigma}}(a^{\sigma}, \ell^{\sigma}, x^{\sigma}) \quad (\text{mod. } a^{\sigma}) \tag{24}$$

$$w \geqq r^{\sigma}\,[-f^{\sigma}_{\ell^{\sigma}}(a^{\sigma}, \ell^{\sigma}, x^{\sigma})] \quad (\text{mod. } \ell^{\sigma}) \tag{25}$$

$$p \geqq r^{\sigma}\,[-f^{\sigma}_{x^{\sigma}}(a^{\sigma}, \ell^{\sigma}, x^{\sigma})] \quad (\text{mod. } x^{\sigma}) \tag{26}$$

$$f^{\sigma}(a^{\sigma}, \ell^{\sigma}, x^{\sigma}) \leqq K^{\sigma} \quad (\text{mod. } r^{\sigma}), \tag{27}$$

where r^{σ} $[r^{\sigma} \geq 0]$ is the vector of imputed rental prices of fixed factors of production of social institution σ.

The following basic identity holds:

$$\pi\, a^{\sigma} - w\ell^{\sigma} - px^{\sigma} = r^{\sigma} K^{\sigma}. \tag{28}$$

Market Equilibrium for the Prototype Model of Social Common Capital

Suppose social common capital taxes with the rate τ are levied upon the use of services of social common capital. Market equilibrium will be obtained if we find prices of produced goods p; wage rates w; prices charged for the use of services of social common capital θ; and prices paid for the provision of services of social common capital π, at which demand and supply are equal for all goods and labor services, and the total provision of services of social common capital is equal to the total use of services of social common capital. The prices charged for the use of services of social common capital θ are higher, by the tax rate τ, than the prices paid for the provision of services of social common capital π; that is,

$$\theta = \pi + \tau \theta. \tag{29}$$

[To simplify the notational system, we are using the same symbol τ for social common capital tax rate τ and impact coefficient $\tau(a)$. To avoid confusion, the impact coefficient is always expressed by the functional form $\tau(a)$.]

The social common capital tax rates are administratively determined by the government and announced prior to the opening of the market. Prices of produced goods p and wage rates w are determined in perfectly competitive markets, so are the prices charged for the use of services of social common capital and paid for the provision of services of social common capital, respectively, denoted by θ and π, where

$$p \geq 0, \quad w \geq 0, \quad \pi > 0, \quad \theta > 0.$$

Market Equilibrium and Social Common Capital

Market equilibrium under the presence of social institutions in charge of social common capital is obtained if the following equilibrium conditions are satisfied:

(i) Each individual ν chooses the combination (c^ν, a^ν) of the vector of consumption c^ν and the use of services of social common capital a^ν in such a manner that the utility of individual ν

$$u^\nu = u^\nu(c^\nu, \varphi^\nu(a)\, a^\nu)$$

is maximized subject to the budget constraint

$$pc^{\nu} + \theta a^{\nu} = y^{\nu},$$

where y^{ν} is the income of individual ν in units of market prices and a is the total amount of services of social common capital used by all members of the society that is assumed to be given when individual ν chooses (c^{ν}, a^{ν}).

(ii) Each private firm μ chooses the combination $(x^{\mu}, \ell^{\mu}, a^{\mu})$ of vectors of production x^{μ}, employment of labor ℓ^{μ}, and use of services of social common capital a^{μ} that maximizes net profit

$$px^{\mu} - w\ell^{\mu} - \theta a^{\mu}$$

over $(x^{\mu}, \ell^{\mu}, a^{\mu}) \in T^{\mu}$.

(iii) Each social institution σ chooses the combination $(a^{\sigma}, \ell^{\sigma}, x^{\sigma})$ of provision of services of social common capital a^{σ}, employment of labor ℓ^{σ}, and use of produced goods x^{σ} that maximizes net value

$$\pi a^{\sigma} - w\ell^{\sigma} - px^{\sigma}$$

over $(a^{\sigma}, \ell^{\sigma}, x^{\sigma}) \in T^{\sigma}$.

(iv) Total amounts of services of social common capital used by all members of the society are equal to total amounts of services of social common capital provided by social institutions σ in charge of social common capital; that is,

$$a = \sum_{\nu} a^{\nu} + \sum_{\mu} a^{\mu} \tag{30}$$

$$a = \sum_{\sigma} a^{\sigma}. \tag{31}$$

(v) At wage rates w, total demand for employment of labor is equal to total supply:

$$\sum_{\nu} \ell^{\nu} = \sum_{\mu} \ell^{\mu} + \sum_{\sigma} \ell^{\sigma}. \tag{32}$$

(vi) At prices of produced goods p, total demand for goods is equal to total supply:

$$\sum_{\mu} x^{\mu} = \sum_{\nu} c^{\nu} + \sum_{\sigma} x^{\sigma}. \tag{33}$$

In the following discussion, we suppose that for any given level of social common capital tax rate τ ($\tau \geq 0$), the state of the economy

$$\mathrm{E} = (c^\nu, a^\nu, x^\mu, \ell^\mu, a^\mu, a^\sigma, \ell^\sigma, x^\sigma, a, p, w, \pi, \theta)$$

that satisfies all conditions for market equilibrium generally exists and is uniquely determined.

Concerning National Income Accounting

Income y^ν of each individual ν is given as the sum of wages, dividend payments of private firms and social institutions, and subsidy payments t^ν:

$$y^\nu = w\ell^\nu + \sum_\mu s^{\nu\mu} r^\mu K^\mu + \sum_\sigma s^{\nu\sigma} r^\sigma K^\sigma + t^\nu,$$

where

$$s^{\nu\mu} \geqq 0, \quad \sum_\nu s^{\nu\mu} = 1, \quad s^{\nu\sigma} \geqq 0, \quad \sum_\nu s^{\nu\sigma} = 1.$$

Subsidy payments $\{t^\nu\}$ for individuals are so arranged that the sum of subsidy payments to all individuals are equal to the sum of social common capital tax payments $\tau\theta a$:

$$\sum_\nu t^\nu = \tau\,\theta a,$$

where

$$\tau\theta = \theta - \pi.$$

National income y is the sum of incomes of all individuals:

$$y = \sum_\nu y^\nu.$$

By taking note of the equilibrium conditions

$$\sum_\mu x^\mu = \sum_\nu c^\nu + \sum_\sigma x^\sigma, \quad \sum_\nu \ell^\nu = \sum_\mu \ell^\mu + \sum_\sigma \ell^\sigma$$

$$a = \sum_\nu a^\nu + \sum_\mu a^\mu, \quad a = \sum_\sigma a^\sigma,$$

we have

$$y = \sum_\nu w\ell^\nu + \sum_\mu r^\mu K^\mu + \sum_\sigma r^\sigma K^\sigma + \tau\theta a$$

$$= \sum_\nu w\ell^\nu + \sum_\mu (px^\mu - w\ell^\mu - \theta a^\mu)$$

$$+ \sum_\sigma (\pi a^\sigma - w\ell^\sigma - px^\sigma) + \tau\theta a$$

$$= \sum_\nu (pc^\nu + \theta a^\nu) - (\theta - \pi)a + \tau\theta a$$

$$= \sum_\nu (pc^\nu + \theta a^\nu).$$

Thus we have established the familiar identity of two definitions of national income.

6. MARKET EQUILIBRIUM AND SOCIAL OPTIMUM

To explore welfare implications of market equilibrium corresponding to the given levels of social common capital tax rates τ, we consider the social utility U defined by

$$U = \sum_\nu \alpha^\nu u^\nu = \sum_\nu \alpha^\nu u^\nu(c^\nu, \varphi^\nu(a)a^\nu),$$

where utility weight α^ν is the inverse of marginal utility of income y^ν of individual ν at market equilibrium.

We consider the following maximum problem:

Maximum Problem for Social Optimum. Find the pattern of consumption and production of goods, employment of labor, use and provision of services of social common capital, and total use of services of social common capital, $(c^\nu, a^\nu, x^\mu, \ell^\mu, a^\mu, a^\sigma, \ell^\sigma, x^\sigma, a)$, that maximizes the social utility

$$U = \sum_\nu \alpha^\nu u^\nu = \sum_\nu \alpha^\nu u^\nu(c^\nu, \varphi^\nu(a)a^\nu) \tag{34}$$

among all feasible patterns of allocation

$$\sum_\nu c^\nu + \sum_\sigma x^\sigma \leqq \sum_\mu x^\mu \tag{35}$$

$$\sum_\mu \ell^\mu + \sum_\sigma \ell^\sigma \leqq \sum_\nu \ell^\nu \tag{36}$$

$$\sum_\nu a^\nu + \sum_\mu a^\mu \leqq a \tag{37}$$

$$a \leqq \sum_\sigma a^\sigma \tag{38}$$

$$f^{\mu}(x^{\mu}, \ell^{\mu}, \varphi^{\mu}(a)\, a^{\mu}) \leqq K^{\mu} \tag{39}$$

$$f^{\sigma}(a^{\sigma}, \ell^{\sigma}, x^{\sigma}) \leqq K^{\sigma}, \tag{40}$$

where utility weights α^{ν} are evaluated at the market equilibrium corresponding to the given level of social common capital tax rate τ.

The maximum problem for social optimum may be solved in terms of the Lagrange method. Let us define the Lagrangian form:

$$\begin{aligned} L(c^{\nu}, a^{\nu}, x^{\mu}, \ell^{\mu}, a^{\mu}, a^{\sigma}, \ell^{\sigma}, x^{\sigma}, a; p, w, \theta, \pi, r^{\mu}, r^{\sigma}) \\ = \sum_{\nu} \alpha^{\nu} u^{\nu}(c^{\nu}, \varphi^{\nu}(a) a^{\nu}) + p \left(\sum_{\mu} x^{\mu} - \sum_{\nu} c^{\nu} - \sum_{\sigma} x^{\sigma} \right) \\ + w \left(\sum_{\nu} \ell^{\nu} - \sum_{\mu} \ell^{\mu} - \sum_{\sigma} \ell^{\sigma} \right) \\ + \theta \left(a - \sum_{\nu} a^{\nu} - \sum_{\mu} a^{\mu} \right) + \pi \left(\sum_{\sigma} a^{\sigma} - a \right) \\ + \sum_{\mu} r^{\mu} [K^{\mu} - f^{\mu}(x^{\mu}, \ell^{\mu}, \varphi^{\mu}(a)\, a^{\mu})] \\ + \sum_{\sigma} r^{\sigma} [K^{\sigma} - f^{\sigma}(a^{\sigma}, \ell^{\sigma}, x^{\sigma})], \end{aligned} \tag{41}$$

where the Lagrange unknowns $p, w, \theta, \pi, r^{\mu}$, and r^{σ} are, respectively, associated with constraints (35), (36), (37), (38), (39), and (40).

The optimum solution may be obtained by partially differentiating the Lagrangian form (41) with respect to unknown variables $c^{\nu}, a^{\nu}, x^{\mu}, \ell^{\mu}, a^{\mu}, a^{\sigma}, \ell^{\sigma}, x^{\sigma}, a$, and putting them equal to 0, where feasibility conditions (35)–(40) are satisfied:

$$\alpha^{\nu} u^{\nu}_{c^{\nu}}(c^{\nu}, \varphi^{\nu}(a)\, a^{\nu}) \leqq p \quad (\text{mod. } c^{\nu}) \tag{42}$$

$$\alpha^{\nu} u^{\nu}_{a^{\nu}}(c^{\nu}, \varphi^{\nu}(a)\, a^{\nu}) \varphi^{\nu}(a) \leqq \theta \quad (\text{mod. } a^{\nu}) \tag{43}$$

$$p \leqq r^{\mu} f^{\mu}_{x^{\mu}}(x^{\mu}, \ell^{\mu}, \varphi^{\mu}(a)\, a^{\mu}) \quad (\text{mod. } x^{\mu}) \tag{44}$$

$$w \geqq r^{\mu} \left[-f^{\mu}_{\ell^{\mu}}(x^{\mu}, \ell^{\mu}, \varphi^{\mu}(a)\, a^{\mu}) \right] \quad (\text{mod. } \ell^{\mu}) \tag{45}$$

$$\theta \geqq r^{\mu} \left[-f^{\mu}_{a^{\mu}}(x^{\mu}, \ell^{\mu}, \varphi^{\mu}(a)\, a^{\mu}) \varphi^{\mu}(a) \right] \quad (\text{mod. } a^{\mu}) \tag{46}$$

$$f^{\mu}(x^{\mu}, \ell^{\mu}, \varphi^{\mu}(a) a^{\mu}) \leqq K^{\mu} \quad (\text{mod. } r^{\mu}) \tag{47}$$

$$\pi \leqq r^{\sigma} f^{\sigma}_{a^{\sigma}}(a^{\sigma}, \ell^{\sigma}, x^{\sigma}) \quad (\text{mod. } a^{\sigma}) \tag{48}$$

$$w \geqq r^\sigma[-f^\sigma_{\ell^\sigma}(a^\sigma, \ell^\sigma, x^\sigma)] \quad (\text{mod. } \ell^\sigma) \tag{49}$$

$$p \geqq r^\sigma[-f^\sigma_{x^\sigma}(a^\sigma, \ell^\sigma, x^\sigma)] \quad (\text{mod. } x^\sigma) \tag{50}$$

$$f^\sigma(a^\sigma, \ell^\sigma, x^\sigma) \leqq K^\sigma \quad (\text{mod. } r^\sigma) \tag{51}$$

$$\theta = \pi + \tau(a)\, a\theta, \tag{52}$$

where $\tau(a)$ is the vector of the impact coefficients of social common capital.

Only equation (52) may need clarification. Partially differentiate the Lagrangian form (41) with respect to a, to obtain

$$\frac{\partial L}{\partial a} = \sum_\nu \alpha^\nu u^\nu_{a^\nu}(c^\nu, \varphi^\nu(a)\, a^\nu)\, [-\tau(a)]\, \varphi^\nu(a)\, a^\nu$$
$$+ \sum_\mu r^\mu \left[f^\mu_{a^\mu}(x^\mu, \ell^\mu, \varphi^\mu(a)\, a^\mu)\, \tau(a)\varphi^\mu(a)\, a^\mu\right] + \theta - \pi$$
$$= -\tau(a)\left[\sum_\nu \theta a^\nu + \sum_\mu \theta a^\mu\right] + \theta - \pi = -\tau(a)\theta a + \theta - \pi.$$

Hence, $\dfrac{\partial L}{\partial a} = 0$ implies equation (52):

Equation (52) may be written as

$$\theta - \pi = \tau\theta, \quad \tau = \tau(a)a, \tag{53}$$

where τ is the social common capital tax rate that is administratively determined prior to the opening of the market.

Applying the classic Kuhn-Tucker theorem on concave programming, Euler-Lagrange equations (42)–(52), together with feasibility conditions (35)–(40), are necessary and sufficient conditions for the optimum solution of the maximum problem for social optimum. [See, for example, Arrow, Hurwicz, and Uzawa (1958). In the mathematical notes at the end of Chapter 1 of Uzawa (2003), a brief description of the Kuhn-Tucker theorem on concave programming is presented.]

It is apparent that Euler-Lagrange equations (42)–(52), together with feasibility conditions (35)–(40), coincide precisely with the equilibrium conditions for market equilibrium with the social common capital tax rate given by (53).

As noted previously, marginality conditions (42) and (43) and the linear homogeneity hypothesis for utility functions $u^\nu(c^\nu, a^\nu)$ imply

$$\alpha^\nu u^\nu(c^\nu, \varphi^\nu(a)a^\nu) = pc^\nu + \theta\, a^\nu = y^\nu,$$

which, by summing over ν, yield

$$U = \sum_{\nu} y^{\nu} = y.$$

We have thus established the following proposition.

Proposition 1. *Consider the social common capital tax scheme with the tax rate τ for the use of services of social common capital given by*

$$\tau = \tau(a)a,$$

where $\tau(a)$ is the vector of impact coefficients of social common capital.

Then market equilibrium obtained under such a social common capital tax scheme is a social optimum in the sense that a set of positive weights for the utilities of individuals $(\alpha^1, \dots, \alpha^n)[\alpha^{\nu} > 0]$ exists such that the social utility

$$U = \sum_{\nu} \alpha^{\nu} u^{\nu} = \sum_{\nu} \alpha^{\nu} u^{\nu}(c^{\nu}, \varphi^{\nu}(a)a^{\nu})$$

is maximized among all feasible patterns of allocation $(c^{\nu}, a^{\nu}, x^{\mu}, \ell^{\mu}, a^{\mu}, a^{\sigma}, \ell^{\sigma}, x^{\sigma}, a)$.

The optimum level of social utility U is equal to national income y:

$$U = y.$$

Social optimum is defined with respect to any social utility

$$U = \sum_{\nu} \alpha^{\nu} u^{\nu} = \sum_{\nu} \alpha^{\nu} u^{\nu}(c^{\nu}, \varphi^{\nu}(a)a^{\nu}),$$

where $(\alpha^1, \dots, \alpha^n)$ is an arbitrarily given set of positive weights for the utilities of individuals. A pattern of allocation $(c^{\nu}, a^{\nu}, x^{\mu}, \ell^{\mu}, a^{\mu}, a^{\sigma}, \ell^{\sigma}, x^{\sigma}, a)$ is a social optimum if the given social utility U is maximized among all feasible patterns of allocation.

Social optimum necessarily implies the existence of the social common capital tax scheme, where the tax rate τ is given by $\tau = \tau(a)a$. However, the budgetary constraints for individuals

$$pc^{\nu} + \theta a^{\nu} = y^{\nu}$$

are not necessarily satisfied. It is apparent that the following proposition holds.

Proposition 2. *Suppose a pattern of allocation* $(c^\nu, a^\nu, x^\mu, \ell^\mu, a^\mu, a^\sigma, \ell^\sigma, x^\sigma, a)$ *is a social optimum; that is, a set of positive weights for the utilities of individuals* $(\alpha^1, \ldots, \alpha^n)$ *exists such that the given pattern of allocation* $(c^\nu, a^\nu, x^\mu, \ell^\mu, a^\mu, a^\sigma, \ell^\sigma, x^\sigma, a)$ *maximizes the social utility*

$$U = \sum_\nu \alpha^\nu u^\nu = \sum_\nu \alpha^\nu u^\nu(c^\nu, \varphi^\nu(a)a^\nu)$$

among all feasible patterns of allocation.

Then, a system $\{t^\nu\}$ *of income transfer among individuals of the society exists such that*

$$\sum_\nu t^\nu = 0,$$

and the given pattern of allocation $(c^\nu, a^\nu, x^\mu, \ell^\mu, a^\mu, a^\sigma, \ell^\sigma, x^\sigma, a)$ *corresponds precisely to the market equilibrium under the social common capital tax scheme with the rate* τ *given by*

$$\tau = \tau(a)a,$$

where $\tau(a)$ *is the vector of impact coefficients of social common capital.*

7. SOCIAL COMMON CAPITAL AND LINDAHL EQUILIBRIUM

The concept of Lindahl equilibrium was originally introduced by Lindahl (1919) to examine the structure of a tax system that is just and equitable, rather than merely efficient. Since then, a large number of contributions were made to clarify welfare implications of Lindahl equilibrium within the theory of public goods, in particular by Johansen (1963), Foley (1967, 1970), Fabre-Sender (1969), Malinvaud (1971), Milleron (1972), Roberts (1974), Kaneko (1977), Mas-Colell (1980), and Mäler and Uzawa (1994), among others.

With respect to global warming, the existence of Lindahl equilibrium and the implications for the welfare effect of global warming were examined in detail by Uzawa (2003). Within the context of global warming, Lindahl equilibrium is obtained when, in each country, the actual level of total CO_2 emissions is exactly equal to the level that would be chosen by each country if it were free to choose the level of total CO_2 emissions most desirable in terms of its preference ordering, assuming that the price it would be paid is equal to its own marginal disutility. With regard to social common capital, the concept of Lindahl equilibrium is similarly defined.

Lindahl Conditions

Let us recall the postulates for the behavior of individuals at market equilibrium. At market equilibrium, conditions for the consumer optimum are obtained if each individual ν chooses the combination (c^ν, a^ν) of vector of consumption c^ν and use of services of social common capital a^ν in such a manner that the utility of individual ν

$$u^\nu = u^\nu(c^\nu, \varphi^\nu(a)\, a^\nu)$$

is maximized subject to the budget constraint

$$pc^\nu + \theta a^\nu = y^\nu.$$

Let us first rewrite the budget constraint as follows:

$$pc^\nu + \theta a^\nu - \tau \theta a^\nu = \widehat{y}^{\,\nu},$$

where

$$\widehat{y}^{\,\nu} = y^\nu - \tau \theta a^\nu.$$

Lindahl conditions are satisfied if a system of individual tax rates $\{\tau^\nu\}$ exists such that

$$\sum_\nu \tau^\nu = \tau, \qquad \tau^\nu \geqq 0 \quad \text{for all } \nu,$$

and for each individual ν, (c^ν, a^ν, a) is the optimum solution to the following virtual maximum problem:

Find $(\overline{c}^\nu, \overline{a}^\nu, \overline{a}^{(\nu)})$ that maximizes

$$u^\nu = \varphi^\nu(\overline{a}^{(\nu)})\, u^\nu(\overline{c}^\nu, \varphi^\nu(\overline{a}^{(\nu)})\, \overline{a}^\nu)$$

subject to the virtual budget constraint

$$p\, \overline{c}^\nu + \theta\, \overline{a}^\nu - \tau^\nu\, \theta\, \overline{a}^{(\nu)} = \hat{y}^\nu.$$

Because (c^ν, a^ν, a) is the optimum solution to the virtual maximum problem for individual ν, the optimum conditions imply

$$\tau^\nu \theta = \alpha^\nu\, u^\nu_{a^\nu}(c^\nu, \varphi^\nu(a)\, a^\nu)\, [\tau\,(a)\, \varphi^\nu(a)\, a^\nu],$$

where α^ν is the inverse of marginal utility of income y^ν of individual ν.

Hence,

$$\tau^{\nu}\theta = \tau(a)\, a^{\nu}\theta,$$

which implies

$$\tau^{\nu}\theta\, a = \tau(a) a^{\nu}\theta\, a = \tau\theta\, a^{\nu}.$$

Thus, Lindahl conditions are always satisfied at market equilibrium.

Lindahl Equilibrium

A pattern of consumption, production, and use and provision of services of social common capital $(c^{\nu}, a^{\nu}, x^{\mu}, \ell^{\mu}, a^{\mu}, a^{\sigma}, \ell^{\sigma}, x^{\sigma}, a)$ is a Lindahl equilibrium if there exist prices of produced goods p; wage rates and user charges for services of social common capital, respectively, denoted by w and θ; and prices paid for the provision of services of social common capital π such that the following conditions are satisfied:

(i) Each individual ν chooses the combination (c^{ν}, a^{ν}) of vector of consumption c^{ν} and use of services of social common capital a^{ν} in such a manner that the utility of individual ν

$$u^{\nu} = u^{\nu}(c^{\nu}, \varphi^{\nu}(a)\, a^{\nu})$$

is maximized subject to the budget constraint

$$pc^{\nu} + \theta a^{\nu} = y^{\nu},$$

where y^{ν} is the income of individual ν in units of market prices and a is the total amount of services of social common capital used by all members of the society:

$$a = \sum_{\nu} a^{\nu} + \sum_{\mu} a^{\mu}.$$

(ii) Each private firm μ chooses the combination $(x^{\mu}, \ell^{\mu}, a^{\mu})$ of vectors of production x^{μ}, employment of labor ℓ^{μ}, and use of services of social common capital a^{μ} that maximizes net profit

$$px^{\mu} - w\ell^{\mu} - \theta a^{\mu}$$

over $(x^{\mu}, \ell^{\mu}, a^{\mu}) \in T^{\mu}$.

(iii) Each social institution σ chooses the combination $(a^\sigma, \ell^\sigma, x^\sigma)$ of provision of services of social common capital a^σ, employment of labor ℓ^σ, and use of produced goods x^σ that maximizes net value

$$\pi a^\sigma - w\ell^\sigma - px^\sigma$$

over $(a^\sigma, \ell^\sigma, x^\sigma) \in T^\sigma$.

(iv) Total amounts of services of social common capital used by all members of the society are equal to total amounts of services of social common capital provided by social institutions σ in charge of social common capital; that is,

$$a = \sum_\nu a^\nu + \sum_\mu a^\mu$$
$$a = \sum_\sigma a^\sigma.$$

(v) At the vector of wage rates w, total demand for the employment of labor is equal to total supply:

$$\sum_\nu \ell^\nu = \sum_\mu \ell^\mu + \sum_\sigma \ell^\sigma.$$

(vi) At the vector of prices for produced goods p, total demand for goods is equal to total supply:

$$\sum_\mu x^\mu = \sum_\nu c^\nu + \sum_\sigma x^\sigma.$$

(vii) Lindahl conditions for individuals are satisfied; that is, for each individual ν, (c^ν, a^ν, a) is the optimum solution to the following virtual maximum problem:

Find $(\overline{c}^\nu, \overline{a}^\nu, \overline{a}^{(\nu)})$ that maximizes

$$u^\nu = \varphi^\nu(\overline{a}^{(\nu)})\, u^\nu(\overline{c}^\nu, \varphi^\nu(\overline{a}^{(\nu)})\, \overline{a}^\nu)$$

subject to the virtual budget constraint

$$p\, \overline{c}^\nu + \theta\, \overline{a}^\nu - \tau^\nu\, \overline{a}^{(\nu)} = \hat{y}^\nu,$$

where

$$\hat{y}^\nu = y^\nu - \tau\theta\, a^\nu.$$

It is apparent that the following proposition holds.

Proposition 3. *Consider the social common capital tax scheme with the tax rate τ for the use of services of social common capital given by*

$$\tau = \tau(a)a,$$

where $\tau(a)$ is the vector of impact coefficients of social common capital.

Then market equilibrium obtained under such a social common capital tax scheme is always a Lindahl equilibrium.

8. ADJUSTMENT PROCESSES OF SOCIAL COMMON CAPITAL

In the previous sections, we examined two patterns of resource allocation involving social common capital: market allocation, on one hand, and social optimum, on the other. Market allocation is obtained as competitive equilibrium with social common capital taxes levied on the use of services of social common capital with the tax rate

$$\tau = \tau(a)a,$$

where $\tau(a)$ is the vector of impact coefficients of social common capital.

Social optimum is defined with respect to the social utility

$$U = \sum_{\nu} \alpha^{\nu} u^{\nu} = \sum_{\nu} \alpha^{\nu} u^{\nu}(c^{\nu}, \varphi^{\nu}(a)a^{\nu}),$$

where $(\alpha^1, \ldots, \alpha^n)$ $[\alpha^{\nu} > 0]$ is an arbitrarily given set of positive weights for the utilities of individuals. A pattern of allocation is social optimum if the social utility U is maximized among all feasible patterns of allocation.

Market equilibrium with social common capital tax rate $\tau = \tau(a)a$ coincides with the social optimum with respect to the social utility

$$U = \sum_{\nu} \alpha^{\nu} u^{\nu} = \sum_{\nu} \alpha^{\nu} u^{\nu}(c^{\nu}, \varphi^{\nu}(a)a^{\nu}),$$

where, for each individual ν, utility weight α^{ν} is the inverse of marginal utility of income y^{ν} at market equilibrium.

We have also shown that market equilibrium with social common capital tax rate $\tau = \tau(a)a$ is always a Lindahl equilibrium.

The tax rate $\tau = \tau(a)a$ is administratively determined and announced prior to the opening of the market, when the total amount of services of social common capital a used by all members of the society is not known. We may need to devise adjustment processes concerning the social common capital tax rate that are stable. We first consider an alternative adjustment process concerning the total amount of services of social common capital a. In the following discussion, we work with the prototype model of social common capital in which only one kind of social common capital exists.

We would first like to examine the relationships between the total amount of services of social common capital and the ensuing level of the social utility.

Let us assume that the total amount of services of social common capital a is announced at the beginning of the adjustment process and consider the pattern of resource allocation at the market equilibrium with the total amount of services of social common capital at the given level a.

Market equilibrium under the presence of social institutions in charge of social common capital is obtained if the following equilibrium conditions are satisfied:

(i) Each individual ν chooses the combination (c^ν, a^ν) of the vector of consumption c^ν and the use of services of social common capital a^ν in such a manner that the utility of individual ν,

$$u^\nu = u^\nu(c^\nu, \varphi^\nu(a)\, a^\nu),$$

is maximized subject to the budget constraint

$$pc^\nu + \theta a^\nu = y^\nu,$$

where y^ν is the income of individual ν in units of market prices and a is the total amount of services of social common capital used by all members of the society that is assumed to be given when individual ν chooses (c^ν, a^ν):

$$a = \sum_\nu a^\nu + \sum_\mu a^\mu.$$

(ii) Each private firm μ chooses the combination (x^μ, ℓ^μ, a^μ) of vectors of production x^μ, use of variable factors of production ℓ^μ, and use of services of social common capital a^μ that maximizes net profit

$$px^\mu - w\ell^\mu - \theta a^\mu$$

over $(x^\mu, \ell^\mu, a^\mu) \in T^\mu$.

(iii) Each social institution σ chooses the combination $(a^\sigma, \ell^\sigma, x^\sigma)$ of provision of services of social common capital a^σ, employment of labor ℓ^σ, and use of produced goods x^σ that maximizes net value

$$\pi a^\sigma - w\ell^\sigma - px^\sigma$$

over $(a^\sigma, \ell^\sigma, x^\sigma) \in T^\sigma$.

(iv) Total amounts of services of social common capital used by all members of the society are equal to total amounts of services of social common capital provided by social institutions σ in charge of social common capital; that is,

$$a = \sum_\nu a^\nu + \sum_\mu a^\mu$$

$$a = \sum_\sigma a^\sigma.$$

(v) At the vector of wage rates w, total demand for the employment of labor is equal to total supply:

$$\sum_\nu \ell^\nu = \sum_\mu \ell^\mu + \sum_\sigma \ell^\sigma.$$

(vi) At the vector of prices for produced goods p, total demand for goods is equal to total supply:

$$\sum_\mu x^\mu = \sum_\nu c^\nu + \sum_\sigma x^\sigma.$$

It may be noted that the total amount of services of social common capital is given at an arbitrarily given level a and announced prior to the opening of the market, whereas social common capital tax rate τ is given at the level satisfying

$$\tau\theta = \theta - \pi, \tag{54}$$

where θ and π are, respectively, the prices charged for the use of social common capital and paid for the provision of services of social common capital determined on the market.

Market equilibrium thus obtained corresponds to the social optimum with respect to the social utility

$$U = \sum_\nu \alpha^\nu u^\nu = \sum_\nu \alpha^\nu u^\nu(c^\nu, \varphi^\nu(a)a^\nu),$$

where, for each individual ν, utility weight α^ν is the inverse of marginal utility of income of individual ν at the market equilibrium and the total amount of services of social common capital at the predetermined level a.

We examine the effect of the marginal change in the total amount of services of social common capital a on the level of the social utility U. The level of the social utility U at market equilibrium is given as the value of the Lagrangian form, as defined by (41):

$$
\begin{aligned}
L &= L(c^\nu, a^\nu, x^\mu, a^\mu, b^\sigma, w^\sigma; p, \pi, \theta, r^\mu, \rho^\sigma) \\
&= \sum_\nu \alpha^\nu u^\nu (c^\nu, \varphi^\nu(a) a^\nu) + p \left(\sum_\mu x^\mu - \sum_\nu c^\nu - \sum_\sigma x^\sigma \right) \\
&\quad + w \left(\sum_\nu \ell^\nu - \sum_\mu \ell^\mu - \sum_\sigma \ell^\sigma \right) \\
&\quad + \theta \left(a - \sum_\nu a^\nu - \sum_\mu a^\mu \right) + \pi \left(\sum_\sigma a^\sigma - a \right) \\
&\quad + \sum_\mu r^\mu [K^\mu - f^\mu(x^\mu, \ell^\mu, \varphi^\mu(a)\, a^\mu)] \\
&\quad + \sum_\sigma r^\sigma [K^\sigma - f^\sigma(a^\sigma, \ell^\sigma, x^\sigma)],
\end{aligned}
$$

where a is not a variable, but rather is regarded as a parameter.

By taking total differentials of both sides of the Lagrangian form L and by noting equilibrium conditions

$$
\frac{\partial L}{\partial c^\nu} = 0, \quad \frac{\partial L}{\partial a^\nu} = 0, \ldots, \quad \frac{\partial L}{\partial a^\sigma} = 0, \quad \frac{\partial L}{\partial \ell^\sigma} = 0, \quad \frac{\partial L}{\partial x^\sigma} = 0, \ldots,
$$

we obtain

$$
dU = [\theta - \pi - \tau(a) a\, \theta] da.
$$

Hence,

$$
\frac{dU}{da} = \theta - \pi - \tau(a) a\, \theta. \tag{55}
$$

The Lagrangian unknown θ may be interpreted as the imputed price for the use of services of social common capital, and it is decreased as the total amount of services of social common capital a is increased. Similarly, the Lagrangian unknown π may be interpreted as the imputed price for the provision of services of social common capital, and it is increased as the total amount of services of social common capital a is increased. Hence, the right-hand side of equation (55) is a decreasing function of a when the following condition is satisfied:

$$\tau(a)a < 1.$$

The tax rate τ at the market equilibrium with the total amount of services of social common capital a is also uniquely determined:

$$\tau\theta = \theta - \pi.$$

We have now established the following proposition.

Proposition 4. *Consider the adjustment process defined by the following differential equation:*

$$\text{(A)} \qquad \dot{a} = k[\theta - \pi - \tau(a)a\theta],$$

where the speed of adjustment k is a positive constant and all variables refer to the state of the economy at the market equilibrium under the social common capital tax scheme with the tax rate τ:

$$\tau\theta = \theta - \pi.$$

Then differential equation (A) is globally stable; that is, for any initial condition a_0, the solution path to differential equation (A) converges to the stationary state a, where

$$\theta - \pi = \tau(a)a\theta, \tau(a)a < 1.$$

Adjustment Processes of Social Common Capital Tax Rate

At the market equilibrium with social common capital tax rate $\tau(a)a$, individual social common capital tax payments are then given by $\tau(a)a\theta\, a^\nu$ $(\nu \in N)$.

We would like to introduce an adjustment process with respect to the social common capital tax rate τ that is globally stable.

For an arbitrarily given social common capital tax rate τ, let us consider the market equilibrium in which income y^ν of each individual ν is given by

$$y^\nu = w\ell^\nu + \left[\sum_\mu s^{\nu\mu} r^\mu K^\mu + \sum_\sigma s^{\nu\sigma} r^\sigma K^\sigma\right] + t^\nu,$$

$$s^{\nu\mu} \geqq 0, \quad \sum_\nu s^{\nu\mu} = 1, \quad s^{\nu\sigma} \geqq 0, \quad \sum_\nu s^{\nu\sigma} = 1,$$

where r^μ and r^σ are, respectively, the imputed rental prices of factors of production of private firm μ and social institution σ, t^ν is the subsidy payments to individual ν, and

$$\sum_\nu t^\nu = \tau\theta a, \quad \tau\theta = \theta - \pi.$$

Such a market equilibrium is characterized by the following conditions, where p, θ, and π are, respectively, the prices of produced goods, the price charged for the use of services of social common capital θ, and the price paid for the provision of services of social common capital:

(i) Each individual ν chooses the combination (c^ν, a^ν) of the vector of consumption c^ν and the use of services of social common capital a^ν in such a manner that the utility of individual ν

$$u^\nu = u^\nu(c^\nu, \varphi^\nu(a)\, a^\nu)$$

is maximized subject to the budget constraint

$$pc^\nu + \theta a^\nu = y^\nu,$$

where y^ν is the income of individual ν in units of market prices and a is the total amount of services of social common capital used by all members of the society that is assumed to be given when individual ν chooses (c^ν, a^ν).

(ii) Each private firm μ chooses the combination (x^μ, ℓ^μ, a^μ) of vectors of production x^μ, employment of labor ℓ^μ, and use of services of social common capital a^μ that maximizes net profit

$$px^\mu - w\ell^\mu - \theta a^\mu$$

over $(x^\mu, \ell^\mu, a^\mu) \in T^\mu$.

(iii) Each social institution σ chooses the combination $(a^\sigma, \ell^\sigma, x^\sigma)$ of provision of services of social common capital a^σ, employment of labor ℓ^σ, and use of produced goods x^σ that maximizes net value

$$\pi a^\sigma - w\ell^\sigma - px^\sigma$$

over $(a^\sigma, \ell^\sigma, x^\sigma) \in T^\sigma$.

(iv) Total amounts of services of social common capital used by all members of the society are equal to total amounts of services of social common capital provided by social institutions σ in charge of social common capital; that is,

$$a = \sum_{\nu} a^{\nu} + \sum_{\mu} a^{\mu}$$

$$a = \sum_{\sigma} a^{\sigma}.$$

(v) At the vector of prices of variable factors of production w, total demand for the use of variable factors of production is equal to total supply:

$$\sum_{\nu} \ell^{\nu} = \sum_{\mu} \ell^{\mu} + \sum_{\sigma} \ell^{\sigma}.$$

(vi) At the vector of prices for produced goods p, total demand for goods is equal to total supply:

$$\sum_{\mu} x^{\mu} = \sum_{\nu} c^{\nu} + \sum_{\sigma} x^{\sigma}.$$

(vii) The price charged for the use of services of social common capital θ exceeds, by the tax rate $\tau\theta$, the price paid for the provision of services of social common capital π:

$$\theta - \pi = \tau\theta.$$

We then consider the adjustment process with respect to the social common capital tax rate τ defined by the following differential equation:

(B) $$\dot{\tau} = k[\tau(a)a - \tau],$$

with initial condition τ_{θ}, where k is an arbitrarily given positive number.

It is apparent that the following proposition holds.

Proposition 5. *The adjustment process defined by differential equation* (B) *is globally stable; that is, for any initial condition* τ_0, *the solution path* τ *to differential equation* (B) *converges to the optimum social common capital tax rate* $\tau(a)a$.

3

Sustainability and Social Common Capital

1. INTRODUCTION

Social common capital involves intergenerational equity and justice. Although the construction and maintenance of social common capital require the use of substantial portions of scarce resources, both human and nonhuman, putting a significant burden on the current generation, future generations will benefit greatly if the construction of social common capital carried out by the current generation is properly arranged.

In this chapter, we examine the problems of the accumulation of social common capital primarily from the viewpoint of the intergenerational distribution of utilities. Our analysis is based on the concept of sustainability introduced in Uzawa (1991b, 2003), and we examine the conditions under which processes of the accumulation of social common capital over time are sustainable. The conceptual framework of the economic analysis of social common capital developed in Chapter 2 are extended to deal with the problems of the irreversibility of processes of the accumulation of social common capital owing to the Penrose effect. The concept of the Penrose effect was originally introduced in Uzawa (1968, 1969) in the context of macroeconomic analysis, and was extensively utilized in the dynamic analysis of global warming as described in Uzawa (2003, Chapter 5). The presentation of the theory of sustainable processes of capital accumulation in this chapter largely reproduces the one introduced there.

The analysis focuses on the examination of the system of imputed prices associated with the time-path of consumption that is dynamically optimum with respect to the intertemporal preference relation, in which the presence of the Penrose effect implies the diminishing marginal rates of investment in private capital and social common capital upon the rates at which private capital and social common capital are accumulated. The sustainable time-path of consumption and investment is characterized by the stationarity of the imputed prices associated with the given intertemporal preference ordering, whereas the efficiency of resource allocation from the short-run point of view is preserved at each time.

Similar concepts may be applied to the general case of accumulation of both private and social common capital. A time-path of consumption and capital accumulation is sustainable when the imputed price of each kind of social common capital remains identical over time. In other words, a time-path of consumption and investment is sustainable if all future generations will face the same imputed prices of various kinds of social common capital as those faced by the current generation. The existence of the sustainable time-path of consumption and capital accumulation starting with an arbitrarily given stock of capital is ensured when the processes of accumulation of various kinds of capital are subject to the Penrose effect that exhibits the law of diminishing marginal rates of investment.

In what follows, we present a way of formulating the concept of sustainability within the theoretical framework of the economic analysis of social common capital and derive propositions that may be consulted in devising institutional arrangements and policy measures likely to be effective in realizing a sustainable state such as that introduced by John Stuart Mill in his classic *Principles of Political Economy* (Mill 1848), particularly in the chapter entitled "On Stationary States." The stationary state, as envisioned by Mill, is interpreted as the state of the economy in which all macroeconomic variables, such as gross domestic product, national income, consumption, investments, prices of all goods and services, wages, and real rates of interest, all remain stationary, whereas, within the society, individuals are actively engaged in economic, social, and cultural activities, new scientific discoveries are incessantly made, and new products are continuously introduced while the natural environment is being preserved at the sustainable state.

The concept of sustainability also involves intergenerational equity and justice. The problems of intergenerational equity and justice have been studied by several economists and philosophers. Our formulation of the concept of sustainability is largely based on contributions by Rawls (1971), Solow (1974a,b), Sen (1982), Norton (1989), Norgaard (1990a,b), Howarth and Norgaard (1990, 1992, 1995), Page (1991, 1997), Uzawa (1991b, 1992a, 1998), Howarth and Monahan (1992), and Pezzey (1992).

2. REVIEW OF THE THEORY OF DYNAMIC OPTIMALITY

We begin our discussion with a review of the theory of optimum capital accumulation that was originally introduced by Ramsey (1928) and elaborated by Arrow (1962a,b; 1965, 1968), Uzawa (1964), Srinivasan (1965), Koopmans (1965), Cass (1965), and Arrow and Kurz (1970). The Ramsey theory of dynamic optimality was further elaborated by Epstein and Haynes (1983), Lucas and Stokey (1984), Roemer (1986), Epstein (1987), and Rebelo (1993). It was later applied by Uzawa (1993, 1996, 1998, 2003) to the problems of capital accumulation involving social common capital such as the atmosphere and the commons.

In examining the processes of sustainability involving the accumulation of social common capital, we take specific note of the contributions made by a large number of economists concerning the problems of optimum economic growth and environmental quality. We cite only a few among these contributions having implications pertinent to the analysis developed in this chapter: d'Arge (1971a,b), Keeler, Spence, and Zeckhauser (1971), Forster (1973), Dasgupta and Heal (1974, 1979), Mäler (1974), Solow (1974b), Krautkraemer (1985), Musu (1990, 1994), Grossman and Helpman (1991), Howarth (1991a,b), Aghion and Howitt (1992), Gradus and Smulders (1993), Huan and Cai (1994), Bovenberg and Smulders (1995), Smulders (1995), and Smulders and Gradus (1996).

The Ramsey–Koopmans–Cass Theory of Optimum Capital Accumulation

The basic premises of the analysis of dynamic optimality are that the intertemporal preference ordering prevailing in the society in question is independent of the technological conditions and processes of capital accumulation, as typically illustrated by the Ramsey–Koopmans–Cass utility integral, and the Pontryagin maximum method in the calculus of variations is effectively utilized.

We consider an aggregative model of capital accumulation whose behavioral characteristics are described by those of the representative consumer and producer. We first consider the simple case in which only one kind of goods serves both for consumption and investment. Those goods that are invested as capital may also be used either for consumption or investment. The utility of the representative consumer is assumed to be cardinal.

The instantaneous level of the utility u_t at each time t is represented by a utility function

$$u_t = u(c_t),$$

where c_t is the quantity of goods consumed by the representative consumer at time t.

We assume that the utility function $u = u(c)$ remains identical over time, is defined for all nonnegative $c \geqq 0$, is continuous and continuously twice-differentiable, and satisfies the following conditions:

$$u(c) > 0, \quad u'(c) > 0, \quad u''(c) < 0 \quad \text{for all } c > 0.$$

We assume that the intertemporal preference ordering over the set of conceivable time-paths of consumption (c_t: $t \geqq 0$) may be expressed by the Ramsey–Koopmans–Cass utility integral

$$U(c) = \int_0^\infty u(c_t)e^{-\delta t}dt, \quad c = (c_t), \tag{1}$$

where $u_t = u(c_t)$ is the utility function expressing the instantaneous level of utility at time t and δ is the utility rate of discount that is assumed to be a positive constant ($\delta > 0$).

The utility rate of discount δ is assumed to be independent of the time-path of consumption and capital accumulation, and to be constant and positive. The conceptual basis of the discount rate has been intensively examined in the literature by Koopmans (1965), Arrow and Kurz (1970), Bradford (1975), Dasgupta (1982a), Lind (1982a,b), Sen (1982), Stiglitz (1982), Stockfish (1982), Cropper and Portney (1992), Wallace (1993), and Weitzman (1993).

We denote by K_t the stock of capital at time t, and by c_t, z_t, respectively, consumption and investment at time t. Then, we have

$$c_t + z_t = f(K_t), \tag{2}$$

where $f(K)$ is the production function that is assumed to be independent of time t.

The production function $f(K)$ expresses the net national product produced from the given stock of capital K. We assume that production function $f(K)$ is defined, continuous, and continuously twice-differentiable for all $K > 0$, that marginal products of capital are always positive, and that production processes are subject to the law of diminishing marginal returns:

$$f'(K) > 0, \quad f''(K) < 0 \quad \text{for all } K > 0.$$

The rate of capital accumulation at time t, $\dot{K}_t$, is given by the dynamic equation

$$\dot{K}_t = \alpha(z_t, K_t), \;\; K_0 = K^0, \tag{3}$$

where K^0 is the initial stock of capital and $\alpha(z_t, K_t)$ is the Penrose function relating the rate of capital accumulation $\dot{K}_t$ to investment z_t and the stock of capital K_t at time t.

The Penrose function $\alpha(z, K)$ expresses the net rate of capital accumulation; thus we may assume that the partial derivative of $\alpha(z, K)$ with respect to z is always positive, whereas with respect to K, it is always negative:

$$\alpha_z = \alpha_z(z, K) > 0, \quad \alpha_K = \alpha_K(z, K) < 0.$$

The Penrose Effect

The *Penrose effect* is expressed by the conditions that the Penrose function $\alpha(z, K)$ is concave and strictly quasi-concave with respect to (z, K):

$$\alpha_{zz} < 0, \quad \alpha_{KK} < 0, \quad \alpha_{zz}\alpha_{KK} - {\alpha_{zK}}^2 \geqq 0.$$

The following condition is usually assumed for the Penrose function $\alpha(z, K)$:

$$\alpha_{zK}(z, K) = \alpha_{Kz}(z, K) < 0.$$

Note that all variables are assumed to be nonnegative:

$$K_t, \; c_t, \; z_t \geqq 0 \quad \text{for all } t \geqq 0.$$

The concept of the Penrose effect was originally introduced by Penrose (1959) to describe the growth processes of an individual firm. It was later formalized by Uzawa (1968, 1969) in the context of a Keynesian analysis of macroeconomic processes of dynamic equilibrium to elucidate the effect of investment activities on the processes of capital accumulation.

Marginal Efficiency of Investment

A particularly important concept associated with the Penrose function $\alpha(z, K)$ is *marginal efficiency of investment*, which plays a crucial role in the analysis of dynamic processes of capital accumulation and economic growth. Marginal efficiency of investment expresses the extent to which the marginal increase in investment z induces the marginal increase in net national product $f(K)$ in the future. The marginal efficiency of investment is composed of two components.

The first component is the marginal increase in net national product $f(K)$ directly induced by the marginal increase $\alpha_z(z, K)$ in the stock of capital due to the marginal increase in investment z; that is,

$$r(K)\alpha_z(z, K),$$

where $r(K) = f'(K)$ is the marginal product of capital.

The second component measures the extent of the marginal effect on future processes of capital accumulation due to the marginal increase in the stock of capital today K; that is,

$$\alpha_K(z, K).$$

Thus, the marginal efficiency of investment $m = m(z, K)$ may be expressed as

$$m = m(z, K) = r(K)\alpha_z(z, K) + \alpha_K(z, K).$$

The marginal efficiency of investment $m = m(z, K)$ is a decreasing function of both investment z and the stock of capital K:

$$m_z(z, K) = \frac{\partial m}{\partial z} = r\alpha_{zz} + \alpha_{Kz} < 0$$

$$m_K(z, K) = \frac{\partial m}{\partial K} = r'\alpha_z + (\alpha_{zK} + \alpha_{KK}) < 0,$$

where $r' = r'(K) = f''(K) < 0$.

In the standard neoclassical theory of investment, the Penrose effect is not recognized; that is,

$$\alpha(z, K) = z \quad \text{for all } z \geqq 0, K \geqq 0.$$

Then,

$$m\,(z, K) = r$$

$$m_z(z, K) = 0, \quad m_K(z, K) = r'(K) < 0 \quad \text{for all } z \geqq 0, K \geqq 0.$$

Dynamic Optimality and Imputed Price of Capital

A time-path of consumption and capital accumulation, $(c, K) = (c_t, K_t)$, is *dynamically optimum* if it maximizes the Ramsey–Koopmans–Cass utility integral

$$U(c) = \int_0^\infty u(c_t)e^{-\delta t}dt, \quad c = (c_t) \tag{4}$$

subject to the constraints that

$$c_t + z_t = f(K_t) \tag{5}$$

$$\dot{K}_t = \alpha(z_t, K_t), K_0 = K^0, \tag{6}$$

where the initial stock of capital K^0 is given and positive ($K^0 > 0$).

The problem of the dynamic optimum may be solved in terms of the concept of imputed price of capital. The imputed price of capital at time t, π_t, is the discounted present value of the marginal increases in outputs in the future measured in units of the utility due to the marginal increase in investment at time t. The marginal increase in outputs at future time τ measured in units of the utility is given by

$$\pi_\tau m_\tau,$$

where π_t is the imputed price of capital at future time τ and m_τ is the marginal efficiency of investment at future time τ:

$$m_\tau = m(z_\tau, K_\tau) = r_\tau \alpha_z(z_\tau, K_\tau) + \alpha_K(z_\tau, K_\tau), \quad r_\tau = f'(K_\tau).$$

Thus the imputed price of capital at time t, π_t, is given by

$$\pi_t = \int_t^\infty \pi_\tau m_\tau e^{-\delta(\tau - t)}d\tau. \tag{7}$$

By differentiating both sides of (7) with respect to time t, we obtain the following differential equation:

$$\dot{\pi}_t = \delta \pi_t - m_t \pi_t. \tag{8}$$

Differential equation (8) is the Euler–Lagrange differential equation in the calculus of variations. In the context of the theory of optimum capital accumulation, it is often referred to as the Ramsey–Keynes equation. The economic meaning of the Ramsey–Keynes equation (8) may be brought out better if we rewrite it as

$$\dot{\pi}_t + m_t \pi_t = \delta \pi_t. \tag{9}$$

We suppose that capital is transacted as an asset on a virtual capital market that is perfectly competitive and the imputed price π_t is identified with the market price at time t. Consider the situation in which the unit of such an asset is held for the short time period $[t, t + \Delta t]$ $(\Delta t > 0)$. The gains obtained by holding such an asset are composed of capital gains $\Delta \pi_t = \pi_{t+\Delta t} - \pi_t$ and "earnings" $m_t \pi_t \Delta t$; that is,

$$\Delta \pi_t + m_t \pi_t \Delta t.$$

On the other hand, the cost of holding such an asset for the time period $[t, t + \Delta t]$ consists of "interest" payment $\delta \pi_t \Delta t$, where the utility rate of discount δ is identified with the "rate of interest." Hence, on a virtual capital market, these two amounts become equal; that is,

$$\Delta \pi_t + m_t \pi_t \Delta t = \delta \pi_t \Delta t.$$

Dividing both sides of this equation by Δt and taking the limit as $\Delta t \to 0$, we obtain relation (9).

By dividing both sides of relation (8) by π_t, we obtain the following equation:

$$\frac{\dot{\pi}_t}{\pi_t} = \delta - m_t. \tag{10}$$

The imputed real national income at time t, H_t, is given by

$$H_t = u(x_t) + \pi_t \alpha(z_t, K_t). \tag{11}$$

The optimum levels of consumption and investment at each time t, (c_t, z_t), are obtained if imputed real national income H_t at time t

is maximized subject to feasibility constraint (5). Let the Lagrangian form be given by

$$L_t = u(c_t) + \pi_t \alpha(z_t, K_t) + p_t[f(K_t) - c_t - z_t],$$

where p_t is the Lagrangian unknown associated with constraint (5).

The optimum conditions are

$$u'(c_t) = p_t \tag{12}$$

$$\pi_t \alpha_z(z_t, K_t) = p_t, \tag{13}$$

where the value of p_t is chosen so that feasibility condition (5) is satisfied.

Lagrange unknown p_t may be interpreted as the imputed price of the output at time t. Equation (12) means that the optimum level of consumption c_t at time t is obtained when marginal utility $u'(c_t)$ is equated with imputed price p_t at time t. Equation (13) means that the optimum level of investment z_t at time t is obtained when the value of the marginal product of investment z_t evaluated at the imputed price π_t of capital is equated with the imputed price p_t of the output at time t.

The dynamically optimum time-path of consumption and capital accumulation, $(c, K) = ((c_t, K_t))$, is obtained if the time-path of the imputed price of capital (π_t) thus obtained satisfies the transversality conditions:

$$\lim_{t \to +\infty} \pi_t K_t e^{-\delta t} = 0.$$

Under the neoclassical conditions imposed on the utility function, the production function, and the Penrose function, the dynamically optimum time-path of consumption and capital accumulation, $(c^o, K^o) = ((c_t^o, K_t^o))$, with an arbitrarily given initial stock of capital K^0 $[K^0 > 0]$ generally exists and is uniquely determined, provided that only one kind of capital goods is involved. For the general case involving several kinds of capital goods, however, the dynamically optimum time-path of consumption and capital accumulation, $(c^o, K^o) = ((c_t^o, K_t^o))$, has been shown to exist only for exceptionally rare circumstances.

3. DYNAMIC OPTIMALITY FOR THE ECONOMY WITH SEVERAL KINDS OF PRODUCED AND CAPITAL GOODS

The optimum theory of capital accumulation, as briefly reviewed in the previous section, may be applied to an economy involving several kinds of produced goods as well as capital goods.

We consider an economy consisting of n individuals and m private firms. Individuals are generically denoted by $\nu = 1, \ldots, n$, and private firms by $\mu = 1, \ldots, m$. Goods produced by private firms are generically denoted by $j = 1, \ldots, J$.

We assume the utility of each individual ν is cardinal and is expressed by the utility function

$$u^\nu = u^\nu(c^\nu),$$

where $c^\nu = (c_j^\nu)$ is the vector of goods consumed by individual ν.

We assume that, for each individual ν, the utility function $u^\nu(c^\nu)$ is continuous, continuously twice-differentiable, concave, strictly quasi-concave, and homogeneous of order 1 with respect to c^ν.

There are several kinds of variable factors of production, to be denoted by $\eta = 1, \ldots,$ H. All variable factor of production are owned by private individuals. The amounts of various kinds of variable factors of production owned by each individual ν are expressed by an H-dimensional vector $\ell^\nu = (\ell_\eta^\nu)$, where ℓ_η^ν denotes the amount of variable factor of production η owned by individual ν. Each individual ν owns at least one type of variable factor of production; that is, $\ell^\nu \geq 0$. Typical variable factors of production are various kinds of labor, so that variable factors of production are often referred to simply as labor.

Capital goods that are needed by private firms to produce goods are generically denoted by $f = 1, \ldots, F$. Quantities of capital goods accumulated in each firm μ are expressed by an F-dimensional vector $K^\mu = (K_f^\mu)$, where K_f^μ denotes the quantity of capital goods f accumulated in firm μ. Each private firm μ owns at least one type of capital goods; that is, $K^\mu \geq 0$. The employment of labor by firm μ is expressed by an H-dimensional vector $\ell^\mu = (\ell_\eta^\mu)$, where ℓ_η^ν denotes the amount of labor of type η employed by firm μ. Quantities of goods produced by firm μ are denoted by an J-dimensional vector $x^\mu = (x_j^\mu)$.

The production possibility set T^μ of private firm μ is given by

$$T^\mu = \{(x^\mu, \ell^\mu)\colon \quad (x^\mu, \ell^\mu) \geqq 0, \quad f^\mu(x^\mu, \ell^\mu) \leqq K^\mu\},$$

where the F-dimensional vector-valued function $f^\mu(x^\mu, \ell^\mu)$ specifies the minimum quantities of capital goods required to produce goods by x^μ with the employment of labor kept at the levels ℓ^μ.

The function $f^\mu(x^\mu, \ell^\mu)$ is assumed to be continuous, continuously twice-differentiable, concave, strictly quasi-concave, and homogeneous of order 1 with respect to (x^μ, ℓ^μ), and

$$f^\mu(x^\mu, \ell^\mu) \geqq 0, \quad f^\mu_{x^\mu}(x^\mu, \ell^\mu) \geqq 0, \quad f^\mu_{\ell^\mu}(x^\mu, \ell^\mu) \leqq 0$$
$$\text{for all } (x^\mu, \ell^\mu) \geqq 0.$$

If we take into consideration investment activities carried out by firm μ, the production possibility set T^μ of firm μ is modified as follows:

$$T^\mu = \left\{(x^\mu, z^\mu, \ell^\mu, c^\mu) \colon (x^\mu, z^\mu, \ell^\mu, c^\mu) \geqq 0, \ell^\mu = \ell^\mu_p + \ell^\mu_i, \right.$$
$$\left. f^\mu\left(x^\mu, \ell^\mu_p\right) + g^\mu(z^\mu, \ell^\mu_i, c^\mu) \leqq K^\mu \right\},$$

where the function $f^\mu(x^\mu, \ell^\mu)$ specifies the minimum quantities of capital goods required to produce goods by x^μ with the employment of labor kept at the levels ℓ^μ, whereas the function $g^\mu(z^\mu, \ell^\mu, c^\mu)$ specifies the minimum quantities of capital goods required for firm μ to increase the stock of capital goods by z^μ with the employment of labor and the use of produced goods, respectively, kept at the levels ℓ^μ and c^μ.

We assume that the function $g^\mu(z^\mu, \ell^\mu, c^\mu)$ is defined, continuous, and continuously twice-differentiable, concave, strictly quasi-convex, and homogeneous of order 1 with respect to (z^μ, ℓ^μ, c^μ), and the following conditions are satisfied:

$$g^\mu(z^\mu, \ell^\mu, c^\mu) \geqq 0, \quad g^\mu_{z^\mu}(z^\mu, \ell^\mu, c^\mu) \geqq 0, \quad g^\mu_{\ell^\mu}(z^\mu, \ell^\mu, c^\mu) \leqq 0,$$
$$g^\mu_{c^\mu}(z^\mu, \ell^\mu, c^\mu) \leqq 0 \quad \text{for all } (z^\mu, \ell^\mu, c^\mu) \geqq 0.$$

The rate of accumulation of the stock of capital goods in firm μ is given by the following system of differential equations:

$$\dot{K}^\mu_t = z^\mu_t - \gamma K^\mu_t, \quad K^\mu_0 = K^\mu_o,$$

where γ is the rate of depreciation of the stock of capital goods. We assume that the rate of depreciation γ is a positive constant.

The Problem of the Dynamic Optimum

The problem of the dynamic optimum for the economy with several kinds of produced goods and capital goods as specified above may be formulated as follows:

Find the pattern of consumption and production of goods, and investment in capital goods at all times t, $(c_t^\nu, x_t^\mu, z_t^\mu)$, such that the ensuing time-path of consumption and capital accumulation, $(c^\nu, K^\mu) = ((c_t^\nu, K_t^\mu))$, maximizes the Ramsey–Koopmans–Cass utility integral

$$U = \int_0^\infty U_t e^{-\delta t} dt, \quad U_t = \sum_\nu u^\nu (c_t^\nu) \tag{14}$$

subject to the feasibility constraints

$$\dot{K}_t^\mu = z_t^\mu - \gamma K_t^\mu, \quad K_0^\mu = K_{\text{o}}^\mu \ (\mu = 1, \ldots, m) \tag{15}$$

$$\sum_\nu c_t^\nu + \sum_\mu c_t^\mu \leqq \sum_\mu x_t^\mu \tag{16}$$

$$\sum_\mu \ell_t^\mu \leqq \sum_\nu \ell^\nu \tag{17}$$

$$f^\mu (x_t^\mu, \ell_{pt}^\mu) + g^\mu (z_t^\mu, \ell_{it}^\mu, c_t^\mu) \leqq K_t^\mu, \quad \ell_t^\mu = \ell_{pt}^\mu + \ell_{it}^\mu \quad (\mu = 1, \ldots, m). \tag{18}$$

The problem of the dynamic optimum, as posited here, may be solved in terms of the Lagrange method. Let us define the Lagrangian form:

$$L = \int_0^\infty L_t e^{-\delta t} dt,$$

where

$$\begin{aligned} L_t = {} & \sum_\nu u^\nu (c_t^\nu) + \sum_\mu \pi_t^\mu (z_t^\mu - \gamma K_t^\mu) + p_t \left[\sum_\mu x_t^\mu - \sum_\nu c_t^\nu - \sum_\mu c_t^\mu \right] \\ & + w_t \left[\sum_\nu \ell^\nu - \sum_\mu \ell_t^\mu \right] + \sum_\mu r_t^\mu [K_t^\mu - f^\mu (x_t^\mu, \ell_{pt}^\mu) - g^\mu (z_t^\mu, \ell_{it}^\mu, c_t^\mu)], \end{aligned} \tag{19}$$

and π_t^μ, p_t, w_t, and r_t^μ are the Lagrange unknowns associated, respectively, with constraints (15), (16), (17), and (18). In terms of the standard usage of terminology in economic analysis, π_t^μ is the vector of imputed prices of capital goods in firm μ, p_t is the vector of prices, w_t is the vector of imputed wages, and r_t^μ is the vector of imputed rental prices of capital goods of firm μ, all at time t.

The optimum solution at time t may be obtained by differentiating the Lagrangian form (19) partially with respect to unknown variables $c_t^\nu, x_t^\mu, z_t^\mu, \ell_{pt}^\mu, \ell_{it}^\mu$, and putting them equal to 0, where feasibility conditions (16)–(18) are satisfied (for the sake of expository brevity, the time suffix t is often omitted):

$$u_{c^\nu}^\nu(c^\nu) \leqq p \quad (\text{mod.}\, c^\mu) \tag{20}$$

$$p \leqq r^\mu f_{x^\mu}^\mu\left(x^\mu, \ell_p^\mu\right) \quad (\text{mod.}\, x^\mu) \tag{21}$$

$$w \geqq r^\mu \left[-f_{\ell_p^\mu}^\mu\left(x^\mu, \ell_p^\mu\right)\right] \quad (\text{mod.}\, \ell_p^\mu) \tag{22}$$

$$\pi^\mu \leqq r^\mu g_{z^\mu}^\mu\left(z^\mu, \ell_i^\mu, c^\mu\right) \quad (\text{mod.}\, z^\mu) \tag{23}$$

$$w \geqq r^\mu \left[-g_{\ell_i^\mu}^\mu\left(z^\mu, \ell_i^\mu, c^\mu\right)\right] \quad (\text{mod.}\, \ell_i^\mu) \tag{24}$$

$$p \geqq r^\mu \left[-g_{c^\mu}^\mu\left(z^\mu, \ell_i^\mu, c^\mu\right)\right] \quad (\text{mod.}\, c^\mu). \tag{25}$$

Applying the classic Kuhn-Tucker theorem on concave programming, the Euler-Lagrange equations (20)–(25), together with feasibility conditions (15)–(18), are necessary and sufficient conditions for the short-run optimum of the problem of the dynamic optimum at time t.

The constant-returns-to-scale hypothesis implies the following relations:

$$u^\nu(c^\nu) = pc^\nu \tag{26}$$

$$px^\mu = w\ell_p^\mu + r^\mu K_p^\mu \tag{27}$$

$$\pi^\mu z^\mu = w\ell_i^\mu + pc^\mu + r^\mu K_i^\mu, \tag{28}$$

where K_p^μ and K_i^μ are the amounts of capital goods in firm μ that are used, respectively, for production and investment activities, and

$$K_p^\mu + K_i^\mu = K^\mu.$$

The imputed prices of the stock of capital goods in firm μ at time t, π_t^μ, are the discounted present values of the marginal increases in the outputs in the future, measured in units of the utility, due to the marginal increase in the stock of capital goods in firm μ at time t; that is,

$$\pi_t^\mu = \int_t^\infty r_\tau^\mu e^{-(\delta+\gamma)(\tau-t)} d\tau. \tag{29}$$

Equation (29) is obtained if we note that the marginal increases in the outputs at future time τ, measured in units of the utility, are given by the vector of the imputed rental prices r_τ^μ of capital goods at time τ, and the depreciation rate of capital goods is γ.

By differentiating both sides of (29) with respect to time t, we obtain the following system of differential equations:

$$\dot{\pi}_t^\mu = (\delta + \mu)\pi_t^\mu - r_t^\mu \quad (\mu = 1, .., m). \tag{30}$$

The dynamically optimum time-path of consumption and capital accumulation, $(c^\mu, K^\mu) = ((c_t^\nu, K_t^\mu))$, is obtained when the control variables $c_t^\nu, x_t^\mu, z_t^\mu, w_t^\mu$ $(\nu = 1, .., n;\ \mu = 1, .., m)$ at all times t are so chosen that the marginality conditions (20)–(25), together with feasibility conditions (15)–(18), are all satisfied and the imputed prices of capital goods π_t^μ $(\mu = 1, .., m)$ satisfy the system of differential equations (30) together with the transversality conditions

$$\lim_{t\to+\infty} \pi_t^\mu K_t^\mu e^{-(\delta+\gamma)t} = 0 \quad (\mu = 1, .., m). \tag{31}$$

Thus, we have derived the conditions for the dynamic optimality for the economy involving several kinds of produced and capital goods. However, the existence of the dynamically optimum time-paths satisfying these optimality conditions is generally not guaranteed. Indeed, the problems of finding dynamic optima are extremely difficult when more than one state variable is involved. Besides the mathematical problems concerning the existence of dynamic optima for the problems of the dynamic optimum as posited here, we may need to be genuinely concerned with the more fundamental issues of perfect foresight and knowledge. The definition of imputed prices of capital goods (29), as is evident in the transversality conditions (31), presupposes that prices of goods, wage rates, the imputed prices of capital goods, and all other relevant variables at all future times are known for certain, a presupposition that is hardly accepted under any circumstances, and any analysis under the hypothesis of perfect foresight would be only of an academic interest, without significant merit from social and policy points of view.

Dynamic Optimality and Perfect Foresight

The optimum conditions for the dynamic optimum are similar to those for *market equilibrium with perfect foresight* concerning the schedule of marginal efficiency of investment in capital goods of individual firms, together with a certain income redistribution scheme.

Market equilibrium for such an economy is obtained when the following conditions are satisfied:

(i) Each individual ν chooses the vector of consumption c^{ν} in such a manner that the utility of individual ν

$$u^{\nu} = u^{\nu}(c^{\nu})$$

is maximized subject to the budget constraint

$$pc^{\nu} = y^{\nu}, \tag{32}$$

where y^{ν} is the income of individual ν in units of market prices. Income y^{ν} of individual ν is given as the sum of dividend payments of private firms subtracted by investment

$$y^{\nu} = \sum_{\mu} s^{\nu\mu}(r^{\mu} K^{\mu} - \pi^{\mu} z^{\mu}), \tag{33}$$

where

$$s^{\nu\mu} \geqq 0, \quad \sum_{\nu} s^{\nu\mu} = 1.$$

(ii) Each firm μ chooses the combination $(x^{\mu}, z^{\mu}, \ell^{\mu}, c^{\mu})$ of production x^{μ}, investment z^{μ}, labor employment ℓ^{μ}, and use of produced goods c^{μ} in such a manner that net profit

$$px^{\mu} + \pi^{\mu} z^{\mu} - w\ell^{\mu} - pc^{\mu}$$

is maximized over $(x^{\mu}, z^{\mu}, \ell^{\mu}, c^{\mu}) \in T^{\mu}$.

(iii) At the vector of prices p, total demand for goods is equal to total supply:

$$\sum_{\nu} c^{\nu} + \sum_{\mu} c^{\mu} = \sum_{\mu} x^{\mu}. \tag{34}$$

(iv) At the vector of wage rates w, total demand for labor employment is equal to total supply:

$$\sum_{\mu} \ell^{\mu} = \sum_{\nu} \ell^{\nu}. \tag{35}$$

Then the equilibrium conditions for market equilibrium at time t are as follows: the consumer optimum

$$\alpha^{\nu} u^{\nu}_{c^{\nu}}(c^{\nu}) \leqq p \quad (\text{mod.}\, c^{\mu}), \tag{36}$$

where α^{ν} is the inverse of marginal utility of income of individual ν; the producer optimum for private firms

$$p \leqq r^{\mu} f^{\mu}_{x^{\mu}}\left(x^{\mu}, \ell^{\mu}_{p}\right) \quad (\text{mod.}\, x^{\mu}) \tag{37}$$

$$w \geqq r^{\mu}\left[-f^{\mu}_{\ell^{\mu}}\left(x^{\mu}, \ell^{\mu}_{p}\right)\right] \quad (\text{mod.}\, \ell^{\mu}_{p}) \tag{38}$$

$$\pi^{\mu} \leqq r^{\mu} g^{\mu}_{z^{\mu}}\left(z^{\mu}, \ell^{\mu}_{i}, c^{\mu}\right) \quad (\text{mod.}\, z^{\mu}) \tag{39}$$

$$w \geqq r^{\mu}\left[-g^{\mu}_{\ell^{\mu}}\left(z^{\mu}, \ell^{\mu}_{i}, c^{\mu}\right)\right] \quad (\text{mod.}\, \ell^{\mu}_{i}) \tag{40}$$

$$p \geqq r^{\mu}\left[-g^{\mu}_{c^{\mu}}\left(z^{\mu}, \ell^{\mu}_{i}, c^{\mu}\right)\right] \quad (\text{mod.}\, c^{\mu}); \tag{41}$$

and perfect foresight and knowledge on the schedules of marginal efficiency of investment in capital goods of individual firms

$$\pi^{\mu} = \int_{t}^{\infty} r^{\mu}_{\tau} e^{-(\delta+\gamma)(\tau-t)} d\tau. \tag{42}$$

Thus the equilibrium conditions for market equilibrium with perfect foresight concerning the schedule of marginal efficiency of investment in capital goods are identical to the optimum conditions for the problem of the dynamic optimum except for the weights $\{\alpha^{\nu}\}$ assigned to individuals ν. To attain the dynamic optimum, we need an income redistribution scheme by which the utilities of all individuals are assigned equal weights.

4. SUSTAINABLE TIME-PATHS OF CONSUMPTION AND CAPITAL ACCUMULATION

In the analysis of dynamic optimality, a crucial role is played by the concept of *imputed price* of capital – either privately owned means of production or social common capital such as forests, oceans, the atmosphere, and social infrastructure. The imputed price of a particular kind of capital expresses the extent to which the marginal increase of the stock of the capital today contributes to the marginal increase of the welfare of the future generations of the society. The concept of *sustainability* introduced in this chapter is defined in terms of imputed price. Dynamic processes involving the accumulation of private and social common capital are sustainable when, at each time, intertemporal allocation of scarce resources is so arranged that the imputed prices of the various kinds of private capital and social common capital are to remain stationary at all future times.

Dynamic optimality may be obtained as market equilibrium with a perfectly competitive market under the hypothesis of perfect foresight with respect to the schedule of marginal efficiency of investment in various kinds of private capital. Sustainability, on the other hand, may be identified as market equilibrium with stationary expectations with respect to the schedules of marginal efficiency of investment in both private and social common capital.

When we try to introduce the concept of sustainability with reference to the imputed price of social common capital such as the natural environment, we must be aware of the intrinsic difficulties involved in making calculations of its magnitude, as argued by Lind and Arrow (1970), Lind (1982b), and others. Nevertheless, in the analysis of the dynamic optimum for global warming, as developed in Uzawa (1991b, 1992a, 1996, 2003), it is possible to find ways by which the processes of economic activities, capital accumulation, and the abatement of greenhouse gas emissions are so harmonized within the market institutions that the ensuing time-paths of consumption and the atmospheric concentrations of greenhouse gases are sustainable. We would like to see if the analytical apparatuses developed for the problem of global warming may be extended to the general circumstances in which several kinds of private capital as well as social common capital are involved.

Sustainability in the Simple Case

To begin, we introduce the concept of sustainability for the simple case in which the same kind of goods serves for both consumption and investment. As in previous sections, the instantaneous level of the utility u_t at each time t is represented by the utility function

$$u_t = u(c_t),$$

where c_t is the quantity of goods consumed by the representative consumer at time t.

The utility function $u = u(c)$ is defined for all nonnegative $c \geqq 0$, is continuous and continuously twice-differentiable, and satisfies the following conditions:

$$u(c) > 0, \quad u'(c) > 0, \quad u''(c) < 0 \quad \text{for all } c > 0.$$

It is assumed that the utility function $u = u(c)$ remains identical over time.

We first consider the case in which only one kind of private capital exists. We denote by K_t the stock of capital at time t and by c_t, z_t, respectively, consumption and investment at time t. Then, we have

$$c_t + z_t = f(K_t),$$

where $f(K)$ is the production function, which is assumed to be given independently of time t.

Production function $f(K)$ is defined, continuous, and continuously twice-differentiable for all $K \geqq 0$ and satisfies the following conditions:

$$f'(K) > 0, \quad f''(K) < 0 \quad \text{for all } K > 0.$$

The rate of capital accumulation at time t, $\dot{K}_t$, is given by

$$\dot{K}_t = \alpha(z_t, K_t), \; K_0 = K^0,$$

where K^0 is the initial stock of capital, and $\alpha(z, K)$ is the Penrose function relating the rate of capital accumulation $\dot{K}_t$ with investment z_t and the stock of capital K_t, at time t.

The imputed price of capital at time t, π_t, is defined as the discounted present value of the marginal increases in the outputs in the future, measured in units of the utility, due to the marginal increase in investment at time t, that is,

$$\pi_t = \int_t^\infty \pi_\tau m_\tau e^{-\delta(\tau - t)} d\tau,$$

where m_τ is the marginal efficiency of investment at future time τ:

$$m_\tau = m(z_\tau, K_\tau) = r_\tau \alpha_z(z_\tau, K_\tau) + \alpha_K(z_\tau, K_\tau), \quad r_\tau = f'(K_\tau).$$

A feasible time-path of consumption and capital accumulation, $(c, K) = ((c_t, K_t))$, is sustainable when the imputed price of capital π_t remains stationary at a certain level π; that is,

$$\pi_t = \pi \quad \text{for all } t \geqq 0.$$

Under conditions of sustainability, we have, from the definition of imputed price, that

$$m(z_t, K_t) = r_t \alpha_z(z_t, K_t) + \alpha_K(z_t, K_t) = \delta \quad \text{for all } t.$$

Thus, if a time-path of consumption is sustainable, then all future generations face the same imputed price of capital as the current generation does. Because the imputed price of capital at each time t expresses the discounted present value of the marginal increases of all future utilities due to the marginal increase in the stock of capital time t, the concept of sustainability thus defined may capture certain aspects of intergenerational equity. However, the more important issue of distributional equity remains to be analyzed. In the following sections, keeping this deficiency of our approach in mind, we see how the level of the imputed price π for sustainable time-paths is determined. The analysis to be introduced in the next few sections reproduces some of the basic results described in Uzawa (2003, Chapter 5).

Sustainable Levels of Consumption and Investment: One-Good Economy

First, we would like to see if the levels of consumption and investment at the sustainable time-path $(c, z) = ((c_t, z_t))$ are uniquely determined. To see this, the conditions for sustainability are put together as follows:

$$\dot{K} = \alpha(z, K) \tag{43}$$

$$c + z = f(K) \tag{44}$$

$$m = r\alpha_z + \alpha_K = \delta, \tag{45}$$

where the time suffix t is omitted.

By taking a differential of both sides of relations (44) and (45), we obtain

$$\begin{pmatrix} 1 & 1 \\ 0 & m_z \end{pmatrix} \begin{pmatrix} dc \\ dz \end{pmatrix} = \begin{pmatrix} r & 0 \\ -m_K & 1 \end{pmatrix} \begin{pmatrix} dK \\ d\delta \end{pmatrix},$$

where

$$m_z = r\alpha_{zz} + \alpha_{Kz} < 0, \quad m_K = r'\alpha_z + (r\alpha_{zK} + \alpha_{KK}) < 0$$
$$[r' = f''(K) < 0].$$

Hence,

$$\begin{pmatrix} dc \\ dz \end{pmatrix} = \begin{pmatrix} 1 & 1 \\ 0 & m_z \end{pmatrix}^{-1} \begin{pmatrix} r & 0 \\ -m_K & 1 \end{pmatrix} \begin{pmatrix} dK \\ d\delta \end{pmatrix}$$
$$= \frac{1}{m_z} \begin{pmatrix} rm_z + m_K & -1 \\ -m_K & 1 \end{pmatrix} \begin{pmatrix} dK \\ d\delta \end{pmatrix}$$

$$\frac{\partial c}{\partial K} = r + \frac{m_K}{m_z} > 0, \; \frac{\partial z}{\partial K} = -\frac{m_K}{m_z} < 0, \; \frac{\partial c}{\partial \delta} = -\frac{1}{m_z} > 0, \; \frac{\partial z}{\partial \delta} = \frac{1}{m_z} < 0.$$

Thus, the levels of consumption and investment (c, z) at the sustainable time-path are uniquely determined. In addition, we have

$$\left.\frac{\partial \alpha}{\partial K}\right|_{\dot{K}=0} = \alpha_z \frac{dz}{dK} + \alpha_K = -\alpha_z \frac{m_K}{m_z} + \alpha_K < 0 \quad [\alpha_z > 0, \alpha_K < 0].$$

Hence, the differential equation (43) has a uniquely determined stationary state, and it is globally stable.

Thus, we have established the following proposition.

Proposition 1. *For an economy with only one kind of capital, the levels (c, z) of consumption and investment at the sustainable time-path are uniquely determined for any given stock of capital $K > 0$.*

The larger the stock of private capital K, the higher the level of consumption c along the sustainable time-path and the lower the level of investment z. The higher the rate of discount δ, the higher the level of consumption c along the sustainable time-path and the lower the level of investment z.

At the sustainable time-path, the levels (c_t, z_t) of consumption and investment approach the long-run stationary state as time t goes to infinity.

For the standard case of the neoclassical world, we have

$$\alpha(z, K) = z \quad \text{for all } z, K \geqq 0$$

$$m(z, K) = f'(K) \quad \text{for all } z, K \geqq 0.$$

Hence, a z that satisfies sustainability conditions does not generally exist.

Sustainable Levels of Consumption and Investment: A General Case with Several Produced and Capital Goods

We denote by $K = (K_f)$ the vector of stock of capital of various kinds, where $f\ (f = 1, \ldots, F)$ generically refers to the type of private capital. The production function is represented by $f(K)$, where all the neoclassical conditions postulated in Chapter 2 are satisfied. That is, $f(K)$ is given independent of time t, is defined for all nonnegative $K \geqq 0$, is continuous and continuously twice-differentiable, and is concave and strictly quasi-concave with respect to K, and marginal products are always positive.

The vector of stock of capital K_t at time t is then determined by the following system of differentiable equations:

$$\dot{K}_f = \alpha_f(z_f, K_f) \quad (f = 1, \ldots, F)$$

with initial condition $K_0 = K_o$, where $K_o \geq 0$ is the vector of the initial stock of private capital, and $\alpha_f(z_f, K_f)$ is the Penrose function with regard to capital of type f, relating to the increase in the stock of capital of type f with investment in capital of type f, z_f, and the existing stock of capital of type f, K_f.

The Penrose effect is expressed by the conditions that, for capital of type f, $\alpha_f(z_f, K_f)$ is a concave and strictly quasi-concave function of (z_f, K_f), and

$$\frac{\partial \alpha_f}{\partial z_f} > 0, \quad \frac{\partial \alpha_f}{\partial K_f} < 0 \quad (f = 1, \ldots, F).$$

Marginal products of investment in various kinds of private capital are given by

$$m_f = \frac{\partial f}{\partial K_f} \frac{\partial \alpha_f}{\partial z_f} + \frac{\partial \alpha_f}{\partial K_f} > 0 \quad (f = 1, \ldots, F).$$

Exactly as in the simple case, the imputed price of the capital of type f at time t, π_{ft}, is defined as the discounted present value of the marginal increases in the output in the future, measured in units of the utility, due to the marginal increase in investment in the capital of type f at time t; that is,

$$\pi_{ft} = \int_t^\infty \pi_{f\tau} m_{f\tau} e^{-\delta(\tau - t)} d\tau,$$

where $m_{f\tau}$ is the marginal efficiency of investment at future time τ:

$$m_{f\tau} = m(z_{f\tau}, K_{f\tau}) = r_{f\tau}\alpha_{z_f}(z_{f\tau}, K_{f\tau}) + \alpha_{K_f}(z_{f\tau}, K_{f\tau}) = \delta.$$

A feasible time-path of consumption and capital accumulation $(c, K) = ((c_t, K_t))$ is sustainable when, for each type f of capital, the imputed price of capital π_{ft} at time t remains constant at a certain level π_f; that is,

$$\pi_{ft} = \pi_f \quad \text{for all } t \geqq 0.$$

Hence, a feasible time-path of consumption and capital accumulation (c_t, K_t) is sustainable if a system of imputed prices of private capital (π_f) exists such that the following conditions are satisfied:

$$\dot{K}_{ft} = \alpha_f(z_{ft}, K_{ft})$$

$$c_t + \sum_\ell z_{\ell t} = f(K_t)$$

$$m_{ft} = m(z_{ft}, K_{ft}) = r_{ft}\alpha_{z_f}(z_{ft}, K_{ft}) + \alpha_{K_f}(z_{ft}, K_{ft}) = \delta,$$
$$r_{\ell t} = f_{K_\ell}(K_t).$$

Proposition 2. *For an economy with several kinds of private capital, the levels of consumption and stock of capital goods (c_t, K_t) with the vector of investment $z_t = (z_{ft})$ at the sustainable time-path are uniquely determined for any vector of given stock of private capital, $K_0 \geq 0$.*

The sustainable time-path of consumption and capital accumulation (c_t, K_t) approaches the long-run stationary state as t goes to infinity.

5. SOCIAL COMMON CAPITAL AND SUSTAINABILITY

The concept of sustainability as introduced in the previous sections may easily be extended to the economy involving social common capital as well as private capital. The following presentation largely reproduces those discussed in Uzawa (2003, Chapter 5).

We denote by V_t the stock of social common capital existing in the society at time t, and the stock of private capital is denoted by K_t. Output $f(K_t)$ at each time t is divided among consumption c_t, investment in private capital z_t, and investment in social common capital w_t:

$$c_t + z_t + w_t = f(K_t),$$

where the production function $f(K)$ satisfies all the neoclassical conditions postulated in the previous sections.

The rate of increase in the stock of private capital, $\dot{K}_t$, is determined in terms of the Penrose function $\alpha(z, K)$:

$$\dot{K}_t = \alpha(z_t, K_t). \tag{46}$$

The Penrose function $\alpha(z, K)$ concerning the accumulation of private capital is assumed to satisfy the following conditions.

The function $\alpha(z, K)$ is defined for all $(z, K) \geqq 0$ and is continuous, continuously twice-differentiable, concave, and strictly quasi-concave with respect to (z, K); that is,

$$\alpha_{zz} < 0, \quad \alpha_{KK} < 0, \quad \alpha_{zz}\alpha_{KK} - {\alpha_{zK}}^2 \geqq 0.$$

It is assumed that

$$\alpha_z(z, K) > 0, \quad \alpha_K(z, K) < 0.$$

We also assume that the effect of investment in social common capital is subject to the Penrose effect, and thus the rate of increase in the stock of social common capital, $\dot{V}_t$, is determined, in terms of the Penrose function $\beta(w, V)$, as

$$\dot{V}_t = \beta(w_t, V_t). \tag{47}$$

The Penrose function $\beta(w, V)$ concerning the accumulation of social common capital is also assumed to satisfy the concavity conditions.

The function $\beta(w, V)$ is defined for all $(w, V) \geqq 0$ and is continuous, continuously twice-differentiable, concave, and strictly quasi-concave with respect to (w, V); that is,

$$\beta_{ww} < 0, \quad \beta_{VV} < 0, \quad \beta_{ww}\beta_{VV} - {\beta_{wV}}^2 \geqq 0.$$

It is assumed that

$$\beta_w(w, V) > 0, \quad \beta_V(w, V) < 0.$$

Note that for the case of global warming as discussed in Uzawa (1991b, 2003), the stock V represents the difference between the critical level and the current level of the accumulation of atmospheric carbon dioxide.

We assume that the utility u_t at each time t is a function of the vector of consumption c_t and the stock of environmental capital V_t,

$$u_t = u(c_t, V_t),$$

where utility function $u(c, V)$ is assumed to be defined for all $(c, V) \geqq 0$, positive valued with positive marginal utilities, continuously twice-differentiable, concave, and strictly quasi-concave with respect to (c, V):

$$u(c, V) > 0, \quad u_c(c, V), \quad u_V(c, V) > 0$$

$$u_{cc}, u_{VV} > 0, \quad u_{cc}u_{VV} - {u_{cV}}^2 \geqq 0 \quad \text{for all } (c, V) \geqq 0.$$

The sustainable time-path of consumption and capital accumulation is obtained in terms of the imputed prices of private capital and social common capital, to be denoted, respectively, by π_t and ψ_t. As with the case of private capital, the imputed price ψ_t of social common capital at time t is the discounted present value of the marginal increases in the outputs in the future due to the marginal increase in the level of investment in social common capital at time t; that is,

$$\psi_t = \int_t^\infty \psi_\tau n_\tau e^{-\delta(\tau - t)} d\tau,$$

where $n_t = n(c_t, w_t, V_t)$ is the marginal efficiency of investment in social common capital at time t.

The marginal efficiency of investment in social common capital $n = n(c, w, V)$ is defined by

$$n = n(c, w, V) = s\beta_w(w, V) + \beta_V(w, V),$$

where $\beta_w(w, V)$ is the marginal product of investment in social common capital, whereas $s = s(c, V)$ is the marginal rate of substitution between consumption and social common capital:

$$s = s(c, V) = \frac{u_V(c, V)}{u_c(c, V)}.$$

We now obtain the following Euler–Lagrange differential equations for the imputed prices of private capital and social common capital, π_t, ψ_t:

$$\frac{\dot{\pi}_t}{\pi_t} = \delta - m_t, \quad m_t = m(z_t, K_t)$$

$$\frac{\dot{\psi}_t}{\psi_t} = \delta - n_t, \quad n_t = n(c_t, w_t, V_t).$$

The time-path $(c_t, z_t, w_t, K_t, V_t)$ is sustainable when the imputed prices of private capital and social common capital, π_t and ψ_t, are determined so that the following conditions are satisfied:

$$m(z_t, K_t) = n(c_t, \ w_t, V_t) = \delta.$$

The imputed real national income at time t is given by

$$H_t = u(c_t, V_t) + \pi_t \alpha(z_t, K_t) + \psi_t \beta(w_t, V_t).$$

The optimum levels of consumption and investment in private capital and social common capital at each time t, c_t, z_t, w_t, are obtained so that the imputed real national income H_t is maximized subject to the constraints

$$c_t + z_t + w_t = f(K_t).$$

Let us denote by p_t the imputed price of output at time t. Then we obtain the following marginality conditions:

$$u_c(c_t, V_t) = p_t$$

$$\pi_t \alpha_z(z_t, K_t) = p_t$$

$$\psi_t \beta_w(w_t, V_t) = p_t.$$

For any given stock of private capital and social common capital, K, V $[K, V > 0]$, the levels of consumption and investment in private capital and social common capital at the sustainable time-path, (c, z, w), are uniquely determined.

To see this, note the following equations:

$$c + z + w = f(K)$$

$$m(z, K) = \delta$$

$$n(c, w, V) = \delta.$$

By taking a differential of both sides of these equations, we obtain

$$\begin{pmatrix} 1 & 1 & 1 \\ 0 & m_z & 0 \\ n_c & 0 & n_w \end{pmatrix} \begin{pmatrix} dc \\ dz \\ dw \end{pmatrix} = \begin{pmatrix} r & 0 & 0 \\ -m_K & 0 & 1 \\ 0 & -n_V & 1 \end{pmatrix} \begin{pmatrix} dK \\ dV \\ d\delta \end{pmatrix}$$

$$\begin{pmatrix} dc \\ dz \\ dw \end{pmatrix} = \begin{pmatrix} 1 & 1 & 1 \\ 0 & m_z & 0 \\ n_c & 0 & n_w \end{pmatrix}^{-1} \begin{pmatrix} r & 0 & 0 \\ -m_K & 0 & 1 \\ 0 & -n_V & 1 \end{pmatrix} \begin{pmatrix} dK \\ dV \\ d\delta \end{pmatrix}$$

$$= \frac{1}{\Delta} \begin{pmatrix} 1 & -\frac{1}{m_z} & -\frac{1}{n_w} \\ 0 & \frac{1}{m_z}\left(1 - \frac{n_c}{n_w}\right) & 0 \\ -\frac{n_c}{n_w} & \frac{1}{m_z}\frac{n_c}{n_w} & \frac{1}{n_w} \end{pmatrix} \begin{pmatrix} r & 0 & 0 \\ -m_K & 0 & 1 \\ 0 & -n_V & 1 \end{pmatrix} \begin{pmatrix} dk \\ dV \\ d\delta \end{pmatrix}$$

$$= \frac{1}{\Delta} \begin{pmatrix} r + \frac{m_K}{m_z} & \frac{n_V}{n_w} & -\frac{1}{m_z} - \frac{1}{n_w} \\ -\frac{m_K}{m_z}\left(1 - \frac{n_c}{n_V}\right) & 0 & \frac{1}{m_z}\left(1 - \frac{n_c}{n_V}\right) \\ -\left(r + \frac{m_K}{m_z}\right)\frac{n_c}{n_V} & -\frac{n_V}{n_w} & \frac{1}{m_z}\frac{n_V}{n_w} + \frac{1}{n_w} \end{pmatrix} \begin{pmatrix} dK \\ dV \\ d\delta \end{pmatrix},$$

where

$$\Delta = 1 - \frac{n_c}{n_w} > 0, m_z, m_K < 0, n_w, n_V < 0, n_c > 0.$$

Hence,

$$\begin{pmatrix} dc \\ dz \\ dw \end{pmatrix} = \begin{pmatrix} + & + & + \\ - & 0 & - \\ + & - & - \end{pmatrix} \begin{pmatrix} dK \\ dV \\ d\delta \end{pmatrix}.$$

On the other hand,

$$\begin{pmatrix} d\dot{K} \\ d\dot{V} \end{pmatrix} = \begin{pmatrix} d\alpha \\ d\beta \end{pmatrix}$$

$$= \begin{pmatrix} \alpha_K - \frac{\alpha_z}{\Delta}\frac{m_K}{m_z}\left(1 - \frac{n_c}{n_V}\right) & 0 \\ -\frac{\beta_w}{\Delta}\left(r + \frac{m_K}{m_z}\right)\frac{n_c}{n_V} & \beta_V - \frac{\beta_w}{\Delta}\left(\frac{1}{m_z}\frac{n_V}{n_w} + \frac{1}{n_w}\right) \end{pmatrix} \begin{pmatrix} dk \\ dV \end{pmatrix},$$

where

$$\alpha_K - \frac{\alpha_z}{\Delta}\frac{m_K}{m_z}\left(1 - \frac{n_c}{n_V}\right) < 0, \quad \beta_V - \frac{\beta_w}{\Delta}\left(\frac{1}{m_z}\frac{n_V}{n_w} + \frac{1}{n_w}\right) < 0.$$

Hence, the system of differential equations, (46) and (47), is globally stable. We have thus established the following proposition.

Proposition 3. *Suppose that there are several kinds of private capital and social common capital. For any given stock of private capital and social common capital, $K, V, (K, V > 0)$, the levels of consumption and investment in private capital and social common capital at the sustainable time-path, (c, z, w), are always uniquely determined.*

The larger the stock of private capital K, the higher the consumption and investment in social common capital along the sustainable time-path, but the lower the investment in private capital. On the other hand, the larger the stock of social common capital V, the higher the consumption and investment in private capital along the sustainable time-path, but the lower is the investment in social common capital. The lower the rate of discount δ, the lower the consumption along the sustainable time-path, whereas investments in private capital and social common capital both increase.

The sustainable time-path of consumption and investment in private capital and social common capital, (c, z, w), approaches the long-run stationary state as t goes to infinity.

6. SUSTAINABILITY FOR THE PROTOTYPE MODEL OF SOCIAL COMMON CAPITAL

The analysis of sustainable processes of consumption and capital accumulation we have introduced in the previous sections may be readily applied to the prototype model of social common capital as introduced in Chapter 2.

As sustainability is defined in terms of the stationarity of the imputed prices of various kinds of capital goods, the conditions for sustainability are identical with those for dynamic optimality except for the optimality conditions in the short run.

We resume the discussion carried out in Chapter 2. Although the basic premises of the model remain identical to those for the prototype model of social common capital introduced in Chapter 2, we must explicitly take care of investment activities in both private firms and social institutions in charge of social common capital. For the sake of expository brevity, we assume that only fixed factors of production are limitational in the production processes of both private firms and social institutions in charge of social common capital, thus abstracting from the role of labor entirely.

Basic Premises of the Prototype Model of Social Common Capital

We consider an economy consisting of n individuals, m private firms, and s social institutions in charge of social common capital. Individuals are generically denoted by $\nu = 1, .., n$, private firms by $\mu = 1, .., m$, and social institutions by $\sigma = 1, .., s$. Goods produced by private firms are generically denoted by $j = 1, \ldots, J$, whereas there is only one kind of social common capital.

The Principal Agency

The utility of each individual ν is cardinal and is expressed by the utility function

$$u^\nu = u^\nu(c^\nu, \varphi^\nu(a)a^\nu),$$

where c^ν is the vector of goods consumed and a^ν is the amount of services of social common capital used, both by individual ν, whereas a is the total amount of services of social common capital used by all members of the society:

$$a = \sum_\nu a^\nu + \sum_\mu a^\mu,$$

where a^μ is the amount of services of social common capital used by private firm μ. The impact index function $\varphi^\nu(a)$ expresses the extent to which the utility of individual ν is affected by the phenomenon of congestion with respect to the use of services of social common capital. The impact coefficients $\tau^\nu(a)$ of social common capital defined by

$$\tau(a) = -\frac{\varphi^{\nu\prime}(a)}{\varphi^\nu(a)}$$

are assumed to be identical for all individuals and satisfy the following conditions:

$$\tau(a) > 0, \quad \tau'(a) > 0.$$

The utility function $u^\nu(c^\nu, a^\nu)$ is assumed to satisfy the following conditions:

(U1) $u^\nu(c^\nu, a^\nu)$ is defined, positive, continuous, and continuously twice-differentiable with respect to (c^ν, a^ν) for all $(c^\nu, a^\nu) \geqq 0$.

(U2) $u^\nu_{c^\nu}(c^\nu, a^\nu) > 0, u^\nu_{a^\nu}(c^\nu, a^\nu) > 0$ for all $(c^\nu, a^\nu) \geqq 0$.

(U3) Marginal rates of substitution between any pair of consumption goods and services of social common capital are diminishing, or more specifically, $u^\nu(c^\nu, a^\nu)$ is strictly quasi-concave with respect to (c^ν, a^ν).

(U4) $u^\nu(c^\nu, a^\nu)$ is homogeneous of order 1 with respect to (c^ν, a^ν).

Private Firms

Processes of production of private firms are also affected by the phenomenon of congestion regarding the use of services derived from social common capital. We assume that, in each private firm μ, the minimum quantities of factors of production that are required to produce goods by x^μ and at the same time to increase the stock of fixed factors of production by $z^\mu = (z^\mu_f)$ with the use of services of social common capital at the level a^μ are specified by the following F-dimensional vector-valued function:

$$f^\mu(x^\mu, z^\mu, \varphi^\mu(a)a^\mu) = \left(f^\mu_f(x^\mu, z^\mu, \varphi^\mu(a)a^\mu)\right),$$

where $\varphi^\mu(a)$ is the impact index with regard to the extent to which the effectiveness of services of social common capital in processes of production in private firm μ is impaired by congestion. For private firm μ, the impact coefficients $\tau^\mu(a)$ of social common capital to be defined by

$$\tau(a) = -\frac{\varphi^{\mu\prime}(a)}{\varphi^\mu(a)}$$

are assumed to be identical for all private firms, identical to those for individuals.

The production possibility set of each private firm μ, T^μ, is composed of all combinations (x^μ, z^μ, a^μ) of vectors of production x^μ and investment z^μ, and use of services of social common capital a^μ that are possible with the organizational arrangements, technological conditions, and given endowments of factors of production K^μ in firm μ. It may be expressed as

$$T^\mu = \{(x^\mu, z^\mu, a^\mu)\colon (x^\mu, z^\mu, a^\mu) \geqq 0,\ f^\mu(x^\mu, z^\mu, \varphi^\mu(a)\, a^\mu) \leqq K^\mu\},$$

where the total amount of services of social common capital used by all members of the society, a, is assumed to be a given parameter.

The following neoclassical conditions are assumed:

($T^\mu 1$) $f^\mu(x^\mu, z^\mu, a^\mu)$ are defined, positive, continuous, and continuously twice-differentiable with respect to (x^μ, z^μ, a^μ).

($T^\mu 2$) $f^\mu_{x^\mu}(x^\mu, z^\mu, a^\mu) > 0,\ f^\mu_{\ell^\mu}(x^\mu, z^\mu, a^\mu) \leqq 0,\ f^\mu_{a^\mu}(x^\mu, z^\mu, a^\mu) \leqq 0.$

($T^\mu 3$) $f^\mu(x^\mu, z^\mu, a^\mu)$ are strictly quasi-convex with respect to (x^μ, z^μ, a^μ).

($T^\mu 4$) $f^\mu(x^\mu, z^\mu, a^\mu)$ are homogeneous of order 1 with respect to (x^μ, z^μ, a^μ).

Social Institutions in Charge of Social Common Capital

Similarly, in each social institution σ, the minimum quantities of factors of production required to provide services of social common capital by a^σ and at the same time to engage in investment activities to accumulate the stock of fixed factors of production by $z^\sigma = (z^\sigma_f)$ with the use of produced goods by $x^\sigma = (x^\sigma_j)$ are specified by an F-dimensional vector-valued function:

$$f^\sigma(a^\sigma, z^\sigma, x^\sigma) = \left(f^\sigma_f(a^\sigma, z^\sigma, x^\sigma)\right).$$

For each social institution σ, the production possibility set T^σ is composed of all combinations $(a^\sigma, z^\sigma, x^\sigma)$ of provision of services of social common capital a^σ, investment z^σ, and use of produced goods x^σ that are possible with the organizational arrangements, technological conditions, and the given endowments of factors of production K^σ of social institution σ. That is, it may be expressed as

$$T^\sigma = \{(a^\sigma, z^\sigma, x^\sigma)\colon (a^\sigma, z^\sigma, x^\sigma) \geqq 0,\ f^\sigma(a^\sigma, z^\sigma, x^\sigma) \leqq K^\sigma\}.$$

The following neoclassical conditions are assumed:

($T^\sigma 1$) $f^\sigma(a^\sigma, z^\sigma, x^\sigma)$ are defined, positive, continuous, and continuously twice-differentiable with respect to $(a^\sigma, z^\sigma, x^\sigma)$ for all $(a^\sigma, z^\sigma, x^\sigma) \geqq 0$.

(T$^\sigma$2) $f^\sigma_{a^\sigma}(a^\sigma, z^\sigma, x^\sigma) > 0$, $f^\sigma_{\ell^\sigma}(a^\sigma, z^\sigma, x^\sigma) < 0$, $f^\sigma_{x^\sigma}(a^\sigma, z^\sigma, x^\sigma) < 0$ for all $(a^\sigma, z^\sigma, x^\sigma) \geqq 0$.

(T$^\sigma$3) $f^\sigma(a^\sigma, z^\sigma, x^\sigma)$ are strictly quasi-convex with respect to $(a^\sigma, z^\sigma, x^\sigma)$ for all $(a^\sigma, z^\sigma, x^\sigma) \geqq 0$.

(T$^\sigma$4) $f^\sigma(a^\sigma, z^\sigma, x^\sigma)$ are homogeneous of order 1 with respect to $(a^\sigma, z^\sigma, x^\sigma)$.

Dynamically Optimum Paths for the Prototype Model of Social Common Capital

The accumulation of the stock of capital goods in firm μ is given by the following differential equation:

$$\dot{K}^\mu_t = z^\mu_t - \gamma K^\mu_t, \quad K^\mu_0 = K^\mu_{\text{o}}, \tag{48}$$

where z^μ_t is the vector specifying the levels of investment in capital goods in firm μ at time t and $\gamma = (\gamma_f)$ is the vector of the rates of depreciation of capital goods.

Similarly, the accumulation of the stock of capital goods in social institution σ is given by the following differential equation

$$\dot{K}^\sigma_t = z^\sigma_t - \gamma K^\sigma_t, \quad K^\sigma_0 = K^\sigma_{\text{o}}, \tag{49}$$

where z^σ_t is the vector specifying the levels of investment in capital goods in social institution σ at time t and $\gamma = (\gamma_f)$ is the vector of the rates of depreciation of capital goods, assumed to be identical to those for private firms.

The dynamically optimum path of consumption and investment for the prototype model of social common capital may be obtained as the optimum solution to the following problem of the dynamic optimum.

The Problem of the Dynamic Optimum. Find the pattern of consumption and investment in private capital and social common capital at all times t, $(c^\nu_t, z^\mu_t, z^\sigma_t)$, that maximizes the Ramsey–Koopmans–Cass utility integral

$$U = \int_0^\infty U_t e^{-\delta t} dt, \quad U_t = \sum_\nu u^\nu(c^\nu_t, a^\nu_t)$$

subject to the feasibility constraints (48), (49), and

$$\sum_{\nu} c_t^{\nu} + \sum_{\sigma} x_t^{\sigma} \leqq \sum_{\mu} x_t^{\mu} \tag{50}$$

$$a_t \leqq \sum_{\sigma} a_t^{\sigma} \tag{51}$$

$$\sum_{\nu} a_t^{\nu} + \sum_{\mu} a_t^{\mu} \leqq a_t \tag{52}$$

$$f^{\mu}\left(x_t^{\mu}, z_t^{\mu}, \varphi^{\mu}(a_t)\, a_t^{\mu}\right) \leqq K_t^{\mu} \tag{53}$$

$$f^{\sigma}\left(a_i^{\sigma}, z_i^{\sigma}, x_i^{\sigma}\right) \leqq K_i^{\sigma}, \tag{54}$$

where a_t^{ν}, a_t^{μ}, a_t^{σ} are, respectively, the amounts of services of social common capital concerning individuals ν, private firms μ, and social institutions σ, and a_t is the total amount of services of social common capital, all at time t.

We introduce the Lagrangian form

$$L = \int_0^{\infty} L_t e^{-\delta t} dt,$$

where

$$\begin{aligned}
L_t = & \sum_{\nu} u^{\nu}\left(c_t^{\nu}, \varphi^{\nu}(a_t) a_t^{\nu}\right) + \sum_{\mu} \psi_t^{\mu}\left(z_t^{\mu} - \gamma K_t^{\mu}\right) + \sum_{\sigma} \psi_t^{\sigma}\left(z_t^{\sigma} - \gamma K_t^{\sigma}\right) \\
& + p_t \left[\sum_{\mu} x_t^{\mu} - \sum_{\nu} c_t^{\nu} - \sum_{\sigma} x_t^{\sigma}\right] + \pi_t \left[\sum_{\sigma} a_t^{\sigma} - a_t\right] \\
& + \theta_t \left[a_t - \sum_{\nu} a_t^{\nu} - \sum_{\mu} a_t^{\mu}\right] + \sum_{\mu} r_t^{\mu}\left[K_t^{\mu} - f^{\mu}\left(x_t^{\mu}, z_t^{\mu}, \varphi^{\mu}(a_t)\, a_t^{\mu}\right)\right] \\
& + \sum_{\sigma} r_t^{\sigma}\left[K_t^{\sigma} - f^{\sigma}\left(a_i^{\sigma}, z_i^{\sigma}, x_i^{\sigma}\right)\right],
\end{aligned}$$

ψ_t^{μ} and ψ_t^{σ} are, respectively, the imputed prices of capital goods in private firm μ and social institution σ; π_t and θ_t are, respectively, the imputed prices of the provision and use of services of social common capital; and r_t^{μ} and r_i^{σ} are, respectively, the imputed rents of capital goods in private firm μ and social institution σ, all at time t.

The dynamically optimum time-path consumption and capital accumulation, $(c_t^{\nu}, K_t^{\mu}, K_i^{\sigma})$, are characterized by the following optimum conditions, where the time suffix t is omitted, in addition to feasibility conditions (48)–(54):

$$u^{\nu}_{c^{\nu}}(c^{\nu}, \varphi^{\nu}(a)a^{\nu}) \leqq p \quad (\text{mod.}\, c^{\nu})$$

$$u^{\nu}_{a^{\nu}}(c^{\nu}, \varphi^{\nu}(a)a^{\nu})\varphi^{\nu}(a) \leqq \theta \quad (\text{mod.}\, a^{\nu})$$

$$p \leqq r^{\mu} f^{\mu}_{x^{\mu}}(x^{\mu}, z^{\mu}, \varphi^{\mu}(a)\, a^{\mu}) \quad (\text{mod.}\, x^{\mu})$$

$$\psi^{\mu} \leqq r^{\mu} f^{\mu}_{z^{\mu}}(x^{\mu}, z^{\mu}, \varphi^{\mu}(a)\, a^{\mu}) \quad (\text{mod.}\, z^{\mu})$$

$$f^{\mu}(x^{\mu}, z^{\mu}, \varphi^{\mu}(a)\, a^{\mu}) \leqq K^{\mu} \quad (\text{mod.}\, r^{\mu})$$

$$\theta \geqq r^{\mu}\left[-f^{\mu}_{a^{\mu}}(x^{\mu}, z^{\mu}, \varphi^{\mu}(a)\, a^{\mu})\varphi^{\mu}(a)\right] \quad (\text{mod.}\, a^{\mu})$$

$$\pi \leqq r^{\sigma} f^{\sigma}_{a^{\sigma}}(a^{\sigma}, z^{\sigma}, x^{\sigma}) \quad (\text{mod.}\, a^{\sigma})$$

$$\psi^{\sigma} \leqq r^{\sigma} f^{\sigma}_{z^{\sigma}}(a^{\sigma}, z^{\sigma}, x^{\sigma}) \quad (\text{mod.}\, z^{\sigma})$$

$$p \geqq r^{\sigma}\,[-f^{\sigma}_{x^{\sigma}}(a^{\sigma}, z^{\sigma}, x^{\sigma})] \quad (\text{mod.}\, x^{\sigma})$$

$$f^{\sigma}(a^{\sigma}, z^{\sigma}, x^{\sigma}) \leqq K^{\sigma} \quad (\text{mod.}\, r^{\sigma})$$

$$\theta - \pi = \tau\theta, \tau = \tau(a)a.$$

The dynamic equations for the imputed prices of private capital and social common capital are given by

$$\dot{\psi}^{\mu} = (\delta + \gamma)\psi^{\mu} - r^{\mu} \tag{55}$$

$$\dot{\psi}^{\sigma} = (\delta + \gamma)\psi^{\sigma} - r^{\sigma}, \tag{56}$$

together with the transversality conditions:

$$\lim_{t\to+\infty} \psi^{\mu}_t K^{\mu}_t e^{-(\delta+\gamma)t} = 0, \qquad \lim_{t\to+\infty} \psi^{\sigma}_t K^{\sigma}_t e^{-(\delta+\gamma)t} = 0.$$

These optimum conditions coincide with those for market equilibrium with perfect foresight concerning the schedules of marginal efficiency of investment in both private capital and social common capital. Thus, it is apparent that the following proposition holds.

Proposition 4. *In the prototype model of social common capital, the optimum conditions for the dynamically optimum time-path of consumption and accumulation of private capital and social common capital coincide precisely with those for market equilibrium with the social common capital tax at the rate $\tau(a)\, y$:*

$$\theta - \pi = \tau\theta, \quad \tau = \tau(a)a,$$

where $\tau(a)$ is the impact coefficient of social common capital, with perfect foresight concerning the schedules of marginal efficiency of investment in both private capital and social common capital.

Sustainable time-paths for the prototype model of social common capital may be similarly obtained. One only has to replace the dynamic equations for the imputed prices (55), (56), and the transversality conditions by the following conditions:

$$\psi^{\mu} = \frac{r^{\mu}}{\delta + \gamma}, \quad \psi^{\sigma} = \frac{r^{\sigma}}{\delta + \gamma}.$$

It is apparent that the following proposition holds.

Proposition 5. *In the prototype model of social common capital, the conditions for the sustainable time-path of consumption and accumulation of both private capital and social common capital coincide precisely with the optimum conditions for market equilibrium with the social common capital tax at the rate $\tau = \tau(a)a$:*

$$\theta - \pi = \tau\theta, \quad \tau = \tau(a)a,$$

with stationary expectations concerning the schedules of marginal efficiency of investment in both private capital and social common capital.

4

A Commons Model of Social Common Capital

1. INTRODUCTION

The natural environment comprises an important component of social common capital. It is generally held as common property resources and is managed as the commons either by local communities or the state authorities. The atmospheric environment, for example, as the largest commons, is to be managed by all nations in the world. The natural environment is in principle not privately appropriated to individual members of the society or transacted through market institutions. In Chapter 1, we formulated simple dynamic models of the fisheries, forestry, and agricultural commons to examine critically the theme of the tragedy of the commons, originally put forward by Hardin (1968). However, the analysis was primarily confined to the cases in which the commons are evaluated in terms of the pecuniary gains accrued to the members of the communities that communally own or control the commons, where the role of the commons as social common capital has been only tangentially noted. When the natural environment is regarded as social common capital, there are two crucial properties that must be explicitly incorporated in any dynamic model. The first property concerns the externalities, both static and dynamic, with respect to the use of the natural environment as a factor of production. The second property concerns the role of the natural environment as an important component of the living environment, significantly affecting the quality of human life.

The institutions of the commons have historically been set up to solve the problems of the optimum use of resources from the natural environment. Some of the more successful historical and traditional commons have been studied in detail in the literature, as recorded in McCay and Acheson (1987) and Berkes (1989).

In this chapter, we introduce a commons model of social common capital in which the interplay of a number of the commons is analyzed in detail and the institutional framework is examined whereby the sustainable pattern of resource allocation may be realized.

2. A COMMONS MODEL OF SOCIAL COMMON CAPITAL

The analysis of the commons model of social common capital in this chapter is carried out within the framework of the prototype model of social common capital introduced in Chapter 2, focusing the analysis on the role of the commons. Virtually all the variables and relations introduced in Chapter 2 are retained.

The commons model of social common capital discussed in this chapter consists of a finite number of commons. Each commons consists of individuals and two types of institutions – private firms that are specialized in producing goods that are transacted on the market and social institutions that are concerned with the provision of services of social common capital. For the sake of expository brevity, the following discussion is carried out in terms of the representative individual, the private firm, and the social institution of each commons. Commons are denoted by ν $(\nu = 1, \ldots, n)$, and goods produced by private firms are generically denoted by $j = 1, \ldots, J$. We consider the situation in which there is only one kind of social common capital.

Utility Functions of the Commons

For each commons ν, the economic welfare is represented by the utility function

$$u^\nu = u^\nu\left(c^\nu, \varphi^\nu(a)a_c^\nu\right),$$

where a is the total amount of services of social common capital used by all members of the economy:

$$a = \sum_\nu a^\nu, \quad a^\nu = a_c^\nu + a_p^\nu \quad (\nu \in N),$$

where, for each commons ν, a^ν is the amount of services of social common capital used by commons ν, whereas a_c^ν and a_p^ν are the amounts of services of social common capital, respectively, used by the representative individual and the private firm of commons ν, and $\varphi^\nu(a)$ is the impact index function of social common capital for commons ν, where

$$\varphi^\nu(a) > 0, \quad \varphi^{\nu\prime}(a) < 0, \quad \varphi^{\nu\prime\prime}(a) < 0.$$

The impact index of social common capital

$$\tau(a) = -\frac{\varphi^{\nu\prime}(a)}{\varphi^\nu(a)},$$

is assumed to be identical for all commons ν. The following conditions are satisfied:

$$\tau(a) > 0, \quad \tau'(a) > 0.$$

The following neoclassical conditions are assumed:

(U1) Utility function $u^\nu(c^\nu, \varphi^\nu(a)a_c^\nu)$ is defined, positive, continuous, and continuously twice-differentiable for all $(c^\nu, a_c^\nu, a) \geqq 0$.

(U2) Marginal utilities are positive both for the consumption of produced goods c^ν and the use of services of social common capital a_c^ν:

$$u^\nu_{c^\nu}(c^\nu, \varphi^\nu(a)a_c^\nu) > 0, \quad u^\nu_{a_c^\nu}(c^\nu, \varphi^\nu(a)a_c^\nu) > 0$$
$$\text{for all } (c^\nu, a_c^\nu, a) \geqq 0.$$

(U3) Utility function $u^\nu(c^\nu, \varphi^\nu(a)a_c^\nu)$ is strictly quasi-concave with respect to (c^ν, a_c^ν, a) for all (c^ν, a_c^ν) for any given $a \geqq 0$.

(U4) Utility function $u^\nu(c^\nu, \varphi^\nu(a)a_c^\nu)$ is homogeneous of order 1 with respect to (c^ν, a_c^ν) for any given $a \geqq 0$; that is,

$$u^\nu(tc^\nu, t\varphi^\nu(a)a_c^\nu) = tu^\nu(c^\nu, \varphi^\nu(a)a_c^\nu)$$
$$\text{for all } t \geqq 0, (c^\nu, a_c^\nu, a) \geqq 0.$$

The Euler identity holds:

$$u^\nu(c^\nu, \varphi^\nu(a)a_c^\nu) = u^\nu_{c^\nu}(c^\nu, \varphi^\nu(a)a_c^\nu)c^\nu + u^\nu_{a_c^\nu}(c^\nu, \varphi^\nu(a)a_c^\nu)\varphi^\nu(a)a_c^\nu.$$

Production Possibility Sets for Private Firms of the Commons

For each commons ν, the production possibility set T^ν of the private firm of commons ν is composed of all combinations (x^ν, a_p^ν) of vectors of production x^ν and use of services of social common capital a_p^ν that are possibly produced with the organizational arrangements and technological conditions of the representative firm of commons ν and the given endowments of factors of production of private firm ν, K^ν. It is expressed as

$$T^\nu = \left\{\left(x^\nu, a_p^\nu\right) : \left(x^\nu, a_p^\nu\right) \geqq 0,\ f^\nu\left(x^\nu, \varphi^\nu(a)\, a_p^\nu\right) \leqq K^\nu\right\}.$$

(T1) $f^\nu(x^\nu, \varphi^\nu(a)\, a_p^\nu)$ is defined, positive, continuous, and continuously twice-differentiable with respect to (c^ν, a_c^ν, a) for all $(x^\nu, a_p^\nu, a) \geqq 0$.

(T2) $f_{x^\nu}^\nu(x^\nu, \varphi^\nu(a)\, a_p^\nu) > 0,\ f_{a_p^\nu}^\nu(x^\nu, \varphi^\nu(a)\, a_p^\nu) \leqq 0$ for all $(x^\nu, a_p^\nu, a) \geqq 0$.

(T3) $f^\nu(x^\nu, \varphi^\nu(a)\, a_p^\nu)$ is strictly quasi-convex with respect to (c^ν, a_c^ν, a) for all $(x^\nu, a_p^\nu, a) \geqq 0$.

(T4) $f^\nu(x^\nu, \varphi^\nu(a)\, a_p^\nu)$ is homogeneous of order 1 with respect to (x^ν, a_p^ν) for any given $a \geqq 0$; that is,

$$f^\nu\left(tx^\nu, t\varphi^\nu(a)\, a_p^\nu\right) = t f^\nu\left(x^\nu, \varphi^\nu(a)\, a_p^\nu\right)$$
$$\text{for all } t \geqq 0,\ (c^\nu, a_c^\nu, a) \geqq 0.$$

The Euler identity holds:

$$f^\nu\left(x^\nu, \varphi^\nu(a)\, a_p^\nu\right) = f_{x^\nu}^\nu\left(x^\nu, \varphi^\nu(a)\, a_p^\nu\right)x^\nu + f_{a_p^\nu}^\nu\left(x^\nu, \varphi^\nu(a)\, a_p^\nu\right)\varphi^\nu(a)\, a_p^\nu.$$

Postulates (T1–T3) imply that the production possibility set T^ν is a closed, convex set of $J + 1$-dimensional vectors (x^ν, a_p^ν). Note, however, that the production possibility set T^ν of the private firm of each commons ν depends on the total use of services of social common capital a.

Production Possibility Sets for Social Institutions of the Commons

For each commons ν, the production possibility set of the social institution in charge of social common capital, S^ν, is composed of all combinations (b^ν, w^ν) of the provision of services of social common capital b^ν and the use of produced goods w^ν that are possible with the organizational arrangements and technological conditions, with given endowments of factors of production of the social institution of the commons ν, V^ν. It is expressed as

$$S^\nu = \{(b^\nu, w^\nu) : (b^\nu, w^\nu) \geqq 0,\ g^\nu(b^\nu, w^\nu) \leqq V^\nu\}.$$

(S1) $g^\nu(b^\nu, w^\nu)$ is defined, positive, continuous, and continuously twice-differentiable for all $(b^\nu, w^\nu) \geqq 0$.

(S2) $g^\nu_{b^\nu}(b^\nu, w^\nu) > 0, g^\nu_{w^\nu}(b^\nu, w^\nu) \leqq 0$ for all $(b^\nu, w^\nu) \geqq 0$.

(S3) $g^\nu(b^\nu, w^\nu)$ are strictly quasi-convex with respect to (b^ν, w^ν) for all $(b^\nu, w^\nu) \geqq 0$.

(S4) $g^\nu(b^\nu, w^\nu)$ are homogeneous of order 1 with respect to (b^ν, w^ν) for all $(b^\nu, w^\nu) \geqq 0$; that is,

$$g^\nu(tb^\nu, tw^\nu) = tg^\nu(b^\nu, w^\nu) \quad \text{for all } t \geqq 0, (b^\nu, w^\nu) \geqq 0.$$

The Euler identity holds:

$$g^\nu(b^\nu, w^\nu) = g^\nu_{b^\nu}(b^\nu, w^\nu)\, b^\nu + g^\nu_{w^\nu}(b^\nu, w^\nu)\, w^\nu.$$

Postulates (S1–S3) imply that the production possibility set S^ν is a closed, convex set of $1 + J$-dimensional vectors (b^ν, w^ν).

3. MARKET EQUILIBRIUM FOR THE COMMONS MODEL OF SOCIAL COMMON CAPITAL

Suppose social common capital taxes with the rate τ are levied on the use of services of social common capital. Market equilibrium is obtained if we find the vector of prices of produced goods p, the price charged for the use of services of social common capital θ, and the price paid for the provision of services of social common capital π such that demand and supply are equal for all goods and the total provision of services of social common capital is equal to the total use of services of social common capital. The price charged for the use of services of social common capital θ is higher, by the tax rate $\tau\theta$, than the price paid for the provision of services of social common capital π; that is,

$$\theta = \pi + \tau\theta.$$

Market equilibrium for the commons model of social common capital is obtained if the following conditions are satisfied:

(i) The representative individual of each commons ν chooses the combination (c^ν, a^ν_c) of the vector of consumption c^ν and the use of services of social common capital a^ν_c in such a manner that the utility of commons ν

$$u^\nu = u^\nu\big(c^\nu, \varphi^\nu(a)\, a^\nu_c\big)$$

is maximized subject to the budget constraint

$$pc^\nu + \theta a_c^\nu = y^\nu,$$

where y^ν is the income of commons ν in units of market prices and a is the total amount of services of social common capital used by all members of the society that is assumed to be given when individual ν chooses (c^ν, a_c^ν):

$$a = \sum_\nu a^\nu, \quad a^\nu = a_c^\nu + a_p^\nu \quad (\nu \in N),$$

where a_p^ν is the amount of services of social common capital used by the private firm of commons ν.

(ii) The private firm of each commons ν chooses the combination (x^ν, a_p^ν) of production vector x^ν and the use of services of social common capital a_p^ν in such a manner that net profit

$$px^\nu - \theta a_p^\nu$$

is maximized over $(x^\nu, a_p^\nu) \in T^\nu$.

(iii) The social institution in charge of social common capital in each commons ν chooses the combination (b^ν, w^ν) of the provision of services of social common capital b^ν and the use of produced goods w^ν in such a manner that net value

$$\pi b^\nu - pw^\nu$$

is maximized over $(b^\nu, w^\nu) \in S^\nu$.

(iv) The total amount of services of social common capital provided by all social institutions in charge of social common capital is equal to the total use of services of social common capital by all commons of the economy; that is,

$$\sum_\nu b^\nu = a.$$

(v) At the price vector p, total demand for goods is equal to total supply:

$$\sum_\nu x^\nu = \sum_\nu c^\nu + \sum_\nu w^\nu.$$

(vi) For each commons ν, the balance-of-payments condition is satisfied; that is,

$$px^{\nu} - pc^{\nu} - pw^{\nu} + \pi(b^{\nu} - a^{\nu}) = 0.$$

Optimum Conditions for Market Equilibrium

Optimum and equilibrium conditions for market equilibrium for the commons model of social common capital, $[c^{\nu}, a_c^{\nu}, x^{\nu}, a_p^{\nu}, b^{\nu}, w^{\nu}$ $(\nu \in N); a, p, \pi, \theta]$, are listed.

The Consumer Optimum

$$pc^{\nu} + \theta a_c^{\nu} = y^{\nu} \tag{1}$$

$$\alpha^{\nu} u_{c^{\nu}}^{\nu}(c^{\nu}, \varphi^{\nu}(a)\, a_c^{\nu}) \leqq p \quad (\text{mod.}\, c^{\nu}) \tag{2}$$

$$\alpha^{\nu} u_{a_c^{\nu}}^{\nu}(c^{\nu}, \varphi^{\nu}(a)\, a_c^{\nu})\varphi^{\nu}(a) \leqq \theta \quad (\text{mod. } a_c^{\nu}) \tag{3}$$

$$\alpha^{\nu} u^{\nu}(c^{\nu}, \varphi^{\nu}(a)\, a_c^{\nu}) = y^{\nu}. \tag{4}$$

The Producer Optimum for Private Firms

$$p \leqq r^{\nu} f_{x^{\nu}}^{\nu}(x^{\nu}, \varphi^{\nu}(a)\, a_p^{\nu}) \quad (\text{mod.}\, x^{\nu}) \tag{5}$$

$$\theta \geqq r^{\nu}[- f_{a_p^{\nu}}^{\nu}(x^{\nu}, \varphi^{\nu}(a)\, a_p^{\nu})\varphi^{\nu}(a)] \quad (\text{mod. } a_p^{\nu}) \tag{6}$$

$$f^{\nu}(x^{\nu}, \varphi^{\nu}(a)\, a_p^{\nu}) \leqq K^{\nu} \quad (\text{mod.}\, r^{\nu}) \tag{7}$$

$$px^{\nu} - \theta a_p^{\nu} = r^{\nu} K^{\nu}. \tag{8}$$

The Producer Optimum for Social Institutions in Charge of Social Common Capital

$$\pi \leqq \rho^{\nu} g_{b^{\nu}}^{\nu}(b^{\nu}, w^{\nu}) \quad (\text{mod.}\, b^{\nu}) \tag{9}$$

$$p \geqq \rho^{\nu}[-g_{w^{\nu}}^{\nu}(b^{\nu}, w^{\nu})] \quad (\text{mod.}\, w^{\nu}) \tag{10}$$

$$g^{\nu}(b^{\nu}, w^{\nu}) \leqq V^{\nu} \quad (\text{mod.}\, \rho^{\nu}) \tag{11}$$

$$\pi b^{\nu} - pw^{\nu} = \rho^{\nu} V^{\nu}. \tag{12}$$

Equilibrium Conditions

$$a = \sum_{\nu} a^{\nu}, \quad a^{\nu} = a_c^{\nu} + a_p^{\nu} \quad (\nu \varepsilon N) \tag{13}$$

$$a = \sum_{\nu} b^{\nu} \tag{14}$$

$$\sum_{\nu} x^{\nu} = \sum_{\nu} c^{\nu} + \sum_{\nu} w^{\nu} \tag{15}$$

$$\theta = \pi + \tau\theta. \tag{16}$$

In the following discussion, we suppose that for any given level of social common capital tax rate τ ($\tau > 0$), the state of the economy

$$\mathrm{E} = \left[c^{\nu}, a_c^{\nu}, x^{\nu}, a_p^{\nu}, b^{\nu}, w^{\nu}\ (\nu \in N); a, p, \pi, \theta\right]$$

that satisfies all optimum and equilibrium conditions for market equilibrium generally exists and is uniquely determined.

National Income Accounting

Income y^{ν} of each commons ν is the sum of factor income $r^{\nu}K^{\nu} + \rho^{\nu}V^{\nu}$ and social common capital tax payments $\tau\theta a^{\nu}$:

$$y^{\nu} = (r^{\nu}K^{\nu} + \rho^{\nu}V^{\nu}) + \tau\theta a^{\nu},$$

where

$$\tau\theta = \theta - \pi.$$

National income y is the sum of incomes of all commons:

$$y = \sum_{\nu} y^{\nu} = \sum_{\nu} r^{\nu}K^{\nu} + \sum_{\nu} \rho^{\nu}V^{\nu} + \tau\theta a.$$

Another definition of national income y is

$$y = \sum_{\nu} px^{\nu} + \sum_{\nu} \pi b^{\nu}.$$

That is, national income y is the aggregate of the values in units of price of produced goods and services of social common capital.

Because the conditions of constant returns to scale prevail, we have relations (8) and (12):

$$px^{\nu} - \theta a_p^{\nu} = r^{\nu}K^{\nu}, \quad \pi b^{\nu} - pw^{\nu} = \rho^{\nu}V^{\nu}.$$

Hence,

$$\sum_\nu px^\nu - \sum_\nu \theta a_p^\nu + \sum_\nu \pi b^\nu - \sum_\nu pw^\nu = \sum_\nu r^\nu K^\nu + \sum_\nu \rho^\nu V^\nu$$

$$\sum_\nu (pc^\nu + \theta a_c^\nu) = \left(\sum_\nu r^\nu K^\nu + \sum_\nu \rho^\nu V^\nu\right) + \sum_\nu \theta a^\nu - \sum_\nu \pi b^\nu$$

$$= \left(\sum_\nu r^\nu K^\nu + \sum_\nu \rho^\nu V^\nu\right) + \tau\theta a.$$

That is, the following familiar identity in national income accounting holds:

$$y = \sum_\nu px^\nu + \sum_\nu \pi b^\nu = \left(\sum_\nu r^\nu K^\nu + \sum_\nu \rho^\nu V^\nu\right) + \tau\theta a.$$

4. MARKET EQUILIBRIUM AND SOCIAL OPTIMUM

To explore welfare implications of market equilibrium for the commons model of social common capital under the given level of social common capital tax rate τ, we consider the social utility U given by

$$U = \sum_{\nu\in N} \alpha^\nu u^\nu = \sum_{\nu\in N} \alpha^\nu u^\nu(c^\nu, \varphi^\nu(a)\, a_c^\nu),$$

where, for each commons ν, the utility weight α^ν is the inverse of the marginal utility of income y^ν of commons ν at market equilibrium.

We consider the following maximum problem:

Maximum Problem for Social Optimum. Find the pattern of consumption and production of goods, use and provision of services of social common capital, and total use of services of social common capital $[c^\nu, a_c^\nu, x^\nu, a_p^\nu, b^\nu, w^\nu (\nu \in N); a]$ that maximizes the social utility

$$U = \sum_{\nu\in N} \alpha^\nu u^\nu = \sum_{\nu\in N} \alpha^\nu u^\nu(c^\nu, \varphi^\nu(a)\, a_c^\nu) \tag{17}$$

among all feasible patterns of allocation:

$$\sum_{\nu\in N} c^\nu + \sum_{\nu\in N} w^\nu \leqq \sum_{\nu\in N} x^\nu \tag{18}$$

$$a = \sum_{\nu\in N} a^\nu, \quad a^\nu = a_c^\nu + a_p^\nu \quad (\nu \in N) \tag{19}$$

$$a = \sum_{\nu \in N} b^\nu \tag{20}$$

$$f^\nu\left(x^\nu, \varphi^\nu(a)\, a_p^\nu\right) \leqq K^\nu \quad (\nu \in N) \tag{21}$$

$$g^\nu(b^\nu, w^\nu) \leqq V^\nu \quad (\nu \in N). \tag{22}$$

The maximum problem for social optimum may be solved in terms of the Lagrange method. Let us define the Lagrangian form:

$$\begin{aligned} &L\left(c^\nu, a_c^\nu, x^\nu, a_p^\nu, b^\nu, w^\nu, a, p, \pi, \theta, r^\nu, \rho^\nu(\nu \in N)\right) \\ &= \sum_{\nu \in N} \alpha^\nu u^\nu\left(c^\nu, \varphi^\nu(a)\, a_c^\nu\right) + p\left[\sum_{\nu \in N} x^\nu - \sum_{\nu \in N} c^\nu - \sum_{\nu \in N} w^\nu\right] \\ &\quad + \theta\left[a - \sum_{\nu \in N} a^\nu\right] + \pi\left[\sum_{\nu \in N} b^\nu - a\right] \\ &\quad + \sum_{\nu \in N} r^\nu\left[K^\nu - f^\nu\left(x^\nu, \varphi^\nu(a)\, a_p^\nu\right)\right] \\ &\quad + \sum_{\nu \in N} \rho^\nu\left[V^\nu - g^\nu(b^\nu, w^\nu)\right]. \end{aligned} \tag{23}$$

The Lagrange unknowns $p, \theta, \pi, r^\nu, \rho^\nu$ are associated, respectively, with constraints (18), (19), (20), (21), and (22). The optimum solution may be obtained by partially differentiating the Lagrangian form (23) with respect to unknown variables $c^\nu, a_c^\nu, x^\nu, a_p^\nu, b^\nu, w^\nu, a$ and putting them equal to 0, where feasibility conditions (18)–(22) are satisfied. That is, for each commons ν $(\nu \in N)$,

$$\alpha^\nu u_{c^\nu}^\nu\left(c^\nu, \varphi^\nu(a)\, a_c^\nu\right) \leqq p \quad (\text{mod.}\, c^\nu) \tag{24}$$

$$\alpha^\nu u_{a_c^\nu}^\nu(c^\nu, \varphi^\nu(a)\, a_c^\nu)\, \varphi^\nu(a) \leqq \theta \quad (\text{mod.}\, a_c^\nu) \tag{25}$$

$$p \leqq r^\nu f_{x^\nu}^\nu\left(x^\nu, \varphi^\nu(a)\, a_p^\nu\right) \quad (\text{mod.}\, x^\nu) \tag{26}$$

$$\theta \geqq r^\nu\left[-f_{a_p^\nu}^\nu\left(x^\nu, \varphi^\nu(a)\, a_p^\nu\right) \varphi^\nu(a)\right] \quad (\text{mod.}\, a_p^\nu) \tag{27}$$

$$f^\nu\left(x^\nu, \varphi^\nu(a)\, a_p^\nu\right) \leqq K^\nu \quad (\text{mod.}\, r^\nu) \tag{28}$$

$$\pi \leqq \rho^\nu g_{b^\nu}^\nu(b^\nu, w^\nu) \quad (\text{mod.}\, b^\nu) \tag{29}$$

$$p \geqq \rho^\nu\left[-g_{w^\nu}^\nu(b^\nu, w^\nu)\right] \quad (\text{mod.}\, w^\nu) \tag{30}$$

$$g^\nu(b^\nu, w^\nu) \leqq V^\nu \quad (\text{mod.}\, \rho^\nu) \tag{31}$$

$$\theta - \pi = \tau(a) a\theta, \tag{32}$$

where $\tau(a)$ is the impact coefficient of social common capital.

Only relation (32) may need clarification. Partially differentiate the Lagrangian form (23) with respect to a, to obtain

$$\begin{aligned}\frac{\partial L}{\partial a} &= \sum_{\nu\in N} \alpha^\nu u^\nu_{a^\nu}(c^\nu, \varphi^\nu(a)\, a^\nu_c)[-\tau(a)]\varphi^\nu(a)\, a^\nu_c \\ &\quad + \sum_{\nu\in N} r^\nu\left[f^\nu_{a^\nu_p}(x^\nu, \varphi^\nu(a)\, a^\nu_p)\, \tau(a)\varphi^\nu(a)\, a^\nu_p\right] + \theta - \pi \\ &= -\tau(a)\left[\sum_{\nu\in N} \theta a^\nu_c + \sum_{\nu\in N} \theta a^\nu_p\right] + \theta - \pi = -\tau(a)\, a\theta + \theta - \pi.\end{aligned}$$

Hence, $\frac{\partial L}{\partial a} = 0$ implies relation (32); relation (32) may be written as

$$\theta - \pi = \tau\theta, \qquad \tau = \tau(a) a, \tag{33}$$

where τ is the social common capital rate administratively determined prior to the opening of the market.

Exactly as in the case of the prototype model of social common capital discussed in Chapter 2, the classic Kuhn-Tucker theorem on concave programming may be enlisted to obtain the proposition that the Euler-Lagrange equations (24)–(32) and feasibility conditions (18)–(22) are necessary and sufficient conditions for the optimum solution of the maximum problem for social optimum.

It is apparent that the Euler-Lagrange equations (24)–(32) and feasibility conditions (18)–(22) coincide precisely with the equilibrium conditions for market equilibrium with the social common capital tax rate $\tau = \tau(a)a$.

Marginality conditions, (24), (25), and the linear homogeneity hypothesis for utility functions $u^\nu(c^\nu, a^\nu)$ imply

$$\alpha^\nu u^\nu(c^\nu, \varphi^\nu(a)\, a^\nu_c) = pc^\nu + \theta a^\nu_c = y^\nu,$$

which, by summing over ν, yield

$$U = \sum_{\nu\in N} y^\nu = y.$$

We have thus established the following proposition.

Proposition 1. *In the commons model of social common capital, we consider the social common capital tax scheme with the tax rate τ for the use of services of social common capital given by*

$$\tau = \tau(a)a,$$

where $\tau(a)$ is the impact coefficient of social common capital.

Then market equilibrium obtained under such a social common capital tax scheme is a social optimum in the sense that a set of positive weights for the utilities of the commons $(\alpha^1, \ldots, \alpha^n)$ $[\alpha^\nu > 0]$ exists such that the social utility

$$U = \sum_{\nu \in N} \alpha^\nu u^\nu = \sum_{\nu \in N} \alpha^\nu u^\nu (c^\nu, \varphi^\nu(a)\, a_c^\nu)$$

is maximized among all feasible patterns of allocation $[c^\nu, a_c^\nu, x^\nu, a_p^\nu, b^\nu, w^\nu (\nu \in N); a]$.

The optimum level of social utility U is equal to national income y:

$$U = y.$$

Social optimum is defined with respect to any social utility

$$U = \sum_{\nu \in N} \alpha^\nu u^\nu = \sum_{\nu \in N} \alpha^\nu u^\nu (c^\nu, \varphi^\nu(a)\, a_c^\nu)$$

where $(\alpha^1, \ldots, \alpha^n)$ is an arbitrarily given set of positive weights for the utilities of commons. A pattern of allocation $(c^\nu, a_c^\nu, x^\nu, a_p^\nu, b^\nu, w^\nu, a)$ is a social optimum if the social utility U thus defined is maximized among all feasible patterns of allocation.

Social optimum necessarily implies the existence of the social common capital tax scheme, where the tax rate τ is given by $\tau = \tau(a)a$. However, the budgetary constraints for the commons

$$pc^\nu + \theta a_c^\nu = y^\nu$$

are not necessarily satisfied. However, exactly the same proof as that introduced in Uzawa (2003, Chapter 1) may be enlisted to see the validity of the following proposition.

Proposition 2. *In the commons model of social common capital, suppose a pattern of allocation $[c^\nu, a_c^\nu, x^\nu, a_p^\nu, b^\nu, w^\nu (\nu \in N); a]$ is a social optimum; that is, a set of positive weights for the utilities of* *commons* $(\alpha^1, \ldots, \alpha^n)$ $[\alpha^\nu > 0]$ *exists such that the given pattern of allocation* $[c^\nu, a_c^\nu, x^\nu, a_p^\nu, b^\nu, w^\nu(\nu \in N); a]$ *maximizes the social utility*

$$U = \sum_{\nu \in N} \alpha^\nu u^\nu = \sum_{\nu \in N} \alpha^\nu u^\nu(c^\nu, \varphi^\nu(a)\, a_c^\nu)$$

among all feasible patterns of allocation.

Then, a system of income transfer among the commons of the economy, $\{t^\nu\}$, *exists such that*

$$\sum_{\nu \in N} t^\nu = 0,$$

and the given pattern of allocation $[c^\nu, a_c^\nu, x^\nu, a_p^\nu, b^\nu, w^\nu(\nu \in N); a]$ *corresponds precisely to the market equilibrium under the social common capital tax scheme with the rate* τ *given by*

$$\tau = \tau(a)a,$$

where $\tau(a)$ *is the impact coefficient of social common capital.*

5. SOCIAL COMMON CAPITAL AND LINDAHL EQUILIBRIUM

In the commons model of social common capital introduced in the previous sections, we would like to see if the market equilibrium under the social common capital tax scheme with the tax rate $\tau = \tau(a)a$ is a Lindahl equilibrium.

Lindahl Conditions

Let us recall the postulates for the behavior of each commons at market equilibrium for the commons model of social common capital. At market equilibrium, conditions for the consumer optimum are obtained if the representative individual of each commons ν chooses the combination (c^ν, a_c^ν) of the vector of consumption c^ν and the use of services of social common capital a_c^ν in such a manner that the utility of commons ν

$$u^\nu = u^\nu(c^\nu, \varphi^\nu(a)\, a_c^\nu)$$

is maximized subject to the budget constraint

$$pc^\nu + \theta a_c^\nu = y^\nu,$$

where income y^ν of each commons ν is given by

$$y^\nu = r^\nu K^\nu + \rho^\nu V^\nu + \tau\theta a^\nu,$$

where r^ν and ρ^ν are, respectively, the imputed rental prices of factors of production of the private firm and the social institution of commons ν, and

$$\tau\theta = \theta - \pi.$$

Lindahl conditions are satisfied if a system of individual tax rates for the commons, $\{\tau^\nu\}$, exists such that

$$\sum_\nu \tau^\nu = \tau, \quad \tau^\nu \geqq 0 \quad \text{for all } \nu,$$

and, for the representative individual of each commons ν, (c^ν, a_c^ν, a) is the optimum solution to the following virtual maximum problem:

Find $(\bar{c}^\nu, \bar{a}_c^\nu, \bar{a}^{(\nu)})$ that maximizes the utility of commons ν:

$$u^\nu = u^\nu\left(\bar{c}^\nu, \varphi^\nu\left(\bar{a}^{(\nu)}\right) \bar{a}_c^\nu\right)$$

subject to the virtual budget constraint

$$p\bar{c}^\nu + \theta\bar{a}_c^\nu - \tau^\nu\theta\bar{a}^{(\nu)} = \hat{y}^\nu,$$

where

$$\hat{y}^\nu = y^\nu - \tau\theta a^\nu.$$

Because (c^ν, a^ν, a) is the optimum solution to the virtual maximum problem for commons ν, the optimum conditions imply

$$\tau^\nu\theta = \alpha^\nu u_{a_c^\nu}^\nu (c^\nu, \varphi^\nu(a)\, a_c^\nu)\, [\tau(a)\varphi^\nu(a)\, a_c^\nu],$$

where α^ν is the inverse of the marginal utility of income of commons ν.

Hence,

$$\tau^\nu\theta = \tau(a)a^\nu\theta,$$

which implies

$$\tau^\nu\theta a = \tau(a)a^\nu\theta a = \tau\theta a^\nu.$$

Thus, Lindahl conditions are always satisfied at market equilibrium with the tax rate τ for the use of services of social common capital given by $\tau = \tau(a)a$.

Lindahl Equilibrium

A pattern of consumption, production, and use and provision of services of social common capital $[c^\nu, a_c^\nu, x^\nu, a_p^\nu, b^\nu, w^\nu (\nu \in N); a]$ is a Lindahl equilibrium if there exist the vector of prices of produced goods p, the price charged for the use of services of social common capital θ, and the price paid for the provision of services of social common capital π such that the following conditions are satisfied:

(i) For each commons ν, the representative individual chooses the combination (c^ν, a_c^ν) of consumption vector c^ν and use of services of social common capital a_c^ν in such a manner that the utility of commons ν

$$u^\nu = u^\nu \left(c^\nu, \varphi^\nu(a)\, a_c^\nu\right)$$

is maximized subject to the budget constraint

$$pc^\nu + \theta a_c^\nu = y^\nu,$$

where y^ν is the income of commons ν given by

$$y^\nu = r^\nu K^\nu + \rho^\nu V^\nu + \tau \theta a^\nu.$$

(ii) For each commons ν, the private firm chooses the combination (x^ν, a_p^ν) of production vector x^ν and the use of services of social common capital a_p^ν in such a manner that net profit

$$px^\nu - \theta a_p^\nu$$

is maximized over $(x^\nu, a_p^\nu) \in T^\nu$.

(iii) For each commons ν, the social institution in charge of social common capital chooses the combination (b^ν, w^ν) of the provision of services of social common capital b^ν and the use of produced goods w^ν in such a manner that net value

$$\pi b^\nu - pw^\nu$$

is maximized over $(b^\nu, w^\nu) \in S^\nu$.

(iv) Prices p are determined so that total demand for goods is equal to total supply:

$$\sum_\nu x^\nu = \sum_\nu c^\nu + \sum_\nu w^\nu.$$

(v) The total amount of services of social common capital is equal to the total use of services of social common capital by all members of the society; that is,

$$a = \sum_{\nu} a^{\nu}, \quad a^{\nu} = a_c^{\nu} + a_p^{\nu} \quad (\nu \in N).$$

(vi) The total amount of services of social common capital provided by all social institutions in charge of social common capital is equal to the total use of services of social common capital by all members of the society; that is,

$$\sum_{\nu} b^{\nu} = a.$$

(vii) Lindahl conditions for individual commons are satisfied; that is, for each commons ν, (c^{ν}, a_c^{ν}, a) is the optimum solution to the following virtual maximum problem:

Find $(\overline{c}^{\nu}, \overline{a}_c^{\nu}, \overline{a}^{(\nu)})$ that maximizes the utility of commons ν:

$$u^{\nu} = u^{\nu}\left(\overline{c}^{\nu}, \varphi^{\nu}\left(\overline{a}^{(\nu)}\right) \overline{a}_c^{\nu}\right)$$

subject to the virtual budget constraint

$$p\overline{c}^{\nu} + \theta \overline{a}_c^{\nu} - \tau^{\nu} \theta \overline{a}^{(\nu)} = \hat{y}^{\nu},$$

where

$$\hat{y}^{\nu} = y^{\nu} - \tau \theta a^{\nu}.$$

Proposition 3. *In the commons model of social common capital, we consider the social common capital tax scheme with the tax rate τ for the use of services of social common capital given by*

$$\tau = \tau(a)\, a,$$

where $\tau(a)$ is the impact coefficient of social common capital.

Then market equilibrium obtained under such a social common capital tax scheme is always a Lindahl equilibrium.

6. THE COOPERATIVE GAME ASSOCIATED WITH THE COMMONS MODEL

We regard the commons model of social common capital introduced in the previous sections as a cooperative game and examine the conditions under which the core of the cooperative game is nonempty.

The players of the cooperative game for the commons model of social common capital are the commons in the society. Each commons may choose as a strategy a combination of the vector of goods consumed and the amount of services of social common capital used by the commons, and the payoff for each commons is simply the utility of the representative individual of the commons. The unit of measurement for the utilities of the commons may be determined prior to the beginning of the game, is decided by the consensus of all the commons involved, and is assumed to remain fixed throughout the game.

A coalition for the social common capital game is any group of the commons, and the value of each coalition is the maximum of the sum of the utilities of the commons in the coalition on the assumption that those commons not belonging to the coalition form their own coalition and try to maximize the sum of their utilities.

The standard definition of the *core* in game theory is adopted. The core of the cooperative game for the commons model of social common capital consists of those allotments of the value of the game among the commons that no coalition can block. On the assumption that the standard neoclassical conditions for utility functions and production possibility sets are satisfied, we would like to examine the conditions under which the core of the social common capital game is nonempty.

As in the case of the cooperative game associated with global warming discussed in Uzawa (1997, 1999, 2003), the concept of the core of the social common capital game adopted in this chapter differs from that of Foley (1970) and those of virtually all game-theoretic contributions, as described in the classic review article by Kurz (1994) on the game-theoretic approach to the problems of public goods, where all the articles referred to are formulated exactly in terms of Foley's specifications. In our formulation of the cooperative game associated with the commons model of social common capital, the sum of the utilities of the commons in coalition S is defined as

$$\sum_{\nu \in S} u^{\nu} = \sum_{\nu \in S} u^{\nu}(c^{\nu}, \varphi^{\nu}(a)\, a_c^{\nu}),$$

where a is the total amount of services of social common capital used by all commons of the economy,

$$a = \sum_{\nu \in N} a^{\nu}, \quad a^{\nu} = a_c^{\nu} + a_p^{\nu} \quad (\nu \in N);$$

a_c^ν and a_p^ν are, respectively, the amounts of services of social common capital used by the representative individual and the private firm of commons ν; and $\varphi^\nu(a)$ is the impact index function of social common capital for commons ν.

On the other hand, in Foley's model, the sum of the utilities of the commons in coalition S is given by

$$\sum_{\nu \in S} u^\nu = \sum_{\nu \in S} u^\nu(c^\nu, \varphi^\nu(a_S)\, a_c^\nu),$$

where a_S is the total amount of services of social common capital used by the commons in coalition S:

$$a_S = \sum_{\nu \in S} a^\nu, \quad a^\nu = a_c^\nu + a_p^\nu \quad (\nu \in S).$$

One of the difficulties involved in the analysis of the cooperative game associated with the commons model of social common capital is that the value of each coalition S is influenced by the choice made by the players in the complementary coalition $N - S$.

Value of Coalition

The value of a coalition S $(N \subset S)$ is defined as the sum of the utilities of the commons in S when coalition S and the complementary coalition $N - S$ are in equilibrium. The core of the social common capital game consists of those allotments of the value of the game among commons that no coalition can block.

A coalition S is simply any subset of $N = \{1, \ldots, n\}$. A pattern of allocation $[c^\nu, a_c^\nu, x^\nu, a_p^\nu, b^\nu, w^\nu(\nu \in S); a_S]$ is feasible with respect to coalition S if

$$\sum_{\nu \in S} c^\nu + \sum_{\nu \in S} w^\nu \leqq \sum_{\nu \in S} x^\nu$$

$$\sum_{\nu \in S} a^\nu \leqq a_S, \quad a^\nu = a_c^\nu + a_p^\nu \quad (\nu \in S)$$

$$a_S \leqq \sum_{\nu \in S} b^\nu$$

$$f^\nu\left(x^\nu, \varphi^\nu(a)\, a_p^\nu\right) \leqq K^\nu \quad (\nu \in S)$$

$$g^\nu(b^\nu, w^\nu) \leqq V^\nu \quad (\nu \in S).$$

A pattern of allocation $[c^\nu, a_c^\nu, x^\nu, a_p^\nu, b^\nu, w^\nu(\nu \in S); a_S]$ is optimum with respect to coalition S if the utility of coalition S

$$U_S = \sum_{\nu \in S} u^\nu = \sum_{\nu \in S} u^\nu(c^\nu, \varphi^\nu(a)\, a_c^\nu)$$

is maximized among all patterns that are feasible with respect to coalition S, where

$$a = a_S + a_{N-S},$$

with the total use of services of social common capital by the commons in the complementary coalition $N - S$ given at the level a_{N-S}.

The assumptions on utility functions and production possibility sets for the commons model of social common capital postulated in the previous sections ensure that, for any coalition S, the pattern of allocation $[c^\nu, a_c^\nu, x^\nu, a_p^\nu, b^\nu, w^\nu(\nu \in S); a_S]$ that is optimum with respect to coalition S always exists and is uniquely determined for any given a_{N-S}.

The given amount a_{N-S} represents the total amount of services of social common capital used by all the commons that do not belong to coalition S:

$$a_{N-S} = \sum_{\nu \in N-S} a^\nu.$$

We suppose that the commons that do not belong to the given coalition S form their own coalition $N - S$ and try to maximize the sum of their utilities

$$U_{N-S} = \sum_{\nu \in N-S} u^\nu = \sum_{\nu \in N-S} u^\nu(c^\nu, \varphi^\nu(a)\, a_c^\nu),$$

among all patterns that are feasible with respect to coalition $N - S$.

A pattern of allocation $[c^\nu, a_c^\nu, x^\nu, a_p^\nu, b^\nu, w^\nu(\nu \in N - S); a_{N-S}]$ is optimum with respect to coalition $N - S$ if the utility of coalition $N - S$, U_{N-S}, is maximized among all patterns that are feasible with respect to coalition $N - S$:

$$\sum_{\nu \in N-S} c^\nu + \sum_{\nu \in N-S} w^\nu \leqq \sum_{\nu \in N-S} x^\nu$$

$$\sum_{\nu \in N-S} a^\nu \leqq a_{N-S}$$

$$a_{N-S} \leqq \sum_{\nu \in N-S} b^{\nu}$$

$$f^{\nu}(x^{\nu}, \varphi^{\nu}(a)\, a_p^{\nu}) \leqq K^{\nu} \quad (\nu \in N - S)$$

$$g^{\nu}(b^{\nu}, w^{\nu}) \leqq V^{\nu} \quad (\nu \in N - S),$$

where

$$a = a_{N-S} + a_S,$$

with total use of services of social common capital by the commons in the complementary coalition S given at the level a_S.

Equilibrium of Coalitions

Two coalitions, S and $N - S$, are in equilibrium if the total amount a_{N-S} of services of social common capital used by the commons belonging to the complementary coalition $N - S$ that the commons belonging to coalition S take as given is exactly equal to the total amount a_{N-S} of services of social common capital actually used by the commons belonging to coalition $N - S$, and vice versa.

In exactly the same manner as in Uzawa (2003, Chapter 7), the pattern of consumption and production of goods for individual commons, the use of services of social common capital by individual commons, and the total use of services of social common capital by all commons, $[c^{\nu}, a_c^{\nu}, x^{\nu}, a_p^{\nu}, b^{\nu}, w^{\nu}\ (\nu \in N); a]$, that satisfy equilibrium conditions for two coalitions, S and $N - S$, are uniquely determined. Thus our cooperative game may be regarded as a legitimate cooperative game in game theory.

We denote the relevant values at the equilibrium for two coalitions S and $N - S$ as follows:

$$c^{\nu}(S), a_c^{\nu}(S), x^{\nu}(S), a_p^{\nu}(S), b^{\nu}(S), w^{\nu}(S), a^{\nu}(S), a(S) \quad \text{for } \nu \in S$$

$$c^{\nu}(N-S), a_c^{\nu}(N-S), x^{\nu}(N-S), a_p^{\nu}(N-S), b^{\nu}(N-S), w^{\nu}(N-S),$$

$$a^{\nu}(N-S), a(N-S) \quad \text{for } \nu \in N - S,$$

where

$$a(S) = a(N-S) = \sum_{\nu \in S} a^{\nu}(S) + \sum_{\nu \in N-S} a^{\nu}(N-S).$$

Then the values of two coalitions S and $N - S$ are given, respectively, by

$$v(S) = \sum_{\nu \in S} \alpha^\nu u^\nu \left[c^\nu(S), \varphi^\nu(a(S))\, a_c^\nu(S)\right]$$

$$v(N-S) = \sum_{\nu \in N-S} \alpha^\nu u^\nu \left[c^\nu(N-S), \varphi^\nu(a(N-S))\, a_c^\nu(N-S)\right].$$

The maximum problem for the equilibrium of two coalitions S and $N - S$ may be solved in terms of the Lagrange method. Let us define the Lagrangian form:

$$\begin{aligned}
L &\left[(c^\nu), (a_c^\nu), (x^\nu), (a_p^\nu), (b^\nu), (w^\nu), a; p_S, p_{N-S}, \pi_S, \pi_{N-S}, \right. \\
&\left. \theta, \theta_S, \theta_{N-S}, (r^\nu), (\rho^\nu)\right] \\
&= \sum_{\nu \in N} \alpha^\nu u^\nu (c^\nu, \varphi^\nu(a)\, a_c^\nu) + p_S \left(\sum_{\nu \in S} x^\nu - \sum_{\nu \in S} c^\nu - \sum_{\nu \in S} w^\nu\right) \\
&\quad + p_{N-S} \left(\sum_{\nu \in N-S} x^\nu - \sum_{\nu \in N-S} c^\nu - \sum_{\nu \in N-S} w^\nu\right) + \theta(a - a_S - a_{N-S}) \\
&\quad + \theta_S \left(a_S - \sum_{\nu \in S} a^\nu\right) + \theta_{N-S} \left(a_{N-S} - \sum_{\nu \in N-S} a^\nu\right) + \pi_S \left(\sum_{\nu \in S} b^\nu - a_S\right) \\
&\quad + \pi_{N-S} \left(\sum_{\nu \in N-S} b^\nu - a_{N-S}\right) + \sum_{\nu \in N} r^\nu \left[K^\nu - f^\nu\left(x^\nu, \varphi^\nu(a)\, a_p^\nu\right)\right] \\
&\quad + \sum_{\nu \in N} \rho^\nu \left[V^\nu - g^\nu(b^\nu, w^\nu)\right].
\end{aligned}$$

The equilibrium of coalitions S and $N - S$ is uniquely obtained by differentiating the Lagrangian form with respect to the relevant variables and equating them to 0.

The Whole Coalition N

A coalition of particular importance is the whole coalition consisting of all commons of the economy, $N = \{1, \ldots, n\}$. A pattern of allocation $[c^\nu, a_c^\nu, x^\nu, a_p^\nu, b^\nu, w^\nu (\nu \in N); a]$ is feasible if

$$\sum_{\nu \in N} c^\nu + \sum_{\nu \in N} w^\nu \leqq \sum_{\nu \in N} x^\nu$$

$$a = \sum_{\nu \in N} a^\nu, \quad a^\nu = a_c^\nu + a_p^\nu \quad (\nu \in N)$$

$$a = \sum_{\nu \in N} b^\nu$$

$$f^\nu(x^\nu, \varphi^\nu(a)\, a_p^\nu) \leqq K^\nu \quad (\nu \in N)$$

$$g^\nu(b^\nu, w^\nu) \leqq V^\nu \quad (\nu \in N).$$

A feasible pattern $[c^\nu, a_c^\nu, x^\nu, a_p^\nu, b^\nu, w^\nu(\nu \in N); a]$ is optimum if it maximizes the aggregate utility

$$U = \sum_{\nu \in N} u^\nu = \sum_{\nu \in N} u^\nu(c^\nu, \varphi^\nu(a)\, a_c^\nu)$$

among all feasible patterns.

The relevant variables for the pattern of allocation $[c^\nu, a_c^\nu, x^\nu, a_p^\nu, b^\nu, w^\nu(\nu \in N); a]$ that is optimum with respect to coalition N and the associated variables may be denoted as follows:

$$c^\nu(N), a_c^\nu(N), x^\nu(N), a_p^\nu(N), b^\nu(N), w^\nu(N), a^\nu(N), a(N),$$

where

$$a(N) = \sum_{\nu \in N} a^\nu(N), \quad a^\nu(N) = a_c^\nu(N) + a_p^\nu(N) \quad (\nu \in N).$$

The value of the whole coalition N is the maximum value of the sum of the utilities of the countries in coalition N; it is denoted by

$$v(N) = \sum_{\nu \in N} u^\nu(c^\nu(N), \varphi^\nu(a(N) a_c^\nu(N))).$$

Optimum Conditions for the Whole Coalition N

The optimum pattern of allocation $[c^\nu(N), a_c^\nu(N), x^\nu(N), a_p^\nu(N), b^\nu(N), w^\nu(N); a(N)]$ and the associated imputed prices $p(N), \pi(N), \theta(N), r^\nu(N), \rho^\nu(N)$ for the coalition N satisfy the following conditions.

$$\sum_{\nu \in N} x^\nu(N) = \sum_{\nu \in N} c^\nu(N) + \sum_{\nu \in N} w^\nu(N)$$

$$a(N) = \sum_{\nu \in N} a^\nu(N), \quad a^\nu(N) = a_c^\nu(N) + a_p^\nu(N) \quad (\nu \in N)$$

$$a(N) = \sum_{\nu \in N} b^\nu(N)$$

$$f^\nu(x^\nu(N), \varphi^\nu(a(N))\, a_p^\nu(N)) = K^\nu \quad (\nu \in N)$$

$$g^\nu(b^\nu(N), w^\nu(N)) = V^\nu \quad (\nu \in N)$$

$$u_{c^\nu}^\nu(c^\nu(N), \varphi^\nu(a(N))\, a_c^\nu(N)) = p(N) \quad (\nu \in N)$$

$$u_{a_c^\nu}^\nu(c^\nu(N), \varphi^\nu(a(N))\, a_c^\nu(N))\varphi^\nu(a(N)) = \theta(N) \quad (\nu \in N)$$

$$p(N) = r^\nu(N) f^\nu_{x^\nu}(x^\nu(N), \varphi^\nu(a(N))\, a^\nu_p(N)) \quad (\nu \in N)$$
$$\theta(N) = r^\nu(N) [- f^\nu_{a^\nu}(x^\nu(N), \varphi^\nu(a(N))\, a^\nu_p(N)) \varphi^\nu(a(N)) \quad (\nu \in N)$$
$$\pi(N) = \rho^\nu(N) g^\nu_{b^\nu}(b^\nu(N), w^\nu(N)) \quad (\nu \in N)$$
$$p(N) = r^\nu(N) [-g^\nu_{w^\nu}(b^\nu(N), w^\nu(N))] \quad (\nu \in N)$$
$$\theta(N) - \pi(N) = \tau(a(N))\, a(N) \theta(N),$$

where, for the sake of expository brevity, all marginality conditions are assumed to be satisfied with equality.

7. THE CORE OF THE COOPERATIVE GAME FOR THE COMMONS MODEL

An allotment of the total value $v(N)$ of a cooperative game $G = (N, v(S))$ with transferable utility is said to be in the core if no coalition of players can block that allotment. Formally, we have the following definition.

An allotment of the value $v(N)$ of the cooperative game $(N, v(S))$ is a vector $\omega = (\omega^\nu)$ that satisfies the efficiency conditions

$$\sum_{\nu \in N} \omega^\nu = v(N).$$

An allotment $\omega = (\omega^\nu)$ is in the core if the following conditions are satisfied:

$$\sum_{\nu \in S} \omega^\nu \geqq v(S) \quad \text{for all coalitions } S \subset N.$$

Bondareva-Shapley's Theorem and the Nonemptiness of the Core

The nonemptiness of the core for any cooperative game is addressed in a classic theorem attributed to Bondareva and Shapley.

Bondareva-Shapley's Theorem. *Let $G = (N, v(S))$ be a cooperative game with characteristic function $v(S)$ $(S \subset N)$. The core of the game $G = (N, v(S))$ is nonempty if, and only if, for any balancing weights (λ_S), the following Bondareva-Shapley inequality holds:*

$$\sum_S \lambda_S v(S) \leqq v(N),$$

where $\sum_S$ means the summation over all possible coalitions $S \subset N$.

Note that a set of weights for all possible coalitions (λ_S) is said to be balancing if the following conditions are satisfied:

$$\lambda_S \geqq 0 \quad \text{for all } S \subset N, \text{ and } \sum_{S \ni \nu} \lambda_S = 1 \quad \text{for all } \nu \in N.$$

Bondareva-Shapley's theorem was originally proved by Bondareva (1962, 1963) and Shapley (1967). Further development of Bondareva-Shapley's theorem was provided by Aumann (1989), Kannai (1992), and others. Bondareva-Shapley's theorem was effectively applied to prove the nonemptiness of the core for the cooperative game associated with global warming, as discussed in detail in Uzawa (2003, Chapter 7).

Proof of Bondareva-Shapley's Theorem

If an allotment $\omega = (\omega^\nu)$ is in the core, then the following conditions are satisfied:

(i) $\sum_{\nu \in N} \omega^\nu = \upsilon(N)$.

(ii) $\sum_{\nu \in S} \omega^\nu \geqq \upsilon(S)$ for all coalitions S.

For any balancing weights (λ_S), we multiply both sides of (ii) by λ_S and sum over all S to obtain

$$\sum_S \lambda_S \upsilon(S) \leqq \sum_S \lambda_S \sum_{\nu \in S} \omega^\nu = \sum_{\nu \in N} \sum_{S - \nu} \lambda_S \omega^\nu = \sum_{\nu \in N} \omega^\nu = \upsilon(N),$$

thus proving the necessity part of Bodareva-Shapley's theorem.

To prove the sufficiency part of Bondareva-Shapley's theorem, let us make the following observation. The relationships between the concept of balancing weights and the definition of the core are easily seen if we consider the following linear programming problem (A) and its dual (B).

(A) Find $\omega = (\omega^\nu)$ that minimizes

$$\sum_{\nu \in N} \omega^\nu$$

subject to the constraints

$$\sum_{\nu \in N} \delta_S^\nu \omega^\nu \geqq \upsilon(S) \quad \text{for all } S \subset N,$$

where $\delta_S^\nu = 1$, if $\nu \in S$, and $\delta_S^\nu = 0$, if $\nu \notin S$.

(B) Find $y = (y_S)$ that maximizes

$$\sum_S \upsilon(S) y_S$$

subject to the constraints

$$\sum_S \delta_S^\nu y_S = 1 \quad \text{for all } \nu \in N$$

$$y_S \geqq 0 \quad \text{for all } S \subset N.$$

The duality theorem of linear programming ensures that the two linear programming problems (A) and (B) have the same value.

As (λ_S) is a set of balancing weights, we know that the value of linear programming problem (B) is equal to $\upsilon(N)$. Hence, linear programming problem (A) also has the value $\upsilon(N)$, which implies the existence of $\omega = (\omega^\nu)$ such that the system of inequalities in linear programming problem (A) is satisfied, and

$$\sum_{\nu \in N} \omega^\nu = \upsilon(N).$$

Such an $\omega = (\omega^\nu)$ clearly belongs to the core of the game $G = (N, \upsilon(S))$. Thus the Bondareva-Shapley theorem has been proved.

Q. E. D.

Nonemptiness of the Core of the Cooperative Game for the Commons

Bondareva-Shapley's theorem is now applied to examine the conditions for the nonemptiness of the core of the cooperative game for the commons model of social common capital.

We first note the following fundamental inequalities concerning the optimum variables of the cooperative game for the commons model of social common capital. For the sake of expository brevity, the values of the relevant variables at the optimum of the whole coalition N, $c^\nu(N)$, $a_c^\nu(N)$, $x^\nu(N)$, $a_p^\nu(N)$, $b^\nu(N)$, $w^\nu(N)$, $a(N)$, $p(N)$, $\pi(N)$, $\theta(N)$, $r^\nu(N)$, and $\rho^\nu(N)$, are, respectively, denoted by c_o^ν, a_{co}^ν, x_o^ν, a_{po}^ν, b_o^ν, w_o^ν, a_o, p_o, π_o, θ_o, r_o^ν, and ρ_o^ν. The value $\upsilon(N)$ of the whole coalition N then is given by

$$\upsilon(N) = \sum_{\nu \in N} \alpha^\nu u^\nu(c_o^\nu, \varphi^\nu(a_o)\, a_{co}^\nu).$$

The following relations are satisfied:

$$\sum_{\nu \in N} c_o^\nu + \sum_{\nu \in N} w_o^\nu = \sum_{\nu \in N} x_o^\nu$$

$$\sum_{\nu \in N} a_{co}^\nu + \sum_{\nu \in N} a_{po}^\nu = a_o$$

$$a_o = \sum_{\nu \in N} a_o^\nu$$

$$a_o = \sum_{\nu \in N} b_o^\nu$$

$$u_{c^\nu}^\nu (c_o^\nu, \varphi^\nu(a_o)\, a_{co}^\nu) = p_o \quad (\nu \in N)$$

$$u_{a_c^\nu}^\nu (c_o^\nu, \varphi^\nu(a_o)\, a_{co}^\nu)\varphi^\nu(a_o) = \theta_o \quad (\nu \in N)$$

$$p_o = r_o^\nu f_{x^\nu}^\nu (x_o^\nu, \varphi^\nu(a_o)\, a_{po}^\nu) \quad (\nu \in N)$$

$$\theta_o = r_o^\nu[- f_{a_p^\nu}^\nu (x_o^\nu, \varphi^\nu(a_o)\, a_{po}^\nu)\varphi^\nu(a_o)] \quad (\nu \in N)$$

$$f^\nu(x_o^\nu, \varphi^\nu(a_o)\, a_{po}^\nu) = K^\nu \quad (\nu \in N)$$

$$\pi_o = \rho_o^\nu g_{b^\nu}^\nu (b_o^\nu, w_o^\nu) \quad (\nu \in N)$$

$$p_o = -\rho_o^\nu g_{w^\nu}^\nu (b_o^\nu, w_o^\nu) \quad (\nu \in N)$$

$$g^\nu(b_o^\nu, w_o^\nu) = V^\nu \quad (\nu \in N)$$

$$\theta_o = \pi_o + \tau(a_o)\, a_o \theta_o.$$

Similar relationships hold for the optimum values of the relevant variables for coalition S:

$$\upsilon(S) = \sum_{\nu \in S} u^\nu(c^\nu(S), \varphi^\nu(a(S))\, a_c^\nu(S)),$$

where the values of the relevant variables at the equilibrium are written as $c^\nu(S)$, $a_c^\nu(S)$, $x^\nu(S)$, $a_p^\nu(S)$, $a^\nu(S)$, $a_S(S)$, and $a(S)$. The Lagrange unknowns $p, \pi, \theta, r^\nu, \rho^\nu$ are associated, respectively, with constraints (18), (19), (20), (21), and (22), where N is replaced by S. The optimum solution may be obtained by partially differentiating the Lagrangian form (23) with respect to unknown variables c^ν, a_c^ν, x^ν, a_p^ν, b^ν, w^ν, a_S, and putting them equal to 0, where feasibility conditions (18)–(22) are satisfied:

$$f^\nu(x^\nu(S), \varphi^\nu(a(S))\, a_*^\nu(S)) = K^\nu \quad (\nu \in S)$$

$$g^\nu(b^\nu(S), w^\nu(S)) = V^\nu \quad (\nu \in S)$$

$$u_{c^\nu}^\nu(c^\nu(S), \varphi^\nu(a(S))\, a_c^\nu(S)) = p(S) \quad (\nu \in S)$$

$$u_{a^\nu}^\nu(c^\nu(S), \varphi^\nu(a(S))\, a_c^\nu(S))\varphi^\nu(a(S)) = \theta(S)$$

$$p(S) = r^\nu(S)\, f_{x^\nu}^\nu(x^\nu(S), \varphi^\nu(a(S))\, a^\nu(S)) \quad (\nu \in S)$$

$$\theta(S) = r^{\nu}(S)\,[-f^{\nu}_{a^{\nu}}(x^{\nu}(S), \varphi^{\nu}(a(S))\,a^{\nu}(S))\varphi^{\nu}(a(S))] \quad (\nu \in S)$$
$$\pi(S) = \rho^{\nu}(S) g^{\nu}_{b^{\nu}}(b^{\nu}(S), w^{\nu}(S)) \quad (\nu \in S)$$
$$p(S) = r^{\nu}(S)\,[-g^{\nu}_{w^{\nu}}(b^{\nu}(S), w^{\nu}(S))] \quad (\nu \in S)$$
$$\theta(S) = \pi(S) + \tau(a(S))\,a(S)\theta(S),$$

where the imputed prices $p(S), \pi(S), \theta(S), r^{\nu}(S), \rho^{\nu}(S)$ are the values of the Lagrange unknowns $p, \pi, \theta, r^{\nu}, \rho^{\nu}$ at the optimum for coalition S. Similar relations hold at the optimum for coalition $N - S$.

We may assume that by taking a suitable utility indicator, $u^{\nu}(c^{\nu}, \varphi^{\nu}(a)\,a^{\nu}_c)$ is concave with respect to (c^{ν}, a^{ν}_c, a). Such a utility indicator may be chosen by a procedure similar to those of the utility indicator in CO_2 standards introduced in Uzawa (2003, Chapter 1). Then, we have the following inequality:

$$\begin{aligned}
&u^{\nu}(c^{\nu}_{o}, \varphi^{\nu}(a_o)a^{\nu}_{co}) - u^{\nu}(c^{\nu}(S), \varphi^{\nu}(a(S))\,a^{\nu}_c(S)) \\
&\quad \geqq u^{\nu}_{c^{\nu}}(c^{\nu}_{o}, \varphi^{\nu}(a_o)a^{\nu}_{co})\,[c^{\nu}_{o} - c^{\nu}(S)] \\
&\qquad + u^{\nu}_{a^{\nu}}(c^{\nu}_{o}, \varphi^{\nu}(a_o)a^{\nu}_{co})\,\varphi^{\nu}(a_o)\,[a^{\nu}_{co} - a^{\nu}_c(S)] \\
&\qquad - u^{\nu}_{a^{\nu}}(c^{\nu}_{o}, \varphi^{\nu}(a_o)a^{\nu}_{o})\,\tau(a_o)\varphi^{\nu}(a_o)a^{\nu}_{co}\,[a_o - a(S)] \\
&= p_o[c^{\nu}_{o} - c^{\nu}(S)] + \theta_o[a^{\nu}_{co} - a^{\nu}_c(S)] - \tau(a_o)\theta_o a^{\nu}_{co}[a_o - a(S)] \quad (\nu \in S).
\end{aligned}$$

Thus, for commons ν in coalition S, we have

$$\begin{aligned}
&u^{\nu}(c^{\nu}_{o}, \varphi^{\nu}(a_o)a^{\nu}_{co}) - u^{\nu}(c^{\nu}(S), \varphi^{\nu}(a(S))\,a^{\nu}_c(S)) \\
&\quad \geqq p_o[c^{\nu}_{o} - c^{\nu}(S)] + \theta_o[a^{\nu}_{co} - a^{\nu}_c(S)] - \tau(a_o)\theta_o a^{\nu}_{co}[a_o - a(S)]. \qquad (34)
\end{aligned}$$

As $a(N - S) = a(S)$, inequality (34) also holds for the commons ν in the complementary coalition $N - S$.

Similarly, as $f^{\nu}(x^{\nu}, \varphi^{\nu}(a)a^{\nu}_p)$ is assumed to be convex with respect to (x^{ν}, a^{ν}_p, a), we have the following inequality:

$$\begin{aligned}
&r^{\nu}_{o}\left[K^{\nu} - f^{\nu}(x^{\nu}_{o}, \varphi^{\nu}(a_o)a^{\nu}_{po})\right] - r^{\nu}_{o}\left[K^{\nu} - f^{\nu}(x^{\nu}(S), \varphi^{\nu}(S)a^{\nu}_p(S))\right] \\
&\quad \geqq -r^{\nu}_{o} f^{\nu}_{x^{\nu}}(x^{\nu}_{o}, \varphi^{\nu}(a_o)a^{\nu}_{po})\,[x^{\nu}_{o} - x^{\nu}(S)] \\
&\qquad - r^{\nu}_{o} f^{\nu}_{a^{\nu}}(x^{\nu}_{o}), \varphi^{\nu}(a_o)a^{\nu}_{po})\,\varphi^{\nu}(a_o)\left[a^{\nu}_{po} - a^{\nu}_p(S)\right] \\
&\qquad + r^{\nu}_{o} f^{\nu}_{a^{\nu}}(x^{\nu}_{o}, \varphi^{\nu}(a_o)a^{\nu}_{po})\tau(a_o)\varphi^{\nu}(a_o)a^{\nu}_{po}[a_o - a(S)] \\
&\quad = -p_o[x^{\nu} - x^{\nu}(S)] + \theta_o\left[a^{\nu}_{po} - a^{\nu}_p(S)\right] - \tau(a_o)\theta_o a^{\nu}_{po}[a_o - a(S)].
\end{aligned} \qquad (35)$$

We also have from the convexity of $g^\nu(b^\nu, w^\nu)$ with respect to (b^ν, w^ν) that

$$\begin{aligned}\rho_o^\nu [V^\nu - g^\nu(b_o^\nu, w_o^\nu)] - \rho_o^\nu [V^\nu - g^\nu(b^\nu(S), w^\nu(S))] \\ \geqq -\pi_o [b_o^\nu - b^\nu(S)] + p_o [w_o^\nu - w^\nu(S)]. \end{aligned} \tag{36}$$

Adding both sides of the inequalities (34)–(36) and noting

$$\begin{aligned}&r_o^\nu \left[K^\nu - f^\nu\left(x_o^\nu, \varphi^\nu(a_o)a_{po}^\nu\right)\right] = 0\\ &r_o^\nu \left[K^\nu - f^\nu\left(x^\nu(S), \varphi^\nu(S)a_p^\nu(S)\right)\right] \geqq 0\\ &\rho_o^\nu [V^\nu - g^\nu(b_o^\nu, w_o^\nu)] = 0\\ &\rho_o^\nu [V^\nu - g^\nu(b^\nu(S), w^\nu(S)] \geqq 0,\end{aligned}$$

we obtain

$$\begin{aligned}&\alpha^\nu u^\nu(c_o^\nu, \varphi^\nu(a_o)a_{co}^\nu) - \alpha^\nu u^\nu(c^\nu(S), \varphi^\nu(a(S))\, a_c^\nu(S))\\ &\quad \geqq p_o[c_o^\nu - c^\nu(S)] + \theta_o[a_{co}^\nu - a_c^\nu(S)] - \tau(a_o)\theta_o a_{co}^\nu [a_o - a(S)]\\ &\qquad - p_o[x^\nu - x^\nu(S)] + \theta_o\left[a_{po}^\nu - a_p^\nu(S)\right] - \tau(a_o)\theta_o a_{po}^\nu [a_o - a(S)]\\ &\qquad - \pi_o[b_o^\nu - b^\nu(S)] + p_o[w_o^\nu - w^\nu(S)].\end{aligned}$$

Hence,

$$\begin{aligned}&u^\nu(c_o^\nu, \varphi^\nu(a_o)a_{co}^\nu) - u^\nu(c^\nu(S), \varphi^\nu(a(S))\, a_c^\nu(S))\\ &\quad \geqq p_o\{[c_o^\nu + w_o^\nu - x_o^\nu] - [c^\nu(S) + w^\nu(S) - x^\nu(S)]\}\\ &\qquad + \left[\theta_o a_o^\nu - \pi_o b_o^\nu - \tau(a_o)a_o\theta_o a_o^\nu\right]\\ &\qquad - \left[\theta_o a^\nu(S) - \pi_o b^\nu(S) - \tau(a_o)\theta_o a_o^\nu a(S)\right] \quad (\nu \in N).\end{aligned} \tag{37}$$

Let $\{\lambda_S\}$ be any set of balancing weights; that is,

$$\lambda_S \geqq 0 \quad \text{for all } S \subset N, \text{ and } \sum_{S \ni \nu} \lambda_S = 1 \quad (\nu \in N).$$

We define the new variables as follows:

$$\begin{aligned}&c^\nu = \sum_{S\ni\nu} \lambda_S c^\nu(S), \quad x^\nu = \sum_{S\ni\nu} \lambda_S x^\nu(S), \quad w^\nu = \sum_{S\ni\nu} \lambda_S w^\nu(S),\\ &a_c^\nu = \sum_{S\ni\nu} \lambda_S a_c^\nu(S), \quad a_p^\nu = \sum_{S\ni\nu} \lambda_S a_p^\nu(S), \quad a^\nu = \sum_{S\ni\nu} \lambda_S a^\nu(S),\\ &b^\nu = \sum_{S\ni\nu} \lambda_S b^\nu(S).\end{aligned}$$

Then, we have

$$a = \sum_{\nu \in N} a^\nu, \quad a = a_c^\nu + a_p^\nu \quad (\nu \in N)$$
$$\sum_{\nu \in N} b^\nu = \sum_S \lambda_S \sum_{\nu \in S} b^\nu(S) = \sum_S \lambda_S \sum_{\nu \in S} a^\nu(S) = \sum_{\nu \in N} a^\nu$$
$$\sum_{\nu \in N} (c^\nu + w^\nu - x^\nu) = \sum_S \lambda_S \sum_{\nu \in S} [c^\nu(S) + w^\nu(S) - x^\nu(S)] = 0$$
$$\theta_o - \pi_o - \tau(a_o)a_o\theta_o = 0.$$

Both sides of inequality (37) may be multiplied by λ_S, summed over $\sum_{\nu \in N} \sum_{S \ni \nu} = \sum_S \sum_{\nu \in S}$ to obtain

$$\sum_{\nu \in N} u^\nu(c_o^\nu, \varphi^\nu(a_o)a_o^\nu) - \sum_S \lambda_S \sum_{\nu \in S} u^\nu(c^\nu(S), \varphi^\nu(a(S))a^\nu(S))$$
$$\geqq -(\theta_o - \pi_o)a + \tau(a_o)\theta_o \sum_S \lambda_S \sum_{\nu \in S} a_o^\nu a(S)$$
$$= \tau(a_o)\theta_o \left\{ \sum_S \lambda_S \sum_{\nu \in S} [a_S(N)a(S) - a(N)a_S(S)] \right\}$$
$$= \tau(a_o)\theta_o \left\{ \sum_S \lambda_S \sum_{\nu \in S} a(N)a(S) \left[\frac{a_S(N)}{a(N)} - \frac{a_S(S)}{a(S)} \right] \right\}.$$

Hence,

$$v(N) - \sum_S \lambda_S v(S)$$
$$\geqq \tau(a_o)\theta_o \left\{ \sum_S \lambda_S \sum_{\nu \in S} a(N)a(S) \left[\frac{a_S(N)}{a(N)} - \frac{a_S(S)}{a(S)} \right] \right\}.$$

Suppose the following condition is satisfied:

$$(*) \qquad \frac{a_S(S)}{a(S)} = \frac{a_S(N)}{a(N)} \quad \text{for all } S \subset N.$$

Then condition $(*)$ implies the Bondareva-Shapley inequality

$$v(N) \geqq \sum_S \lambda_S v(S), \ \text{ for all balancing weights } \{\lambda_S\}.$$

Thus, we have established the following proposition.

Proposition 4. *Let $G = (N, v(S))$ be the cooperative game associated with the commons model of social common capital game. Then the* *core of cooperative game $G = (N, v(S))$ is nonempty if condition $(*)$ is satisfied.*

$$(*) \qquad \frac{a_S(S)}{a(S)} = \frac{a_S(N)}{a(N)} \quad \text{for all } S \subset N.$$

Condition $(*)$ for the nonemptiness of the core of the cooperative game associated with the commons model of social common capital, as is the case with the global warming game, is so stringent that it may be satisfied only for an extremely limited class of the commons model of social common capital.

8. AN ALTERNATIVE DEFINITION OF THE CORE OF THE COOPERATIVE GAME FOR THE COMMONS MODEL

The discussion of the value of coalition for the cooperative game associated with the commons model of social common capital, as developed in the previous sections, assumes the strictly game-theoretic circumstances concerning the outcome of the choice of the strategy for each coalition S and its complementary $N - S$. That is, the commons belonging to coalition S presuppose that the total amount a of services of social common capital being used by all commons in the economy reflects the amount a of services of social common capital being used by the commons of coalition S, on the assumption that the amount a_{N-S} of the complementary coalition $N - S$ remains as it is now.

Two coalitions S and $N - S$ are in equilibrium if their respective amounts of services of social common capital, a_S and a_{N-S}, satisfy the equilibrium conditions

$$a = a_S + a_{N-S}.$$

Proposition 4 above states that for any coalitions S and $N - S$, the equilibrium always exists and is uniquely determined. Thus, the cooperative game associated with the commons model of social common capital is defined, with the value of coalition S being the sum of the utilities of the commons of coalition S at the equilibrium.

In this section, we examine the implications of an alternative definition of the value of coalition for the cooperative game associated with the commons model of social common capital. Let us denote by u_S and u_{N-S} the sums of the utilities of the commons in coalitions S

and $N - S$, respectively, by

$$u_S = \sum_{\nu \in S} u^\nu, \quad u_{N-S} = \sum_{\nu \in N-S} u^\nu.$$

A pair of the utilities (u_S, u_{N-S}) is admissible if there is no pair $(u_S{}', u_{N-S}{}')$ associated with allocations that are feasible with respect to coalitions S and $N - S$ such that

$$u_S \leqq u_S{}', \quad u_{N-S} \leqq u_{N-S}{}'$$

with strict inequality for either S or $N - S$.

The cooperative game associated with the commons model of social common capital may alternatively be conceived if the values of each coalition S and its complementary $N - S$ are defined by

$$v(S) = \sum_{\nu \in S} \alpha^\nu u^\nu(c^\nu, \varphi^\nu(a)\, a_c^\nu), \quad v(N - S) = \sum_{\nu \in N-S} \alpha^\nu u^\nu(c^\nu, \varphi^\nu(a)\, a_c^\nu)$$

for any allocations $\{c^\nu, a_c^\nu\ (\nu \in S); a_S\}$ and $\{c^\nu, a_c^\nu\ (\nu \in N - S); a_{N-S}\}$ that are admissible with respect to coalitions S and $N - S$.

If an allotment is in the core of the cooperative game associated with the commons model under the alternative definition, it is a fortiori in the core of the cooperative game under the original definition. The alternative definition of the value of coalition, however, does not satisfy the standard condition required for cooperative games with transferable utility, for admissible pairs (u_S, u_{N-S}) are not uniquely defined.

In terms of assumptions (U1–U3) and (T1–T3), a pair of feasible allocations, $\{c^\nu, a_c^\nu, x^\nu, a_p^\nu, b^\nu, w^\nu (\nu \in S); a_S\}$ and $\{c^\nu, a_c^\nu, x^\nu, a_p^\nu, b^\nu, w^\nu (\nu \in N - S); a_{N-S}\}$, is admissible if, and only if, a pair of positive weights $\beta = (\beta_S, \beta_{N-S}),\ (\beta_S, \beta_{N-S} > 0)$, exists such that the weighted sum of utilities of two coalitions

$$\begin{aligned} U &= \beta_S U_S + \beta_{N-S} U_{N-S} \\ &= \beta_S \sum_{\nu \in S} u^\nu(c^\nu, \varphi^\nu(a)\, a_c^\nu) + \beta_{N-S} \sum_{\nu \in S} u^\nu(c^\nu, \varphi^\nu(a)\, a_c^\nu) \end{aligned}$$

is maximized subject to the constraints:

$$\sum_{\nu \in S} c^\nu + \sum_{\nu \in S} w^\nu \leqq \sum_{\nu \in S} x^\nu$$

$$a = \sum_{\nu \in S} a^\nu + a_{N-S}, \quad a^\nu = a_c^\nu + a_p^\nu \quad (\nu \in S)$$

$$f^\nu(x^\nu, \varphi^\nu(a)\, a_*^\nu) \leqq K^\nu \quad (\nu \in S)$$
$$g^\nu(b^\nu, w^\nu) \leqq V^\nu \quad (\nu \in S),$$

where a_{N-S}, b_{N-S} are the relevant amounts for the complementary coalition $N - S$. The similar constraints are for the complementary coalition $N - S$.

The values of the relevant variables at the optimum for the maximum problem above are uniquely determined and they may be denoted by

$$c^\nu(S, \beta), x^\nu(S, \beta), a^\nu(S, \beta), a_S(S, \beta), a(S, \beta), \text{ and so on.}$$

The values of the sums of the utilities for coalitions S and $N - S$ at the optimum may be denoted, respectively, by $\upsilon(S, \beta)$ and $\upsilon(N - S, \beta)$.

Then, for any pair $\beta = (\beta_S, \beta_{N-S})$ of positive weights β_S, β_{N-S}, the values thus defined, $\upsilon(S, \beta)$ and $\upsilon(N - S, \beta)$, are considered, respectively, to be the values of coalitions S and $N - S$ for the alternative cooperative game associated with the commons model of social common capital.

Balancedness of Coalitions for the Cooperative Game Associated with the Commons Model

A coalition S and its complementary $N - S$ are defined as being *balanced* if a pair of positive weights $\beta = (\beta_S, \beta_{N-S})$ exists such that

$$a_S(S, \beta) = t_S a(S, \beta), \quad a_{N-S}(S, \beta) = t_{N-S} a(S, \beta),$$

where

$$t_S = \frac{a_S(N)}{a(N)}, \quad t_{N-S} = \frac{a_{N-S}(N)}{a(N)}, \quad t_S, t_{N-S} > 0, \quad t_S + t_{N-S} = 1.$$

The cooperative game associated with the cooperative game for the commons model introduced in this section is balanced if the value $\upsilon(S)$ of each coalition S is given by

$$\upsilon(S) = \sum_{\nu \in S} u^\nu(c^\nu(S, \beta), \varphi^\nu(a(S, \beta))\, a_c^\nu(S, \beta)),$$

where $\beta = (\beta_S, \beta_{N-S})$ is the pair of positive weights with respect to which coalition S and $N - S$ are balanced.

We now have the following proposition, which may be proved in a manner exactly the same as the one described in Uzawa (2003, Chapter 7).

Proposition 5. *Let $G(N, \upsilon(S))$ be the cooperative game with transferable utility associated with the commons model of social common capital, where conditions (U1–U3) and (T1–T3) are assumed. Then, for any coalition S, $(S \subset N)$, there exists a pair of positive weights, $\beta = (\beta_S, \beta_{N-S})$, $\beta_S, \beta_{N-S} > 0$, with respect to which coalition S and its complementary $N - S$ are balanced, and the value $\upsilon(S)$ of the cooperative game associated with $G(N, \upsilon(S))$ is defined as the sum of the utilities of the commons belonging to coalition S when coalition S and its complementary $N - S$ are balanced.*

The core of the cooperative game associated with the commons model of social common capital $G(N, \upsilon(S))$ is always nonempty.

5

Energy and Recycling of Residual Wastes

1. INTRODUCTION

In this chapter, we formulate a model of social common capital in which the energy use and recycling of residual waste are explicitly taken into consideration and the optimal arrangements concerning the pricing of energy and recycling of residual wastes are examined within the framework of the prototype model of social common capital introduced in Chapter 2.

The disposal of residual wastes – industrial, urban, and otherwise – has become one of the more menacing problems faced by any contemporary society. In this chapter, we explore the possibility of converting the disposed stock of residual wastes to an "urban mine" from which precious metals and other materials are extracted to be used as raw materials for the industrial processes of production, particularly for the production of energy.

In the model of social common capital introduced in this chapter, we consider a particular type of social institution that is specialized in reprocessing disposed residual wastes and converting them to raw materials to be used as inputs for the production processes of energy-producing firms.

As in the case of the models of social common capital introduced in the previous chapters, all factors of production that are necessary for the professional provision of services of social common capital are either privately owned or are managed as though they are privately owned. As was discussed in detail in the Introduction, services of social common capital are subject to the phenomenon of congestion, resulting in the divergence between private and social costs. Therefore, to obtain efficient allocation of scarce resources, it becomes necessary to levy taxes on the disposal of residual wastes and to pay subsidies for the reprocessing of disposed residual wastes. Subsidy payments are made to the social institutions specialized in the recycling of disposed residual wastes based on the imputed price of the disposed residual wastes, whereas members of the society are levied taxes for the disposal of residual wastes at exactly the same rate as the subsidy payments made to social institutions in charge of the recycling of residual wastes. One of the crucial problems is to see how the optimum tax and subsidy rates are determined for the recycling model of residual wastes, as was the case with the various components of social common capital discussed in the previous chapters.

2. SPECIFICATIONS OF THE RECYCLING MODEL OF SOCIAL COMMON CAPITAL

The society in question consists of a finite number of individuals, private firms, and social institutions in charge of social common capital. There are two types of private firms: those specialized in producing goods that are transacted on the market, on the one hand, and those that are engaged in the production of energy, on the other. The residual wastes that are disposed of in the processes of consumption and production activities by members of the society are partly recycled by social institutions in charge of social common capital and converted into the raw materials to be used for energy production. Social institutions in charge of social common capital are primarily concerned with the management of residual wastes from a social point of view, but the ownership arrangements of the institutions are private in the sense that all the shares issued by social institutions are owned by private individuals.

Social common capital taxes are charged for the disposal of residual wastes, with the rates to be administratively determined by the government and announced prior to the opening of the market. Social institutions in charge of social common capital recycle the residual wastes disposed of by members of the society and convert them to the raw materials used in the processes of energy production. Subsidy payments are made to social institutions for the recycling of residual wastes, at the rates exactly equal to the tax rates charged on the disposal of residual wastes. The raw materials produced by social institutions in charge of the recycling of residual wastes are sold, on a competitive market, to private firms engaged in the production of energy.

As in Chapter 2, one of the crucial roles of the government is to determine the tax rates on the disposal of residual wastes in such a manner that the ensuing pattern of resource allocation is optimum in a certain well-defined, socially acceptable sense.

Individuals are generically denoted by $\nu = 1, \dots, n$, and private firms that are specialized in producing goods and energy are, respectively, denoted by $\mu = 1, \dots, m$ and $\varepsilon = 1, \dots, e$. Social institutions in charge of waste management are denoted by $\sigma = 1, \dots, s$. Goods produced by private firms are generically denoted by $j = 1, \dots, J$. There are two types of factors of production, variable and fixed. Variable factors of production are generically denoted by $\eta = 1, \dots,$ H and fixed factors of production by $f = 1, \dots, F$. We often refer to variable factors of production as labor, whereas fixed factors of production are referred to as capital goods.

Quantities of capital goods accumulated in each private firm μ are expressed by $K^\mu = (K_f^\mu)$, where K_f^μ denotes the quantity of capital goods f accumulated in firm μ. Quantities of goods produced by firm μ are denoted by $x^\mu = (x_j^\mu)$, where x_j^μ denotes the quantity of goods j produced by firm μ, net of the quantities of goods used by firm μ itself. The amounts of various types of labor employed by firm μ are expressed by $\ell^\mu = (\ell_\eta^\mu)$, where ℓ_η^μ denotes the amount of labor of type η employed by firm μ. To carry out productive activities, private firms use energy; the amount of energy used by firm μ is denoted by b^μ. The amount of residual wastes disposed of by firm μ is denoted by a^μ.

Quantities of capital goods accumulated in energy-producing firm ε are expressed by $K^\varepsilon = (K_f^\varepsilon)$. The amount of energy produced by firm ε is denoted by b^ε, net of the amount of energy used by firm ε itself. To carry out productive activities, energy-producing firms use raw materials. The amount of raw materials used by firm ε is denoted by q^ε, whereas the employment of labor and the use of produced goods by firm ε are, respectively, denoted by $\ell^\mu = (\ell_\eta^\mu)$ and $x^\varepsilon = (x_j^\varepsilon)$. The amount of residual wastes disposed of by firm ε is denoted by a^ε.

The manner in which social institutions in charge of waste management convert residual wastes to raw materials used in energy production is similarly postulated. Quantities of capital goods accumulated in social institution σ are expressed by $K^\sigma = (K_f^\sigma)$. We denote by q^σ the amount of raw materials for energy production used by social institution σ. The employment of labor and the use of produced goods by social institution σ are denoted, respectively, by $\ell^\sigma = (\ell_\eta^\sigma)$ and $x^\sigma = (x_j^\sigma)$. The amount of residual wastes recycled by social institution σ is denoted by a^σ.

Principal Agency of the Society

The principal agency of the society is each individual who consumes goods produced by private firms, uses energy provided by energy-producing firms, and disposes of the residual wastes in relation to consumption activities. The vector of goods consumed by each individual ν is denoted by $c^\nu = (c_j^\nu)$ and the amount of energy used by individual ν is denoted by b^ν, whereas the amount of residual wastes disposed of by individual ν is denoted by a^ν.

We assume that both private firms and social institutions in charge of waste management are owned by individuals. We denote by $s^{\nu\mu}$, $s^{\nu\varepsilon}$, and $s^{\nu\sigma}$, respectively, the shares of private firms μ, ε, and social institution σ owned by individual ν, where

$$s^{\nu\mu} \geqq 0, \quad \sum_\nu s^{\nu\mu} = 1; \quad s^{\nu\varepsilon} \geqq 0, \quad \sum_\nu s^{\nu\varepsilon} = 1; \quad s^{\nu\sigma} \geqq 0, \quad \sum_\nu s^{\nu\sigma} = 1.$$

The economic welfare of each individual ν is expressed by a preference ordering represented by the utility function

$$u^\nu = u^\nu(c^\nu, b^\nu, a^\nu),$$

where c^ν is the vector of goods consumed, b^ν is the amount of energy used, and a^ν denotes the amount of residual wastes disposed of by individual ν.

Neoclassical Conditions for Utility Functions

For each individual ν, the utility function $u^\nu = u^\nu(c^\nu, b^\nu, a^\nu)$ satisfies the following neoclassical conditions:

(U1) $u^\nu(c^\nu, b^\nu, a^\nu)$ is defined, positive, continuous, and continuously twice-differentiable with respect to (c^ν, b^ν, a^ν).

(U2) Marginal utilities are always positive for the consumption of produced goods c^ν, the amount of energy used b^ν, and the amount of residual wastes disposed a^ν; that is,

$$u^\nu_{c^\nu}(c^\nu, b^\nu, a^\nu) > 0, \quad u^\nu_{b^\nu}(c^\nu, b^\nu, a^\nu) > 0, \quad u^\nu_{a^\nu}(c^\nu, b^\nu, a^\nu) > 0.$$

(U3) Marginal rates of substitution between any pair of the consumption of produced goods c^ν, the use of energy b^ν, and the disposal of residual wastes a^ν are always diminishing, or more specifically, $u^\nu(c^\nu, b^\nu, a^\nu)$ is strictly quasi-concave with respect to (c^ν, b^ν, a^ν).

(U4) $u^\nu(c^\nu, b^\nu, a^\nu)$ is homogeneous of order 1 with respect to (c^ν, b^ν, a^ν); that is,

$$u^\nu(tc^\nu, tb^\nu, ta^\nu) = tu^\nu(c^\nu, b^\nu, a^\nu) \quad \text{for all } t \geqq 0.$$

The linear homogeneity hypothesis (U4) implies the Euler identity:

$$u^\nu(c^\nu, b^\nu, a^\nu) = u^\nu_{c^\nu}(c^\nu, b^\nu, a^\nu)\, c^\nu + u^\nu_{b^\nu}(c^\nu, b^\nu, a^\nu)\, b^\nu + u^\nu_{a^\nu}(c^\nu, b^\nu, a^\nu)\, a^\nu.$$

Effects of Accumulated Residual Wastes

The quality of the environment, both natural and urban, is diminished by the accumulation of residual wastes. The extent to which the quality of the environment is diminished by the accumulation of residual wastes may be expressed by the postulate that utility level u^ν of each individual ν is a decreasing function of the accumulation of residual wastes W:

$$u^\nu = \phi^\nu(W) u^\nu(c^\nu, b^\nu, a^\nu).$$

The function $\phi^\nu(W)$ expresses the extent to which the utility of individual ν is negatively affected by the accumulation of residual wastes. It is referred to as the impact index of the accumulation of residual wastes. The impact index $\phi^\nu(W)$ for each individual ν is assumed to satisfy the following conditions:

$$\phi^\nu(W) > 0, \quad \phi^{\nu\prime}(W) < 0, \quad \phi^{\nu\prime\prime}(W) < 0 \quad \text{for all } W \geqq 0.$$

The relative rate of the marginal change in the impact index due to the marginal increase in the accumulation of residual wastes is defined by

$$\tau^\nu(W) = -\frac{\phi^{\nu\prime}(W)}{\phi^\nu(W)}.$$

It is referred to as the impact coefficient of the disposal of residual wastes.

As in the case of the prototype model of social common capital, we assume that the impact coefficients $\tau^\nu(W)$ are identical for all individuals:

$$\tau^\nu(W) = \tau(W) \quad \text{for all } \nu.$$

The impact coefficient function $\tau(W)$ satisfies the following conditions:

$$\tau(W) > 0, \quad \tau'(W) > 0.$$

The impact index function $\phi(W)$ of the following form is often postulated, originally introduced in Uzawa (1991b) and extensively utilized in Uzawa (2003):

$$\phi(W) = (\widehat{W} - W)^\beta, \quad W < \widehat{W},$$

where $\widehat{W}$ is the critical level of the accumulation of residual wastes and β is the sensitivity parameter, $0 < \beta < 1$.

With respect to this impact index function $\phi(W)$, the impact coefficient $\tau(W)$ is given by

$$\tau(W) = \frac{\beta}{\widehat{W} - W}.$$

The Consumer Optimum

We assume markets for produced goods are perfectly competitive; prices of goods are denoted by an J-dimensional vector $p = (p_j)$ $(p \geq 0)$. The price of energy is denoted by π $(\pi > 0)$, and the tax rate charged to the disposal of residual wastes by θ $(\theta \geqq 0)$.

Each individual ν chooses the combination (c^ν, b^ν, a^ν) of consumption of goods c^ν, use of energy b^ν, and disposal of residual wastes a^ν that maximizes individual ν's utility function

$$u^\nu = \phi^\nu(W)u^\nu(c^\nu, b^\nu, a^\nu)$$

subject to the budget constraint

$$pc^\nu + \pi\, b^\nu + \theta\, a^\nu = y^\nu, \tag{1}$$

where y^ν is individual ν's income.

The optimum combination (c^ν, b^ν, a^ν) of consumption of goods c^ν, use of energy b^ν, and disposal of residual wastes a^ν is characterized by the following marginality conditions:

$$\alpha^\nu \phi^\nu(W) u^\nu_{c^\nu}(c^\nu, b^\nu, a^\nu) \leqq p \quad (\text{mod. } c^\nu) \tag{2}$$

$$\alpha^\nu \phi^\nu(W) u^\nu_{b^\nu}(c^\nu, b^\nu, a^\nu) \leqq \pi \quad (\text{mod. } b^\nu) \tag{3}$$

$$\alpha^\nu \phi^\nu(W) u^\nu_{a^\nu}(c^\nu, b^\nu, a^\nu) \leqq \theta \quad (\text{mod. } a^\nu), \tag{4}$$

where α^ν $(\alpha^\nu > 0)$ is the inverse of the marginal utility of individual ν's income y^ν.

Relation (2) expresses the principle that the marginal utility of each good is exactly equal to the market price when the utility is measured in units of market price. Relation (3) means that the marginal utility of energy is equal to the price of energy, whereas relation (4) means that the marginal utility of the disposal of residual wastes is equal to the tax rate charged for the disposal of residual wastes.

By multiplying both sides of relations (2), (3), and (4), respectively, by c^ν, b^ν, a^ν and adding them, we obtain

$$\alpha^\nu \phi^\nu(W)\left[u^\nu_{c^\nu}(c^\nu, b^\nu, a^\nu)\, c^\nu + u^\nu_{b^\nu}(c^\nu, b^\nu, a^\nu)\, b^\nu + u^\nu_{a^\nu}(c^\nu, b^\nu, a^\nu)\, a^\nu\right]$$
$$= p c^\nu + \pi\, b^\nu + \theta\, a^\nu.$$

On the other hand, in view of the Euler identity for utility function $u^\nu(c^\nu, b^\nu, a^\nu)$ and budgetary constraint (1), we have

$$\alpha^\nu \phi^\nu(W) u^\nu(c^\nu, b^\nu, a^\nu) = y^\nu. \tag{5}$$

Relation (5) means that, at the consumer optimum, the level of utility of individual ν, when expressed in units of market price, is exactly equal to income y^ν of individual ν.

Production Possibility Sets of Firms Producing Goods

As in the case of the prototype model of social common capital, the conditions concerning the production of goods by firm μ are specified by the production possibility set T^μ that summarizes the technological possibilities and organizational arrangements of firm μ; the endowments of capital goods of firm μ are given as K^μ.

In firm μ, the minimum quantities of capital goods required to produce goods by the vector x^μ with the employment of labor, the use of energy, and the disposal of residual wastes, respectively, at ℓ^μ, b^μ, and a^μ are specified by an F-dimensional vector-valued function,

$$f^\mu(x^\mu, \ell^\mu, b^\mu, a^\mu) = \left(f_f^\mu(x^\mu, \ell^\mu, b^\mu, a^\mu)\right).$$

We assume that marginal rates of substitution between any pair of the production of goods, the employment of labor, the use of energy, and the disposal of residual wastes are smooth and diminishing, that there are always trade-offs among them, and that the conditions of constant returns to scale prevail. That is, we assume

($T^\mu 1$) $f^\mu(x^\mu, \ell^\mu, b^\mu, a^\mu)$ are defined, positive, continuous, and continuously twice-differentiable with respect to $(x^\mu, \ell^\mu, b^\mu, a^\mu)$.

($T^\mu 2$) $f_{x^\mu}^\mu(x^\mu, \ell^\mu, b^\mu, a^\mu) > 0, \quad f_{\ell^\mu}^\mu(x^\mu, \ell^\mu, b^\mu, a^\mu) < 0,$
$f_{b^\mu}^\mu(x^\mu, \ell^\mu, b^\mu, a^\mu) < 0, \quad f_{a^\mu}^\mu(x^\mu, \ell^\mu, b^\mu, a^\mu) < 0.$

($T^\mu 3$) $f^\mu(x^\mu, \ell^\mu, b^\mu, a^\mu)$ are strictly quasi-convex with respect to $(x^\mu, \ell^\mu, b^\mu, a^\mu)$.

($T^\mu 4$) $f^\mu(x^\mu, \ell^\mu, b^\mu, a^\mu)$ are homogeneous of order 1 with respect to $(x^\mu, \ell^\mu, b^\mu, a^\mu)$.

From the constant-returns-to-scale condition ($T^\mu 4$), we have the Euler identity:

$$\begin{aligned} f^\mu(x^\mu, \ell^\mu, b^\mu, a^\mu) = {} & f_{x^\mu}^\mu(x^\mu, \ell^\mu, b^\mu, a^\mu)x^\mu + f_{\ell^\mu}^\mu(x^\mu, \ell^\mu, b^\mu, a^\mu)\ell^\mu \\ & + f_{b^\mu}^\mu(x^\mu, \ell^\mu, b^\mu, a^\mu)b^\mu + f_{a^\mu}^\mu(x^\mu, \ell^\mu, b^\mu, a^\mu)a^\mu. \end{aligned}$$

The production possibility set of firm μ, T^μ, is composed of all combinations $(x^\mu, \ell^\mu, b^\mu, a^\mu)$ of vector of production x^μ, employment of labor ℓ^μ, use of energy b^μ, and disposal of residual wastes a^μ that are possible with the organizational arrangements, technological conditions, and given endowments of capital goods K^μ in firm μ. Thus, it may be expressed as

$$T^\mu = \{(x^\mu, \ell^\mu, b^\mu, a^\mu)\colon (x^\mu, \ell^\mu, b^\mu, a^\mu) \geqq 0,\ f^\mu(x^\mu, \ell^\mu, b^\mu, a^\mu) \leqq K^\mu\}.$$

Postulates ($T^\mu 1$–$T^\mu 3$) imply that the production possibility set T^μ is a closed, convex set of $J + \mathrm{H} + 1 + 1$-dimensional vectors $(x^\mu, \ell^\mu, b^\mu, a^\mu)$.

The Producer Optimum for Firms Producing Goods

Prices of goods on a perfectly competitive market are denoted by a price vector p, wage rates by w, the price of energy by π, and the tax rate charged for the disposal of residual wastes by θ.

Each firm μ chooses the combination $(x^\mu, \ell^\mu, b^\mu, a^\mu)$ of vector of production x^μ, employment of labor ℓ^μ, use of energy b^μ, and disposal of residual wastes a^μ that maximizes net profit

$$px^\mu - w\ell^\mu - \pi b^\mu - \theta a^\mu$$

over $(x^\mu, \ell^\mu, b^\mu, a^\mu) \in T^\mu$.

Conditions (T^μ1–T^μ3) postulated above ensure that, for any combination of price vector p, wage rates w, price of energy π, and tax rate charged for the disposal of residual wastes θ, the optimum combination $(x^\mu, \ell^\mu, b^\mu, a^\mu)$ of vector of production x^μ, employment of labor ℓ^μ, use of energy b^μ, and disposal of residual wastes a^μ always exists and is uniquely determined.

To examine how the optimum combination of vector of production x^μ, employment of labor ℓ^μ, use of energy b^μ, and disposal of residual wastes a^μ is determined, let us denote the vector of imputed rental prices of capital goods by $r^\mu = (r_f^\mu)$ $[r_f^\mu \geqq 0]$. Then the optimum conditions are

$$p \leqq r^\mu f_{x^\mu}^\mu(x^\mu, \ell^\mu, b^\mu, a^\mu) \quad (\text{mod. } x^\mu) \tag{6}$$

$$w \geqq r^\mu[-f_{\ell^\mu}^\mu(x^\mu, \ell^\mu, b^\mu, a^\mu)] \quad (\text{mod. } \ell^\mu) \tag{7}$$

$$\pi \geqq r^\mu[-f_{b^\mu}^\mu(x^\mu, \ell^\mu, b^\mu, a^\mu)] \quad (\text{mod. } b^\mu) \tag{8}$$

$$\theta \geqq r^\mu[-f_{a^\mu}^\mu(x^\mu, \ell^\mu, b^\mu, a^\mu) \quad (\text{mod. } a^\mu) \tag{9}$$

$$f^\mu(x^\mu, \ell^\mu, b^\mu, a^\mu) \leqq K^\mu \quad (\text{mod. } r^\mu). \tag{10}$$

Condition (6) means that the choice of production technologies and the levels of production are adjusted so as to equate marginal factor costs with output prices.

Condition (7) means that the employment of labor is adjusted so that the marginal gains due to the marginal increase in the employment of various types of labor are equal to the wage rates w.

Condition (8) means that the use of energy is adjusted so that the marginal gains due to the marginal increase in the use of energy are equal to the price of energy π.

Condition (9) means that the disposal of residual wastes is controlled so that the marginal gains due to the marginal decrease in the disposal of residual wastes are equal to the tax rate charged for the disposal of residual wastes θ.

Condition (10) means that the use of factor of production f does not exceed the endowments K^μ_f, and the conditions of full employment are satisfied whenever imputed rental price r^μ_f is positive.

We have assumed that the technologies are subject to constant returns to scale (T$^\mu$4), and thus, in view of the Euler identity, conditions (6)–(9) imply that

$$\begin{aligned} px^\mu - w\ell^\mu - \pi b^\mu - \theta a^\mu &= r^\mu\big[f^\mu_{x^\mu}(x^\mu, \ell^\mu, b^\mu, a^\mu)\, x^\mu \\ &\quad + f^\mu_{\ell^\mu}(x^\mu, \ell^\mu, b^\mu, a^\mu)\ell^\mu \\ &\quad + f^\mu_{b^\mu}(x^\mu, \ell^\mu, b^\mu, a^\mu)b^\mu \\ &\quad + f^\mu_{a^\mu}(x^\mu, \ell^\mu, b^\mu, a^\mu)a^\mu\big] \\ &= r^\mu f^\mu(x^\mu, \ell^\mu, b^\mu, a^\mu) = r^\mu K^\mu. \quad (11) \end{aligned}$$

That is, for each firm μ, the net evaluation of output is equal to the sum of the imputed rental payments to all factors of production of firm μ. The meaning of relation (11) may be better brought out if we rewrite it as

$$px^\mu = w\ell^\mu + \pi b^\mu + \theta a^\mu + r^\mu K^\mu.$$

That is, the value of output measured in market prices px^μ is equal to the sum of wages $w\ell^\mu$, payments for the use of energy πb^μ, tax payments for the disposal of residual wastes θa^μ, and payments in terms of the imputed rental prices made for the use of fixed factors of production endowed within firm μ, $r^\mu K^\mu$. Thus, the validity of the Menger-Wieser principle of imputation is assured.

Production Possibility Sets of Firms Producing Energy

Firms specialized in the production of energy are generically denoted by ε. The conditions concerning the production of energy by firm ε are specified by the production possibility set T^ε that summarizes the technological possibilities and organizational arrangements of firm ε, with the endowments of capital goods accumulated in firm ε given as K^ε.

In firm ε, the minimum quantities of factors of production that are required to produce energy by the amount b^ε with the employment of labor, the use of raw materials, and the disposal of residual wastes, respectively, at ℓ^μ, q^ε, and a^ε are specified by an F-dimensional vector-valued function

$$f^\varepsilon(b^\varepsilon, \ell^\varepsilon, q^\varepsilon, a^\varepsilon) = \left(f^\varepsilon_f(b^\varepsilon, \ell^\varepsilon, q^\varepsilon, a^\varepsilon)\right).$$

For the sake of expository brevity, we assume that no produced goods are used in the processes of energy production. The following discussion will be easily extended to the general case in which produced goods are used in the processes of energy production.

We assume that marginal rates of substitution between any pair of the production of energy, the employment of labor, the use of raw materials, and the disposal of residual wastes are smooth and diminishing, that there are always trade-offs among them, and that the conditions of constant returns to scale prevail. That is, we assume

($T^\varepsilon 1$) $f^\varepsilon(b^\varepsilon, \ell^\varepsilon, q^\varepsilon, a^\varepsilon)$ are defined, positive, continuous, and continuously twice-differentiable with respect to $(b^\varepsilon, \ell^\varepsilon, q^\varepsilon, a^\varepsilon)$.

($T^\varepsilon 2$) $f^\varepsilon_{b^\varepsilon}(b^\varepsilon, \ell^\varepsilon, q^\varepsilon, a^\varepsilon) > 0, \quad f^\varepsilon_{\ell^\varepsilon}(b^\varepsilon, \ell^\varepsilon, q^\varepsilon, a^\varepsilon) < 0,$
$f^\varepsilon_{q^\varepsilon}(b^\varepsilon, \ell^\varepsilon, q^\varepsilon, a^\varepsilon) < 0, \quad f^\varepsilon_{a^\varepsilon}(b^\varepsilon, \ell^\varepsilon, q^\varepsilon, a^\varepsilon) < 0.$

($T^\varepsilon 3$) $f^\varepsilon(b^\varepsilon, \ell^\varepsilon, q^\varepsilon, a^\varepsilon)$ are strictly quasi-convex with respect to $(b^\varepsilon, \ell^\varepsilon, q^\varepsilon, a^\varepsilon)$.

($T^\varepsilon 4$) $f^\varepsilon(b^\varepsilon, \ell^\varepsilon, q^\varepsilon, a^\varepsilon)$ are homogeneous of order 1 with respect to $(b^\varepsilon, \ell^\varepsilon, q^\varepsilon, a^\varepsilon)$.

From the constant returns to scale conditions ($T^\varepsilon 4$), we have the Euler identity:

$$\begin{aligned} f^\varepsilon(b^\varepsilon, \ell^\varepsilon, q^\varepsilon, a^\varepsilon) = {} & f^\varepsilon_{b^\varepsilon}(b^\varepsilon, \ell^\varepsilon, q^\varepsilon, a^\varepsilon)b^\varepsilon + f^\varepsilon_{\ell^\varepsilon}(b^\varepsilon, \ell^\varepsilon, q^\varepsilon, a^\varepsilon)\ell^\varepsilon \\ & + f^\varepsilon_{q^\varepsilon}(b^\varepsilon, \ell^\varepsilon, q^\varepsilon, a^\varepsilon)q^\varepsilon + f^\varepsilon_{a^\varepsilon}(b^\varepsilon, \ell^\varepsilon, q^\varepsilon, a^\varepsilon)a^\varepsilon. \end{aligned}$$

The production possibility set of firm ε, T^ε, is composed of all combinations $(b^\varepsilon, \ell^\varepsilon, q^\varepsilon, a^\varepsilon)$ of production of energy b^ε, employment of labor ℓ^ε, use of raw materials q^ε, and disposal of residual wastes a^ε that are possible with the organizational arrangements and technological conditions in firm ε and the given endowments of factors of production K^ε of firm ε. It may be expressed as

$$T^\varepsilon = \{(b^\varepsilon, \ell^\varepsilon, q^\varepsilon, a^\varepsilon)\colon (b^\varepsilon, \ell^\varepsilon, q^\varepsilon, a^\varepsilon) \geqq 0,\ f^\varepsilon(b^\varepsilon, \ell^\varepsilon, q^\varepsilon, a^\varepsilon) \leqq K^\varepsilon\}.$$

Postulates (T^ε1–T^ε3) imply that the production possibility set T^ε is a closed, convex set of $1 + H + 1 + 1$-dimensional vectors $(b^\varepsilon, \ell^\varepsilon, q^\varepsilon, a^\varepsilon)$.

The Producer Optimum for Firms Producing Energy

The price of energy is denoted by π, the wage rates by w, the price of raw materials for energy production by λ, and the tax rate charged for the disposal of residual wastes by θ.

Firm ε chooses the combination $(b^\varepsilon, \ell^\varepsilon, q^\varepsilon, a^\varepsilon)$ of energy production b^ε, labor employment ℓ^ε, use of raw materials q^ε, and disposal of residual wastes a^ε that maximizes net profit

$$\pi b^\varepsilon - w\ell^\varepsilon - \lambda q^\varepsilon - \theta a^\varepsilon$$

over $(b^\varepsilon, \ell^\varepsilon, q^\varepsilon, a^\varepsilon) \in T^\varepsilon$.

Conditions (T^ε1–T^ε3) postulated above ensure that, for any combination of energy price π, wage rates w, price of raw materials λ, and tax rate charged for the disposal of residual wastes θ, the optimum combination $(b^\varepsilon, \ell^\varepsilon, q^\varepsilon, a^\varepsilon)$ of energy production b^ε, labor employment ℓ^ε, use of raw materials q^ε, and disposal of residual wastes a^ε always exists and is uniquely determined.

To see how the optimum combination of energy production b^ε, labor employment ℓ^ε, use of raw materials q^ε, and disposal of residual wastes a^ε, $(b^\varepsilon_o, \ell^\varepsilon_o, q^\varepsilon_o, a^\varepsilon_o)$, is determined, let us denote the vector of imputed rental prices of factors of production by $r^\varepsilon = (r^\varepsilon_\ell)$ $[r^\varepsilon_\ell \geqq 0]$. Then the optimum conditions are

$$\pi \leqq r^\varepsilon f^\varepsilon_{b^\varepsilon}(b^\varepsilon, \ell^\varepsilon, q^\varepsilon, a^\varepsilon) \quad (\text{mod. } b^\varepsilon) \tag{12}$$

$$w \geqq r^\varepsilon[-f^\varepsilon_{\ell^\varepsilon}(b^\varepsilon, \ell^\varepsilon, q^\varepsilon, a^\varepsilon)] \quad (\text{mod. } \ell^\varepsilon) \tag{13}$$

$$\lambda \geqq r^\varepsilon[-f^\varepsilon_{q^\varepsilon}(b^\varepsilon, \ell^\varepsilon, q^\varepsilon, a^\varepsilon)] \quad (\text{mod. } q^\varepsilon) \tag{14}$$

$$\theta \geqq r^\varepsilon[-f^\varepsilon_{a^\varepsilon}(b^\varepsilon, \ell^\varepsilon, q^\varepsilon, a^\varepsilon)] \quad (\text{mod. } a^\varepsilon) \tag{15}$$

$$f^\varepsilon(b^\varepsilon, \ell^\varepsilon, q^\varepsilon, a^\varepsilon) \leqq K^\varepsilon \quad (\text{mod. } r^\varepsilon). \tag{16}$$

Condition (12) means that the choice of production technologies and the levels of production are adjusted so as to equate marginal factor costs with the price of energy π.

Condition (13) means that the employment of labor is adjusted so that the marginal gain due to the marginal increase in the employment of labor of type η is equal to wage rate w_η.

Condition (14) means that the use of raw materials is adjusted so that the marginal gain due to the marginal increase in the use of raw materials is equal to the price of raw materials λ.

Condition (15) means that the disposal of residual wastes is controlled so that the marginal gain due to the marginal increase in the disposal of residual wastes is equal to the tax rate charged for the disposal of residual wastes θ.

Condition (16) means that the use of factor of production f does not exceed the endowments K_f^ε and the conditions of full employment are satisfied whenever imputed rental price r_f^ε is positive.

We have assumed that the technologies are subject to constant returns to scale ($T^\varepsilon 4$), and thus, in view of the Euler identity, conditions (12)–(16) imply that

$$\begin{aligned}\pi b^\varepsilon - w\ell^\varepsilon - \lambda q^\varepsilon - \theta a^\varepsilon = r^\varepsilon\big[&f_{b^\varepsilon}^\varepsilon(b^\varepsilon, \ell^\varepsilon, q^\varepsilon, a^\varepsilon)b^\varepsilon + f_{\ell^\varepsilon}^\varepsilon(b^\varepsilon, \ell^\varepsilon, q^\varepsilon, a^\varepsilon)\ell^\varepsilon \\ &+ f_{q^\varepsilon}^\varepsilon(b^\varepsilon, \ell^\varepsilon, q^\varepsilon, a^\varepsilon)q^\varepsilon + f_{a^\varepsilon}^\varepsilon(b^\varepsilon, \ell^\varepsilon, q^\varepsilon, a^\varepsilon)a^\varepsilon\big] \\ = r^\varepsilon &f^\varepsilon(b^\varepsilon, \ell^\varepsilon, q^\varepsilon, a^\varepsilon) = r^\varepsilon K^\varepsilon. \qquad (17)\end{aligned}$$

That is, for each firm ε, the net evaluation of output is equal to the sum of the imputed rental payments to all fixed factors of production of firm ε. The meaning of relation (17) may be better brought out if we rewrite it as

$$\pi b^\varepsilon = w\ell^\varepsilon + \lambda q^\varepsilon + \theta a^\varepsilon + r^\varepsilon K^\varepsilon.$$

That is, the value of energy output measured in market prices πb^ε is equal to the sum of wages $w\ell^\varepsilon$, payments for the use of raw materials λq^ε, tax payments for the disposal of residual wastes θa^ε, and payments in terms of the imputed rental prices for the use of fixed factors of production accumulated in firm ε, $r^\varepsilon K^\varepsilon$. Thus, the validity of the Menger-Wieser principle of imputation is assured for energy-producing firms, too.

Production Possibility Sets for Social Institutions in Charge of Recycling of Residual Wastes

As in the case of firms producing goods and energy, the conditions concerning the processes of recycling of residual wastes for each social institution σ are specified by the production possibility set T^σ that summarizes the technological possibilities and organizational arrangements for social institution σ; the endowments of factors of production in social institution σ are given. The quantities of fixed factors of production accumulated in social institution σ are given as K^σ.

In social institution σ, the minimum quantities of factors of production required to produce raw materials for energy production by quantity q^σ through the recycling processes of residual wastes by the amount a^σ with the employment of labor ℓ^σ and the use of energy b^σ are specified by an F-dimensional vector-valued function:

$$f^\sigma(q^\sigma, a^\sigma, \ell^\sigma, b^\sigma) = \left(f_f^\sigma(q^\sigma, a^\sigma, \ell^\sigma, b^\sigma)\right).$$

We assume that for each social institution σ, marginal rates of substitution between any pair of the production of raw materials for energy production, the recycling of residual wastes, the employment of labor, the use of energy, and the use of produced goods are smooth and diminishing, that there are always trade-offs among them, and that the conditions of constant returns to scale prevail. That is, we assume

($T^\sigma 1$) $f^\sigma(q^\sigma, a^\sigma, \ell^\sigma, b^\sigma)$ are defined, positive, continuous, and continuously twice-differentiable with respect to $(q^\sigma, a^\sigma, \ell^\sigma, b^\sigma)$.

($T^\sigma 2$) $f^\sigma_{q^\sigma}(q^\sigma, a^\sigma, \ell^\sigma, b^\sigma) > 0, \quad f^\sigma_{a^\sigma}(q^\sigma, a^\sigma, \ell^\sigma, b^\sigma) > 0,$
$f^\sigma_{\ell^\sigma}(q^\sigma, a^\sigma, \ell^\sigma, b^\sigma) < 0, \quad f^\sigma_{b^\sigma}(q^\sigma, a^\sigma, \ell^\sigma, b^\sigma) < 0.$

($T^\sigma 3$) $f^\sigma(q^\sigma, a^\sigma, \ell^\sigma, b^\sigma)$ are strictly quasi-convex with respect to $(q^\sigma, a^\sigma, \ell^\sigma, b^\sigma)$.

($T^\sigma 4$) $f^\sigma(q^\sigma, a^\sigma, \ell^\sigma, b^\sigma)$ are homogeneous of order 1 with respect to $(q^\sigma, a^\sigma, \ell^\sigma, b^\sigma)$.

From the constant-returns-to-scale conditions ($T^\sigma 4$), we have the Euler identity:

$$\begin{aligned} f^\sigma(q^\sigma, a^\sigma, \ell^\sigma, b^\sigma) = {} & f^\sigma_{q^\sigma}(q^\sigma, a^\sigma, \ell^\sigma, b^\sigma)q^\sigma + f^\sigma_{a^\sigma}(q^\sigma, a^\sigma, \ell^\sigma, b^\sigma)a^\sigma \\ & + f^\sigma_{\ell^\sigma}(q^\sigma, a^\sigma, \ell^\sigma, b^\sigma)\ell^\sigma + f^\sigma_{b^\sigma}(q^\sigma, a^\sigma, \ell^\sigma, b^\sigma)b^\sigma. \end{aligned}$$

For each social institution σ in charge of recycling of residual wastes, the production possibility set T^σ is composed of all combinations $(q^\sigma, a^\sigma, \ell^\sigma, b^\sigma)$ of production of raw materials q^σ, recycling of residual wastes a^σ, labor employment ℓ^σ, and energy input b^σ that are possible with the organizational arrangements, technological conditions of social institution σ, and given endowments of fixed factors of production K^σ:

$$T^\sigma = \{(q^\sigma, a^\sigma, \ell^\sigma, b^\sigma)\colon (q^\sigma, a^\sigma, \ell^\sigma, b^\sigma) \geqq 0, f^\sigma(q^\sigma, a^\sigma, \ell^\sigma, b^\sigma) \leqq K^\sigma\}.$$

Postulates ($\mathrm{T}^\sigma 1$–$\mathrm{T}^\sigma 3$) imply that the production possibility set T^σ of social institution σ is a closed, convex set of $1 + 1 + \mathrm{H} + 1$-dimensional vectors $(q^\sigma, a^\sigma, \ell^\sigma, b^\sigma)$.

The Producer Optimum for Social Institutions in Charge of Recycling of Residual Wastes

Each social institution σ chooses the combination $(q^\sigma, a^\sigma, \ell^\sigma, b^\sigma)$ of production of raw materials q^σ, use of residual wastes a^σ, labor employment ℓ^σ, and energy input b^σ that maximizes net profit

$$\lambda q^\sigma + \theta a^\sigma - w\ell^\sigma - \pi q^\sigma$$

over $(b^\varepsilon, \ell^\varepsilon, q^\varepsilon, a^\varepsilon) \in T^\varepsilon$.

Conditions ($\mathrm{T}^\sigma 1$–$\mathrm{T}^\sigma 3$) postulated for social institution σ ensure that for any combination of price of produced raw materials λ, rate of subsidy payments for the use of residual wastes θ, wage rates w, and energy price π, the optimum combination $(q^\sigma, a^\sigma, \ell^\sigma, b^\sigma)$ of production of raw materials q^σ, use of residual wastes a^σ, labor employment ℓ^σ, and energy input b^σ always exists and is uniquely determined.

The optimum combination $(q^\sigma, a^\sigma, \ell^\sigma, b^\sigma)$ of production of raw materials q^σ, recycling of residual wastes a^σ, labor employment ℓ^σ, and energy input b^σ may be characterized by the following marginality conditions:

$$\lambda \leqq r^\sigma f^\sigma_{q^\sigma}(q^\sigma, a^\sigma, \ell^\sigma, b^\sigma) \quad (\text{mod. } q^\sigma) \tag{18}$$

$$\theta \leqq r^\sigma f^\sigma_{a^\sigma}(q^\sigma, a^\sigma, \ell^\sigma, b^\sigma) \quad (\text{mod. } a^\sigma) \tag{19}$$

$$w \geqq r^\sigma[-f^\sigma_{\ell^\sigma}(q^\sigma, a^\sigma, \ell^\sigma, b^\sigma)] \quad (\text{mod. } \ell^\sigma) \tag{20}$$

$$\pi = r^\sigma[-f^\sigma_{b^\sigma}(q^\sigma, a^\sigma, \ell^\sigma, b^\sigma)] \quad (\text{mod. } b^\sigma) \tag{21}$$

$$f^\sigma(q^\sigma, a^\sigma, \ell^\sigma, b^\sigma) \leqq K^\sigma \quad (\text{mod. } r^\sigma), \tag{22}$$

where r^σ is the vector of imputed rental prices of fixed factors of production of social institution σ.

Condition (18) means that the choice of production technologies and the output of raw materials are adjusted so as to equate marginal factor costs with the price of raw materials λ.

Condition (19) means that the recycling of residual wastes is adjusted so that the marginal gains due to the marginal increase in the disposal of residual wastes are equal to the tax rate charged for the disposal of residual wastes θ.

Condition (20) means that the employment of labor is adjusted so that the marginal gain due to the marginal increase in the employment of labor of type η is equal to wage rate w_η.

Condition (21) means that the use of energy is adjusted so that the marginal gain due to the marginal increase in the use of energy is equal to the price of energy π.

Condition (22) means that the use of factor of production f does not exceed the endowments K_f^σ and the conditions of full employment are satisfied whenever imputed rental price r_f^σ is positive.

We have assumed that the technologies are subject to constant returns to scale (T$^\sigma$4), and thus, in view of the Euler identity, conditions (18)–(22) imply that

$$\begin{aligned}\lambda q^\sigma + \theta a^\sigma - w\ell^\sigma - \pi q^\sigma &= r^\sigma \big[f_{q^\sigma}^\sigma(q^\sigma, a^\sigma, \ell^\sigma, b^\sigma) q^\sigma \\ &\quad + f_{a^\sigma}^\sigma(q^\sigma, a^\sigma, \ell^\sigma, b^\sigma) a^\sigma \\ &\quad + f_{\ell^\sigma}^\sigma(q^\sigma, a^\sigma, \ell^\sigma, b^\sigma) \ell^\sigma \\ &\quad + f_{b^\sigma}^\sigma(q^\sigma, a^\sigma, \ell^\sigma, b^\sigma) b^\sigma \big] \\ &= r^\sigma f^\sigma(q^\sigma, a^\sigma, \ell^\sigma, b^\sigma) = r^\sigma K^\sigma.\end{aligned}$$

Thus,

$$\lambda q^\sigma + \theta a^\sigma - w\ell^\sigma - \pi q^\sigma = r^\sigma K^\sigma. \tag{23}$$

The meaning of relation (23) may be better brought out if we rewrite it as

$$\lambda q^\sigma + \theta a^\sigma = w\ell^\sigma + \pi q^\sigma + r^\sigma K^\sigma.$$

That is, the sum of the value of output of raw materials measured in market prices λq^σ and the subsidy payments for the use of residual wastes θa^σ is equal to the sum of wage bills $w\ell^\sigma$, payments for the use of energy πq^σ, and payments in terms of imputed rental prices made to the fixed factors of production accumulated in social institution

σ, $r^\varepsilon K^\varepsilon$. Thus, the validity of the Menger-Wieser principle of imputation is assured for social institution σ, too.

3. MARKET EQUILIBRIUM FOR THE ENERGY-RECYCLING MODEL OF SOCIAL COMMON CAPITAL

We first recapitulate the basic premises of the energy-recycling model of social common capital introduced in the previous sections.

The Consumer Optimum

The preference ordering of each individual ν is expressed by the utility function

$$u^\nu = \phi^\nu(W)u^\nu(c^\nu, b^\nu, a^\nu),$$

where c^ν is the vector of goods consumed by individual ν, b^ν is the amount of energy used by individual ν, and a^ν is the amount of residual wastes disposed of by individual ν. The impact index $\phi^\nu(W)$ indicates the extent of the damage to the environment caused by the accumulation of residual wastes. The impact coefficient of the disposal of residual wastes

$$\tau(W) = -\frac{\phi^{\nu\prime}(W)}{\phi^\nu(W)}$$

is assumed to be identical for all individuals.

Each individual ν chooses the combination (c^ν, b^ν, a^ν) of the vector of consumption of goods c^ν, the use of energy b^ν, and the disposal of residual wastes a^ν in such a manner that individual ν's utility

$$\phi^\nu(W)u^\nu(c^\nu, b^\nu, a^\nu)$$

is maximized subject to the budget constraint

$$pc^\nu + \pi b^\nu + \theta a^\nu = y^\nu, \tag{24}$$

where p is the price vector of goods, π is the price of energy, θ is the tax rate charged to the disposal of residual wastes, and y^ν is the income of individual ν.

The optimum combination (c^ν, b^ν, a^ν) of consumption of goods c^ν, use of energy b^ν, and disposal of residual wastes a^ν is characterized by the following marginality conditions:

$$\alpha^\nu \phi^\nu(W) u^\nu_{c^\nu}(c^\nu, b^\nu, a^\nu) \leqq p \quad (\mathrm{mod.}\ c^\nu) \tag{25}$$

$$\alpha^\nu \phi^\nu(W) u^\nu_{b^\nu}(c^\nu, b^\nu, a^\nu) \leqq \pi \quad (\mathrm{mod.}\ b^\nu) \tag{26}$$

$$\alpha^\nu \phi^\nu(W) u^\nu_{a^\nu}(c^\nu, b^\nu, a^\nu) \leqq \theta \quad (\mathrm{mod.}\ a^\nu), \tag{27}$$

where $\alpha^\nu (\alpha^\nu > 0)$ is the inverse of the marginal utility of individual ν's income y^ν.

The following basic identity holds:

$$\alpha^\nu \phi^\nu(W) u^\nu(c^\nu, b^\nu, a^\nu) = pc^\nu + \pi b^\nu + \theta a^\nu = y^\nu. \tag{28}$$

The Producer Optimum for Private Firms Producing Goods

The conditions concerning the production of goods in each private firm μ are specified by the production possibility set T^μ:

$$T^\mu = \{(x^\mu, \ell^\mu, b^\mu, a^\mu)\colon (x^\mu, \ell^\mu, b^\mu, a^\mu) \geqq 0, f^\mu(x^\mu, \ell^\mu, b^\mu, a^\mu) \leqq K^\mu\},$$

where $f^\mu(x^\mu, \ell^\mu, b^\mu, a^\mu)$ is the function specifying the minimum quantities of capital goods required to produce goods by x^μ with the employment of labor, the use of energy, and the disposal of residual wastes, respectively, at ℓ^μ, b^μ and a^μ.

Each firm μ chooses the combination $(x^\mu, \ell^\mu, b^\mu, a^\mu)$ of vectors of production x^μ, employment of labor ℓ^μ, use of energy b^μ, and disposal of residual wastes a^μ that maximizes net profit

$$px^\mu - w\ell^\mu - \pi b^\mu - \theta a^\mu \quad (x^\mu, \ell^\mu, b^\mu, a^\mu) \in T^\mu,$$

where p is the price vector, w is the vector of wage rates, π is the price of energy, and θ is the tax rate charged to the disposal of residual wastes.

The producer optimum for private firm μ is characterized by the following marginality conditions:

$$p \leqq r^\mu f^\mu_{x^\mu}(x^\mu, \ell^\mu, b^\mu, a^\mu) \quad (\mathrm{mod.}\ x^\mu) \tag{29}$$

$$w \geqq r^\mu[-f^\mu_{\ell^\mu}(x^\mu, \ell^\mu, b^\mu, a^\mu)] \quad (\mathrm{mod.}\ \ell^\mu) \tag{30}$$

$$\pi \geqq r^\mu[-f^\mu_{b^\mu}(x^\mu, \ell^\mu, b^\mu, a^\mu)] \quad (\mathrm{mod.}\ b^\mu) \tag{31}$$

$$\theta \geqq r^{\mu}[-f^{\mu}_{a^{\mu}}(x^{\mu}, \ell^{\mu}, b^{\mu}, a^{\mu})] \quad (\text{mod. } a^{\mu}) \tag{32}$$

$$f^{\mu}(x^{\mu}, \ell^{\mu}, b^{\mu}, a^{\mu}) \leqq K^{\mu} \quad (\text{mod. } r^{\mu}), \tag{33}$$

where r^{μ} is the vector of imputed rental prices of capital goods.

$$px^{\mu} - w\ell^{\mu} - \pi b^{\mu} - \theta a^{\mu} = r^{\mu} K^{\mu}. \tag{34}$$

The Producer Optimum for Firms Producing Energy

The production possibility set of energy-producing firm ε, T^{ε}, is composed of all combinations $(b^{\varepsilon}, \ell^{\varepsilon}, q^{\varepsilon}, a^{\varepsilon})$ of energy production b^{ε}, labor employment ℓ^{ε}, use of raw materials q^{ε}, and disposal of residual wastes a^{ε} that are possible with the organizational arrangements and technological conditions in firm ε and the given endowments of factors of production K^{ε} of firm ε:

$$T^{\varepsilon} = \{(b^{\varepsilon}, \ell^{\varepsilon}, q^{\varepsilon}, a^{\varepsilon}): \quad (b^{\varepsilon}, \ell^{\varepsilon}, q^{\varepsilon}, a^{\varepsilon}) \geqq 0, \quad f^{\varepsilon}(b^{\varepsilon}, \ell^{\varepsilon}, q^{\varepsilon}, a^{\varepsilon}) \leqq K^{\varepsilon}\}.$$

Firm ε chooses the combination $(b^{\varepsilon}, \ell^{\varepsilon}, q^{\varepsilon}, a^{\varepsilon})$ of energy production b^{ε}, labor employment ℓ^{ε}, use of raw materials q^{ε}, and disposal of residual wastes a^{ε} that maximizes net profit

$$\pi b^{\varepsilon} - w\ell^{\varepsilon} - \lambda q^{\varepsilon} - \theta a^{\varepsilon}$$

over $(b^{\varepsilon}, \ell^{\varepsilon}, q^{\varepsilon}, a^{\varepsilon}) \in T^{\varepsilon}$, where π is the price of energy, w is the vector of wage rates, λ is the price of raw materials for energy production, and θ is the tax rate charged for the disposal of residual wastes. The optimum conditions are

$$\pi \leqq r^{\varepsilon} f^{\varepsilon}_{b^{\varepsilon}}(b^{\varepsilon}, \ell^{\varepsilon}, q^{\varepsilon}, a^{\varepsilon}) \quad (\text{mod. } b^{\varepsilon}) \tag{35}$$

$$w \geqq r^{\varepsilon}[-f^{\varepsilon}_{\ell^{\varepsilon}}(b^{\varepsilon}, \ell^{\varepsilon}, q^{\varepsilon}, a^{\varepsilon})] \quad (\text{mod. } \ell^{\varepsilon}) \tag{36}$$

$$\lambda \geqq r^{\varepsilon}[-f^{\varepsilon}_{q^{\varepsilon}}(b^{\varepsilon}, \ell^{\varepsilon}, q^{\varepsilon}, a^{\varepsilon})] \quad (\text{mod. } q^{\varepsilon}) \tag{37}$$

$$\theta \geqq r^{\varepsilon}[-f^{\varepsilon}_{a^{\varepsilon}}(b^{\varepsilon}, \ell^{\varepsilon}, q^{\varepsilon}, a^{\varepsilon})] \quad (\text{mod. } a^{\varepsilon}) \tag{38}$$

$$f^{\varepsilon}(b^{\varepsilon}, \ell^{\varepsilon}, q^{\varepsilon}, a^{\varepsilon}) \leqq K^{\varepsilon} \quad (\text{mod. } r^{\varepsilon}), \tag{39}$$

where r^{ε} is the vector of imputed rental prices of factors of production of energy-producing firm ε

$$\pi b^{\varepsilon} - w\ell^{\varepsilon} - \lambda q^{\varepsilon} - \theta a^{\varepsilon} = r^{\varepsilon} K^{\varepsilon}. \tag{40}$$

The Producer Optimum for Social Institutions in Charge of Recycling of Residual Wastes

For each social institution σ in charge of recycling of residual wastes, the production possibility set T^σ is composed of all combinations $(q^\sigma, a^\sigma, \ell^\sigma, b^\sigma)$ of production of raw materials q^σ, use of residual wastes a^σ, labor employment ℓ^σ, and energy input b^σ that are possible with the organizational arrangements, technological conditions of social institution σ, and given endowments of fixed factors of production K^σ:

$$T^\sigma = \{(q^\sigma, a^\sigma, \ell^\sigma, b^\sigma): (q^\sigma, a^\sigma, \ell^\sigma, b^\sigma) \geqq 0,\ \ f^\sigma(q^\sigma, a^\sigma, \ell^\sigma, b^\sigma) \leqq K^\sigma\},$$

where the function $f^\sigma(q^\sigma, a^\sigma, \ell^\sigma, b^\sigma)$ specifies the minimum quantities of factors of production required to produce raw materials for energy production by the quantity q^σ through the recycling processes of residual wastes by the amount a^σ with employment of labor ℓ^σ and use of energy b^σ

Each social institution σ chooses the combination $(q^\sigma, a^\sigma, \ell^\sigma, b^\sigma)$ of production of raw materials q^σ, use of residual wastes a^σ, labor employment ℓ^σ, and energy input b^σ that maximizes net profit

$$\lambda q^\sigma + \theta a^\sigma - w\ell^\sigma - \pi q^\sigma$$

over $(b^\varepsilon, \ell^\varepsilon, q^\varepsilon, a^\varepsilon) \in T^\varepsilon$. The optimum conditions are

$$\lambda \leqq r^\sigma f^\sigma_{q^\sigma}(q^\sigma, a^\sigma, \ell^\sigma, b^\sigma) \quad (\text{mod. } q^\sigma) \tag{41}$$

$$\theta \leqq r^\sigma f^\sigma_{a^\sigma}(q^\sigma, a^\sigma, \ell^\sigma, b^\sigma) \quad (\text{mod. } a^\sigma) \tag{42}$$

$$w \geqq r^\sigma[-f^\sigma_{\ell^\sigma}(q^\sigma, a^\sigma, \ell^\sigma, b^\sigma)] \quad (\text{mod. } \ell^\sigma) \tag{43}$$

$$\pi \geqq r^\sigma[-f^\sigma_{b^\sigma}(q^\sigma, a^\sigma, \ell^\sigma, b^\sigma)] \quad (\text{mod. } b^\sigma) \tag{44}$$

$$f^\sigma(q^\sigma, a^\sigma, \ell^\sigma, b^\sigma) \leqq K^\sigma \quad (\text{mod. } r^\sigma), \tag{45}$$

where r^σ is the vector of imputed rental prices of fixed factors of production of social institution σ

$$\pi b^\varepsilon - w\ell^\varepsilon - \lambda q^\varepsilon - \theta a^\varepsilon = r^\sigma K^\sigma. \tag{46}$$

Market Equilibrium of the Energy-Recycling Model of Social *Common* Capital

Suppose social common capital taxes with the rate θ are levied on the disposal of residual wastes and announced prior to the opening of the market. Social institutions in charge of waste management receive the subsidy payments for the recycling of residual wastes at the rate θ. Market equilibrium will be obtained if we find prices of produced goods p and prices of energy and raw materials, π and λ, at which demand and supply are equal for all goods, energy, and raw materials.

Equilibrium conditions are

Markets for Produced Goods

$$\sum_{\mu} x^{\mu} = \sum_{\nu} c^{\nu} \tag{47}$$

Market for Labor Employment

$$\sum_{\nu} \ell^{\nu} = \sum_{\mu} \ell^{\mu} + \sum_{\varepsilon} \ell^{\varepsilon} + \sum_{\sigma} \ell^{\sigma} \tag{48}$$

Markets for Energy

$$\sum_{\varepsilon} b^{\varepsilon} = \sum_{\nu} b^{\nu} + \sum_{\mu} b^{\mu} + \sum_{\sigma} b^{\sigma} \tag{49}$$

Markets for Raw Materials for Energy Production

$$\sum_{\sigma} q^{\sigma} = \sum_{\varepsilon} q^{\varepsilon}. \tag{50}$$

Net accumulation of residual wastes a is given by

$$a = \sum_{\nu} a^{\nu} + \sum_{\mu} a^{\mu} + \sum_{\varepsilon} a^{\varepsilon} - \sum_{\sigma} a^{\sigma}. \tag{51}$$

Hence, the accumulation of residual wastes $\dot{W}$ is given by

$$\dot{W} = a. \tag{52}$$

In the following discussion, we suppose that for any given level of social common capital tax rate θ, the state of the economy that satisfies all conditions for market equilibrium generally exists and is uniquely determined.

Concerning National Income Accounting

Income y^{ν} of each individual ν is given as the sum of wage payments for the supply of labor $w\ell^{\nu}$ and tax payments for the disposal of residual wastes θa^{ν}, and the dividends for the shares of private firms and social institutions:

$$y^{\nu} = w\ell^{\nu} + \sum_{\mu} s^{\nu\mu} r^{\mu} K^{\mu} + \sum_{\varepsilon} s^{\nu\varepsilon} r^{\varepsilon} K^{\varepsilon} + \sum_{\sigma} s^{\nu\sigma} r^{\sigma} K^{\sigma},$$

where

$$s^{\nu\mu} \geqq 0, \quad \sum_{\nu} s^{\nu\mu} = 1, \quad s^{\nu\varepsilon} \geqq 0, \quad \sum_{\nu} s^{\nu\varepsilon} = 1, \quad s^{\nu\sigma} \geqq 0, \quad \sum_{\nu} s^{\nu\sigma} = 1.$$

National income y is the sum of incomes of all individuals and social common capital tax payments:

$$y = \sum_{\nu} y^{\nu} + \theta a.$$

Hence,

$$\begin{aligned} y &= \sum_{\nu} w\ell^{\nu} + \sum_{\mu} r^{\mu} K^{\mu} + \sum_{\varepsilon} r^{\varepsilon} K^{\varepsilon} + \sum_{\sigma} r^{\sigma} K^{\sigma} + \theta a \\ &= \sum_{\nu} w\ell^{\nu} + \sum_{\mu} (px^{\mu} - w\ell^{\mu} - \pi b^{\mu} - \theta a^{\mu}) \\ &\quad + \sum_{\varepsilon} (\pi b^{\varepsilon} - w\ell^{\varepsilon} - \lambda q^{\varepsilon} - \theta a^{\varepsilon}) \\ &\quad + \sum_{\sigma} (\lambda q^{\sigma} + \theta a^{\sigma} - w\ell^{\sigma} - \pi q^{\sigma}) + \theta a \\ &= \sum_{\nu} (pc^{\nu} + \pi b^{\nu} + \theta a^{\nu}). \end{aligned}$$

Thus the fundamental identity in national accounting has been established.

4. MARKET EQUILIBRIUM AND SOCIAL OPTIMUM

To explore the welfare implications of market equilibrium corresponding to the given level of social common capital tax rate θ, we consider the social utility U given by

$$U = \sum_{\nu} \alpha^{\nu} u^{\nu} = \sum_{\nu} \alpha^{\nu} \phi^{\nu}(W) u^{\nu}(c^{\nu}, b^{\nu}, a^{\nu}),$$

where utility weight α^{ν} is the inverse of marginal utility of income of individual ν at market equilibrium. We consider the following maximum problem:

Maximum Problem for Social Optimum. Find the pattern of the consumption and production of goods, energy, and raw materials for energy production, and the disposal and use of residual wastes

$(c^\nu, b^\nu, a^\nu, x^\mu, \ell^\mu, b^\mu, a^\mu, b^\varepsilon, \ell^\varepsilon, q^\varepsilon, a^\varepsilon, q^\sigma, a^\sigma, \ell^\sigma, b^\sigma, a)$ that maximizes the social utility

$$U = \sum_\nu \alpha^\nu u^\nu = \sum_\nu \alpha^\nu \phi^\nu(W) u^\nu(c^\nu, b^\nu, a^\nu) \tag{53}$$

subject to the constraints

$$\sum_\nu c^\nu \leqq \sum_\mu x^\mu \tag{54}$$

$$\sum_\mu \ell^\mu + \sum_\varepsilon \ell^\varepsilon + \sum_\sigma \ell^\sigma \leqq \sum_\nu \ell^\nu \tag{55}$$

$$\sum_\nu b^\nu + \sum_\mu b^\mu + \sum_\sigma b^\sigma \leqq \sum_\varepsilon b^\varepsilon \tag{56}$$

$$\sum_\varepsilon q^\varepsilon \leqq \sum_\sigma q^\sigma \tag{57}$$

$$a = \sum_\nu a^\nu + \sum_\mu a^\mu + \sum_\varepsilon a^\varepsilon - \sum_\sigma a^\sigma \tag{58}$$

$$f^\mu(x^\mu, \ell^\mu, b^\mu, a^\mu) \leqq K^\mu \tag{59}$$

$$f^\varepsilon(b^\varepsilon, \ell^\varepsilon, q^\varepsilon, a^\varepsilon) \leqq K^\varepsilon \tag{60}$$

$$f^\sigma(q^\sigma, a^\sigma, \ell^\sigma, b^\sigma) \leqq K^\sigma, \tag{61}$$

where utility weights α^ν are evaluated at the market equilibrium corresponding to the given level of social common capital tax rate θ and, similarly, a is the net level of the total disposal of residual wastes at the market equilibrium.

The maximum problem for social optimum may be solved in terms of the Lagrange method. Let us define the Lagrangian form

$$\begin{aligned} L &= L(c^\nu, b^\nu, a^\nu, x^\mu, \ell^\mu, b^\mu, a^\mu, b^\varepsilon, \ell^\varepsilon, q^\varepsilon, a^\varepsilon, q^\sigma, a^\sigma, \ell^\sigma, b^\sigma, \\ &\qquad p, w, \pi, \lambda, \theta, r^\mu, r^\varepsilon, r^\sigma) \\ &= \sum_\nu \alpha^\nu \phi^\nu(W) u^\nu(c^\nu, b^\nu, a^\nu) + p\left[\sum_\mu x^\mu - \sum_\nu c^\nu\right] \\ &\quad + w\left[\sum_\nu \ell^\nu - \sum_\mu \ell^\mu - \sum_\varepsilon \ell^\varepsilon - \sum_\sigma \ell^\sigma\right] + \lambda\left[\sum_\varepsilon q^\varepsilon - \sum_\sigma q^\sigma\right] \\ &\quad + \theta\left[a - \sum_\nu a^\nu - \sum_\mu a^\mu - \sum_\varepsilon a^\varepsilon + \sum_\sigma a^\sigma\right] \end{aligned}$$

$$+ \sum_{\mu} r^{\mu}[K^{\mu} - f^{\mu}(x^{\mu}, \ell^{\mu}, b^{\mu}, a^{\mu})] + \sum_{\varepsilon} r^{\varepsilon}[K^{\varepsilon} - f^{\varepsilon}(b^{\varepsilon}, \ell^{\varepsilon}, q^{\varepsilon}, a^{\varepsilon})]$$

$$+ \sum_{\sigma} r^{\sigma}[K^{\sigma} - f^{\sigma}(q^{\sigma}, a^{\sigma}, \ell^{\sigma}, b^{\sigma})], \tag{62}$$

where the Lagrange unknowns $p, w, \pi, \lambda, \theta, r^{\mu}, r^{\varepsilon}$, and r^{σ} are associated, respectively, with constraints (54), (55), (56), (57), (58), (59), (60), and (61). At the risk of confusion, the same symbol θ is used for both the Lagrangian unknown and the given level of social common capital tax rate with respect to which the market equilibrium is obtained.

The optimum solution is obtained by partially differentiating the Lagrangian form (62) with respect to the variables $c^{\nu}, b^{\nu}, a^{\nu}, x^{\mu}, \ell^{\mu}, b^{\mu}, a^{\mu}, b^{\varepsilon}, \ell^{\varepsilon}, q^{\varepsilon}, a^{\varepsilon}, q^{\sigma}, a^{\sigma}, \ell^{\sigma}, b^{\sigma}$ and putting them equal to 0, where feasibility conditions (54)–(61) are satisfied:

$$\alpha^{\nu}\phi^{\nu}(W)u^{\nu}_{c^{\nu}}(c^{\nu}, b^{\nu}, a^{\nu}) \leqq p \quad (\text{mod. } c^{\nu}) \tag{63}$$

$$\alpha^{\nu}\phi^{\nu}(W)u^{\nu}_{b^{\nu}}(c^{\nu}, b^{\nu}, a^{\nu}) \leqq \pi \quad (\text{mod. } b^{\nu}) \tag{64}$$

$$\alpha^{\nu}\phi^{\nu}(W)u^{\nu}_{a^{\nu}}(c^{\nu}, b^{\nu}, a^{\nu}) \leqq \theta \quad (\text{mod. } a^{\nu}) \tag{65}$$

$$p \leqq r^{\mu} f^{\mu}_{x^{\mu}}(x^{\mu}, \ell^{\mu}, b^{\mu}, a^{\mu}) \quad (\text{mod. } x^{\mu}) \tag{66}$$

$$w \geqq r^{\mu}[-f^{\mu}_{\ell^{\mu}}(x^{\mu}, \ell^{\mu}, b^{\mu}, a^{\mu})] \quad (\text{mod. } \ell^{\mu}) \tag{67}$$

$$\pi \geqq r^{\mu}[-f^{\mu}_{b^{\mu}}(x^{\mu}, \ell^{\mu}, b^{\mu}, a^{\mu})] \quad (\text{mod. } b^{\mu}) \tag{68}$$

$$\theta \geqq r^{\mu}[-f^{\mu}_{a^{\mu}}(x^{\mu}, \ell^{\mu}, b^{\mu}, a^{\mu})] \quad (\text{mod. } a^{\mu}) \tag{69}$$

$$f^{\mu}(x^{\mu}, \ell^{\mu}, b^{\mu}, a^{\mu}) \leqq K^{\mu} \quad (\text{mod. } r^{\mu}) \tag{70}$$

$$\pi \leqq r^{\varepsilon} f^{\varepsilon}_{b^{\varepsilon}}(b^{\varepsilon}, \ell^{\varepsilon}, q^{\varepsilon}, a^{\varepsilon}) \quad (\text{mod. } b^{\varepsilon}) \tag{71}$$

$$w \geqq r^{\varepsilon}[-f^{\varepsilon}_{\ell^{\varepsilon}}(b^{\varepsilon}, \ell^{\varepsilon}, q^{\varepsilon}, a^{\varepsilon})] \quad (\text{mod. } \ell^{\varepsilon}) \tag{72}$$

$$\lambda \geqq r^{\varepsilon}[-f^{\varepsilon}_{q^{\varepsilon}}(b^{\varepsilon}, \ell^{\varepsilon}, q^{\varepsilon}, a^{\varepsilon})] \quad (\text{mod. } q^{\varepsilon}) \tag{73}$$

$$\theta \geqq r^{\varepsilon}[-f^{\varepsilon}_{a^{\varepsilon}}(b^{\varepsilon}, \ell^{\varepsilon}, q^{\varepsilon}, a^{\varepsilon})] \quad (\text{mod. } a^{\varepsilon}) \tag{74}$$

$$\lambda \leqq r^{\sigma} f^{\sigma}_{q^{\sigma}}(q^{\sigma}, a^{\sigma}, \ell^{\sigma}, b^{\sigma}) \quad (\text{mod. } q^{\sigma}) \tag{75}$$

$$\theta \leqq r^{\sigma} f^{\sigma}_{a^{\sigma}}(q^{\sigma}, a^{\sigma}, \ell^{\sigma}, b^{\sigma}) \quad (\text{mod. } a^{\sigma}) \tag{76}$$

$$w \geqq r^{\sigma}[-f^{\sigma}_{\ell^{\sigma}}(q^{\sigma}, a^{\sigma}, \ell^{\sigma}, b^{\sigma})] \quad (\text{mod. } \ell^{\sigma}) \tag{77}$$

$$\pi \geqq r^\sigma[-f^\sigma_{b^\sigma}(q^\sigma, a^\sigma, \ell^\sigma, b^\sigma)] \quad (\text{mod. } b^\sigma) \tag{78}$$

$$f^\sigma(q^\sigma, a^\sigma, \ell^\sigma, b^\sigma) \leqq K^\sigma \quad (\text{mod. } r^\sigma). \tag{79}$$

As with the case of the prototype model of social common capital discussed in Chapter 2, the classic Kuhn-Tucker theorem on concave programming ensures that Euler-Lagrange equations (63)–(79) are necessary and sufficient conditions for the optimum solution of the maximum problem for social optimum.

It is straightforward to see that Euler-Lagrange equations (63)–(79) coincide precisely with the equilibrium conditions for market equilibrium with the social common capital tax rate θ.

As noted previously, marginality conditions (63)–(79), and the linear homogeneity hypothesis for utility functions $u^\nu(c^\nu, b^\nu, a^\nu)$ imply

$$\alpha^\nu \phi^\nu(W) u^\nu(c^\nu, b^\nu, a^\nu) = y^\nu,$$

which, by summing over ν, yield

$$U = \sum_\nu y^\nu = y.$$

We have thus established the following proposition.

Proposition 1. *Consider the social common capital tax scheme with the rate θ for the disposal of residual wastes in the energy-recycling model of social common capital.*

Then market equilibrium obtained under such a social common capital tax scheme is a social optimum with respect to the given net level of the total disposal of residual wastes a in the sense that a set of positive weights for the utilities of individuals $(\alpha^1, \ldots, \alpha^n)$ exists such that the pattern of consumption and production of goods, energy, and raw materials for energy production, and disposal and use of residual wastes at the market equilibrium $(c^\nu, b^\nu, a^\nu, x^\mu, \ell^\mu, b^\mu, a^\mu, b^\varepsilon, \ell^\varepsilon, q^\varepsilon, a^\varepsilon, q^\sigma, a^\sigma, \ell^\sigma, b^\sigma)$ maximizes the social utility

$$U = \sum_\nu \alpha^\nu u^\nu = \sum_\nu \alpha^\nu \phi^\nu(W) u^\nu(c^\nu, b^\nu, a^\nu)$$

among all feasible patterns of allocation, where utility weight α^ν is the inverse of marginal utility of income of individual ν at the market equilibrium and a is the given net level of the total disposal of residual wastes at the market equilibrium.

The optimum level of social utility U is equal to national income y:

$$U = y.$$

Optimum Taxation for the Disposal of Residual Wastes

To examine the adverse effect of the accumulation of residual wastes on the welfare of the society, we calculate the imputed price of the disposal of residual wastes. The imputed price of the disposal of residual wastes ψ is defined as the discounted present value of the marginal decrease in the social utility of the economy due to the marginal increase in the accumulation of residual wastes. At each time t, the accumulated amount of residual wastes is denoted by W, and the social utility is defined by

$$U = \sum_{\nu} \alpha^{\nu} u^{\nu} = \sum_{\nu} \alpha^{\nu} \phi^{\nu}(W) u^{\nu}(c^{\nu}, b^{\nu}, a^{\nu}),$$

where utility weight α^{ν} is the inverse of marginal utility of income of individual ν at the market equilibrium and the net level of the total disposal of residual wastes is the level a at the market equilibrium.

The marginal increase in the accumulation of residual wastes induces the marginal increase in the stock of accumulated residual wastes, and the corresponding marginal decrease in social utility U is given by

$$\begin{aligned} -\frac{\partial U}{\partial W} &= \sum_{\nu} \alpha^{\nu}[-\varphi^{\nu\prime}(W)] u^{\nu}(c^{\nu}, b^{\nu}, a^{\nu}) \\ &= \tau(W) \sum_{\nu} \alpha^{\nu} \varphi^{\nu}(W) u^{\nu}(c^{\nu}, b^{\nu}, a^{\nu}), \end{aligned}$$

where $\tau(W)$ is the impact coefficient of the disposal of residual wastes and y is the national income at the market equilibrium. Hence, in view of Proposition 1, we have

$$-\frac{\partial U}{\partial W} = \tau(W) y.$$

Assuming that the social rate of discount is a positive constant δ ($\delta > 0$), we have the following formula for the imputed price of the disposal of residual wastes ψ:

$$\psi = \frac{\tau(W) y}{\delta}.$$

Now we would like to calculate the effect of the marginal increase in the net level of total disposal of residual wastes a on the level of social utility

$$U = \sum_{\nu} \alpha^{\nu} u^{\nu} = \sum_{\nu} \alpha^{\nu} \phi^{\nu}(W) u^{\nu}(c^{\nu}, b^{\nu}, a^{\nu}),$$

where the resulting marginal increase in the accumulation of residual wastes W is explicitly taken into account.

By taking total differentials of both sides of (62) and noting optimum conditions

$$\frac{\partial L}{\partial c^{\nu}} = 0, \ \frac{\partial L}{\partial b^{\nu}} = 0, \ \frac{\partial L}{\partial a^{\nu}} = 0, \ldots, \ \frac{\partial L}{\partial q^{\sigma}} = 0, \ \frac{\partial L}{\partial a^{\sigma}} = 0, \ \frac{\partial L}{\partial \ell^{\sigma}} = 0, \ \frac{\partial L}{\partial b^{\sigma}} = 0,$$

we obtain

$$dU = \frac{\partial L}{\partial a} da - \psi dW = \left[\theta - \frac{\tau(W) y}{\delta} \right] da.$$

Hence,

$$\frac{dU}{da} = \theta - \frac{\tau(W) y}{\delta}.$$

Thus, the optimum net level of the total disposal of residual wastes a is obtained when

$$\theta = \frac{\tau(W) y}{\delta}.$$

We have thus established the following proposition.

Proposition 2. *In the energy-recycling model of social common capital, consider the social common capital tax scheme with the rate θ for the disposal of residual wastes:*

$$\theta = \frac{\tau(W) y}{\delta},$$

where $\tau(W)$ is the impact coefficient of the disposal of residual wastes, y is the national income at the market equilibrium, and δ is the social rate of discount.

Then market equilibrium obtained under such a social common capital tax scheme is a social optimum in the sense that a set of positive weights for the utilities of individuals $(\alpha^1, \ldots, \alpha^n)$ exists such that the pattern of consumption and production of goods, energy, and raw materials for energy production, and disposal and use of residual *wastes at the market equilibrium* $(c^\nu, b^\nu, a^\nu, x^\mu, \ell^\mu, b^\mu, a^\mu, b^\varepsilon, \ell^\varepsilon, q^\varepsilon, a^\varepsilon, q^\sigma, a^\sigma, \ell^\sigma, b^\sigma, a)$ *maximizes the social utility*

$$U = \sum_\nu \alpha^\nu u^\nu = \sum_\nu \alpha^\nu \phi^\nu(W) u^\nu(c^\nu, b^\nu, a^\nu)$$

among all feasible patterns of allocation, where utility weight α^ν *is the inverse of the marginal utility of income of individual* ν *at the market equilibrium.*

The optimum level of the social utility U *is equal to national income* y*:*

$$U = y.$$

Social Optimum and Market Equilibrium

Social optimum is defined with respect to any social utility

$$U = \sum_\nu \alpha^\nu u^\nu = \sum_\nu \alpha^\nu \varphi^\nu(W) u^\nu(c^\nu, b^\nu, a^\nu)$$

where $(\alpha^1, \ldots, \alpha^n)$ is an arbitrarily given set of positive weights for the utilities of individuals. A pattern of consumption and production of goods, energy, and raw materials for energy production, and disposal and use of residual wastes at the market equilibrium $(c^\nu, b^\nu, a^\nu, x^\mu, \ell^\mu, b^\mu, a^\mu, b^\varepsilon, \ell^\varepsilon, q^\varepsilon, a^\varepsilon, q^\sigma, a^\sigma, \ell^\sigma, b^\sigma, a)$ is a social optimum if the social utility U thus defined is maximized among all feasible patterns of allocation.

Social optimum necessarily implies the existence of the social common capital tax scheme, where the tax rate θ is given by $\theta = \frac{\tau(W)y}{\delta}$. However, the budgetary constraints for individuals

$$pc^\nu + \pi\, b^\nu + \theta a^\nu = y^\nu$$

are not necessarily satisfied. It is straightforward to see the validity of the following proposition.

Proposition 3. *Suppose an allocation* $(c^\nu, b^\nu, a^\nu, x^\mu, \ell^\mu, b^\mu, a^\mu, b^\varepsilon, \ell^\varepsilon, q^\varepsilon, a^\varepsilon, q^\sigma, a^\sigma, \ell^\sigma, b^\sigma, a)$ *is a social optimum; that is, a set of positive weights for the utilities of individuals* $(\alpha^1, \ldots, \alpha^n)$ *exists such that the given pattern of allocation maximizes the aggregate utility*

$$U = \sum_\nu \alpha^\nu u^\nu = \sum_\nu \alpha^\nu \varphi^\nu(W) u^\nu(c^\nu, b^\nu, a^\nu)$$

among all feasible patterns of allocation.

Then, a system of income transfer among individuals of the society, $\{t^\nu\}$, exists such that

$$\sum_\nu t^\nu = 0,$$

and the given pattern of allocation corresponds precisely to the market equilibrium under the social common capital tax scheme with the tax rate θ given by

$$\theta = \frac{\tau(W)y}{\delta},$$

where $\tau(W)$ is the impact coefficient of the disposal of residual wastes, y is the national income at the market equilibrium, and δ is the social rate of discount.

Adjustment Processes of Social Common Capital Tax Rates

In the previous sections, we examined two patterns of resource allocation involving social common capital: market allocation, on one hand, and social optimum, on the other. Market allocation $(c^\nu, b^\nu, a^\nu, x^\mu, \ell^\mu, b^\mu, a^\mu, b^\varepsilon, \ell^\varepsilon, q^\varepsilon, a^\varepsilon, q^\sigma, a^\sigma, \ell^\sigma, b^\sigma, a)$ is obtained as competitive equilibrium with social common capital taxes levied on the disposal of residual wastes with the tax rate θ given by

$$\theta = \frac{\tau(W)y}{\delta},$$

where $\tau(W)$ is the impact coefficient of the disposal of residual wastes, y is the national income at the market equilibrium, and δ is the social rate of discount.

Social optimum $(c^\nu, b^\nu, a^\nu, x^\mu, \ell^\mu, b^\mu, a^\mu, b^\varepsilon, \ell^\varepsilon, q^\varepsilon, a^\varepsilon, q^\sigma, a^\sigma, \ell^\sigma, b^\sigma, a)$ is defined with respect to the social utility

$$U = \sum_\nu \alpha^\nu u^\nu = \sum_\nu \alpha^\nu \phi^\nu(W) u^\nu(c^\nu, b^\nu, a^\nu),$$

where $(\alpha^1, \ldots, \alpha^n)$ is an arbitrarily given set of positive weights for the utilities of individuals. A pattern of allocation is social optimum if social utility U is maximized among all feasible patterns of allocation.

Market equilibrium with social common capital tax rate $\theta = \frac{\tau(W)y}{\delta}$ coincides with the social optimum with respect to the social utility

$$U = \sum_\nu \alpha^\nu u^\nu = \sum_\nu \alpha^\nu \varphi^\nu(W) u^\nu(c^\nu, b^\nu, a^\nu),$$

where, for each individual ν, utility weight α^ν is the inverse of marginal utility of individual ν's income y^ν at the market equilibrium.

The tax rate $\theta = \frac{\tau(W)y}{\delta}$ is administratively determined and announced prior to the opening of the market when the level of national income y is not known.

We consider the adjustment process with respect to the social common capital tax rate θ defined by the following differential equation:

$$\text{(A)} \qquad \dot{\theta} = k\left[\frac{\tau(W)y}{\delta} - \theta\right],$$

with initial condition θ_o, where k is an arbitrarily given positive speed of adjustment.

An increase in the social common capital tax rate θ results in a decrease in the level of national income y. Hence, the right-hand side of differential equation (A) is a decreasing function of θ. Thus, the following proposition is easily established.

Proposition 4. *The adjustment process defined by differential equation (A) is globally stable; that is, for any initial condition θ_o, the solution path θ to differential equation (A) converges to the optimum tax rate* $\frac{\tau(w)y}{\delta}$.

6

Agriculture and Social Common Capital

1. INTRODUCTION

Agriculture concerns not only economic and industrial aspects but also virtually every aspect of human life – cultural, social, and natural. It provides us with food and the raw materials such as wood, cotton, silk, and others that are indispensable in sustaining our existence. It also has sustained, with few exceptions, the natural environment such as forests, lakes, wetlands, soil, subterranean water, and the atmosphere.

Agriculture has made possible a harmonious and sustainable interaction between nature and humankind through the social institution of the rural community in many East Asian countries, particularly Japan. This does not, however, necessarily imply that the traditional, conventional social institutions prevailing in most of the agricultural communities are justifiable or desirable.

Land ownership is probably the single most serious and complex problem in Japan. Japan is noted for a high population density and a long history of agricultural development. Land had been cultivated literally to the top of the mountains, and forestry had been subject to a myriad of property rights arrangements. The modern Civil Law, enacted in 1898, adopted an extremely narrow definition of land ownership, voiding traditional forms of property ownership for villages as the commons to manage and control the natural resources to be directly or indirectly obtained from land, forests, and other natural environments. The conflict between the modern Civil Law and traditional institutions of the commons occupied the majority of the legal suits brought before the Grand Court before the Second World War. The land reform measures implemented during the occupation by the Allied powers did not help resolve the dilemma either. Postwar Japan has seen a large number of conflicts, occasionally serious, between the state and its citizens, mostly farmers, in the processes of land expropriation for building the infrastructure.

Since the end of the Second World War, the Narita airport project is probably one of the thorniest problems Japan has faced regarding infrastructure construction, bringing far more extensive damage to the society than the scope and magnitude of the infrastructure facilities as originally planned would have brought. It began on July 4, 1966, when the Cabinet decided to construct the New Tokyo International Airport at Sanrizuka in Narita, without first consulting the inhabitants of the community or the local authorities. Thirty years of conflict claimed close to 10,000 casualties on both sides, leading to a large number of human tragedies, unprecedented in peacetime Japan. The conflict was peacefully brought to an end on May 24, 1993, when the minister of transportation and the representatives of the Airport Opposition Alliance jointly declared that neither side would resort to any forceful measures but instead would cooperate in devising a comprehensive regional development plan, including the completion of the airport, that would be acceptable to all those involved. As part of the peaceful resolution of the Narita conflict, a commission was appointed to draw a blueprint for the Sanrizuka Agricultural Commons that would serve not only as the core organization for the comprehensive regional development plan, but also the prototype of the organizational renovation to revitalize Japanese agriculture.

In this chapter, we formulate the basic premises of the Sanrizuka Agricultural Commons as a model for agriculture as social common capital and examine the conditions for the sustainable development of social common capital and privately owned scarce resources.

2. AN AGRARIAN MODEL OF SOCIAL COMMON CAPITAL

We consider a society that consists of two sectors: the agricultural sector and the industrial sector. The agricultural sector consists of a finite number of villages, each located around a forest and composed of a finite number of farmers engaged in the maintenance of the forest and agricultural activities. The forest of each village is regarded as social common capital and managed as common property resources. The resources of the forest are used by farmers in the village for agricultural activities, primarily for the production of food and other necessities. The forests of the agricultural sector also play an important role in the maintenance of a decent cultural environment.

The industrial sector consists of a finite number of private firms, each engaged in the production of industrial goods that are either consumed by individuals of the society or used by the agricultural and industrial sectors in the processes of production activities. All the factors of production that are necessary for the activities carried on by private firms and in the villages are either owned by private individuals or managed as if they were privately owned.

Subsidy payments are made by the central government to the villages for the maintenance and preservation of the forests of the villages. At the same time, social common capital taxes are levied by each village to be paid by the farmers in the village for the use of natural resources from the forest of the village. Social common capital subsidy and tax rates are administratively determined by either the central government or the villages and are announced prior to the opening of the market.

Industrial and agricultural goods are transacted on perfectly competitive markets. Labor is assumed to be variable and inelastically supplied to a perfectly competitive labor market.

As in other models of social common capital discussed in this book, the primary functions of the central government and the villages are, respectively, to determine the subsidy rate for the maintenance and preservation of the forests of the villages and to determine the tax rates for the use of resources of natural capital in the forests of the villages in such a manner that the ensuing patterns of resource allocation and income distribution are optimum in a certain well-defined, socially acceptable sense.

Basic Premises of the Agrarian Model of Social Common Capital

Individuals are generically denoted by $\nu = 1, \ldots, n$, and villages in the agricultural sector by $\sigma = 1, \ldots, s$, whereas private firms in the industrial sector are denoted by $\mu = 1, \ldots, m$.

Products of the agricultural sector are generically denoted by $i = 1, \ldots, I$, and produced goods of the industrial sector by $j = 1, \ldots, J$. The stock of natural capital in each forest is expressed in certain well-defined units, such as the acreage of the forest or the number of trees in the forest.

There are two types of factors of production: variable and fixed. Typical variable factors of production are various kinds of labor, so we refer to them as labor. In this chapter, we assume that there is only one kind of labor.

Fixed factors of production in the present context are those means of production that are made as fixed, specific components of villages or private firms. In the following discussion, we occasionally refer to fixed factors of production as capital goods. Fixed factors of production are generically denoted by $f = 1, \ldots, F$.

Principal Agency of the Society

The principal agency of the society in question is each individual who consumes goods produced by private firms in the industrial sector and products of the agricultural sector. Goods consumed by individual ν are denoted by a combination (c^ν, b^ν) of two vectors $c^\nu = (c^\nu_j)$ and $b^\nu = (b^\nu_i)$, where c^ν_j and b^ν_i are, respectively, the quantities of good j produced in the industrial sector and good i produced in the agricultural sector.

The amount of labor of each individual ν is denoted by ℓ^ν, which is assumed to be inelastically supplied to the market.

We also assume that both private firms in the industrial sector and farms in the agricultural sector are owned by individuals. We denote by $s^{\nu\mu}$ and $s^{\nu\sigma}$, respectively, the shares of private firm μ and the forest of village σ owned by individual ν, where

$$s^{\nu\mu} \geqq 0, \quad \sum_\nu s^{\nu\mu} = 1; \qquad s^{\nu\sigma} \geqq 0, \quad \sum_\nu s^{\nu\sigma} = 1.$$

It is generally the case that $s^{\nu\sigma} = 0$ for those individuals ν not residing in village σ.

Private Firms in the Industrial Sector

Quantities of fixed factors of production accumulated in each firm μ in the industrial sector are expressed by a vector $K^\mu = (K^\mu_f)$, where K^μ_f denotes the quantity of factor of production f accumulated in firm μ. Quantities of goods produced by each firm μ are denoted by a vector $x^\mu = (x^\mu_j)$, where x^μ_j denotes the quantity of goods j produced by firm μ, net of the quantities of goods used by firm μ itself. The amount of labor employed by firm μ to carry out production activities is denoted by ℓ^{μ}. To carry out productive activities, private firms in the industrial sector use products of the agricultural sector. The amounts of products of the agricultural sector used by firm μ are denoted by a vector $a^{\mu} = (a_i^{\mu})$, where a_i^{μ} denotes the amount of product of type i used by firm μ.

Villages in the Agricultural Sector

The manner in which farmers in the villages are engaged in agricultural activities by using resources extracted from the forests as natural capital is similarly postulated. Farmers in the villages are also engaged in the activities related to the maintenance and reforestation of the forests of the villages.

Farmers in village σ are generically denoted by σ_ν $(\nu = 1, \ldots, n_\sigma)$. Amounts of agricultural products produced by each farmer σ_ν are expressed by a vector $b^{\sigma_\nu} = (b_i^{\sigma_\nu})$, where $b_i^{\sigma_\nu}$ denotes the amount of agricultural product i produced by farmer σ_ν, net of the amounts of agricultural products used by farmer σ_ν himself or herself. The amount of labor employed by farmer σ_ν for agricultural activities is denoted by $\ell_p^{\sigma_\nu}$, whereas the amount of natural capital in the forest of village σ that is depleted in the processes of agricultural activities carried out by farmer σ_ν is denoted by a^{σ_ν}. The increase in the stock of natural capital in the forest of village σ that is enhanced by the reforestation activities carried out by farmer σ_ν is denoted by z^{σ_ν}. The amount of labor employed by farmer σ_ν for reforestation activities is denoted by $\ell_i^{\sigma_\nu}$, whereas the vector x^{σ_ν} specifies the amounts of industrial goods used by farmer σ_ν for reforestation activities.

Quantities of fixed factors of production accumulated in village σ are expressed by a vector $K^{\sigma} = (K_f^{\sigma})$, where K_f^{σ} denotes the quantity of fixed factor of production f accumulated in village σ. It is assumed that $K^{\sigma} \geq 0$. The stock of natural capital in the forests of village σ is denoted by V^{σ}.

3. SPECIFICATIONS OF THE AGRARIAN MODEL OF SOCIAL COMMON CAPITAL

We assume that markets for produced goods of the industrial and agricultural sectors are perfectly competitive; prices of industrial and agricultural goods are, respectively, denoted by vectors $p = (p_j)$ and $\pi = (\pi_i)$, where $p \geq 0, \pi \geq 0$. The market for labor is also assumed to be perfectly competitive, and wage rate is denoted by w $(w > 0)$.

Utility Functions and the Natural Environment

The economic welfare of each individual ν is expressed by a preference ordering that is represented by the utility function:

$$u^\nu = u^\nu(c^\nu, b^\nu),$$

where $c^\nu = (c_j^\nu)$ and $b^\nu = (b_i^\nu)$ are, respectively, the vectors of industrial and agricultural goods consumed by individual ν.

We assume that, for each individual ν, the utility function $u^\nu(c^\nu, b^\nu)$ satisfies the following neoclassical conditions:

(U1) Utility function $u^\nu(c^\nu, b^\nu)$ is defined, positive, continuous, and continuously twice-differentiable for all $(c^\nu, b^\nu) \geqq 0$.

(U2) Marginal utilities are positive for the consumption of both industrial and agricultural goods c^ν and b^ν; that is,

$$u_{c^\nu}^\nu(c^\nu, b^\nu) > 0, \quad u_{b^\nu}^\nu(c^\nu, b^\nu) > 0 \quad \text{for all } (c^\nu, b^\nu) \geqq 0.$$

(U3) Marginal rates of substitution between any pair of the consumption of industrial and agricultural goods are diminishing, or more specifically, $u^\nu(c^\nu, b^\nu)$ is strictly quasi-concave with respect to (c^ν, b^ν).

(U4) Utility function $u^\nu(c^\nu, b^\nu)$ is homogenous of order 1 with respect to (c^ν, b^ν).

The linear homogeneity hypothesis (U4) implies the following Euler identity:

$$u^\nu(c^\nu, b^\nu) = u_{c^\nu}^\nu(c^\nu, b^\nu)\, c^\nu + u_{b^\nu}^\nu(c^\nu, b^\nu)\, b^\nu \quad \text{for all } (c^\nu, b^\nu) \geqq 0.$$

The level of utility of each individual is affected by the presence of the natural environment. We assume that the utility function of individual ν may be expressed as

$$u^\nu = \phi^\nu(V) u^\nu(c^\nu, b^\nu),$$

where the function $\phi^\nu(V)$ specifies the extent to which the presence of the natural environment affects the level of utility of individual ν, V

is the aggregate sum of the stock of natural capital in all forests in the villages

$$V = \sum_{\sigma} V^{\sigma},$$

where V^{σ} is the stock of natural capital in the forest of village σ.

The function $\phi^{\nu}(V)$ is referred to as the impact index of natural capital for individual ν. It may be assumed that the impact index $\phi^{\nu}(V)$ is increased as the total stock of natural capital V is increased, although with diminishing marginal effects. These conditions may be stated as follows:

$$\phi^{\nu}(V) > 0, \quad \phi^{\nu\prime}(V) > 0, \quad \phi^{\nu\prime\prime}(V) < 0 \quad \text{for all } V > 0.$$

The impact coefficient of natural capital for individual ν, $\tau^{\nu}(V)$, is the relative rate of the marginal change in the impact index due to the marginal increase in the total stock of natural capital V; that is

$$\tau^{\nu}(V) = \frac{\phi^{\nu\prime}(V)}{\phi^{\nu}(V)}.$$

In the following discussion, we assume that the impact coefficients $\tau^{\nu}(V)$ of natural capital are identical for all individuals ν; that is,

$$\tau^{\nu}(V) = \tau(V) \quad \text{for all } \nu.$$

The impact coefficients $\tau(V)$ satisfy the following relations:

$$\tau(V) > 0, \quad \tau'(V) < 0 \quad \text{for all } V > 0.$$

The Consumer Optimum

Each individual ν chooses the combination of consumption of industrial and agricultural goods, (c^{ν}, b^{ν}), that maximizes the utility function of individual ν

$$u^{\nu} = \phi^{\nu}(V)u^{\nu}(c^{\nu}, b^{\nu})$$

subject to the budget constraint

$$pc^{\nu} + \pi b^{\nu} = y^{\nu}, \tag{1}$$

where y^{ν} is income of individual ν.

The optimum combination (c^ν, b^ν) of consumption of industrial and agricultural goods is characterized by the following marginality conditions:

$$\phi^\nu(V)u^\nu_{c^\nu}(c^\nu, b^\nu) \leqq \lambda^\nu p \quad (\text{mod. } c^\nu)$$
$$\phi^\nu(V)u^\nu_{b^\nu}(c^\nu, b^\nu) \leqq \lambda^\nu \pi \quad (\text{mod. } b^\nu),$$

where $\lambda^\nu > 0$ is the Lagrange unknown associated with budgetary constraint (1). Lagrange unknown λ^ν is nothing but the marginal utility of income y^ν of individual ν.

To express the marginality relations above in units of market price, we divide both sides of these relations by λ^ν to obtain the following relations:

$$\alpha^\nu\phi^\nu(V)u^\nu_{c^\nu}(c^\nu, b^\nu) \leqq p \quad (\text{mod. } c^\nu) \tag{2}$$
$$\alpha^\nu\phi^\nu(V)u^\nu_{b^\nu}(c^\nu, b^\nu) \leqq \pi \quad (\text{mod. } b^\nu), \tag{3}$$

where $\alpha^\nu = \dfrac{1}{\lambda^\nu} > 0$.

Relations (2) and (3) express the familiar principle that the marginal utility of each good is exactly equal to the market price when the utility is measured in units of market price.

We derive a relation that will play a central role in our analysis of natural capital. By multiplying both sides of relations (2) and (3), respectively, by c^ν and b^ν and adding them, we obtain

$$\alpha^\nu\phi^\nu(V)\,[u^\nu_{c^\nu}(c^\nu, b^\nu)c^\nu + u^\nu_{b^\nu}(c^\nu, b^\nu)b^\nu] = pc^\nu + \pi b^\nu.$$

On the other hand, in view of the Euler identity for utility function $u^\nu(c^\nu, a^\nu)$ and budgetary constraint (1), we have

$$\alpha^\nu\phi^\nu(V)u^\nu(c^\nu, b^\nu) = y^\nu. \tag{4}$$

Relation (4) means that, at the consumer optimum, the level of utility of individual ν, when expressed in units of market price, is precisely equal to income y^ν of individual ν.

Production Possibility Sets of Private Firms in the Industrial Sector

The conditions concerning the production of goods for each private firm μ in the industrial sector are specified by the production possibility set T^μ that summarizes the technological possibilities and organizational arrangements for firm μ with the endowments of fixed factors of production available in firm μ given. The quantities of fixed factors of production accumulated in private firm μ are expressed by a vector $K^\mu = (K_f^\mu)$. It is assumed that $K^\mu \geq 0$.

In each firm μ, the minimum quantities of factors of production that are required to produce goods by $x^\mu = (x_j^\mu)$ with the employment of labor by ℓ^μ and the use of agricultural goods $b^\mu = (b_i^\mu)$ are specified by an F-dimensional vector-valued function:

$$f^\mu(x^\mu, \ell^\mu, b^\mu) = \left(f_f^\mu(x^\mu, \ell^\mu, b^\mu)\right).$$

We assume that marginal rates of substitution between any pair of the production of industrial goods, the employment of labor, and the use of agricultural goods are smooth and diminishing, that there are always trade-offs among them, and that the conditions of constant returns to scale prevail. That is, we assume

(T$^\mu$1) $f^\mu(x^\mu, \ell^\mu, b^\mu)$ are defined, positive, continuous, and continuously twice-differentiable with respect to (x^μ, ℓ^μ, b^μ).

(T$^\mu$2) $f_{x^\mu}^\mu(x^\mu, \ell^\mu, b^\mu) > 0$, $f_{\ell^\mu}^\mu(x^\mu, \ell^\mu, b^\mu) \leqq 0$, $f_{b^\mu}^\mu(x^\mu, \ell^\mu, b^\mu) \leqq 0$.

(T$^\mu$3) $f^\mu(x^\mu, \ell^\mu, b^\mu)$ are strictly quasi-convex with respect to (x^μ, ℓ^μ, b^μ).

(T$^\mu$4) $f^\mu(x^\mu, \ell^\mu, b^\mu)$ are homogeneous of order 1 with respect to (x^μ, ℓ^μ, b^μ).

From constant-return-to-scale condition (T$^\mu$4), we have the Euler identity:

$$f^\mu(x^\mu, \ell^\mu, b^\mu) = f_{x^\mu}^\mu(x^\mu, \ell^\mu, b^\mu)x^\mu + f_{\ell^\mu}^\mu(x^\mu, \ell^\mu, b^\mu)\ell^\mu + f_{b^\mu}^\mu(x^\mu, \ell^\mu, b^\mu)b^\mu.$$

The production possibility set of each firm μ in the industrial sector, T^μ, is composed of all combinations (x^μ, ℓ^μ, b^μ) of production of industrial goods x^μ, employment of labor ℓ^μ, and use of agricultural goods b^μ that are possible with the organizational arrangements, technological conditions, and given endowments of factors of production K^μ in firm μ. Hence, it may be expressed as

$$T^\mu = \{(x^\mu, \ell^\mu, b^\mu)\colon (x^\mu, \ell^\mu, b^\mu) \geqq 0,\ f^\mu(x^\mu, \ell^\mu, b^\mu) \leqq K^\mu\}.$$

Postulates ($T^\mu 1$–$T^\mu 3$) imply that the production possibility set T^μ of each firm μ is a closed, convex set of $J + 1 + I$-dimensional vectors (x^μ, ℓ^μ, b^μ).

The Producer Optimum for Industrial Firms

Each industrial firm μ chooses the combination (x^μ, ℓ^μ, b^μ) of production of industrial goods, employment of labor, and use of agricultural goods that maximizes net profit

$$px^\mu - w\ell^\mu - \pi b^\mu$$

over $(x^\mu, \ell^\mu, b^\mu) \in T^\mu$.

Conditions ($T^\mu 1$–$T^\mu 3$) postulated above ensure that for any combination of prices p, π, and wage rate w, the optimum combination (x^μ, ℓ^μ, b^μ) of production of industrial goods x^μ, employment of labor ℓ^μ, and use of agricultural goods b^μ always exists and is uniquely determined.

To see how the optimum levels of production, employment of labor, and use of agricultural goods are determined, let us denote the vector of imputed rental prices of fixed factors of production by $r^\mu = (r^\mu_f)$ $[r^\mu_f \geqq 0]$. Then the optimum conditions are

$$p \leqq r^\mu f^\mu_{x^\mu}(x^\mu, \ell^\mu, b^\mu) \quad (\text{mod. } x^\mu) \tag{5}$$

$$w \geqq r^\mu \left[-f^\mu_{\ell^\mu}(x^\mu, \ell^\mu, b^\mu) \right] \quad (\text{mod. } \ell^\mu) \tag{6}$$

$$\pi \geqq r^\mu \left[-f^\mu_{b^\mu}(x^\mu, \ell^\mu, b^\mu) \right] \quad (\text{mod. } b^\mu) \tag{7}$$

$$f^\mu(x^\mu, \ell^\mu, b^\mu) \leqq K^\mu \quad (\text{mod. } r^\mu). \tag{8}$$

Condition (5) means that the choice of production technologies and levels of production is adjusted so as to equate marginal factor costs with output prices.

Condition (6) means that the employment of labor is adjusted so that the marginal gains due to the marginal increase in the employment of labor are equal to wage rate w when $\ell^\mu > 0$, and are not larger than w when $\ell^\mu = 0$.

Condition (7) similarly means that the use of agricultural goods is controlled so that the marginal gains due to the marginal increase in the use of agricultural goods are equal to price π_i when $b_i^\mu > 0$, and are not larger than π_i when $b_i^\mu = 0$.

Condition (8) means that the employment of factors of production does not exceed the endowments and the conditions of full employment are satisfied whenever imputed rental price r_f^μ is positive.

The technologies are subject to constant returns to scale ($T^\mu 4$), and thus, in view of the Euler identity, conditions (5)–(8) imply that

$$\begin{aligned} px^\mu - w\ell^\mu - \pi b^\mu &= r^\mu \left[f_{x^\mu}^\mu(x^\mu, \ell^\mu, b^\mu)\, x^\mu + f_{\ell^\mu}^\mu(x^\mu, \ell^\mu, b^\mu)\ell^\mu \right. \\ &\quad \left. + f_{b^\mu}^\mu(x^\mu, \ell^\mu, b^\mu)\, b^\mu \right] \\ &= r^\mu f^\mu(x^\mu, \ell^\mu, b^\mu) = r^\mu K^\mu. \end{aligned} \tag{9}$$

That is, for each private firm μ, the net evaluation of output is equal to the sum of the imputed rental payments to all fixed factors of production of private firm μ. The meaning of relation (9) may be brought out better if we rewrite it as

$$px^\mu = w\ell^\mu + \pi b^\mu + r^\mu K^\mu.$$

That is, the value of output measured in market prices px^μ is equal to the sum of wages $w\ell^\mu$, the payments for the use of agricultural goods πb^μ, and the payments, in terms of imputed rental prices, made for the employment of fixed factors of production $r^\mu K^\mu$. Thus, the validity of the Menger-Wieser principle of imputation is assured with respect to processes of production of private firms in the industrial sector.

Production Possibility Sets of Villages in the Agricultural Sector

The conditions concerning the production of agricultural goods and the reforestation of the forest of village σ that are carried out by the farmers in village σ are specified by the production possibility set T^σ that summarizes the technological possibilities and organizational arrangements of village σ; the stock of natural capital in the forest of village σ and endowments of factors of production in village σ are given and are denoted, respectively, by V^σ and $K^\sigma = (K_f^\sigma)$. It is assumed $V^\sigma > 0$ and $K^\sigma \geq 0$.

Farmers in village σ are generically denoted by σ_ν $(\nu = 1, \ldots, n_\sigma)$. Amounts of agricultural products produced by each farmer σ_ν are denoted by a vector $b^{\sigma_\nu} = (b_i^{\sigma_\nu})$, where $b_i^{\sigma_\nu}$ denotes the amount of agricultural product i produced by farmer σ_ν, net of the amounts of agricultural products used by farmer σ_ν himself or herself. The amount of labor employed by farmer σ_ν for agricultural activities is denoted by $\ell_p^{\sigma_\nu}$, whereas the amount of natural capital in the forest of village σ that is depleted in the processes of agricultural activities carried out by farmer σ_ν is denoted by a^{σ_ν}. The increase in the stock of natural capital in the forest of village σ that is enhanced by the reforestation activities carried out by farmer σ_ν is denoted by z^{σ_ν}. The amount of labor employed by farmer σ_ν for reforestation activities is denoted by $\ell_i^{\sigma_\nu}$, whereas the vector x^{σ_ν} specifies the amounts of industrial goods used by farmer σ_ν for reforestation activities.

Conditions for the Production of Agricultural Goods

The minimum quantities of factors of production required for farmer σ_ν to produce agricultural products by b^{σ_ν} with the employment of labor for agricultural activities by $\ell_p^{\sigma_\nu}$ and the depletion of natural capital of village σ at the level a^{σ_ν} are specified by an F-dimensional vector-valued function:

$$f^{\sigma_\nu}\left(b^{\sigma_\nu}, \ell_p^{\sigma_\nu}, a^{\sigma_\nu}\right) = \left(f_f^{\sigma_\nu}\left(b^{\sigma_\nu}, \ell_p^{\sigma_\nu}, a^{\sigma_\nu}\right)\right).$$

We assume that, for each farmer σ_ν in village σ, marginal rates of substitution between any pair of the production of agricultural products, the employment of labor, and the depletion of natural capital are smooth and diminishing, that there are always trade-offs among them, and that the conditions of constant returns to scale prevail. That is, we assume

($\mathrm{T}_p^\sigma 1$) $f^{\sigma_\nu}(b^{\sigma_\nu}, \ell_p^{\sigma_\nu}, a^{\sigma_\nu})$ are defined, positive, continuous, and continuously twice-differentiable with respect to $(b^{\sigma_\nu}, \ell_p^{\sigma_\nu}, a^{\sigma_\nu})$.

($\mathrm{T}_p^\sigma 2$) $f_{b^{\sigma_\nu}}^{\sigma_\nu}(b^{\sigma_\nu}, \ell_p^{\sigma_\nu}, a^{\sigma_\nu}) > 0, \quad f_{\ell_p^{\sigma_\nu}}^{\sigma_\nu}(b^{\sigma_\nu}, \ell_p^{\sigma_\nu}, a^{\sigma_\nu}) < 0,$ $f_{a^{\sigma_\nu}}^{\sigma_\nu}(b^{\sigma_\nu}, \ell_p^{\sigma_\nu}, a^{\sigma_\nu}) < 0.$

($\mathrm{T}_p^\sigma 3$) $f^{\sigma_\nu}(b^{\sigma_\nu}, \ell_p^{\sigma_\nu}, a^{\sigma_\nu})$ are strictly quasi-convex with respect to $(b^{\sigma_\nu}, \ell_p^{\sigma_\nu}, a^{\sigma_\nu})$.

($\mathrm{T}_p^\sigma 4$) $f^{\sigma_\nu}(b^{\sigma_\nu}, \ell_p^{\sigma_\nu}, a^{\sigma_\nu})$ are homogeneous of order 1 with respect to $(b^{\sigma_\nu}, \ell_p^{\sigma_\nu}, a^{\sigma_\nu})$.

Effects of Congestion on Agricultural Activities in the Villages

Agricultural activities in the villages are affected by the phenomenon of congestion concerning the use of resources extracted from the forests of the villages. We assume that, for each farmer σ_ν in village σ, the minimum quantities of factors of production required for farmer σ_ν to produce agricultural products by b^{σ_ν} with the employment of labor for agricultural activities by $\ell_p^{\sigma_\nu}$ and the depletion of natural capital in the forest of village σ at the level a^{σ_ν} are specified by the F-dimensional vector-valued function

$$f^{\sigma_\nu}\left(b^{\sigma_\nu}, \ell_p^{\sigma_\nu}, \varphi^{\sigma_\nu}\left(\frac{a^\sigma}{V^\sigma}\right)a^{\sigma_\nu}\right) = \left(f_f^{\sigma_\nu}\left(b^{\sigma_\nu}, \ell_p^{\sigma_\nu}, \varphi^{\sigma_\nu}\left(\frac{a^\sigma}{V^\sigma}\right)a^{\sigma_\nu}\right)\right),$$

where $\varphi^{\sigma_\nu}\left(\frac{a^\sigma}{V^\sigma}\right)$ is the impact index expressing the extent to which the effectiveness of services of natural capital in the processes of production of agricultural goods by farmer σ_ν in village σ is impaired by the phenomenon of congestion, $\frac{a^\sigma}{V^\sigma}$ expresses the degree of congestion, where V^σ is the stock of natural capital in village σ; and a^σ is the depletion of the stock of natural capital in the forest of village σ resulting from the agricultural activities carried out by all farmers in village σ; that is,

$$a^\sigma = \sum_\nu a^{\sigma_\nu}.$$

It is assumed that the following conditions are satisfied:

$$\varphi^{\sigma_\nu}\left(\frac{a^\sigma}{V^\sigma}\right) > 0, \quad \varphi^{\sigma_\nu\prime}\left(\frac{a^\sigma}{V^\sigma}\right) < 0, \quad \varphi^{\sigma_\nu\prime\prime}\left(\frac{a^\sigma}{V^\sigma}\right) < 0.$$

The impact coefficient of natural capital for farmer σ_ν, $\tau^{\sigma_\nu}\left(\frac{a^\sigma}{V^\sigma}\right)$, is defined as the relative rate of the marginal change in the impact index $\varphi^{\sigma_\nu}\left(\frac{a^\sigma}{V^\sigma}\right)$ due to the marginal increase in the total stock of natural capital V; that is

$$\tau^{\sigma_\nu}\left(\frac{a^\sigma}{V^\sigma}\right) = -\frac{\varphi^{\sigma_\nu\prime}\left(\frac{a^\sigma}{V^\sigma}\right)}{\varphi^{\sigma_\nu}\left(\frac{a^\sigma}{V^\sigma}\right)}.$$

We assume that the impact coefficients $\tau^{\sigma_\nu}\left(\frac{a^\sigma}{V^\sigma}\right)$ of natural capital in village σ are identical for all farmers in village σ; that is,

$$\tau^{\sigma_\nu}\left(\frac{a^\sigma}{V^\sigma}\right) = \tau^\sigma\left(\frac{a^\sigma}{V^\sigma}\right) \quad \text{for all } \sigma_\nu \text{ and } \frac{a^\sigma}{V^\sigma} > 0.$$

It is assumed that the following conditions are satisfied:

$$\tau^{\sigma}\left(\frac{a^{\sigma}}{V^{\sigma}}\right) > 0, \quad \tau^{\sigma\prime}\left(\frac{a^{\sigma}}{V^{\sigma}}\right) > 0 \quad \text{for all } \frac{a^{\sigma}}{V^{\sigma}} > 0.$$

Hence, we may assume, without loss of generality, that the impact index functions $\varphi^{\sigma_\nu}\left(\frac{a^{\sigma}}{V^{\sigma}}\right)$ are identical for all farmers σ_ν in village σ; that is,

$$\varphi^{\sigma_\nu}\left(\frac{a^{\sigma}}{V^{\sigma}}\right) = \varphi^{\sigma}\left(\frac{a^{\sigma}}{V^{\sigma}}\right) \quad \text{for all } \frac{a^{\sigma}}{V^{\sigma}} > 0.$$

Conditions for the Reforestation of the Forests in the Villages

The minimum quantities of factors of production required for farmer σ_ν in village σ to reforest the forest of village σ at the level z^{σ_ν} with the employment of labor for reforestation activities by $\ell_I^{\sigma_\nu}$ and the use of industrial goods by x^{σ_ν} are specified by an F-dimensional vector-valued function:

$$g^{\sigma_\nu}(z^{\sigma_\nu}, \ell_i^{\sigma_\nu}, x^{\sigma_\nu}) = \left(g_f^{\sigma_\nu}(z^{\sigma_\nu}, \ell_i^{\sigma_\nu}, x^{\sigma_\nu})\right).$$

We assume that, for each farmer σ_ν in village σ, marginal rates of substitution between any pair of the level of reforestation, the employment of labor for reforestation activities, and the use of industrial goods are smooth and diminishing, that there are always trade-offs among them, and that the conditions of constant returns to scale prevail. That is, we assume:

(T_i^{σ}1) $g^{\sigma_\nu}(z^{\sigma_\nu}, \ell_i^{\sigma_\nu}, x^{\sigma_\nu})$ are defined, positive, continuous, and continuously twice-differentiable with respect to $(z^{\sigma_\nu}, \ell_i^{\sigma_\nu}, x^{\sigma_\nu})$.

(T_i^{σ}2) $g_{z^{\sigma_\nu}}^{\sigma_\nu}(z^{\sigma_\nu}, \ell_i^{\sigma_\nu}, a^{\sigma_\nu}) > 0, \quad g_{\ell_i^{\sigma_\nu}}^{\sigma_\nu}(z^{\sigma_\nu}, \ell_i^{\sigma_\nu}, a^{\sigma_\nu}) < 0,$
$g_{a^{\sigma_\nu}}^{\sigma_\nu}(z^{\sigma_\nu}, \ell_i^{\sigma_\nu}, a^{\sigma_\nu}) < 0.$

(T_i^{σ}3) $g^{\sigma_\nu}(z^{\sigma_\nu}, \ell_i^{\sigma_\nu}, x^{\sigma_\nu})$ are strictly quasi-convex with respect to $(z^{\sigma_\nu}, \ell_i^{\sigma_\nu}, x^{\sigma_\nu})$.

(T_i^{σ}4) $g^{\sigma_\nu}(z^{\sigma_\nu}, \ell_i^{\sigma_\nu}, x^{\sigma_\nu})$ are homogeneous of order 1 with respect to $(z^{\sigma_\nu}, \ell_i^{\sigma_\nu}, x^{\sigma_\nu})$.

Production Possibility Sets of the Villages

For each village σ, we denote the amount of agricultural products, the level of reforestation, the employment of labor, the use of produced goods, and the depletion of natural capital in the forest of village σ, respectively, by b^σ, z^σ, ℓ^σ, x^σ, and a^σ. For each village σ, the production possibility set T^σ consists of all combinations of $(b^\sigma, z^\sigma, \ell^\sigma, x^\sigma, a^\sigma)$ such that

$$b^\sigma = \sum_\nu b^{\sigma_\nu}, \quad z^\sigma = \sum_\nu z^{\sigma_\nu}, \quad \ell^\sigma = \sum_\nu \ell^{\sigma_\nu} \quad (\ell^{\sigma_\nu} = \ell_p^{\sigma_\nu} + \ell_i^{\sigma_\nu}),$$

$$x^\sigma = \sum_\nu x^{\sigma_\nu}, \quad a^\sigma = \sum_\nu a^{\sigma_\nu}$$

$$\sum_\nu f^{\sigma_\nu}\left(b^{\sigma_\nu}, \ell_p^{\sigma_\nu}, \varphi^\sigma\left(\frac{a^\sigma}{V^\sigma}\right) a^{\sigma_\nu}\right) + \sum_\nu g^{\sigma_\nu}(z^{\sigma_\nu}, \ell_i^{\sigma_\nu}, x^{\sigma_\nu}) \leqq K^\sigma.$$

Postulates ($\mathrm{T}_p^\sigma 1$–$\mathrm{T}_p^\sigma 3$) and ($\mathrm{T}_i^\sigma 1$–$\mathrm{T}_i^\sigma 3$) imply that the production possibility set T^σ for the production of agricultural goods in village σ is a closed, convex set of $J + 1 + 1 + I + 1$-dimensional vectors $(b^\sigma, z^\sigma, \ell^\sigma, x^\sigma, a^\sigma)$.

The Producer Optimum for the Production of Agricultural Goods

As in the case of industrial firms, conditions of the producer optimum for the production of agricultural goods and the reforestation of the forest in the villages may be obtained. We denote by θ^σ the imputed price of resources in the forest of village σ.

Each village σ chooses the combination $(b^\sigma, z^\sigma, \ell^\sigma, x^\sigma, a^\sigma)$ of production of agricultural goods b^σ, level of reforestation z^σ, employment of labor ℓ^σ, and depletion of natural capital a^σ that maximizes net profit

$$\pi b^\sigma + \psi^\sigma z^\sigma - w\ell^\sigma - p x^\sigma - \theta^\sigma a^\sigma,$$

over $(b^\sigma, z^\sigma, \ell^\sigma, x^\sigma, a^\sigma) \in T^\sigma$, where ψ^σ and θ^σ are, respectively, the imputed prices of the stock of natural capital and resources in the forest of village σ.

Postulates ($\mathrm{T}_p^\sigma 1$–$\mathrm{T}_p^\sigma 3$) and ($\mathrm{T}_i^\sigma 1$–$\mathrm{T}_i^\sigma 3$) for the agricultural and reforestation activities in village σ ensure that for any combination of prices of agricultural goods π, imputed price of stock of natural capital ψ^σ, wage rate w, and imputed price of resources in the forest θ^σ, the optimum combination $(b^\sigma, z^\sigma, \ell^\sigma, x^\sigma, a^\sigma)$ always exists and is uniquely determined.

The optimum combination $(b^\sigma, z^\sigma, \ell^\sigma, x^\sigma, a^\sigma)$ may be characterized by the marginality conditions, in exactly the same manner as in the case of private firms in the industrial sector. If we denote by $r^\sigma = (r_f^\sigma)$

$[r_f^\sigma \geqq 0]$ the vector of imputed rental prices of fixed factors of production in village σ, the optimum conditions are

$$\pi \leqq r^\sigma f^{\sigma_\nu}_{b^{\sigma_\nu}}\left(b^{\sigma_\nu}, \ell_p^{\sigma_\nu}, \varphi^\sigma\left(\frac{a^\sigma}{V^\sigma}\right)a^{\sigma_\nu}\right) \quad (\text{mod.}\, b^{\sigma_\nu}) \tag{10}$$

$$w \geqq r^\sigma\left[-f^{\sigma_\nu}_{\ell^{\sigma_\nu}}\left(b^{\sigma_\nu}, \ell_p^{\sigma_\nu}, \varphi^\sigma\left(\frac{a^\sigma}{V^\sigma}\right)a^{\sigma_\nu}\right)\right] \quad (\text{mod.}\, \ell_p^{\sigma_\nu}) \tag{11}$$

$$\theta^\sigma \geqq r^\sigma\left[-f^{\sigma_\nu}_{a^{\sigma_\nu}}\left(b^{\sigma_\nu}, \ell_p^{\sigma_\nu}, \varphi^\sigma\left(\frac{a^\sigma}{V^\sigma}\right)a^{\sigma_\nu}\right)\varphi^\sigma\left(\frac{a^\sigma}{V^\sigma}\right)\right] \quad (\text{mod.}\, a^{\sigma_\nu}) \tag{12}$$

$$\psi^\sigma \leqq r^\sigma g^{\sigma_\nu}_{z^{\sigma_\nu}}\left(z^{\sigma_\nu}, \ell_i^{\sigma_\nu}, x^{\sigma_\nu}\right) \quad (\text{mod.}\, z^{\sigma_\nu}) \tag{13}$$

$$w \geqq r^\sigma\left[-g^{\sigma_\nu}_{\ell_I^{\sigma_\nu}}\left(z^{\sigma_\nu}, \ell_i^{\sigma_\nu}, x^{\sigma_\nu}\right)\right] \quad (\text{mod.}\, \ell_i^{\sigma_\nu}) \tag{14}$$

$$\theta^\sigma \geqq r^\sigma\left[-g^{\sigma_\nu}_{x^{\sigma_\nu}}\left(z^{\sigma_\nu}, \ell_i^{\sigma_\nu}, x^{\sigma_\nu}\right)\right] \quad (\text{mod.}\, x^{\sigma_\nu}) \tag{15}$$

$$\sum_\nu f^{\sigma_\nu}\left(b^{\sigma_\nu}, \ell_p^{\sigma_\nu}, \varphi^\sigma\left(\frac{a^\sigma}{V^\sigma}\right)a^{\sigma_\nu}\right) + \sum_\nu g^{\sigma_\nu}\left(z^{\sigma_\nu}, \ell_i^{\sigma_\nu}, x^{\sigma_\nu}\right) \leqq K^\sigma \quad (\text{mod.}\, r^\sigma), \tag{16}$$

where

$$b^\sigma = \sum_\nu b^{\sigma_\nu}, \quad z^\sigma = \sum_\nu z^{\sigma_\nu}, \quad \ell^\sigma = \sum_\nu \ell^{\sigma_\nu} \quad \left(\ell^{\sigma_\nu} = \ell_p^{\sigma_\nu} + \ell_i^{\sigma_\nu}\right),$$
$$x^\sigma = \sum_\nu x^{\sigma_\nu}, \quad a^\sigma = \sum_\nu a^{\sigma_\nu}.$$

Condition (10) expresses the principle that the choice of production technologies and levels of agricultural production by farmer σ_ν in village σ are adjusted so as to equate marginal factor costs with the prices of agricultural goods.

Condition (11) means that employment of labor for agricultural activities is adjusted so that the marginal gains due to the marginal increase in the employment are equal to wage rate w when $\ell_p^{\sigma_\nu} > 0$ and are not larger than w when $\ell_p^{\sigma_\nu} = 0$.

Condition (12) means that the use of resources in the forest of village σ by farmer σ_ν in village σ is adjusted so that the marginal gains due to the marginal increase in the use of resources in the forest of village σ are equal to imputed price θ^σ when $a^{\sigma_\nu} > 0$ and are not larger than θ^σ when $a^{\sigma_\nu} = 0$.

Condition (13) expresses the principle that the choice of production technologies and the levels of reforestation by farmer σ_ν in village σ

are adjusted so as to equate marginal factor costs with the imputed price of the stock of capital.

Condition (14) means that employment of labor for reforestation activities is adjusted so that the marginal gains due to the marginal increase in the employment are equal to wage rate w when $\ell_P^{\sigma_\nu} > 0$ and are not larger than w when $\ell_P^{\sigma_\nu} = 0$.

Condition (15) means that the use of industrial goods by farmer σ_ν in village σ is adjusted so that the marginal gains due to the marginal increase in the use of industrial goods are equal to price p_j when $x_j^\nu > 0$ and are not larger than p_j when $x_j^\nu = 0$.

Condition (16) means that the employments of fixed factors of production do not exceed the endowments, and the conditions of full employment are satisfied for factor of production f whenever imputed rental price r_f^σ is positive.

We have assumed that the technologies are subject to constant returns to scale ($T_p^\sigma 4$) and ($T_i^\sigma 4$), and thus, in view of the Euler identity, conditions (10)–(13) imply that

$$
\begin{aligned}
&\pi b^\sigma + \psi^\sigma z^\sigma - w\ell^\sigma - px^\sigma - \theta^\sigma a^\sigma \\
&\quad = \pi \sum_\nu b^{\sigma_\nu} + \psi^\sigma \sum_\nu z^{\sigma_\nu} - w\left[\sum_\nu \ell_p^{\sigma_\nu} + \sum_\nu \ell_i^{\sigma_\nu}\right] \\
&\qquad - p\sum_\nu x^{\sigma_\nu} - \theta^\sigma \sum_\nu a^{\sigma_\nu} \\
&\quad = \sum_\nu \left[\pi b^{\sigma_\nu} - w\ell_p^{\sigma_\nu} - \theta^\sigma a^{\sigma_\nu}\right] + \sum_\nu \left[\psi^\sigma z^{\sigma_\nu} - w\ell_i^{\sigma_\nu} - px^{\sigma_\nu}\right] \\
&\quad = \sum_\nu r^\sigma \left[f_{b^{\sigma_\nu}}^{\sigma_\nu}\left(b^{\sigma_\nu}, \ell_p^{\sigma_\nu}, \varphi^\sigma\left(\frac{a^\sigma}{V^\sigma}\right)a^{\sigma_\nu}\right) b^{\sigma_\nu} \right. \\
&\qquad + f_{\ell^{\sigma_\nu}}^{\sigma_\nu}\left(b^{\sigma_\nu}, \ell_p^{\sigma_\nu}, \varphi^\sigma\left(\frac{a^\sigma}{V^\sigma}\right)a^{\sigma_\nu}\right) \ell_p^{\sigma_\nu} \\
&\qquad \left. + f_{a^{\sigma_\nu}}^{\sigma_\nu}\left(b^{\sigma_\nu}, \ell_p^{\sigma_\nu}, \varphi^\sigma\left(\frac{a^\sigma}{V^\sigma}\right)a^{\sigma_\nu}\right) \varphi^\sigma\left(\frac{a^\sigma}{V^\sigma}\right)a^{\sigma_\nu}\right] \\
&\qquad + \sum_\nu r^\sigma \left[g_{z^{\sigma_\nu}}^{\sigma_\nu}(z^{\sigma_\nu}, \ell_i^{\sigma_\nu}, x^{\sigma_\nu}) z^{\sigma_\nu} \right. \\
&\qquad \left. + g_{\ell_i^{\sigma_\nu}}^{\sigma_\nu}(z^{\sigma_\nu}, \ell_i^{\sigma_\nu}, x^{\sigma_\nu})\, \ell_i^{\sigma_\nu} + g_{x^{\sigma_\nu}}^{\sigma_\nu}(z^{\sigma_\nu}, \ell_i^{\sigma_\nu}, x^{\sigma_\nu})\, x^{\sigma_\nu}\right] \\
&\quad = r^\sigma \left[\sum_\nu f^{\sigma_\nu}\left(b^{\sigma_\nu}, \ell_p^{\sigma_\nu}, \varphi^\sigma\left(\frac{a^\sigma}{V^\sigma}\right)a^{\sigma_\nu}\right) + \sum_\nu g^{\sigma_\nu}(z^{\sigma_\nu}, \ell_i^{\sigma_\nu}, x^{\sigma_\nu})\right] \\
&\quad = r^\sigma K^\sigma. \qquad (17)
\end{aligned}
$$

That is, for each village σ, the net evaluation of agricultural activities carried out by farmers in the village is equal to the sum of the imputed rental payments to fixed factors of production in village σ. As in the case for industrial firms, the meaning of relation (17) may be better brought out, if we rewrite it as

$$\pi b^\sigma + \psi^\sigma z^\sigma = w\ell^\sigma + px^\sigma + \theta^\sigma a^\sigma + r^\sigma K^\sigma.$$

For each village σ, the sum of the values of agricultural output $\pi\, b^\sigma$ and reforestation $\psi^\sigma z^\sigma$ is equal to the sum of wages $w\ell^\sigma$, payments for industrial goods px^σ, payments for the use of resources in the forest $\theta^\sigma a^\sigma$, and payments in terms of the imputed rental prices made to fixed factors of production $r^\sigma K^\sigma$. The validity of the Menger-Wieser principle of imputation is assured for the case of the production of agricultural goods and the reforestation of the forest.

4. MARKET EQUILIBRIUM FOR THE AGRARIAN MODEL OF SOCIAL COMMON CAPITAL

We first recapitulate the basic premises of the model of agriculture as social common capital introduced in the previous sections.

The Consumer Optimum

Each individual ν chooses the combination of consumption of industrial and agricultural goods, (c^ν, b^ν), that maximizes the utility of individual ν

$$u^\nu = \phi^\nu(V)u^\nu(c^\nu, b^\nu)$$

subject to the budget constraint

$$pc^\nu + \pi b^\nu = y^\nu, \tag{18}$$

where y^ν is the income of individual ν, $\phi^\nu(V)$ is the impact index of natural capital for individual ν, V is the aggregate sum of the stock of natural capital in all forests in the society,

$$V = \sum_\sigma V^\sigma,$$

and V^σ is the stock of natural capital in the forest of village σ.

The optimum combination of consumption of industrial and agricultural goods, (c^ν, b^ν), is characterized by the following marginality conditions:

$$\alpha^\nu \phi^\nu(V) u^\nu_{c^\nu}(c^\nu, b^\nu) \leqq p \quad (\text{mod. } c^\nu) \tag{19}$$

$$\alpha^\nu \phi^\nu(V) u^\nu_{b^\nu}(c^\nu, b^\nu) \leqq \pi \quad (\text{mod. } b^\nu). \tag{20}$$

The following basic identity holds:

$$\alpha^\nu u^\nu(c^\nu, \varphi^\nu(a) a^\nu) = pc^\nu + \theta a^\nu = y^\nu. \tag{21}$$

The Producer Optimum for Private Firms in the Industrial Sector

Each private firm μ in the industrial sector chooses the combination (x^μ, ℓ^μ, b^μ) of production of industrial goods x^μ, employment of labor ℓ^μ, and use of agricultural goods b^μ that maximizes net profit

$$px^\mu - w\ell^\mu - \pi b^\mu$$

over $(x^\mu, \ell^\mu, b^\mu) \in T^\mu$, where T^μ is the production possibility set of firm μ:

$$T^\mu = \{(x^\mu, \ell^\mu, b^\mu): (x^\mu, \ell^\mu, b^\mu) \geqq 0,\ f^\mu(x^\mu, \ell^\mu, b^\mu) \leqq K^\mu\}.$$

The optimum conditions are

$$p \leqq r^\mu f^\mu_{x^\mu}(x^\mu, \ell^\mu, b^\mu) \quad (\text{mod. } x^\mu) \tag{22}$$

$$w \geqq r^\mu \left[-f^\mu_{\ell^\mu}(x^\mu, \ell^\mu, b^\mu)\right] \quad (\text{mod. } \ell^\mu) \tag{23}$$

$$\pi \geqq r^\mu \left[-f^\mu_{b^\mu}(x^\mu, \ell^\mu, b^\mu)\right] \quad (\text{mod. } b^\mu) \tag{24}$$

$$f^\mu(x^\mu, \ell^\mu, b^\mu) \leqq K^\mu \quad (\text{mod. } r^\mu), \tag{25}$$

where r^μ is the vector of imputed rental prices of fixed factors of production of firm μ.

The following basic identity holds:

$$px^\mu - w\ell^\mu - \pi b^\mu = r^\mu K^\mu. \tag{26}$$

The Producer Optimum for the Villages

Each village σ choose the combination $(b^\sigma, z^\sigma, \ell^\sigma, x^\sigma, a^\sigma)$ of production of agricultural goods b^σ, level of reforestation z^σ, employment of labor ℓ^σ, and depletion of natural capital a^σ that maximizes net profit

$$\pi b^\sigma + \psi^\sigma z^\sigma - w\ell^\sigma - px^\sigma - \theta^\sigma a^\sigma$$

over $(b^\sigma, z^\sigma, \ell^\sigma, x^\sigma, a^\sigma) \in T^\sigma$, where ψ^σ and θ^σ are, respectively, the imputed price of stock of natural capital and that of resources in the forest of village σ.

The optimum conditions are

$$\pi \leqq r^\sigma f^{\sigma_\nu}_{b^{\sigma_\nu}}\left(b^{\sigma_\nu}, \ell^{\sigma_\nu}_p, \varphi^\sigma\left(\frac{a^\sigma}{V^\sigma}\right)a^{\sigma_\nu}\right) \quad (\text{mod.}\, b^{\sigma_\nu}) \tag{27}$$

$$w \geqq r^\sigma\left[-f^{\sigma_\nu}_{\ell^{\sigma_\nu}_p}\left(b^{\sigma_\nu}, \ell^{\sigma_\nu}_p, \varphi^\sigma\left(\frac{a^\sigma}{V^\sigma}\right)a^{\sigma_\nu}\right)\right] \quad (\text{mod.}\, \ell^{\sigma_\nu}_p) \tag{28}$$

$$\theta^\sigma \geqq r^\sigma\left[-f^{\sigma_\nu}_{a^{\sigma_\nu}}\left(b^{\sigma_\nu}, \ell^{\sigma_\nu}_p, \varphi^\sigma\left(\frac{a^\sigma}{V^\sigma}\right)a^{\sigma_\nu}\right)\varphi^\sigma\left(\frac{a^\sigma}{V^\sigma}\right)\right] \quad (\text{mod.}\, a^{\sigma_\nu}) \tag{29}$$

$$\psi^\sigma \leqq r^\sigma g^{\sigma_\nu}_{z^{\sigma_\nu}}(z^{\sigma_\nu}, \ell^{\sigma_\nu}_i, x^{\sigma_\nu}) \quad (\text{mod.}\, z^{\sigma_\nu}) \tag{30}$$

$$w \geqq r^\sigma\left[-g^{\sigma_\nu}_{\ell^{\sigma_\nu}_I}(z^{\sigma_\nu}, \ell^{\sigma_\nu}_i, x^{\sigma_\nu})\right] \quad (\text{mod.}\, \ell^{\sigma_\nu}_i) \tag{31}$$

$$\theta^\sigma \geqq r^\sigma\left[-g^{\sigma_\nu}_{x^{\sigma_\nu}}(z^{\sigma_\nu}, \ell^{\sigma_\nu}_i, x^{\sigma_\nu})\right] \quad (\text{mod.}\, x^{\sigma_\nu}) \tag{32}$$

$$\sum_\nu f^{\sigma_\nu}\left(b^{\sigma_\nu}, \ell^{\sigma_\nu}_p, \varphi^\sigma\left(\frac{a^\sigma}{V^\sigma}\right)a^{\sigma_\nu}\right) + \sum_\nu g^{\sigma_\nu}(z^{\sigma_\nu}, \ell^{\sigma_\nu}_i, x^{\sigma_\nu}) \leqq K^\sigma \quad (\text{mod.}\, r^\sigma), \tag{33}$$

where r^σ is the vector of imputed rental prices of natural capital in village σ, and

$$b^\sigma = \sum_\nu b^{\sigma_\nu}, \quad z^\sigma = \sum_\nu z^{\sigma_\nu}, \quad \ell^\sigma = \sum_\nu \ell^{\sigma_\nu} \quad (\ell^{\sigma_\nu} = \ell^{\sigma_\nu}_p + \ell^{\sigma_\nu}_i),$$
$$a^\sigma = \sum_\nu a^{\sigma_\nu}, \quad x^\sigma = \sum_\nu x^{\sigma_\nu}.$$

The following basic identity holds:

$$\pi b^\sigma + \psi^\sigma z^\sigma - w\ell^\sigma - px^\sigma - \theta^\sigma a^\sigma = r^\sigma K^\sigma. \tag{34}$$

Market Equilibrium for the Agrarian Model of Social Common Capital

We consider the institutional arrangements whereby subsidy payments are made by the government to the villages for the maintenance and reforestation of the forests of the villages. Subsidy payments are made at the rate τ for the reforestation of the forest of village σ, and taxes at the same rate are levied upon the depletion of resources of the forest of village σ. Thus, the subsidy payments to each village σ are given by

$$\tau(z^\sigma - a^\sigma),$$

where z^σ is the level of reforestation in the forest of village σ and a^σ is the stock of natural capital in the forest of village σ that are depleted by the agricultural activities carried on by the farmers in village σ.

On the other hand, village σ makes arrangements whereby farmers in village σ are required to pay social common taxes at the rate θ^σ for the use of natural resources in the forest of village σ. Total payments of social common taxes made by the farmers in village σ for the depletion of resources in the forest of village is given by $\theta^\sigma a^\sigma$.

Prices of industrial and agricultural goods, p, π, and wage rate w are determined on perfectly competitive markets. The social common capital subsidy rate τ is administratively determined by the central government, whereas the social common capital tax rates $\{\theta^\sigma\}$ are determined by the villages, both announced prior to the opening of the market.

Market equilibrium will be obtained if we find prices of industrial and agricultural goods p and π and wage rate w at which demand and supply are equal for all goods and labor.

At market equilibrium, the following equilibrium conditions must be satisfied in addition to optimality conditions (18)–(20), (22)–(25), and (27)–(33):

(i) At prices of industrial and agricultural goods p and π, total demand for goods are equal to total supply:

$$\sum_\mu x^\mu = \sum_\nu c^\nu + \sum_\sigma x^\sigma \quad \left(x^\sigma = \sum_\nu x^{\sigma_\nu}\right) \tag{35}$$

$$\sum_\sigma b^\sigma = \sum_\nu b^\nu + \sum_\mu b^\mu \quad \left(b^\sigma = \sum_\nu b^{\sigma_\nu}\right). \tag{36}$$

(ii) At wage rate w, total demand for employment of labor is equal to total supply:

$$\sum_{\nu} \ell^{\nu} = \sum_{\mu} \ell^{\mu} + \sum_{\sigma} \ell^{\sigma} \quad \left(\ell^{\sigma} = \sum_{\nu} \ell^{\sigma_{\nu}}, \ \ell^{\sigma_{\nu}} = \ell_{p}^{\sigma_{\nu}} + \ell_{i}^{\sigma_{\nu}} \right). \tag{37}$$

(iii) In each village σ, the stock of natural capital in the forest of village σ that is depleted, a^{σ}, is equal to the sum of resources in the forest of village σ used by the farmers in village σ for agricultural activities:

$$a^{\sigma} = \sum_{\nu} a^{\sigma_{\nu}}. \tag{38}$$

Subsidy payments made by the central government to the villages are given by

$$\tau \sum_{\sigma} (z^{\sigma} - a^{\sigma}),$$

and the net income of each village σ is given by

$$\tau (z^{\sigma} - a^{\sigma}) + \theta^{\sigma} a^{\sigma} - \psi^{\sigma} z^{\sigma},$$

where ψ^{σ} is the imputed price of the forest of village σ.

In the following discussion, we suppose that for any given levels of social common capital subsidy rate τ that is paid by the central government to the villages and social common capital tax rates θ^{σ} that are levied by the villages upon the farmers in the villages for the depletion of resources in the forests of the villages, the state of the economy that satisfies all conditions for market equilibrium generally exists and is uniquely determined.

The change of the stock of natural capital V^{σ} in the forest of each village σ, $\dot{V}^{\sigma}$, is given by

$$\dot{V}^{\sigma} = \gamma^{\sigma}(V^{\sigma}) + z^{\sigma} - a^{\sigma}, \tag{39}$$

where $\gamma^{\sigma}(V^{\sigma})$ is the ecological rate of increase in the stock of natural capital, z^{σ} is the increase in the stock of natural capital, and a^{σ} is the stock of natural capital depleted by the agricultural activities of the farmers in village σ. The function $\gamma^{\sigma}(V^{\sigma})$ specifies the rate of change in the stock of natural capital in the forest of village σ that is determined by the ecological and climatic conditions. It is assumed that for each village σ, $\gamma^\sigma(V^\sigma)$ is a concave function of the stock of natural capital in the forest of village σ; that is,

$$\gamma^{\sigma\prime\prime}(V^\sigma) < 0 \quad \text{for all } V^\sigma > 0.$$

Concerning National Income Accounting

Income y^ν of each individual ν is given as the sum of wages and dividend payments of private firms and social institutions, subtracted by the tax payments t^ν:

$$y^\nu = w\ell^\nu + \sum_\mu s^{\nu\mu} r^\mu K^\mu + \sum_\sigma s^{\nu\sigma}[r^\sigma K^\sigma - \psi^\sigma z^\sigma + \theta^\sigma a^\sigma + \tau(z^\sigma - a^\sigma)] - t^\nu, \quad (40)$$

where

$$s^{\nu\mu} \geqq 0, \quad \sum_\nu s^{\nu\mu} = 1, \quad s^{\nu\sigma} \geqq 0, \quad \sum_\nu s^{\nu\sigma} = 1.$$

Tax payments $\{t^\nu\}$ for individuals are arranged so that the sum of tax payments of all individuals is equal to the sum of social common capital subsidy payments made by the central government to the villages:

$$\sum_\nu t^\nu = \sum_\sigma \tau(z^\sigma - a^\sigma).$$

A word of explanation may be necessary for the definition of income y^ν of each individual ν given by (40), particularly regarding the way the net income of the villages are calculated; that is,

$$r^\sigma K^\sigma - \psi^\sigma z^\sigma + \theta^\sigma a^\sigma + \tau(z^\sigma - a^\sigma).$$

The first item, $r^\sigma K^\sigma$, is the net income each village σ receives from the agricultural activities and the management of the forest of the village, whereas the investment expenditures for the reforestation, $\psi^\sigma z^\sigma$, is subtracted from the net income. The third item, $\theta^\sigma a^\sigma$, is the payments made by the farmers in village σ to the village authorities for the depletion of the stock of natural capital in the forest of the village, whereas the fourth item, $\tau(z^\sigma - a^\sigma)$, is the subsidy payments made by the central government to village σ for the accumulation of the stock, net of depletion, of natural capital in the forest of village σ.

National income y is the sum of incomes of all individuals:

$$y = \sum_{\nu} y^{\nu} = \sum_{\nu} \left\{ w\ell^{\nu} + \sum_{\mu} s^{\nu\mu} r^{\mu} K^{\mu} + \sum_{\sigma} s^{\nu\sigma} [r^{\sigma} K^{\sigma} - \psi^{\sigma} z^{\sigma} + \theta^{\sigma} a^{\sigma} + \tau(z^{\sigma} - a^{\sigma})] - t^{\nu} \right\}.$$

By taking note of the equilibrium conditions

$$\sum_{\mu} x^{\mu} = \sum_{\nu} c^{\nu} + \sum_{\sigma} x^{\sigma}, \quad \sum_{\sigma} b^{\sigma} = \sum_{\nu} b^{\nu} + \sum_{\mu} b^{\mu}, \quad a = \sum_{\sigma} a^{\sigma},$$
$$\sum_{\nu} \ell^{\nu} = \sum_{\mu} \ell^{\mu} + \sum_{\sigma} \ell^{\sigma},$$

we have

$$\begin{aligned} y &= \sum_{\nu} w\ell^{\nu} + \sum_{\mu} r^{\mu} K^{\mu} + \sum_{\sigma} r^{\sigma} K^{\sigma} - \sum_{\sigma} \psi^{\sigma} z^{\sigma} \\ &\quad + \sum_{\sigma} \theta^{\sigma} a^{\sigma} + \sum_{\sigma} \tau(z^{\sigma} - a^{\sigma}) - \sum_{\nu} t^{\nu} \\ &= \sum_{\nu} w\ell^{\nu} + \sum_{\mu} (px^{\mu} - w\ell^{\mu} - \pi b^{\mu}) \\ &\quad + \sum_{\sigma} (\pi b^{\sigma} + \psi^{\sigma} z^{\sigma} - w\ell^{\sigma} - px^{\sigma} - \theta^{\sigma} a^{\sigma}) \\ &\quad - \sum_{\sigma} \psi^{\sigma} z^{\sigma} + \sum_{\sigma} \theta^{\sigma} a^{\sigma} = \sum_{\nu} (pc^{\nu} + \pi b^{\nu}). \end{aligned}$$

Thus we have established the familiar identity of two definitions of national income.

Imputed Prices of the Stock of Natural Capital and the Resources in the Forests of the Villages

Market equilibrium is obtained under the institutional arrangements whereby subsidy payments, at the administratively determined rate τ, are made by the central government to the villages for the maintenance and reforestation of the forests of the villages. The subsidy payments to each village σ are given by

$$\tau(z^{\sigma} - a^{\sigma}),$$

where z^{σ} is the level of reforestation in the forest of village σ and a^{σ} is the stock of natural capital in the forest of village σ that is depleted by the agricultural activities carried on by the farmers in village σ.

When each village σ determines the imputed price ψ^σ of the stock of natural capital in the forest of village σ, the effect on the net income of village σ is taken into account and is expressed by marginal social benefit of the stock of natural capital in the forest of village σ, to be denoted by MSB^σ. It concerns the marginal increase in the level of social utility U enhanced by the marginal decrease in the degree of congestion $\varphi^\sigma\left(\frac{a^\sigma}{V^\sigma}\right)$ with respect to the use of resources in the forest of village σ resulting from the marginal increase in the stock of natural capital V^σ in the forest of village σ. MSB^σ is given by

$$\begin{aligned}\mathrm{MSB}^\sigma &= -\frac{\partial}{\partial V^\sigma}\sum_\nu r^\sigma f^{\sigma_\nu}\left(b^{\sigma_\nu}, \ell_p^{\sigma_\nu}, \varphi^\sigma\left(\frac{a^\sigma}{V^\sigma}\right)a^{\sigma_\nu}\right) \\ &= -\sum_\nu r^\sigma f^{\sigma_\nu}_{a^{\sigma_\nu}}\left(b^{\sigma_\nu}, \ell_p^{\sigma_\nu}, \varphi^\sigma\left(\frac{a^\sigma}{V^\sigma}\right)a^{\sigma_\nu}\right)\tau^\sigma\left(\frac{a^\sigma}{V^\sigma}\right)\varphi^\sigma\left(\frac{a^\sigma}{V^\sigma}\right)\frac{a^\sigma}{V^\sigma}\frac{a^{\sigma_\nu}}{V^\sigma} \\ &= \sum_\nu \theta^\sigma\tau^\sigma\left(\frac{a^\sigma}{V^\sigma}\right)\frac{a^\sigma}{V^\sigma}\frac{a^{\sigma_\nu}}{V^\sigma} = \theta^\sigma\tau^\sigma\left(\frac{a^\sigma}{V^\sigma}\right)\left(\frac{a^\sigma}{V^\sigma}\right)^2.\end{aligned}$$

Thus, the imputed price of the stock of natural capital in the forest of village σ, ψ^σ, is given by

$$\psi^\sigma = \frac{1}{\delta}\left[\tau + \psi^\sigma\gamma^{\sigma\prime}(V^\sigma) + \theta^\sigma\tau^\sigma\left(\frac{a^\sigma}{V^\sigma}\right)\left(\frac{a^\sigma}{V^\sigma}\right)^2\right], \tag{41}$$

where $\gamma^{\sigma\prime}(V^\sigma)$ is the marginal rate of change in the stock of natural capital in the forest of village σ and δ is the social rate of discount that is assumed to be a given positive constant.

When each village σ determines the level of social common tax rate θ^σ that the farmers in village σ must pay for the depletion of natural capital in the forest of village σ, the effect on the net income of village σ is taken into account and is expressed by marginal social costs of the use of resources in the forest of village σ, to be denoted by MSC^σ. MSC^σ consists of two components. The first component is the decrease in the level of social utility due to the marginal decrease in the stock of natural capital in the forest of village σ that is represented by the imputed price ψ^σ of the stock of natural capital in the forest of village σ.

The second component is the marginal decrease in the net income of village σ that is induced by the marginal increase in the use of resources in the forest of village σ. It is given as the marginal decrease in the value, measured in imputed rental prices r^σ, of the minimum quantities of factors of production of village σ; that is,

$$\frac{\partial}{\partial a^\sigma}\sum_\nu r^\sigma\left[f^{\sigma_\nu}\left(b^{\sigma_\nu}, \ell_p^{\sigma_\nu}, \varphi^\sigma\left(\frac{a^\sigma}{V^\sigma}\right)a^{\sigma_\nu}\right)\right]$$

$$=\sum_\nu r^\sigma\left[-f_{a^{\sigma_\nu}}^{\sigma_\nu}\left(b^{\sigma_\nu}, \ell_p^{\sigma_\nu}, \varphi^\sigma\left(\frac{a^\sigma}{V^\sigma}\right)a^{\sigma_\nu}\right)\tau^\sigma\left(\frac{a^\sigma}{V^\sigma}\right)\varphi^\sigma\left(\frac{a^\sigma}{V^\sigma}\right)\frac{a^{\sigma_\nu}}{V^\sigma}\right]$$

$$=\sum_\nu \theta^\sigma\tau^\sigma\left(\frac{a^\sigma}{V^\sigma}\right)\frac{a^{\sigma_\nu}}{V^\sigma}=\theta^\sigma\tau^\sigma\left(\frac{a^\sigma}{V^\sigma}\right)\frac{a^\sigma}{V^\sigma}.$$

Hence, MSC^σ is given by

$$\text{MSC}^\sigma = \psi^\sigma + \theta^\sigma\tau^\sigma\left(\frac{a^\sigma}{V^\sigma}\right)\frac{a^\sigma}{V^\sigma}.$$

Thus, for the optimum level of social common tax rate θ^σ for village σ, the following relation is satisfied:

$$\theta^\sigma = \psi^\sigma + \theta^\sigma\tau^\sigma\left(\frac{a^\sigma}{V^\sigma}\right)\frac{a^\sigma}{V^\sigma}. \tag{42}$$

5. MARKET EQUILIBRIUM AND SOCIAL OPTIMUM

To explore the welfare implications of market equilibrium corresponding to the given level of social common capital subsidy rate τ and the prices θ^σ charged for the use of resources in the forests of villages σ, we consider the social utility U^* given by

$$U^* = \sum_\nu \alpha^\nu\phi^\nu(V)u^\nu(c^\nu, b^\nu) + \psi^\sigma[\gamma^\sigma(V^\sigma) + z^\sigma - a^\sigma],$$

where α^ν is the inverse of marginal utility of income of individual ν, c^ν and b^ν are, respectively, the quantities of industrial and agricultural goods consumed by individual ν, $\phi^\nu(V)$ is the impact index of natural capital for individual ν, V is the aggregate sum of the stock of natural capital in all forests in the society:

$$V = \sum_\sigma V^\sigma,$$

where V^σ is the stock of natural capital in the forest of village σ, ψ^σ is the imputed price of the stock of natural capital in the forest of each village σ, z^σ and a^σ are, respectively, the levels of reforestation and depletion of resources in the forest of village σ.

We consider the following maximum problem:

Maximum Problem for Social Optimum. Find the pattern of consumption and production of industrial and agricultural goods, employment of labor, depletion of natural capital and reforestation in the forests of the villages, $(c^\nu, b^\nu, x^\mu, \ell^\mu, b^\mu, b^{\sigma_\nu}, z^{\sigma_\nu}, \ell_p^{\sigma_\nu}.\ell_i^{\sigma_\nu}, x^{\sigma_\nu}, a^{\sigma_\nu}, a^\sigma)$, that maximizes the social utility

$$U^* = \sum_\nu \alpha^\nu \phi^\nu(V) u^\nu(c^\nu, b^\nu) + \psi^\sigma[\gamma^\sigma(V^\sigma) + z^\sigma - a^\sigma]$$

among all feasible patterns of allocation

$$\sum_\nu c^\nu + \sum_\sigma x^\sigma \leqq \sum_\mu x^\mu \tag{43}$$

$$\sum_\nu b^\nu + \sum_\mu b^\mu \leqq \sum_\sigma b^\sigma \tag{44}$$

$$\sum_\mu \ell^\mu + \sum_\sigma \ell^\sigma \leqq \sum_\nu \ell^\nu \tag{45}$$

$$a^\sigma \geqq \sum_\nu a^{\sigma_\nu} \tag{46}$$

$$f^\mu(x^\mu, \ell^\mu, b^\mu) \leqq K^\mu \tag{47}$$

$$\sum_\nu f^{\sigma_\nu}\left(b^{\sigma_\nu}, \ell_p^{\sigma_\nu}, \varphi^\sigma\left(\frac{a^\sigma}{V^\sigma}\right) a^{\sigma_\nu}\right) + \sum_\nu g^{\sigma_\nu}(z^{\sigma_\nu}, \ell_i^{\sigma_\nu}, x^{\sigma_\nu}) \leqq K^\sigma, \tag{48}$$

where

$$b^\sigma = \sum_\nu b^{\sigma_\nu}, \quad z^\sigma = \sum_\nu z^{\sigma_\nu}, \quad \ell^\sigma = \sum_\nu \ell^{\sigma_\nu} \quad \left(\ell^{\sigma_\nu} = \ell_p^{\sigma_\nu} + \ell_i^{\sigma_\nu}\right),$$
$$x^\sigma = \sum_\nu x^{\sigma_\nu}.$$

The maximum problem for social optimum may be solved in terms of the Lagrange method. Let us define the Lagrangian form:

$$L\left(c^\nu, b^\nu, x^\mu, \ell^\mu, b^\mu, b^{\sigma_\nu}, z^{\sigma_\nu}, \ell_p^{\sigma_\nu}.\, \ell_i^{\sigma_\nu}, x^{\sigma_\nu}, a^{\sigma_\nu}, a^\sigma; p, \pi, w, \theta^\sigma, r^\mu, r^\sigma\right)$$
$$= \sum_\nu \alpha^\nu \phi^\nu(V) u^\nu(c^\nu, b^\nu) + \sum_\sigma \psi^\sigma[\gamma^\sigma(V^\sigma) + z^\sigma - a^\sigma]$$
$$+ p\left(\sum_\mu x^\mu - \sum_\nu c^\nu - \sum_\sigma x^\sigma\right) + \pi\left(\sum_\sigma b^\sigma - \sum_\nu b^\nu - \sum_\mu b^\mu\right)$$

$$+ w\left(\sum_\nu \ell^\nu - \sum_\mu \ell^\mu - \sum_\sigma \ell^\sigma\right) + \sum_\sigma \theta^\sigma \left(a^\sigma - \sum_\nu a^{\sigma_\nu}\right)$$

$$+ \sum_\mu r^\mu [K^\mu - f^\mu(x^\mu, \ell^\mu, b^\mu)] + \sum_\sigma r^\sigma$$

$$\times \left[K^\sigma - \sum_\nu f^{\sigma_\nu}\left(b^{\sigma_\nu}, \ell_p^{\sigma_\nu}, \varphi^\sigma\left(\frac{a^\sigma}{V^\sigma}\right)a^{\sigma_\nu}\right) - \sum_\nu g^{\sigma_\nu}(z^{\sigma_\nu}, \ell_i^{\sigma_\nu}, x^{\sigma_\nu})\right], \tag{49}$$

where

$$b^\sigma = \sum_\nu b^{\sigma_\nu}, \quad z^\sigma = \sum_\nu z^{\sigma_\nu}, \quad \ell^\sigma = \sum_\nu \ell^{\sigma_\nu} \quad (\ell^{\sigma_\nu} = \ell_p^{\sigma_\nu} + \ell_i^{\sigma_\nu}),$$

$$x^\sigma = \sum_\nu x^{\sigma_\nu}.$$

The Lagrange unknowns $p, \pi, w, \theta^\sigma, r^\mu$, and r^σ are, respectively, associated with constraints (43), (44), (45), (46), (47), and (48).

The optimum solution may be obtained by differentiating the Lagrangian form (49) partially with respect to unknown variables $c^\nu, b^\nu, x^\mu, \ell^\mu, b^\mu, b^{\sigma_\nu}, z^{\sigma_\nu}, \ell_p^{\sigma_\nu}, \ell_i^{\sigma_\nu}, x^{\sigma_\nu}, a^{\sigma_\nu}, a^\sigma$, and putting them equal to 0, where feasibility conditions (43)–(48) are satisfied:

$$\alpha^\nu \phi^\nu(V) u_{c^\nu}^\nu(c^\nu, b^\nu) \leqq p \quad (\text{mod.}\, c^\nu) \tag{50}$$

$$\alpha^\nu \phi^\nu(V) u_{b^\nu}^\nu(c^\nu, b^\nu) \leqq \pi \quad (\text{mod.}\, b^\nu) \tag{51}$$

$$p \leqq r^\mu f_{x^\mu}^\mu(x^\mu, \ell^\mu, b^\mu) \quad (\text{mod.}\, x^\mu) \tag{52}$$

$$w \geqq r^\mu [-f_{\ell^\mu}^\mu(x^\mu, \ell^\mu, b^\mu)] \quad (\text{mod.}\, \ell^\mu) \tag{53}$$

$$\pi \geqq r^\mu [-f_{a^\mu}^\mu(x^\mu, \ell^\mu, b^\mu)] \quad (\text{mod.}\, b^\mu) \tag{54}$$

$$f^\mu(x^\mu, \ell^\mu, b^\mu) \leqq K^\mu \quad (\text{mod.}\, r^\mu) \tag{55}$$

$$\pi \leqq r^\sigma f_{b^{\sigma_\nu}}^{\sigma_\nu}\left[b^{\sigma_\nu}, \ell_p^{\sigma_\nu}, \varphi^\sigma\left(\frac{a^\sigma}{V^\sigma}\right)a^{\sigma_\nu}\right] \quad (\text{mod.}\, b^{\sigma_\nu}) \tag{56}$$

$$w \geqq r^\sigma \left[-f_{\ell_p^{\sigma_\nu}}^{\sigma_\nu}\left(b^{\sigma_\nu}, \ell_p^{\sigma_\nu}, \varphi^\sigma\left(\frac{a^\sigma}{V^\sigma}\right)a^{\sigma_\nu}\right)\right] \quad (\text{mod.}\, \ell_p^{\sigma_\nu}) \tag{57}$$

$$\theta^\sigma \geqq r^\sigma \left[-f_{a^{\sigma_\nu}}^{\sigma_\nu}\left(b^{\sigma_\nu}, \ell_p^{\sigma_\nu}, \varphi^\sigma\left(\frac{a^\sigma}{V^\sigma}\right)a^{\sigma_\nu}\right)\varphi^\sigma\left(\frac{a^\sigma}{V^\sigma}\right)\right] \quad (\text{mod.}\, a^{\sigma_\nu}) \tag{58}$$

$$\psi^\sigma \leqq r^\sigma g^{\sigma_\nu}_{z^{\sigma_\nu}}\left(z^{\sigma_\nu}, \ell^{\sigma_\nu}_i, x^{\sigma_\nu}\right) \quad (\text{mod. } z^{\sigma_\nu}) \tag{59}$$

$$w \geqq r^\sigma \left[-g^{\sigma_\nu}_{\ell^{\sigma_\nu}_i}\left(z^{\sigma_\nu}, \ell^{\sigma_\nu}_i, x^{\sigma_\nu}\right)\right] \quad (\text{mod. } \ell^{\sigma_\nu}_i) \tag{60}$$

$$\theta^\sigma \geqq r^\sigma \left[-g^{\sigma_\nu}_{a^{\sigma_\nu}}\left(z^{\sigma_\nu}, \ell^{\sigma_\nu}_i, x^{\sigma_\nu}\right)\right] \quad (\text{mod. } a^{\sigma_\nu}) \tag{61}$$

$$\sum_\nu f^{\sigma_\nu}\left[b^{\sigma_\nu}, \ell^{\sigma_\nu}_p, \varphi^\sigma\left(\frac{a^\sigma}{V^\sigma}\right) a^{\sigma_\nu}\right] + \sum_\nu g^{\sigma_\nu}\left(z^{\sigma_\nu}, \ell^{\sigma_\nu}_i, x^{\sigma_\nu}\right) \leqq K^\sigma \quad (\text{mod. } r^\sigma) \tag{62}$$

$$\theta^\sigma = \psi^\sigma + \theta^\sigma \tau^\sigma \left(\frac{a^\sigma}{V^\sigma}\right)\frac{a^\sigma}{V^\sigma}, \tag{63}$$

where $\tau^\sigma\left(\frac{a^\sigma}{V^\sigma}\right)$ is the impact coefficient of resources of natural capital in the forest of village σ.

Only equation (63) may need clarification. Partially differentiate Lagrangian form (49) with respect to a^σ, to obtain

$$\begin{aligned}
\frac{\partial L}{\partial a^\sigma} &= -\psi^\sigma + \theta^\sigma - \frac{\partial}{\partial a^\sigma}\sum_\nu r^\sigma f^{\sigma_\nu}\left[b^{\sigma_\nu}, \ell^{\sigma_\nu}_p, \varphi^\sigma\left(\frac{a^\sigma}{V^\sigma}\right) a^{\sigma_\nu}\right] \\
&= -\psi^\sigma + \theta^\sigma - \sum_\nu r^\sigma \left[- f^{\sigma_\nu}_{a^{\sigma_\nu}}\left(b^{\sigma_\nu}, \ell^{\sigma_\nu}_p, \varphi^\sigma\left(\frac{a^\sigma}{V^\sigma}\right) a^{\sigma_\nu}\right)\right. \\
&\qquad \left. \times \tau^\sigma\left(\frac{a^\sigma}{V^\sigma}\right)\varphi^\sigma\left(\frac{a^\sigma}{V^\sigma}\right)\frac{a^{\sigma_\nu}}{V^\sigma}\right] \\
&= -\psi^\sigma + \theta^\sigma - \sum_\nu \theta^\sigma \tau^\sigma\left(\frac{a^\sigma}{V^\sigma}\right)\frac{a^{\sigma_\nu}}{V^\sigma} \\
&= -\psi^\sigma + \theta^\sigma - \theta^\sigma \tau^\sigma\left(\frac{a^\sigma}{V^\sigma}\right)\frac{a^\sigma}{V^\sigma} = 0.
\end{aligned}$$

Thus, equation (63) is obtained.

Equation (63) means that the Lagrangian unknown θ^σ is nothing more than the imputed price of resources in the forest of village σ, as given by (42).

Applying the classic Kuhn-Tucker theorem on concave programming, the Euler-Lagrange equations (50)–(63), together with feasibility conditions (43)–(48), are necessary and sufficient conditions for the optimum solution of the maximum problem for social optimum.

It is apparent that the Euler-Lagrange equations (50)–(63), together with feasibility conditions (43)–(48), coincide precisely with the equilibrium conditions for market equilibrium where the price θ^σ charged for the use of resources in the forest of each village σ is equal to the imputed price of resources of natural capital in the forest of each village σ as given by (42):

$$\theta^\sigma = \psi^\sigma + \theta^\sigma \tau^\sigma \left(\frac{a^\sigma}{V^\sigma}\right) \frac{a^\sigma}{V^\sigma}.$$

As noted previously, marginality conditions (50) and (51) and the linear homogeneity hypothesis for utility functions $u^\nu(c^\nu, a^\nu)$ imply

$$\alpha^\nu u^\nu(c^\nu, \varphi^\nu(a)a^\nu) = pc^\nu + \theta\ a^\nu = y^\nu,$$

which, by summing over ν, yields

$$U = \sum_\nu y^\nu = y.$$

We have thus established the following proposition.

Proposition 1. *Consider an agrarian model of social common capital, where subsidy payments at the rate τ are made by the central government to the villages for the reforestation of the forests, whereas, in each village σ, social common taxes at the rate θ^σ are charged to the depletion of resources in the forest of village σ, where θ^σ is equal to the imputed price of resources in the forest of village σ, as given by*

$$\theta^\sigma = \psi^\sigma + \theta^\sigma \tau^\sigma \left(\frac{a^\sigma}{V^\sigma}\right) \frac{a^\sigma}{V^\sigma},$$

and ψ^σ is the imputed price of the stock of natural capital in the forest of village σ, as given by

$$\psi^\sigma = \frac{1}{\delta}\left[\tau + \psi^\sigma \gamma^{\sigma\prime}(V^\sigma) + \theta^\sigma \tau^\sigma \left(\frac{a^\sigma}{V^\sigma}\right)\left(\frac{a^\sigma}{V^\sigma}\right)^2\right].$$

Then market equilibrium obtained under such a social common capital tax scheme is a social optimum in the sense that a set of positive weights for the utilities of individuals $(\alpha^1, \ldots, \alpha^n)$ $[\alpha^\nu > 0]$ exists such that the imputed social utility U^* given by

$$U^* = \sum_\nu \alpha^\nu \phi^\nu(V) u^\nu(c^\nu, b^\nu) + \psi^\sigma\,[\gamma^\sigma(V^\sigma) + z^\sigma - a^\sigma]$$

is maximized among all feasible patterns of allocation $(c^\nu, b^\nu, x^\mu, \ell^\mu, b^\mu, b^\sigma, z^\sigma, \ell^\sigma, x^\sigma, a^\sigma)$.

The level of social utility U at the social optimum is equal to national income y:

$$U = \sum_\nu \alpha^\nu \phi^\nu(V) u^\nu(c^\nu, b^\nu) = y.$$

Social optimum is defined with respect to the imputed social utility

$$U^* = \sum_\nu \alpha^\nu \phi^\nu(V) u^\nu(c^\nu, b^\nu) + \psi^\sigma[\gamma^\sigma(V^\sigma) + z^\sigma - a^\sigma],$$

where $(\alpha^1, \ldots, \alpha^n)$ is an arbitrarily given set of positive weights for the utilities of individuals. A pattern of allocation $(c^\nu, b^\nu, x^\mu, \ell^\mu, b^\mu, b^\sigma, z^\sigma, \ell^\sigma, x^\sigma, a^\sigma)$ is social optimum if the social utility U thus defined is maximized among all feasible patterns of allocation.

Social optimum necessarily implies the existence of the social common capital tax scheme, where the tax rate τ is given by $\tau = \tau(a)a$. However, the budgetary constraints for individuals

$$pc^\nu + \theta a^\nu = y^\nu$$

are not necessarily satisfied.

The Imputed Price of Natural Capital in the Forests of the Villages

The imputed price of the stock of natural capital in the forest of each village σ, ψ^σ, measures the extent to which the marginal increase in the stock of natural capital V^σ in village σ enhances the marginal increase in the level of social utility U, as expressed by

$$U = \sum_\nu \alpha^\nu \phi^\nu(V) u^\nu(c^\nu, b^\nu),$$

where α^ν is the inverse of marginal utility of income of individual ν, $\phi^\nu(V)$ is the impact index of natural capital for individual ν, V is the aggregate sum of the stock of natural capital in all forests in the society,

$$V = \sum_\sigma V^\sigma,$$

and V^σ is the stock of natural capital in the forest of village σ.

The effect of the marginal increase in the stock of natural capital V^σ in village σ on the level of social utility U is twofold. The first effect is the marginal increase in the level of social utility U resulting directly from the marginal increase in the total stock of natural capital V. As the marginal increase in the stock of natural capital V^σ in village σ induces the corresponding marginal increase in the total stock of natural capital V, the first effect is given by

$$\frac{\partial U}{\partial V} = \tau(V) \sum_\nu \alpha^\nu \phi^\nu(V) u^\nu(c^\nu, b^\nu) = \tau(V) y,$$

where y is national income

$$y = \sum_\nu y^\nu.$$

The second effect concerns the marginal increase in the level of social utility U enhanced by the marginal decrease in the degree of congestion $\varphi^\sigma\left(\frac{a^\sigma}{V^\sigma}\right)$ with respect to the use of resources of the forest in village σ resulting from the marginal increase in the stock of natural capital V^σ in village σ. As calculated above, the second effect is given by

$$-\frac{\partial}{\partial V^\sigma} \sum_\nu r^\sigma f^{\sigma_\nu}\left(b^{\sigma_\nu}, \ell^{\sigma_\nu}, \varphi^\sigma\left(\frac{a^\sigma}{V^\sigma}\right) a^{\sigma_\nu}\right) = \theta^\sigma \tau^\sigma \left(\frac{a^\sigma}{V^\sigma}\right)\left(\frac{a^\sigma}{V^\sigma}\right)^2.$$

Thus, the imputed price of the stock of natural capital in the forest of each village σ, ψ^σ, is given by

$$\psi^\sigma = \frac{1}{\delta}\left[\tau + \psi^\sigma \gamma^{\sigma\prime}(V^\sigma) + \theta^\sigma \tau^\sigma \left(\frac{a^\sigma}{V^\sigma}\right)\left(\frac{a^\sigma}{V^\sigma}\right)^2\right]. \tag{64}$$

The market equilibrium under the subsidy scheme at the rate τ corresponds to the sustainable allocation of scarce resources if, and only if, the imputed price ψ^σ of the stock of natural capital under the subsidy scheme at the rate τ is equal to the imputed price ψ^σ of natural capital in the forest of the village σ as given by (64); that is,

$$\tau = \tau(V) y.$$

We have thus established the following propositions.

Proposition 2. *Consider an agrarian model of social common capital in which subsidy payments at the rate τ are made by the central government to the villages for the reforestation of the forests, whereas, in each village*

σ, social common taxes at the rate θ^σ are charged to the farmers of the village σ for the depletion of resources in the forest of the village σ, as given by

$$\theta^\sigma = \psi^\sigma + \theta^\sigma \tau^\sigma \left(\frac{a^\sigma}{V^\sigma}\right) \frac{a^\sigma}{V^\sigma},$$

where ψ^σ is the imputed price of natural capital in the forest of the village σ, as given by

$$\psi^\sigma = \frac{1}{\delta}\left[\tau + \psi^\sigma \gamma^{\sigma\prime}(V^\sigma) + \theta^\sigma \tau^\sigma \left(\frac{a^\sigma}{V^\sigma}\right)\left(\frac{a^\sigma}{V^\sigma}\right)^2\right].$$

The rate of change in the stock of natural capital in the forest of each village σ, V^σ, is given by

$$\dot{V}^\sigma = \gamma^\sigma(V^\sigma) + z^\sigma - a^\sigma,$$

where $\gamma^\sigma(V^\sigma)$ is the ecological rate of increase in the stock of natural capital, z^σ is the investment in the stock of natural capital, and a^σ is the stock of natural capital depleted by the agricultural activities of the farmers in village σ.

Then market equilibrium obtained under such a social common capital subsidy and tax scheme induces a sustainable time-path of patterns of resource allocation if, and only if,

$$\tau = \tau(V)y,$$

where $\tau(V)$ is the impact coefficient of the welfare effect of forests and V is the total stock of natural capital in the forests of the villages.

Proposition 3. *Suppose a pattern of allocation $(c^\nu, b^\nu, x^\mu, \ell^\mu, b^\mu, b^\sigma, z^\sigma, \ell^\sigma, x^\sigma, a^\sigma)$ is a social optimum; that is, a set of positive weights for the utilities of individuals $(\alpha^1, \ldots, \alpha^n)$ exists such that the given pattern of allocation $(c^\nu, b^\nu, x^\mu, \ell^\mu, b^\mu, b^\sigma, z^\sigma, \ell^\sigma, x^\sigma, a^\sigma)$ maximizes the imputed social utility*

$$U^* = \sum_\nu \alpha^\nu \phi^\nu(V) u^\nu(c^\nu, b^\nu) + \psi^\sigma[\gamma^\sigma(V^\sigma) + z^\sigma - a^\sigma]$$

among all feasible patterns of allocation.

Then, a system $\{t^\nu\}$ of income transfer among individuals of the society exists such that

$$\sum_\nu t^\nu = 0,$$

and the given pattern of allocation $(c^\nu, b^\nu, x^\mu, \ell^\mu, b^\mu, b^\sigma, z^\sigma, \ell^\sigma, x^\sigma, a^\sigma)$ corresponds precisely to the market equilibrium under the social common capital tax scheme with the rate τ given by

$$\tau = \tau(V)y,$$

where $\tau(V)$ is the impact coefficient of the welfare effect of forests and V is the total stock of natural capital in the forests of the villages.

6. NATURAL CAPITAL AND LINDAHL EQUILIBRIUM

Lindahl Conditions

Let us recall the postulates for the behavior of individuals at market equilibrium in the agrarian model of social common capital. At market equilibrium, conditions for the consumer optimum are obtained if each individual ν chooses the combination (c^ν, b^ν) of the vectors of consumption of industrial and agricultural goods, c^ν and b^ν, in such a manner that the utility of individual ν

$$u^\nu = \phi^\nu(V)u^\nu(c^\nu, b^\nu)$$

is maximized subject to the budget constraint

$$pc^\nu + \pi b^\nu = y^\nu.$$

Let us first rewrite the budget constraint as follows:

$$pc^\nu + \pi b^\nu - \tau V^\nu = \hat{y}^\nu,$$

where

$$\hat{y}^\nu = y^\nu - \tau V^\nu, \quad \tau = \tau(V)y,$$

and, for each individual ν, V^ν expresses the virtual ownership of the forests of villages:

$$V^\nu = \sum_\sigma s^{\nu\sigma} V^\sigma \quad \left(s^{\nu\sigma} \geqq 0, \sum_\nu s^{\nu\sigma} = 1\right).$$

Lindahl conditions are satisfied if a system of individual tax rates $\{\tau^\nu\}$ exists such that

$$\sum_\nu \tau^\nu = \tau \quad (\tau^\nu \geqq 0 \quad \text{for all } \nu),$$

and for each individual ν, (c^ν, b^ν, V^ν) is the optimum solution to the following virtual maximum problem:

Find $(\bar{c}^\nu, \bar{b}^\nu, \overline{V}^{(\nu)})$ that maximizes

$$u^\nu = \phi^\nu(\overline{V}^{(\nu)})u^\nu(\bar{c}^\nu, \bar{b}^\nu)$$

subject to the virtual budget constraint

$$p\bar{c}^\nu + \theta\bar{b}^\nu - \tau^\nu\overline{V}^{(\nu)} = \hat{y}^\nu.$$

Because (c^ν, b^ν, V^ν) is the optimum solution of the virtual maximum problem for individual ν, the optimum conditions imply

$$\tau^\nu = \alpha^\nu\tau(V)\phi^\nu(V)u^\nu(c^\nu, b^\nu) = \tau(V)y^\nu,$$

where α^ν is the inverse of marginal utility of income y^ν of individual ν.

Hence,

$$\tau(V)yV^\nu = \tau(V)y^\nu V.$$

Thus, Lindahl conditions are satisfied if, and only if,

$$\tau(V)yV^\nu = \tau(V)y^\nu V \Leftrightarrow \frac{y^\nu}{y} = \frac{V^\nu}{V}.$$

Thus we have established the following proposition.

Proposition 4. *Consider an agrarian model of social common capital in which subsidy payments at the rate $\tau = \tau(V)y$ are made by the central government to the villages for the reforestation of the forests, where $\tau(V)$ is the impact coefficient of the welfare effect of forests and V is the total stock of natural capital in the forests of the villages.*

Then market equilibrium obtained under such a social common capital tax scheme is a Lindahl equilibrium if, and only if, income of individual ν, y^ν, is proportional to the virtual ownership of the forests of villages:

$$\frac{y^\nu}{y} = \frac{V^\nu}{V},$$

where, for each individual ν*,* V^ν *is the virtual ownership of the forests of the villages in the agricultural sector of the society*

$$V^\nu = \sum_\sigma s^{\nu\sigma} V^\sigma,$$

where $\{s^{\nu\sigma}\}$ *is the shares of forests in the villages owned by individual* ν*:*

$$s^{\nu\sigma} \geqq 0, \quad \sum_\nu s^{\nu\sigma} = 1.$$

7. ADJUSTMENT PROCESSES OF SOCIAL COMMON CAPITAL TAX RATES

In the previous sections, we have examined two patterns of resource allocation involving natural capital for the model of agriculture as social common capital: market allocation, on one hand, and social optimum, on the other.

Market allocation for the model of agriculture as social common capital is obtained as competitive equilibrium when subsidy payments at the rate $\tau = \tau(V)y$ are made by the central government to the villages for the reforestation of the forests, where $\tau(V)$ is the impact coefficient of the welfare effect of forests and V is the total stock of natural capital in the forests of the villages.

Social optimum is defined with respect to the imputed social utility

$$U^* = \sum_\nu \alpha^\nu \phi^\nu(V) u^\nu(c^\nu, b^\nu) + \psi^\sigma[\gamma^\sigma(V^\sigma) + z^\sigma - a^\sigma],$$

where $(\alpha^1, \ldots, \alpha^n)$ $[\alpha^\nu > 0]$ is an arbitrarily given set of positive weights for the utilities of individuals, where α^ν is the inverse of marginal utility of income of individual ν, $\phi^\nu(V)$ is the impact index of natural capital for individual ν, V is the aggregate sum of the stock of natural capital in all forests in the society,

$$V = \sum_\sigma V^\sigma,$$

and V^σ is the stock of natural capital in the forest of village σ, and for village σ, ψ^σ is the imputed price of the stock of natural capital in the forest of village σ, $\gamma^\sigma(V^\sigma)$ is the ecological rate of increase in the stock of natural capital, z^σ is the increase in the stock of natural capital, and a^σ is the stock of natural capital depleted by the agricultural activities of the farmers in the forest of village σ. A pattern of allocation is social optimum if the social utility U^* is maximized among all feasible patterns of allocation.

Market equilibrium with subsidy payments at the rate τ coincides with the social optimum with respect to the social utility U^* if, and only if, the subsidy rate τ is equal to the optimum rate $\tau(V)y$; that is,

$$\tau = \tau(V)y.$$

As the social common capital subsidy rate τ is to be announced prior to the opening of the market, we must devise adjustment processes with respect to the social common capital subsidy rate τ that are stable.

Let us consider the adjustment process with respect to the social common capital subsidy rate τ by the following differential equation:

$$\text{(A)} \qquad \dot{\tau} = k[\tau(V)y - \tau],$$

where the speed of adjustment k is a positive constant and all variables refer to the state of the economy at the market equilibrium with the social common capital subsidy rate τ.

Regarding the market equilibrium with the social common capital subsidy rate τ, the imputed price ψ^σ of the stock of natural capital in the forest of each village σ is given by

$$\psi^\sigma = \frac{1}{\delta}\left[\tau + \psi^\sigma \gamma^{\sigma\prime}(V^\sigma) + \theta^\sigma \tau^\sigma \left(\frac{a^\sigma}{V^\sigma}\right)\left(\frac{a^\sigma}{V^\sigma}\right)^2\right].$$

As the social utility U^* may be written as

$$U^* = y + \sum_\sigma \psi^\sigma \left[\gamma^\sigma(V^\sigma) + z^\sigma - a^\sigma\right],$$

an increase in the subsidy rate τ implies an increase in the imputed price ψ^σ, resulting in a decrease in national income y. Hence, the right-hand side of differential equation (A) is a decreasing function of the subsidy rate τ. Hence, we have established the following proposition.

Proposition 5. *Consider the adjustment process with respect to the social common capital subsidy rate τ defined by the differential equation*

$$\text{(A)} \qquad \dot{\tau} = k[\tau(V)y - \tau],$$

where the speed of adjustment k is a positive constant and all variables refer to the state of the economy at the market equilibrium with the social common capital subsidy rate τ.

Then differential equation (A) *is globally stable; that is, for any initial condition* τ_0, *the solution path to differential equation* (A) *converges to the stationary state, where*

$$\tau = \tau(V)y.$$

7

Global Warming and Sustainable Development

1. INTRODUCTION

The atmospheric concentration of greenhouse gases, particularly carbon dioxide, has been increasing since the Industrial Revolution, with an accelerated rate in the past three decades. According to the IPCC reports (1991a, 1992, 1996a, 2001a, 2002), it is estimated that if the emission of CO_2 and other greenhouse gases and the disruption of tropical rain forests were to continue at the present pace, global average air surface temperature toward the end of the twenty-first century would be 3–6°C higher than the level prevailing before the Industrial Revolution, resulting in drastic changes in climatic conditions and the disruption of the biological and ecological environments.

The problems of global warming are genuinely dynamic. From past human activities we have inherited an excess concentration of atmospheric CO_2, and the choices we make today concerning the use of fossil fuels and related activities significantly affect all future generations through the phenomenon of global warming that is brought about by the atmospheric concentrations of CO_2 due to the combustion of fossil fuels today. Thus, we explicitly have to take into account the changes in the welfare levels of all future generations caused by the increases in the atmospheric accumulations of CO_2.

In this chapter, we are primarily concerned with the economic analysis of global warming within the theoretical framework of dynamic analysis of global warming, as introduced in Uzawa (1991b, 2003). We are particularly concerned with the policy arrangements of a proportional carbon tax scheme under which the tax rate is made proportional either to the level of the per capita national income of the countries where greenhouse gases are emitted or to the sum of the national incomes of all countries in the world. In the first part of this chapter, we consider the case in which the oceans are the earth's only reservoir of CO_2, whereas in the second part, we explicitly take into consideration the role of the terrestrial forests in moderating processes of global warming by absorbing the atmospheric accumulation of CO_2, on the one hand, and in affecting the level of the welfare of people in the society by providing a decent and cultural environment, on the other.

2. CARBON DIOXIDE ACCUMULATED IN THE ATMOSPHERE

We denote by V_t the amount of CO_2 that has accumulated in the atmosphere at time t. The quantity V_t is measured in actual tons (in weights of carbon content) or in terms of the density of CO_2 in the atmosphere. We also adopt as the origin of the measurement the stable pre–Industrial Revolution level of 600 GtC (gigatons[10^9 tons] of carbon), approximately corresponding to the density of 280 ppm (parts per million). The current level of 750 GtC (approximately 360 ppm) is expressed as $V_t = 150$ GtC.

The premises of the dynamic model introduced in this chapter are primarily based on the scientific findings on global warming and related subjects reported by Keeling (1968, 1983), Dyson and Marland (1979), Takahashi et al. (1980), Marland (1988), Myers (1988), Ramanathan et al. (1985), and IPCC (1991a,b, 1996a,b, 2000, 2001a,b, 2002), among others, and a detailed description of the model was presented in Uzawa (1991b, 2003).

Changes of CO_2 Accumulations Owing to Natural Causes

The atmospheric accumulations of CO_2 change over time as the result of natural and anthropogenic factors. A certain portion of atmospheric concentrations of CO_2 is absorbed by the oceans (roughly estimated at 50%) and to a lesser extent by living terrestrial plants. In the simple dynamic model postulated in this section, the exchange of CO_2 between the atmosphere and the terrestrial biosphere is not taken into consideration.

Approximately 75–90 GtC of carbon are annually exchanged between the atmosphere and the surface oceans. The mechanisms by which atmospheric CO_2 is absorbed into the surface oceans are complicated. They partly depend on the extent to which the surface waters of the oceans are saturated with CO_2, on the one hand, and on the extent to which CO_2 has accumulated in the atmosphere in excess of the equilibrium level, on the other. Studies made by several meteorologists and oceanologists – in particular, Keeling (1968, 1983) and Takahashi et al. (1980) – suggest that the rate of ocean uptake is closely related to the atmospheric accumulations of CO_2 in excess of the stable, pre–Industrial Revolution level of 280 ppm.

In the simple dynamic model introduced in this chapter, we assume that the amount of atmospheric CO_2 annually absorbed by the oceans is given by μV_t, where V_t is the atmospheric concentrations of CO_2 measured in actual tons of CO_2, with the pre–Industrial Revolution level of 600 GtC as the origin of measurement, and the rate of absorption μ is a certain constant that is rather difficult to estimate. The studies made by Takahashi et al. (1980) and others indicate that the rate of absorption μ would have a magnitude of 2–4 percent. In what follows, we assume that $\mu = 0.04$.

In the simple dynamic model, we assume that the anthropogenic change in atmospheric CO_2 is exclusively caused by the combustion of fossil fuels in connection with industrial, agricultural, and urban activities.

The change in the atmospheric level of CO_2 is given by

$$\dot{V}_t = a_t - \mu V_t,$$

where a_t is the annual rate of increase in the atmospheric level of CO_2 due to anthropogenic activities and μV_t is the amount of atmospheric CO_2 annually absorbed by the oceans.

The rate of anthropogenic change in the atmospheric level of CO_2, a_t, is determined by the combustion of fossil fuels and is closely related to the levels of production and consumption activities conducted during the year observed.

3. THE SIMPLE DYNAMIC MODEL OF GLOBAL WARMING

We postulate that each greenhouse gas is measured so as to equate the greenhouse effect with that of CO_2. We postulate that the welfare effect of global warming is measured in relation to the stock of greenhouse gases that have accumulated in the atmosphere.

There are a finite number of individual countries in the world economy that share the earth's atmosphere as a common environment. Each country is generically denoted by $\nu = 1, \ldots, n$.

The behavioral characteristics of individual countries are expressed in the aggregate by two representative economic agents – the consumers, who are concerned with the choice of economic activities related to consumption, on the one hand, and the producers, who are in charge of the choice of technologies and levels of productive activities, on the other.

Specifications of the Utility Functions

We assume that the utility function for each country ν is expressed in the following manner:

$$u^\nu = u^\nu\left(c^\nu, a_c^\nu, V\right),$$

where $c^\nu = (c_j^\nu)$ is the vector of goods consumed in country ν, a_c^ν is the amount of CO_2 emissions released during the processes of consumption, and V is the atmospheric concentration of CO_2 measured in tons of carbon in CO_2.

We assume that for each country ν, utility function $u^\nu(c^\nu, a_c^\nu, V)$ satisfies the following neoclassical conditions:

(U1) Utility function $u^\nu(c^\nu, a_c^\nu, V)$ is defined, continuous, and continuously twice-differentiable for all $(c^\nu, a_c^\nu, V) \geqq 0$.

(U2) Marginal utilities are positive for the consumption of private goods c^ν, but the atmospheric concentrations of carbon dioxide have a negative marginal utility; that is,

$$u^\nu_{c^\nu}\left(c^\nu, a_c^\nu, V\right) > 0, \quad u^\nu_{a_c^\nu}\left(c^\nu, a_c^\nu, V\right) > 0, \quad u^\nu_V\left(c^\nu, a_c^\nu, V\right) < 0.$$

(U3) Marginal rates of substitution between any pair of consumption goods and CO_2 emissions are diminishing; or more specifically, $u^\nu(c^\nu, a_c^\nu, V)$ is strictly quasi-concave with respect to (c^ν, a_c^ν) for any given $V > 0$.

For each country ν, we also assume that utility function $u^\nu(c^\nu, a_c^\nu, V)$ is strongly separable with respect to (c^ν, a_c^ν) and V in the sense originally introduced by Goldman and Uzawa (1964), as discussed in detail in Uzawa (1991b, 2003); that is,

$$u^\nu = \varphi^\nu(V)\, u^\nu\,(c^\nu, a_c^\nu)\,.$$

As in the case of the models of social common capital introduced in the previous chapters, the function $\phi^\nu(V)$ expresses the extent to which people in country ν are adversely affected by global warming, which is referred to as the impact index of global warming. We assume that the impact index function $\phi^\nu(V)$ of global warming for each country ν satisfies the following conditions:

$$\phi^\nu(V) > 0, \quad \phi^{\nu\prime}(V) < 0, \quad \phi^{\nu\prime\prime}(V) < 0 \quad \text{for all } V > 0.$$

The impact coefficient of global warming for country ν is the relative rate of the marginal change in the impact index due to the marginal increase in the atmospheric accumulation of CO_2; that is,

$$\tau^\nu(V) = -\frac{\phi^{\nu\prime}(V)}{\phi^\nu(V)}.$$

We assume that the impact coefficients of global warming $\tau^\nu(V)$ are identical for all countries ν:

$$\tau^\nu(V) = \tau(V) \quad \text{for all } V > 0 \text{ and } \nu.$$

The impact coefficient function $\tau(V)$ satisfies the following conditions:

$$\tau(V) > 0, \quad \tau'(V) > 0 \quad \text{for all } V > 0.$$

As in Uzawa (1991b, 2003), the impact index function $\phi(V)$ of the following form is often postulated:

$$\phi(V) = (\hat{V} - V)^\beta, \quad 0 < V < \hat{V},$$

where $\hat{V}$ is the critical level of the atmospheric accumulation of CO_2 and β is the sensitivity parameter $(0 < \beta < 1)$. The critical level $\hat{V}$ of the atmospheric accumulation of CO_2 is usually assumed to be twice the level prevailing before the Industrial Revolution; that is, $\hat{V} = 600$ GtC. The impact coefficient $\tau(V)$ is given by

$$\tau(V) = \frac{\beta}{\hat{V} - V}.$$

Utility functions $u^\nu(c^\nu, a_c^\nu)$ satisfy the following neoclassical conditions:

(U′1) Utility function $u^\nu(c^\nu, a_c^\nu)$ is defined, positive, continuous, and continuously twice-differentiable for all $(c^\nu, a_c^\nu) \geqq 0$.

(U′2) Marginal utilities are positive for both the consumption of goods c^ν and CO_2 emissions a_c^ν:

$$u_{c^\nu}^\nu(c^\nu, a_c^\nu) \geqq 0, \quad u_{a_c^\nu}^\nu(c^\nu, a_c^\nu) \geqq 0 \quad \text{for all } (c^\nu, a_c^\nu) \geqq 0.$$

(U′3) Utility function $u^\nu(c^\nu, a_c^\nu)$ is strictly quasi-concave with respect to $(c^\nu, a_c^\nu) \geqq 0$.

(U′4) Utility function $u^\nu(c^\nu, a_c^\nu)$ is homogeneous of order 1 with respect to c^ν:

$$u^\nu(tc^\nu, ta_c^\nu) = tu^\nu(c^\nu, a_c^\nu) \quad \text{for all } (c^\nu, a_c^\nu) \geqq 0.$$

The Euler identity holds:

$$u^\nu(c^\nu, a_c^\nu) = u_{c^\nu}^\nu(c^\nu, a_c^\nu)\, c^\nu + u_{a_c^\nu}^\nu(c^\nu, a_c^\nu)\, a_c^\nu \quad \text{for all } (c^\nu, a_c^\nu) \geqq 0.$$

The Consumer Optimum

The world markets for produced goods are assumed to be perfectly competitive and prices of goods are denoted by a nonzero, nonnegative vector p ($p \geq 0$). Suppose carbon taxes at the rate θ^ν are levied upon the emission of CO_2 in each country ν. Carbon tax rate θ^ν is assumed to be nonnegative: $\theta^\nu \geqq 0$.

Suppose national income of country ν in units of world prices is given by y^ν. Then, the consumers in country ν chooses consumption vector c^ν and CO_2 emissions a_c^ν that maximize country ν's utility function

$$u^\nu(c^\nu, V) = \phi^\nu(V)\, u^\nu(c^\nu, a_c^\nu)$$

subject to the budget constraints

$$pc^\nu + \theta^\nu a_c^\nu = y^\nu, \quad (c^\nu, a_c^\nu) \geqq 0.$$

The optimum combination of consumption vector c^ν and CO_2 emissions a_c^ν is characterized by the following marginality conditions:

$$\alpha^\nu \phi^\nu(V)\, u_{c^\nu}^\nu(c^\nu, a_c^\nu) \leqq p \quad (\text{mod. } c^\nu) \tag{1}$$

$$\alpha^\nu \phi^\nu(V)\, u_{a_c^\nu}^\nu(c^\nu, a_c^\nu) \leqq \theta^\nu \quad (\text{mod. } a_c^\nu), \tag{2}$$

where α^ν is the inverse of the marginal utility of income y^ν of country ν.

If we note the Euler identity for the utility function $u^\nu(c^\nu, a_c^\nu)$ of each country ν, we have the following basic relation:

$$\alpha^\nu \phi^\nu(V) u^\nu\left(c^\nu, a_c^\nu\right) = pc^\nu + \theta^\nu a_c^\nu = y^\nu. \quad (3)$$

Specifications for Production Possibility Sets

The conditions concerning the production of goods in each country ν are specified by the production possibility set T^ν that summarizes the technological possibilities and organizational arrangements for country ν; the endowments of factors of production available in country ν are given.

We assume that there is a finite number of factors of production that are essentially needed in the production of goods. They are generically denoted by f $(f = 1, \ldots, F)$. Without loss of generality, we may assume that the factors of production needed in productive activities are the same for all countries involved.

The endowments of factors of production available in each country ν are expressed by an F-dimensional vector $K^\nu = (K_f^\nu)$, where $K^\nu \geq 0$.

In each country ν, the minimum quantities of factors of production required to produce goods by the vector of production $x^\nu = (x_j^\nu)$ with CO_2 emissions at the level a_p^ν are specified by an F-dimensional vector-valued function:

$$f^\nu\left(x^\nu, a_p^\nu\right) = \left(f_f^\nu\left(x^\nu, a_p^\nu\right)\right).$$

We assume that marginal rates of substitution between any pair of the production of goods and the emission of CO_2 are smooth and diminishing, there are always trade-offs among them, and the conditions of constant returns to scale prevail. That is, we assume

(T1) $f^\nu(x^\nu, a_p^\nu)$ are defined, positive, continuous, and continuously twice-differentiable for all $(x^\nu, a_p^\nu) \geqq 0$.

(T2) $f_{x^\nu}^\nu(x^\nu, a_p^\nu) > 0, \quad f_{a_p^\nu}^\nu(x^\nu, a_p^\nu) \leqq 0$ for all $(x^\nu, a_p^\nu) \geqq 0$.

(T3) $f^\nu(x^\nu, a_p^\nu)$ are strictly quasi-convex with respect to (x^ν, a_p^ν) for all $(x^\nu, a_p^\nu) \geqq 0$;

(T4) $f^\nu(x^\nu, a_p^\nu)$ are homogeneous of order 1 with respect to (x^ν, a_p^ν) for all $(x^\nu, a_p^\nu) \geqq 0$.

Hence, the following Euler identity holds:

$$f^\nu\left(x^\nu, a_p^\nu\right) = f_{x^\nu}^\nu\left(x^\nu, a_p^\nu\right) x^\nu + f_{a_p^\nu}^\nu\left(x^\nu, a_p^\nu\right) a_p^\nu \quad \text{for all } \left(x^\nu, a_p^\nu\right) \geqq 0.$$

The production possibility set of each country ν, T^ν, is composed of all combinations (x^ν, a_p^ν) of vectors of production x^ν and CO_2 emissions a_p^ν that are possibly produced with the organizational arrangements and technological conditions in country ν and the given endowments of factors of production K^ν of country ν. Hence, it may be expressed as

$$T^\nu = \left\{\left(x^\nu, a_p^\nu\right): \left(x^\nu, a_p^\nu\right) \geqq 0,\ f^\nu\left(x^\nu, a_p^\nu\right) \leqq K^\nu\right\}.$$

Postulates (T1–T3) imply that the production possibility set T^ν is a closed, convex set of $J+1$-dimensional vectors (x^ν, a_p^ν).

The Producer Optimum

The producers in country ν choose the combination (x^ν, a_p^ν) of vector of production x^ν and CO_2 emissions a^ν that maximizes net profit

$$px^\nu - \theta^\nu a_p^\nu$$

over $(x^\nu, a_p^\nu) \in T^\nu$.

Conditions (T1–T3) postulated above ensure that for any combination of price vector p and carbon tax rate θ^ν, the optimum combination (x^ν, a_p^ν) of vector of production x^ν and CO_2 emissions a_p^ν always exists and is uniquely determined.

To see how the optimum levels of production and CO_2 emissions are determined, let us denote the vector of imputed rental prices of factors of production by $r^\nu = (r_f^\nu)$, $[r_f^\nu \geqq 0]$. Then the optimum conditions are

$$p \leqq r^\nu f_{x^\nu}^\nu\left(x^\nu, a_p^\nu\right) \qquad (\text{mod. } x^\nu) \tag{4}$$

$$\theta^\nu \geqq r^\nu\left[-f_{a_p^\nu}^\nu\left(x^\nu, a_p^\nu\right)\right] \qquad (\text{mod. } a_p^\nu) \tag{5}$$

$$f^\nu\left(x^\nu, a_p^\nu\right) \leqq K^\nu \qquad (\text{mod. } r^\nu). \tag{6}$$

Condition (4) means the familiar principle that the choice of production technologies and the levels of production are adjusted so as to equate marginal factor costs with output prices.

Condition (5) similarly means that CO_2 emissions are controlled so that the marginal loss due to the marginal increase in CO_2 emissions is equal to carbon tax rate θ^ν when $a_p^\nu > 0$ and is not larger than θ^ν when $a_p^\nu = 0$.

Condition (5) means that the utilization of factors of production does not exceed the endowments and the conditions of full employment are satisfied whenever rental price r_f^ν is positive.

We have assumed that the technologies are subject to constant returns to scale (T4), and thus, in view of the Euler identity, conditions (2)–(4) imply that

$$\begin{aligned} px^\nu - \theta^\nu a_p^\nu &= r^\nu \left[f_{x^\nu}^\nu \left(x^\nu, a_p^\nu\right) x^\nu + f_{a_p^\nu}^\nu \left(x^\nu, a_p^\nu\right) a_p^\nu \right] \\ &= r^\nu f^\nu \left(x^\nu, a_p^\nu\right) = r^\nu K^\nu. \end{aligned}$$

That is, the net evaluation of output is equal to the sum of the rental payments to all factors of production.

Suppose all factors of production are owned by individual members of the country ν. Then, national income y^ν of country ν is equal to the sum of the rental payments $r^\nu K^\nu$ and the tax payments $\theta^\nu a^\nu$ ($a^\nu = a_c^\nu + a_p^\nu$) made for the emission of CO_2 in country ν; that is,

$$\begin{aligned} y^\nu &= r^\nu K^\nu + \theta^\nu a^\nu = \left(px^\nu - \theta^\nu a_p^\nu\right) + \theta^\nu a^\nu \\ &= pc^\nu + \theta^\nu a_c^\nu. \end{aligned}$$

Hence, national income y^ν of country ν is equal to the aggregate sum of the expenditures, thus conforming with the standard practice in national income accounting.

Market Equilibrium and Global Warming

We consider the situation in which carbon taxes at the rate of θ^ν are levied on the emission of CO_2 in each country ν.

Market equilibrium for the world economy is obtained if we find the prices of goods p at which total demand is equal to total supply:

$$\sum_\nu c^\nu = \sum_\nu x^\nu.$$

Total CO_2 emissions a are given by

$$a = \sum_\nu a^\nu, \quad a^\nu = a_c^\nu + a_p^\nu.$$

(i) Demand conditions in each country ν are obtained by maximizing utility function

$$u^\nu = \phi^\nu(V)\, u^\nu\,(c^\nu, a_c^\nu)$$

subject to budget constraints

$$pc^\nu + \theta^\nu a_c^\nu = y^\nu,$$

where y^ν is the national income of country ν.

(ii) Supply conditions in each country ν are obtained by maximizing net profits

$$px^\nu - \theta^\nu a_p^\nu$$

over $(x^\nu, a_p^\nu) \in T^\nu$.

(iii) Total CO_2 emissions in the world, a, are given as the sum of CO_2 emissions in all countries; that is,

$$a = \sum_\nu a^\nu, \quad a^\nu = a_c^\nu + a_p^\nu.$$

Deferential Equilibrium for Global Warming

Deferential equilibrium is obtained if, when each country chooses the levels of consumption production activities today, it takes into account the negative impact on the future levels of its own utilities brought about by the CO_2 emissions of that country today.

We suppose a virtual world in which the atmospheric accumulation of CO_2, V, is divided into $\{V^\nu\}$ such that

$$V = \sum_\nu V^\nu, \tag{7}$$

where V^ν is the atmospheric accumulation of CO_2 emitted by country ν since the time of the Industrial Revolution.

The rate of change in the atmospheric level of CO_2 emitted by each country ν, $\dot{V}^\nu$, is given by

$$\dot{V}^\nu = a^\nu - \mu V^\nu, \tag{8}$$

where a^ν is the annual rate of increase in the atmospheric level of CO_2 due to anthropogenic activities in country ν, and μ is the amount of atmospheric carbon dioxide annually absorbed by the oceans.

Consider the situation in which a combination (x^ν, a^ν) of production vector and CO_2 emissions is chosen in country ν. Suppose CO_2 emissions in country ν are increased by a marginal amount. This would induce a marginal increase in the aggregate amount of CO_2 emissions in the world, effecting a marginal increase in the atmospheric level of CO_2. The resulting marginal increase in the degree of future global warming would cause a marginal decrease in country ν's utility. Deferential equilibrium is obtained if this marginal decrease in country ν's future utility due to the marginal increase in CO_2 emissions today in country ν is taken into consideration in determining the levels of consumption, production, and CO_2 emissions today in country ν.

The marginal decrease in country ν's utility due to the marginal increase in CO_2 emissions in country ν today is given by the partial derivative, with minus sign, of the level of country ν's utility, measured in units of world prices

$$\alpha^\nu u^\nu = \alpha^\nu \phi^\nu(V)\, u^\nu\left(c^\nu, a_c^\nu\right),$$

where α^ν is the inverse of the marginal utility of income y^ν of country ν, with respect to atmospheric accumulations of CO_2 in country ν, V^ν; that is,

$$\begin{aligned} -\frac{\partial\left(\alpha^\nu u^\nu\right)}{\partial V} &= -\alpha^\nu \phi^{\nu\prime}(V)\, u^\nu\left(c^\nu, a_c^\nu\right) = \tau(V)\alpha^\nu \phi^\nu(V)\, u^\nu\left(c^\nu, a_c^\nu\right) \\ &= \tau(V) y^\nu, \end{aligned}$$

where $\tau(V)$ is the impact coefficient of global warming.

We assume that future utilities of country ν are discounted at a rate δ that is exogenously given. We also assume that the rate of utility discount δ is a positive constant and is identical for all countries in the world. As atmospheric carbon dioxide is annually absorbed by the rate μ, the imputed price ψ^ν of the atmospheric accumulations of CO_2 of each country ν is given by the discounted present value, with the discount rate $\delta + \mu$, of the marginal decrease in country ν's utility due to the marginal increase in CO_2 emissions in country ν; that is,

$$\psi^\nu = \frac{1}{\delta + \mu} \tau(V) y^\nu. \tag{9}$$

The choice of the levels of consumption, production, and CO_2 emissions for each country ν under the deferential behavioristic postulates then may be viewed as the optimum solution to the following maximum problem:

Find the combination $(c^\nu, x^\nu, a_c^\nu, a_p^\nu, a^\nu)$ of consumption vector, production vector, and CO_2 emissions that maximizes the imputed utility of country ν

$$u_*^\nu = \alpha^\nu \phi^\nu(V)\, u^\nu\,(c^\nu, a_c^\nu) - \psi^\nu a^\nu$$

subject to the constraints that

$$pc^\nu = px^\nu \tag{10}$$

$$f^\nu\left(x^\nu, a_p^\nu\right) \leqq K^\nu \tag{11}$$

$$a^\nu = a_c^\nu + a_p^\nu, \tag{12}$$

where V and ψ^ν are given.

The maximum problem is solved in terms of the Lagrangian form

$$\begin{aligned} &L^\nu\left(c^\nu, x^\nu, a_c^\nu, a_p^\nu, a^\nu; \lambda^\nu, \lambda^\nu r^\nu\right) \\ &\quad = [\alpha^\nu \phi^\nu(V)\, u^\nu\,(c^\nu, a_c^\nu) - \psi^\nu a^\nu] + \lambda^\nu\,(px^\nu - pc^\nu) \\ &\qquad + \lambda^\nu r^\nu\left[K^\nu - f^\nu\left(x^\nu, a_p^\nu\right)\right] + \lambda^\nu \theta^\nu\left(a^\nu - a_c^\nu - a_p^\nu\right), \end{aligned}$$

where the variables $\lambda^\nu, \lambda^\nu r^\nu, \lambda^\nu \theta^\nu$ are the Lagrangian unknowns associated with constraints (10), (11), and (12), respectively.

The optimum conditions are

$$\alpha^\nu \phi^\nu(V)\, u_{c^\nu}^\nu\,(c^\nu,\, a_c^\nu) \leqq p \quad (\text{mod. } c^\nu) \tag{13}$$

$$\alpha^\nu \phi^\nu(V)\, u_{a_c^\nu}^\nu\,(c^\nu,\, a_c^\nu) \leqq \theta^\nu \quad (\text{mod. } a_c^\nu) \tag{14}$$

$$p \leqq r^\nu f_{x^\nu}^\nu\left(x^\nu, a_p^\nu\right) \quad (\text{mod. } x^\nu) \tag{15}$$

$$\theta^\nu \geqq r^\nu\left[- f_{a_p^\nu}^\nu\left(x^\nu, a_p^\nu\right)\right] \quad (\text{mod. } a_p^\nu) \tag{16}$$

$$f^\nu\left(x^\nu, a_p^\nu\right) \leqq K^\nu \quad (\text{mod. } r^\nu), \tag{17}$$

where it may be assumed that with an appropriate change in notation, $\lambda^\nu = 1$ and

$$\theta^\nu = \psi^\nu = \frac{1}{\delta + \mu}\tau(V) y^\nu. \tag{18}$$

Marginality conditions (16) and (17) imply that net profits

$$px^\nu - \theta^\nu a_p^\nu$$

are maximized over the technological possibility set $(x^\nu, a_p^\nu) \in T^\nu$.

Hence, the conditions for deferential equilibrium in the dynamic context are identical to those for a standard market equilibrium when carbon taxes with rate θ^ν given by (18) are levied; that is,

(i) For each country ν, the combination (c^ν, a_c^ν) of consumption vector c^ν and CO_2 emissions a_p^ν maximizes country ν's utility function

$$u^\nu = \phi^\nu(V)\, u^\nu\,(c^\nu, a_c^\nu)$$

subject to the budgetary constraints

$$pc^\nu + \theta^\nu a_c^\nu = y^\nu,$$

where y^ν is the national income of country ν and the aggregate level of atmospheric CO_2 accumulations, V, is assumed to be given.

(ii) For each country ν, the combination (x^ν, a_p^ν) of production vector x^ν and CO_2 emissions a_p^ν that maximizes net profits

$$px^\nu - \theta^\nu a_p^\nu$$

over the technological possibility set $(x^\nu, a_p^\nu) \in T^\nu$, where tax rate θ^ν in each country ν is given by

$$\theta^\nu = \frac{1}{\delta + \mu} \tau(V) y^\nu.$$

Differential equilibrium for the world economy then is obtained if we find the prices of goods p at which total demand is equal to total supply:

$$\sum_\nu c^\nu = \sum_\nu x^\nu$$

and total CO_2 emissions, a, are given by

$$a = \sum_\nu a^\nu.$$

The preceding discussion may be summarized as the following proposition.

Proposition 1. *Deferential equilibrium corresponds precisely to the standard market equilibrium under the system of carbon taxes, where, in each country* ν, *carbon taxes are levied with the rate* θ^ν *that is proportional to the national income* y^ν *of each country* ν *with the discounted present value* $\frac{\tau(V)}{\delta+\mu}$ *of the impact coefficient of global warming* $\tau(V)$ *as the coefficient of proportion; that is,*

$$\theta^\nu = \frac{\tau(V)}{\delta+\mu} y^\nu,$$

where $\tau(V)$ *is the impact coefficient of global warming,*

$$\tau(V) = -\frac{\phi^{\nu\prime}(V)}{\phi^\nu(V)},$$

δ *is the rate of utility discount, and* μ *is the rate at which atmospheric carbon dioxide is annually absorbed by the oceans.*

In terms of the concept of sustainability introduced in Chapter 3, the sustainable time-path of development with respect to global warming is obtained if, and only if, deferential equilibrium is obtained at each moment in time.

4. UNIFORM CARBON TAXES AND SOCIAL OPTIMUM

In the previous section, we saw that deferential equilibrium may be obtained as the standard market equilibrium provided the carbon tax rate θ^ν in each country ν is equal to

$$\theta^\nu = \frac{\tau(V)}{\delta+\mu} y^\nu,$$

where y^ν is the national income of country ν and $\tau(V)$ is the impact coefficient of global warming. We now examine the implications of market equilibrium when the uniform carbon taxes with the rate θ given by

$$\theta = \frac{\tau(V)}{\delta+\mu} y, \quad y = \sum_\nu y^\nu \tag{19}$$

are levied.

The conditions for market equilibrium under the uniform carbon tax scheme are:

(i) For each country ν, the combination (c^ν, a_c^ν) of consumption vector c^ν and CO_2 emissions a_p^ν maximizes country ν's utility function

$$u^\nu = \phi^\nu(V)\, u^\nu\,(c^\nu, a_c^\nu)$$

subject to the budgetary constraint

$$pc^\nu + \theta a_c^\nu = y^\nu,$$

where y^ν is the national income of country ν and the aggregate level of atmospheric CO_2 accumulations, V, is assumed to be given.

(ii) For each country ν, the combination (x^ν, a_p^ν) of production vector x^ν and CO_2 emissions a_p^ν maximizes net profits

$$px^\nu - \theta a_p^\nu$$

over the technological possibility set $(x^\nu, a_p^\nu) \in T^\nu$; that is,

$$f^\nu\,(x^\nu, a_p^\nu) \leqq K^\nu. \tag{20}$$

(iii) Prices of goods p are determined so that total demand is equal to total supply:

$$\sum_\nu c^\nu = \sum_\nu x^\nu. \tag{21}$$

(iv) Total CO_2 emissions a are given by

$$a = \sum_\nu a^\nu, \quad a^\nu = a_c^\nu + a_p^\nu \quad (\nu \in N). \tag{22}$$

The optimum conditions are

$$\alpha^\nu \phi^\nu(V)\, u_{c^\nu}^\nu\,(c^\nu, a_c^\nu) \leqq p \quad (\text{mod. } c^\nu) \tag{23}$$

$$\alpha^\nu \phi^\nu(V)\, u_{a_c^\nu}^\nu\,(c^\nu, a_c^\nu) \leqq \theta \quad (\text{mod. } a_c^\nu) \tag{24}$$

$$p \leqq r^\nu f_{x^\nu}^\nu\,(x^\nu, a_p^\nu) \quad (\text{mod. } x^\nu) \tag{25}$$

$$\theta \geqq r^\nu[-f_{a_p^\nu}^\nu\,(x^\nu, a_p^\nu)] \quad (\text{mod. } a_p^\nu) \tag{26}$$

$$f^\nu(x^\nu, a_p^\nu) \leqq K^\nu \quad (\text{mod. } r^\nu). \tag{27}$$

The following relation holds for each country ν:

$$\alpha^\nu \phi^\nu(V) u^\nu (c^\nu, a_c^\nu) = pc^\nu + \theta a_c^\nu = y^\nu. \tag{28}$$

We now define the world utility U by

$$U = \sum_\nu \alpha^\nu \phi^\nu(V)\, u^\nu (c^\nu, a_c^\nu),$$

which, in view of (28), may be written as

$$U = \sum_\nu y^\nu = y.$$

The imputed price ψ of the atmospheric concentrations of CO_2 with respect to the world utility U is given by

$$\psi = \frac{1}{\delta + \mu} \left[-\frac{\partial U}{\partial V} \right] = \frac{1}{\delta + \mu} \sum_\nu \alpha^\nu \tau(V)\, \phi^\nu(V)\, u^\nu (c^\nu, a_c^\nu),$$

which, in view of relation (28), may be written

$$\psi = \frac{\tau(V)}{\delta + \mu} y.$$

That is, the imputed price ψ of the atmospheric concentrations of CO_2 with respect to the world utility U is equal to the uniform carbon tax rate θ given by (19):

$$\psi = \theta.$$

If we take into account the loss in the level of world utility U due to total CO_2 emissions a to be evaluated at the imputed price ψ of the atmospheric concentrations of CO_2, the imputed world utility may be given by

$$U^* = \sum_\nu \alpha^\nu \phi^\nu(V)\, u^\nu (c^\nu, a_c^\nu) - \psi a.$$

The Problem of the Social Optimum. Find the pattern of consumption and production of goods for individual countries, the pattern of CO_2 emissions by individual countries, and the total CO_2 emissions of the world, $(c^\nu, x^\nu, a_{c,}^\nu, a_p^\nu, a^\nu\ (\nu \in N); a)$, that maximizes the imputed world utility U^*:

$$U^* = \sum_\nu \alpha^\nu \phi^\nu(V) u^\nu (c^\nu, a_c^\nu) - \psi a$$

among all feasible patterns of allocation $(c^\nu, x^\nu, a_{c,}^\nu, a_p^\nu, a^\nu\ (\nu \in N), a)$:

$$\sum_\nu c^\nu = \sum_\nu x^\nu, \quad a = \sum_\nu a^\nu, \quad a^\nu = a_c^\nu + a_p^\nu, \quad (x^\nu, a_p^\nu) \in T^\nu,$$

where V and ψ are, respectively, the atmospheric concentrations of CO_2 and the imputed price of the atmospheric concentrations of CO_2 with respect to world utility U.

The problem of the social optimum may be solved in terms of the Lagrangian form

$$\begin{aligned} &L(c^\nu, x^\nu, a_{c,}^\nu, a_p^\nu, a^\nu, a; p, \theta, r^\nu\ (\nu \in N)) \\ &= \left[\sum_\nu \alpha^\nu \phi^\nu(V) u^\nu (c^\nu, a_c^\nu) - \psi a\right] + \left[\sum_\nu x^\nu - \sum_\nu c^\nu\right] \\ &\quad + \theta \left[a - \sum_\nu a^\nu\right] + \sum_\nu r^\nu \left[K^\nu - f^\nu (x^\nu, a_p^\nu)\right], \end{aligned}$$

where p, θ, and r^ν are the Lagrangian unknowns associated with constraints (21), (22), and (20), respectively.

It is apparent that marginal conditions (23)–(27) are the Euler–Lagrange conditions for the problem of the social optimum. Thus, we have established the following propositions.

Proposition 2. *Consider the uniform carbon tax scheme, where the rate θ is proportional to the aggregate income of the world y with the discounted present value $\frac{\tau(V)}{\delta + \mu}$ of the impact coefficient of global warming $\tau(V)$ as the coefficient of proportion:*

$$\theta = \frac{\tau(V)}{\delta + \mu} y,$$

where $\tau(V)$ is the impact coefficient of global warming and y is the world national income:

$$\tau(V) = -\frac{\phi^{\nu\prime}(V)}{\phi^\nu(V)}, \quad y = \sum_\nu y^\nu.$$

Then the market equilibrium obtained under such a uniform carbon tax scheme is a social optimum in the sense that a set of positive weights exists for the utilities of individual countries $(\alpha^1, \ldots, \alpha^n)$, $[\alpha^\nu > 0]$ *such that the imputed world utility*

$$U^* = \sum_\nu \alpha^\nu \phi^\nu(V)\, u^\nu(c^\nu, a_c^\nu) - \psi a$$

is maximized among all feasible patterns of allocation $(c^\nu, x^\nu, a_{c,}^\nu, a_p^\nu, a^\nu$ $(\nu \in N), a)$:

$$\sum_\nu c^\nu = \sum_\nu x^\nu, \quad a = \sum_\nu a^\nu, \quad a^\nu = a_c^\nu + a_p^\nu \quad (x^\nu, a_p^\nu) \in T^\nu,$$

where V *and* ψ *are, respectively, the atmospheric concentrations of* CO_2 *and the imputed price of the atmospheric concentrations of* CO_2 *with respect to world utility* U.

Then the world utility U *is equal to the aggregate national income of the world* y:

$$U = \sum_\nu \alpha^\nu \phi^\nu(V)\, u^\nu(c^\nu, a_{c,}^\nu) = y,$$

and the imputed price ψ *of the atmospheric concentrations of* CO_2 *is equal to the uniform carbon tax rate* θ:

$$\psi = \theta.$$

Proposition 3. *There always exists a set of positive weights for the utilities of individual countries* $(\alpha^1, \ldots, \alpha^n)$, $[\alpha^\nu > 0]$ *such that the social optimum in the dynamic sense with respect to the imputed world utility,*

$$U^* = \sum_\nu \alpha^\nu \phi^\nu(V)\, u^\nu(c^\nu, a_c^\nu) - \psi a,$$

where ψ *is the imputed price of the atmospheric concentrations of* CO_2 *with respect to world utility* U:

$$U = \sum_\nu \alpha^\nu \phi^\nu(V)\, u^\nu(c^\nu, a_{c,}^\nu),$$

satisfies the balance-of-payments requirements

$$pc^\nu = px^\nu$$

and, accordingly, the corresponding pattern of allocation $(c^\nu, x^\nu, a_{c,}^\nu,$ $a_p^\nu, a^\nu (\nu \in N), a)$, *in conjunction with prices of goods* p *and the carbon tax scheme with the uniform rate* $\theta = \dfrac{\tau(V)}{\delta + \mu} y$, *constitutes a market equilibrium for the world.*

The dynamical stability of the process of the atmospheric accumulation of CO_2 under the uniform carbon tax scheme is established by the following proposition, the proof of which may be given in exactly the same manner as in Uzawa (2003).

Proposition 4. *The process of the atmospheric accumulation of* CO_2 *with the uniform carbon tax rate* $\theta = \frac{\tau(V)}{\delta + \mu} y$ *is dynamically stable. That is, solution paths for the dynamic equation*

$$\dot{V} = a - \mu V,$$

where a *is the level of total emissions of* CO_2 *at time* t *and* μ *is the rate at which atmospheric concentrations of* CO_2 *are annually absorbed by the oceans, always converge to the stationary level* V_* *to be given by the stationarity condition*

$$a_* = \mu V_*,$$

where a_* *is the total* CO_2 *emissions at the market equilibrium under the uniform carbon tax scheme with the atmospheric concentrations of* CO_2 *at the level* V_*.

5. GLOBAL WARMING AND FORESTS

The economic analysis of global warming developed in the previous sections may be extended to examine the role of terrestrial forests in moderating processes of global warming, on the one hand, and in affecting the level of the welfare of people in the society by providing a decent and cultural environment, on the other.

A Simple Dynamic Model of Global Warming and Forests

In the simple, dynamic analysis of global warming introduced in the previous sections, we have assumed that the combustion of fossil fuels is the only cause for atmospheric instability and that the surface ocean is the only reservoir of carbon on the earth's surface that exchanges carbon with the atmosphere. In this section, we consider the role of terrestrial forests, particularly tropical rain forests, in stabilizing the processes of atmospheric equilibrium.

Terrestrial forests are regarded as social common capital and managed by social institutions with an organizational structure similar to that of private enterprise except for the manner in which prices of the forests themselves and products from the forests are determined. We assume that the amount of atmospheric CO_2 absorbed by the terrestrial forest per hectare in each country ν ($\nu = 1, \ldots, n$) is a certain constant on the average to be denoted by $\gamma^\nu > 0$. Then the basic dynamic equation concerning the change in the atmospheric concentrations of CO_2 $\dot{V}$ may be modified to take into account the amount of atmospheric CO_2 absorbed by terrestrial forests. We have

$$\dot{V} = a - \mu V - \sum_\nu \gamma^\nu R^\nu, \tag{29}$$

where a is the total CO_2 emissions in the world,

$$a = \sum_\nu a^\nu,$$

μ is the rate at which atmospheric CO_2 is absorbed by the oceans, and R^ν is the acreage of terrestrial forests of country ν ($\nu = 1, \ldots, n$).

According to Dyson and Marland (1979), the carbon sequester rate for temperate forests is estimated at around 7.5 tC/ha/yr. For tropical rain forests, it is estimated at 9.6–10.0 tC/ha/yr according to Marland (1988) and Myers (1988). See also IPCC (1991a,b, 1996a,b, 2000, 2001a,b), World Resources Institute (1991, 1996), and Uzawa (1991b, 1992a, 1993, 2003).

The change in the acreages of the terrestrial forests R^ν in each country ν is determined first by the levels of reforestation activities and second by various economic activities carried out in country ν during the year in question – particularly by agricultural and lumber industries and by processes of urbanization. We denote by z^ν the acreages of terrestrial forests annually reforested and by b^ν the acreages of terrestrial forests in country ν lost annually lost as a result of economic activities. Then the acreages of terrestrial forests R^ν in each country ν are subject to the following dynamic equations:

$$\dot{R}^\nu = z^\nu - b^\nu \quad (\nu = 1, \ldots, n). \tag{30}$$

Specifications for Utility Functions

We assume that the utility level u^ν of each country ν is influenced by the acreages of terrestrial forests R^ν in country ν, in addition to the atmospheric concentrations of CO_2, V. That is, the utility function for each country ν is expressed in the following manner:

$$u^\nu = u^\nu\left(c^\nu, a_c^\nu, R^\nu, V\right),$$

where $c^\nu = (c_j^\nu)$ is the vector of goods consumed in country ν, a_c^ν is the amount of CO_2 emitted by the consumers in country ν, R^ν is the acreage of terrestrial forests in country ν, and V is the atmospheric concentration of CO_2 that has accumulated in the atmosphere, all at time t.

For each country ν, we assume that utility function $u^\nu(c^\nu, a_c^\nu, R^\nu, V)$ is strongly separable with respect to (c^ν, a_c^ν), R^ν, and V in the sense originally introduced by Goldman and Uzawa (1964), as postulated in Uzawa (1991b, 2003); that is,

$$u^\nu(c^\nu, a_c^\nu, R^\nu, V) = \phi^\nu(V)\varphi^\nu(R^\nu)\, u^\nu(c^\nu, a_c^\nu).$$

As in the case discussed in the previous sections, the function $\phi^\nu(V)$ expresses the extent to which people in country ν are adversely affected by global warming, which is referred to as the impact index of global warming. Similarly, the function $\phi^\nu(V)$ expresses the extent to which people in country ν are positively affected by the presence of the terrestrial forests in country ν, which is referred to as the impact index of forests. We assume that the impact indices, $\phi^\nu(V)$ and $\varphi^\nu(R^\nu)$, satisfy the following conditions:

$$\phi^\nu(V) > 0, \quad \phi^{\nu\prime}(V) < 0, \quad \phi^{\nu\prime\prime}(V) < 0,$$
$$\varphi^\nu(R^\nu) > 0, \quad \varphi^{\nu\prime}(R^\nu) > 0, \quad \varphi^{\nu\prime\prime}(R^\nu) < 0.$$

The impact coefficients of global warming and forests are, respectively, defined by

$$\tau^\nu(V) = -\frac{\phi^{\nu\prime}(V)}{\phi^\nu(V)}, \quad \tau^\nu(R^\nu) = \frac{\varphi^{\nu\prime}(R^\nu)}{\varphi^\nu(R^\nu)}.$$

(At the risk of confusion, the symbol τ^ν is used for both the impact coefficients of global warming and forests.)

We assume that the impact coefficients of global warming $\tau^\nu(V)$ are identical for all countries ν:

$$\tau^\nu(V) = \tau(V) \quad \text{for all } \nu \text{ and } V.$$

The impact coefficient functions, $\tau(V)$ and $\tau^\nu(R^\nu)$, satisfy the following conditions:

$$\tau(V) > 0, \ \ \tau'(V) > 0; \quad \tau^\nu(R^\nu) > 0, \ \ \tau^{\nu\prime}(R^\nu) < 0.$$

We assume that for each country ν, the utility function $u^\nu(c^\nu, a_c^\nu)$ satisfies the conditions (U′1)–(U′4), as introduced in Section 3.

The Consumer Optimum

The consumers in country ν choose the vector of consumption c^ν and CO_2 emissions a_c^ν that maximizes country ν's utility function

$$u^\nu(c^\nu, a_c^\nu, R^\nu, V) = \phi^\nu(V)\varphi^\nu(R^\nu)\, u^\nu(c^\nu, a_c^\nu)$$

subject to the budget constraint

$$pc^\nu + \theta^\nu a_c^\nu = y^\nu,$$

where y^ν is the national income of country ν in units of world prices.

The optimum combination of consumption c^ν and CO_2 emissions a_c^ν is characterized by the following marginality conditions:

$$\alpha^\nu \phi^\nu(V)\varphi^\nu(R^\nu)\, u_{c^\nu}^\nu(c^\nu, a_c^\nu) \leqq p \quad (\text{mod. } c^\nu) \tag{31}$$

$$\alpha^\nu \phi^\nu(V)\varphi^\nu(R^\nu)\, u_{a_c^\nu}^\nu(c^\nu, a_c^\nu) \leqq \theta^\nu \quad (\text{mod. } a_c^\nu), \tag{32}$$

where α^ν is the inverse of the marginal utility of income y^ν of country ν.

The linear homogeneity hypothesis for the utility function $u^\nu(c^\nu, a_c^\nu)$ implies that

$$\alpha^\nu \phi^\nu(V)\varphi^\nu(R^\nu)u^\nu(c^\nu, a_c^\nu) = pc^\nu + \theta^\nu a_c^\nu = y^\nu.$$

Specifications for Production Possibility Sets

The conditions concerning the production of goods in each country ν are specified by the production possibility set T^ν in exactly the same manner as in the previous sections.

In each country ν, the minimum quantities of factors of production needed to produce goods by the vector of production $x^\nu = (x_j^\nu)$ with the use of the natural resources of the forests by the amount b^ν and the CO_2 emission at the level a_p^ν are specified by an F-dimensional vector-valued function,

$$f^\nu\left(x^\nu, b^\nu, a_p^\nu\right) = \left(f_f^\nu\left(x^\nu, b^\nu, a_p^\nu\right)\right).$$

Similarly, the minimum quantities of factors of production needed to engage in reforestation activities at the level z^ν are specified by an F-dimensional vector-valued function,

$$g^\nu(z^\nu) = \left(g^\nu_f(z^\nu)\right).$$

In exactly the same manner as in the previous sections, we assume that marginal rates of substitution between any pair of the production of goods, the use of the natural resources of forests, reforestation activities, and the emission of CO_2 are smooth and diminishing, trade-offs always exist among them, and the conditions of constant returns to scale prevail. That is, we assume that

(T′1) $f^\nu(x^\nu, b^\nu, a^\nu_p)$, $g^\nu(z^\nu)$ are defined, positive valued, continuous, and continuously twice-differentiable for all $(x^\nu, b^\nu, a^\nu_p) \geqq 0$ and $z^\nu \geqq 0$, respectively.

(T′2) $f^\nu_{x^\nu}(x^\nu, b^\nu, a^\nu_p) \geqq 0, \quad f^\nu_{b^\nu}(x^\nu b^\nu, a^\nu_p) < 0, \quad f^\nu_{a^\nu_p}(x^\nu b^\nu, a^\nu_p) < 0$ for all $(x^\nu b^\nu, a^\nu_p) \geqq 0$; and $g^\nu_{z^\nu}(z^\nu) \geqq 0 \quad$ for all $z^\nu \geqq 0$.

(T′3) $f^\nu(x^\nu, b^\nu, a^\nu_p)$ and $g^\nu(z^\nu)$ are strictly quasi-convex with respect to (x^ν, b^ν, a^ν_p) and z^ν, respectively.

(T′4) $f^\nu(x^\nu, b^\nu, a^\nu_p)$ and $g^\nu(z^\nu)$ are homogeneous of order 1 with respect to (x^ν, b^ν, a^ν_p) and z^ν, respectively.

The production possibility set T^ν is given by

$$\begin{aligned} T^\nu = \big\{ & \left(x^\nu, z^\nu, b^\nu, a^\nu_p\right) : \left(x^\nu, z^\nu, b^\nu, a^\nu_p\right) \geqq 0, \\ & f^\nu\left(x^\nu, b^\nu, a^\nu_p\right) + g^\nu(z^\nu) \leqq K^\nu \big\}, \end{aligned}$$

where K^ν is the vector of endowments of fixed factors of production in country ν.

Postulates (T′1–T′3), as specified above, imply that the production possibility set T^ν is a closed convex set of $J + 1 + 1 + 1$-dimensional vectors $(x^\nu, z^\nu, b^\nu, a^\nu_p)$.

The Producer Optimum

Suppose that prices of goods are given by $p = (p_j)$ and the imputed price of forests in each country ν by π^ν, whereas carbon taxes at the rate θ^ν are levied upon the emission of CO_2 in country ν.

Forests are generally regarded as social common capital, and there are no markets on which either the ownership of forests or the entitlements for the products from forests are transacted. Hence, prices of forests are generally not market prices but imputed prices. The imputed price of the ownership of a particular forest is the discounted present value of the stream of the marginal utilities of the forest and the expected value of the entitlements for the natural resources in the forest in the future.

The producers in country ν choose the combination $(x^\nu, z^\nu, b^\nu, a_p^\nu)$ of vectors of production x^ν, levels of reforestation z^ν, use of resources of forests b^ν, and CO_2 emissions a_p^ν that maximizes net profit

$$px^\nu + \pi^\nu(z^\nu - b^\nu) - \theta^\nu a^\nu$$

over $(x^\nu, z^\nu, b^\nu, a_p^\nu) \in T^\nu$; that is, subject to the constraints,

$$f^\nu\left(x^\nu, b^\nu, a_p^\nu\right) + g^\nu(z^\nu) \leqq K^\nu.$$

Marginality conditions for the producer optimum are

$$p \leqq r^\nu f_{x^\nu}^\nu\left(x^\nu, b^\nu, a_p^\nu\right) \quad (\text{mod. } x^\nu) \tag{33}$$

$$\pi^\nu \geqq r^\nu\left[-f_{b^\nu}^\nu\left(x^\nu, b^\nu, a_p^\nu\right)\right] \quad (\text{mod. } b^\nu) \tag{34}$$

$$\theta^\nu \geqq r^\nu\left[-f_{a_p^\nu}^\nu\left(x^\nu, b^\nu, a_p^\nu\right)\right] \quad (\text{mod. } a_p^\nu) \tag{35}$$

$$\pi^\nu \leqq r^\nu g_{z^\nu}^\nu(z^\nu) \quad (\text{mod. } z^\nu) \tag{36}$$

$$f^\nu\left(x^\nu, b^\nu, a_p^\nu\right) + g^\nu(z^\nu) \leqq K^\nu \quad (\text{mod. } r^\nu), \tag{37}$$

where $r^\nu = (r_f^\nu)\,[r_f^\nu \geqq 0]$ denotes the vector of imputed rental prices of factors of production.

The meaning of these conditions is simple. Condition (33) means that the choice of production technologies and the levels of production are adjusted so as to equate marginal factor costs with output prices.

Condition (34) means that the use of resources of forests is determined so that the marginal gain due to the marginal increase in the use of resources of forests is equal to the imputed price of forests π^ν when $b^\nu > 0$ and is not larger than π^ν when $b^\nu = 0$.

Condition (35) means that CO_2 emissions are controlled so that the marginal gain due to the marginal increase in CO_2 emissions is equal to carbon tax rate θ^ν when $a_p^\nu > 0$ and is not larger than θ^ν when $a_p^\nu = 0$.

Condition (36) means that the level of reforestation activities is determined so that the marginal gain due to the marginal increase in the use of resources of forests is equal to the imputed price of forests π^ν when $z^\nu > 0$ and is not larger than π^ν when $z^\nu = 0$.

Condition (37) means that the employment of factors of production does not exceed the endowment and that the conditions of full employment are satisfied whenever the rental price is positive.

We have assumed that the technologies are subject to constant returns to scale, and thus, in view of the Euler identity, conditions (33)–(37) imply that

$$\begin{aligned}
&px^\nu + \pi^\nu(z^\nu - b^\nu) - \theta^\nu a_p^\nu \\
&\quad = r^\nu\big[f_{x^\nu}^\nu(x^\nu, b^\nu, a_p^\nu)x^\nu + f_{b^\nu}^\nu(x^\nu, b^\nu, a_p^\nu)b^\nu \\
&\qquad + f_{a_p^\nu}^\nu(x^\nu, b^\nu, a_p^\nu)a_p^\nu + g_{z^\nu}^\nu(z^\nu)z^\nu\big] \\
&\quad = r^\nu\big[f_{x^\nu}^\nu(x^\nu, b^\nu, a_p^\nu)x^\nu + g_{z^\nu}^\nu(z^\nu)z^\nu \\
&\qquad - f_{b^\nu}^\nu(x^\nu, b^\nu, a_p^\nu)b^\nu - f_{a_p^\nu}^\nu(x^\nu, b^\nu, a_p^\nu)a_p^\nu\big] \\
&\quad = r^\nu\left[f^\nu(x^\nu, b^\nu, a_p^\nu)\, x^\nu + g^\nu(z^\nu)\right] = r^\nu K^\nu.
\end{aligned}$$

That is, the net evaluation of output is equal to the sum of the rental payments to all factors of production.

6. FORESTS AND DEFERENTIAL EQUILIBRIUM

Exactly as in Section 3 of this chapter, deferential equilibrium is obtained if, when the individuals and producers in each country choose the levels of consumption, production, and reforestation activities, they take into account the impact on the future levels of the country's utilities brought about by CO_2 emissions of that country as well as the reforestation activities carried out today.

Imputed Prices of Atmospheric Concentrations of CO_2 and Forests

Consider the situation in which a combination $(c^\nu, a_c^\nu, x^\nu, z^\nu, b^\nu, a_p^\nu)$ of vectors of consumption and production, c^ν, x^ν, level of reforestation activities z^ν, CO_2 emissions a_c^ν, and a_p^ν $(a^\nu = a_c^\nu + a_p^\nu)$ is chosen in country ν. Imputed prices of atmospheric concentrations of CO_2 and forests are defined as follows.

Suppose CO_2 emissions in country ν, a^ν, are increased by the marginal amount. This would induce the marginal increase in the aggregate amount of CO_2 emissions in the world, causing the marginal increase in the atmospheric level of CO_2. The resulting marginal increase in the degree of future global warming would cause the marginal decrease in country ν's utility.

The marginal decrease in country ν's utility due to the marginal increase in CO_2 emissions in country ν today is given by the partial derivative, with minus sign, of the utility of country ν,

$$u^\nu = \alpha^\nu \phi^\nu(V)\varphi^\nu(R^\nu)\, u^\nu(c^\nu, a_c^\nu),$$

with respect to atmospheric accumulations of CO_2, V; that is,

$$-\frac{\partial u^\nu}{\partial V} = \tau(V)\phi^\nu(V)\varphi^\nu(R^\nu)\, u^\nu(c^\nu, a_c^\nu),$$

where $\tau(V)$ is the impact coefficient of global warming.

We assume that future utilities of country ν are discounted at a certain constant rate δ that is exogenously given. We also assume that the rate of utility discount δ is positive and identical for all countries in the world. We have assumed that the rate at which atmospheric CO_2 is annually absorbed by the oceans is a certain constant μ. Hence, for each country ν, the imputed price ψ^ν of the atmospheric accumulations of CO_2, in units of utility of country ν, is given by the discounted present value of the marginal decrease in utility of country ν due to the marginal increase in CO_2 emissions in country ν today; that is,

$$\psi^\nu = \frac{\tau(V)}{\delta + \mu}\phi^\nu(V)\varphi^\nu(R^\nu)\, u^\nu(c^\nu, a_c^\nu).$$

Hence, the imputed price θ^ν of the atmospheric accumulations of CO_2 for country ν, in units of world prices, is given by

$$\theta^\nu = \alpha^\nu \psi^\nu = \frac{\tau(V)}{\delta + \mu} y^\nu, \tag{38}$$

where α^ν is the inverse of the marginal utility of national income y^ν of country ν.

Similarly, the imputed prices of forests, in units of world price, are defined as follows. Suppose the acreages of forests of country ν, R^ν, are increased by the marginal amount. On one hand, this would induce a marginal increase in the level of the utility of country ν and, on the other hand, the marginal increase in the utility of country ν in the future due to the marginal decrease in the atmospheric level of CO_2 induced by the absorbing capacity of forests in country ν.

The first component is the marginal utility with respect to the acreage of forests of country ν, R^ν, in units of world prices. It is given by

$$\frac{\partial u^\nu}{\partial R^\nu} = \tau^\nu(R^\nu)\alpha^\nu\phi^\nu(V)\varphi^\nu(R^\nu)u^\nu(c^\nu, a_c^\nu) = \tau^\nu(R^\nu)y^\nu.$$

The second component is the marginal increase in country ν's utility in the future due to the marginal decrease in the atmospheric level of CO_2 induced by the absorbing capacity of forests in country ν. It is given by

$$\gamma^\nu\theta^\nu = \gamma^\nu\frac{\tau(V)}{\delta+\mu}y^\nu.$$

Hence, the imputed price π^ν of forests of country ν, in units of world prices, is given by the discounted present value of the sum of these two components:

$$\pi^\nu = \frac{1}{\delta}\left[\tau^\nu(R^\nu) + \gamma^\nu\frac{\tau(V)}{\delta+\mu}\right]y^\nu. \tag{39}$$

Forests and Deferential Equilibrium

Conditions for deferential equilibrium for each country ν are obtained in the same manner as those derived in Section 3 of this chapter, except for the introduction of the vector of acreage of forests in each country ν as a new variable.

We assume as given the atmospheric concentrations of CO_2, V, and the acreage of forests in each country ν, R^ν, both at time t. Deferential behavioristic postulates for each country ν may be viewed as the optimum solution to the following maximum problem.

Find the combination $(c^\nu, a_c^\nu, x^\nu, z^\nu, b^\nu, a_p^\nu)$ of vectors of consumption and production c, x^ν, level of reforestation activities z^ν, and CO_2 emissions a_c^ν, a_p^ν, a^ν that maximizes the imputed utility of country ν,

$$u_*^\nu = \phi^\nu(V)\varphi^\nu(R^\nu)u^\nu(c^\nu, a_c^\nu) + \xi^\nu(z^\nu - b^\nu) - \psi^\nu(a^\nu - \gamma^\nu R^\nu),$$

subject to the constraints

$$pc^\nu = px^\nu \tag{40}$$

$$f^\nu(x^\nu, b^\nu, a_p^\nu) + g^\nu(z^\nu) \leqq K^\nu \tag{41}$$

$$a^\nu = a_c^\nu + a_p^\nu, \tag{42}$$

where ψ^ν and ξ^ν are, respectively, the imputed prices of atmospheric concentrations of CO_2 and forests for country ν, measured in units of utility of country ν.

The maximum problem for deferential equilibrium for country ν may be solved in terms of the Lagrangian form

$$\begin{aligned} L^\nu & \left(c^\nu, a_c^\nu, x^\nu, z^\nu, b^\nu, a_p^\nu, a^\nu; \lambda^\nu, \lambda^\nu r^\nu, \lambda^\nu \theta^\nu\right) \\ &= \phi^\nu(V)\varphi^\nu(R^\nu)u^\nu\left(c^\nu, a_c^\nu\right) + \xi^\nu(z^\nu - b^\nu) - \psi^\nu(a^\nu - \gamma^\nu R^\nu) \\ &\quad + \lambda^\nu(px^\nu - pc^\nu) + \lambda^\nu r^\nu\left[K^\nu - f^\nu\left(x^\nu, b^\nu, a_p^\nu\right) - g^\nu(z^\nu)\right] \\ &\quad + \lambda^\nu\theta^\nu\left(a^\nu - a_c^\nu - a_p^\nu\right), \end{aligned} \tag{43}$$

where the variables $\lambda^\nu, \lambda^\nu r^\nu, \lambda^\nu\theta^\nu$ are the Lagrangian unknowns, respectively, associated with constraints (40), (41), and (42).

When expressed in units of market price, the marginality conditions at the optimum are

$$\alpha^\nu\phi^\nu(V)\varphi^\nu(R^\nu)\,u_{c^\nu}^\nu\left(c^\nu, a_c^\nu\right) \leqq p \quad (\text{mod. } c^\nu) \tag{44}$$

$$\alpha^\nu\phi^\nu(V)\varphi^\nu(R^\nu)\,u_{a_c^\nu}^\nu\left(c^\nu, a_c^\nu\right) \leqq \theta^\nu \quad (\text{mod. } a_c^\nu) \tag{45}$$

$$p \leqq r^\nu f_{x^\nu}^\nu\left(x^\nu, b^\nu, a_p^\nu\right) \quad (\text{mod. } x^\nu) \tag{46}$$

$$\pi^\nu \leqq r^\nu\left[-f_{x^\nu}^\nu\left(x^\nu, b^\nu, a_p^\nu\right)\right] \quad (\text{mod. } b^\nu) \tag{47}$$

$$\theta^\nu \geqq r^\nu\left[-f_{a_p^\nu}^\nu\left(x^\nu, b^\nu, a_p^\nu\right)\right] \quad (\text{mod. } a_p^\nu) \tag{48}$$

$$\pi^\nu \leqq r^\nu g_{z^\nu}^\nu(z^\nu) \quad (\text{mod. } z^\nu), \tag{49}$$

where $\alpha^\nu = \frac{1}{\lambda^\nu}$ is the inverse of the marginal utility of country ν's income, and θ^ν, π^ν are, respectively, the imputed prices of atmospheric concentrations of CO_2 and forests, both measured in units of market price:

$$\theta^\nu = \alpha^\nu\psi^\nu = \frac{\tau(V)}{\delta+\mu}y^\nu$$

$$\pi^\nu = \alpha^\nu\xi^\nu = \frac{1}{\delta}\left[\tau^\nu(R^\nu) + \gamma^\nu\frac{\tau(V)}{\delta+\mu}\right]y^\nu,$$

where

$$y^\nu = pc^\nu + \theta^\nu a_c^\nu.$$

Conditions (46)–(49) taken together mean that the combination $(x^\nu, z^\nu, b^\nu, a_p^\nu)$ of vector of production x^ν, level of reforestation activities z^ν, depletion of natural resources of forests b^ν, and CO_2 emissions a_p^ν maximizes net profit

$$px^\nu + \pi^\nu(z^\nu - b^\nu) - \theta^\nu a_p^\nu$$

over $(x^\nu, z^\nu, b^\nu, a_p^\nu) \in T^\nu$.

Deferential equilibrium for the world economy, then, is obtained if we find the prices of goods p at which total demand is equal to total supply:

$$\sum_\nu c^\nu = \sum_\nu x^\nu.$$

Total CO_2 emissions, a, are given by

$$a = \sum_\nu a^\nu, \quad a^\nu = a_c^\nu + a_p^\nu \quad (\nu = 1, \ldots, n).$$

The discussion above may be summarized in the following proposition.

Proposition 5. *Deferential equilibrium corresponds precisely to the standard market equilibrium under the following system of proportional carbon taxes for the emission of CO_2 and tax subsidy measures for the reforestation and depletion of resources of forests:*
(i) *In each country ν, the carbon taxes are levied with the tax rate θ^ν that is proportional to the national income y^ν:*

$$\theta^\nu = \frac{\tau(V)}{\delta + \mu} y^\nu,$$

where $\tau(V)$ is the impact coefficient of global warming, δ is the rate of utility discount, and μ is the rate at which atmospheric CO_2 is annually absorbed by the oceans.
(ii) *In each country ν, tax subsidy arrangements are made for the reforestation and depletion of resources of forests with the rate π^ν that is proportional to the national income y^ν, to be given by*

$$\pi^\nu = \frac{1}{\delta}\left[\tau^\nu(R^\nu) + \gamma^\nu \frac{\tau(V)}{\delta + \mu}\right] y^\nu,$$

where $\tau^\nu(R^\nu)$ is the impact coefficient of forests of country ν.

7. FORESTS AND SOCIAL OPTIMUM

In the previous section, we saw that deferential equilibrium may be obtained as the standard market equilibrium provided a system of proportional carbon taxes for the emission of CO_2 and tax subsidy measures for the reforestation and depletion of resources of forests are adopted. The proportional carbon tax rate θ^ν in each country ν is equal to

$$\theta^\nu = \frac{\tau(V)}{\delta + \mu} y^\nu,$$

where y^ν is the national income of country ν.

We next examine the implications of market equilibrium when the uniform carbon taxes, with the rate θ, are levied:

$$\theta = \frac{\tau(V)}{\delta + \mu} y,$$

where y is the sum of national incomes y^ν of all countries in the world, given by

$$y = \sum_\nu y^\nu.$$

In each country ν, tax subsidy arrangements are made for the reforestation and depletion of resources of the forests with the rate π^ν that is proportional to the national income y^ν, to be given by

$$\pi^\nu = \frac{1}{\delta}\left[\tau^\nu(R^\nu) + \gamma^\nu \frac{\tau(V)}{\delta + \mu}\right] y^\nu,$$

where $\tau^\nu(R^\nu)$ is the impact coefficient of forests of country ν.

Forests and Uniform Carbon Taxes

The conditions for market equilibrium under the uniform carbon tax scheme involving forests are obtained in exactly the same manner as discussed in Section 3 of this chapter.

The representative consumers and producers in each country ν must solve the following maximization problems:

(i) Find the combination of vector of consumption c^ν and CO_2 emissions a_c^ν that maximizes country ν's utility

$$u^\nu(c^\nu, a_c^\nu, R^\nu, V) = \phi^\nu(V)\varphi^\nu(R^\nu)\, u^\nu(c^\nu, a_c^\nu)$$

subject to the budget constraints

$$pc^\nu + \theta^\nu a_c^\nu = y^\nu,$$

where y^ν is the national income of country ν in units of world prices.

(ii) Find the combination $(x^\nu, z^\nu, b^\nu, a_p^\nu)$ of vector of production x^ν, level of reforestation z^ν, use of resources of forests b^ν, and CO_2 emissions a_p^ν that maximizes net profit

$$px^\nu + \pi^\nu(z^\nu - b^\nu) - \theta^\nu a_p^\nu$$

over $(x^\nu, z^\nu, b^\nu, a_p^\nu) \in T^\nu$; that is, subject to the constraints

$$f^\nu(x^\nu, b^\nu, a_p^\nu) + g^\nu(z^\nu) \leqq K^\nu,$$

where π^ν is the imputed price of the forests in country ν, in units of market price, to be given by (39).

Market equilibrium for the world economy, then, is obtained if we find the prices of goods p at which total demand is equal to total supply:

$$\sum_\nu c^\nu = \sum_\nu x^\nu.$$

Total CO_2 emissions a are given by

$$a = \sum_\nu a^\nu.$$

When expressed in units of market price, the optimum marginality conditions are

$$\alpha^\nu \phi^\nu(V)\varphi^\nu(R^\nu)\, u_{c^\nu}^\nu(c^\nu, a_c^\nu) \leqq p \quad (\text{mod. } c^\nu) \tag{50}$$

$$\alpha^\nu \phi^\nu(V)\varphi^\nu(R^\nu)\, u_{a_c^\nu}^\nu(c^\nu, a_c^\nu) \leqq \theta \quad (\text{mod. } a_c^\nu) \tag{51}$$

$$p \leqq r^\nu f_{x^\nu}^\nu(x^\nu, b^\nu, a_p^\nu) \quad (\text{mod. } x^\nu) \tag{52}$$

$$\pi^\nu \geqq r^\nu[-f_{b^\nu}^\nu(x^\nu, b^\nu, a_p^\nu)] \quad (\text{mod. } b^\nu) \tag{53}$$

$$\theta \geqq r^\nu[-f_{a_p^\nu}^\nu(x^\nu, b^\nu, a_p^\nu)] \quad (\text{mod. } a_p^\nu) \tag{54}$$

$$\pi^\nu \leqq r^\nu g_{z^\nu}^\nu(z^\nu), \quad (\text{mod. } z^\nu), \tag{55}$$

where α^ν is the inverse of the marginal utility of national income of country ν,

$$\theta = \frac{\tau(V)}{\delta + \mu} y, \quad y = \sum_\nu y^\nu$$

$$\pi^\nu = \frac{1}{\delta}\left[\tau^\nu(R^\nu) + \gamma^\nu \frac{\tau(V)}{\delta + \mu}\right] y^\nu$$

$$y^\nu = pc^\nu + \theta^\nu a_c^\nu.$$

By multiplying both sides of relations (50) and (51), respectively, by c^ν and a_c^ν, and by noting the Euler identity for utility function $u^\nu(c^\nu, a_c^\nu)$, we obtain

$$\alpha^\nu \phi^\nu(V)\varphi^\nu(R^\nu)u^\nu\left(c^\nu, a_c^\nu\right) = pc^\nu + \theta a_c^\nu.$$

Hence,

$$\alpha^\nu \phi^\nu(V)\varphi^\nu(R^\nu)u^\nu\left(c^\nu, a_c^\nu\right) = y^\nu. \tag{56}$$

We now define the world utility U by

$$U = \sum_\nu \alpha^\nu \phi^\nu(V)\varphi^\nu(R^\nu)u^\nu\left(c^\nu, a_c^\nu\right),$$

which, in view of (56), implies

$$U = \sum_\nu y^\nu = y.$$

By taking partial derivatives of U with respect to V, we obtain

$$\frac{\partial U}{\partial V} = -\tau(V)\sum_\nu \alpha^\nu \phi^\nu(V)\varphi^\nu(R^\nu)u^\nu\left(c^\nu, a_c^\nu\right).$$

By noting relation (56), we obtain

$$\frac{\partial U}{\partial V} = -\tau(V)\sum_\nu y^\nu = -\tau(V)y.$$

The imputed price ψ of the atmospheric concentrations of CO_2 with respect to the world utility U is defined by

$$\psi = \frac{1}{\delta + \mu}\left[-\frac{\partial U}{\partial V}\right] = \frac{\tau(V)}{\delta + \mu} y.$$

Hence,

$$\psi = \theta.$$

The imputed price ψ of the atmospheric concentrations of CO_2 with respect to the world utility U is equal to the uniform carbon tax rate θ that is initially given.

If we take into account the loss in the level of world utility U due to total CO_2 emissions a to be evaluated at the imputed price ψ of the atmospheric concentrations of CO_2 in addition to the gains due to the net increase in the acreage of forests in each country ν, the imputed world utility U_* may be defined by

$$U_* = \sum_\nu \alpha^\nu \phi^\nu(V)\varphi^\nu(R^\nu)u^\nu(c^\nu, a_c^\nu) + \sum_\nu \pi^\nu(z^\nu - b^\nu) - \psi a,$$

where π^ν is the imputed price of forests in country ν and ψ is the imputed price of the atmospheric concentrations of CO_2, respectively, given by

$$\pi^\nu = \frac{1}{\delta}\left[\tau^\nu(R^\nu) + \gamma^\nu \frac{\tau(V)}{\delta + \mu}\right] y^\nu$$

$$\theta = \frac{\tau(V)}{\delta + \mu} y, \quad y = \sum_\nu y^\nu.$$

Social Optimum in the Dynamic Context. Find the pattern of allocation $[c^\nu, a_c^\nu, x^\nu, z^\nu, b^\nu, a_p^\nu, a^\nu (\nu \in N)]$ that maximizes the imputed world utility

$$U_* = \sum_\nu \alpha^\nu \phi^\nu(V)\varphi^\nu(R^\nu)u^\nu(c^\nu, a_c^\nu) + \sum_\nu \pi^\nu(z^\nu - b^\nu) - \psi a,$$

among all feasible patterns of allocation $[c^\nu, a_c^\nu, x^\nu, z^\nu, b^\nu, a_p^\nu, a^\nu$ $(\nu \in N)]$ such that

$$\sum_\nu c^\nu = \sum_\nu x^\nu, \quad a = \sum_\nu a^\nu, \quad (x^\nu, z^\nu, b^\nu, a_p^\nu) \in T^\nu.$$

The social optimum may be obtained in terms of the Lagrangian form

$$\begin{aligned} &L\left(c^\nu, a_c^\nu, x^\nu, z^\nu, b^\nu, a_p^\nu, a^\nu, a; p, r^\nu, \theta\right) \\ &= \sum_\nu \alpha^\nu \phi^\nu(V)\varphi^\nu(R^\nu)u^\nu(c^\nu, a_c^\nu) + \sum_\nu \pi^\nu(z^\nu - b^\nu) - \psi a \\ &+ p\left[\sum_\nu x^\nu - \sum_\nu c^\nu\right] + \sum_\nu r^\nu [K^\nu - f^\nu(x^\nu, b^\nu, a_p^\nu) - g^\nu(z^\nu)] \\ &+ \theta\left[a - \sum_\nu a^\nu\right], \qquad a^\nu = a_c^\nu + a_p^\nu \quad (\nu \in N), \end{aligned}$$

where variables p, r^ν, θ are the Lagrangian unknowns.

It is apparent that

$$\theta = \psi,$$

and the Euler-Lagrange equations for this Lagrangian form are identical to (50)–(55).

Thus, we have established the following proposition.

Proposition 6. *Consider the uniform carbon tax scheme with the same rate θ everywhere in the world, where the rate θ is proportional to the sum y of the national incomes of all countries in the world with the discounted present value $\frac{\tau(V)}{\delta+\mu}$ of the impact coefficient of global warming $\tau(V)$ as the coefficient of proportion:*

$$\theta = \frac{\tau(V)}{\delta+\mu}\, y, \quad y = \sum_\nu y^\nu.$$

Then the market equilibrium obtained under such a uniform carbon tax scheme is a social optimum in the sense that there exists a set of positive weights for the utilities of individual countries $(\alpha^1, \ldots, \alpha^n)$ $[\alpha^\nu > 0]$ such that the net level of world utility defined by

$$U_* = \sum_\nu \alpha^\nu \phi^\nu(V)\varphi^\nu(R^\nu)u^\nu(c^\nu, a_c^\nu) + \sum_\nu \pi^\nu(z^\nu - b^\nu) - \psi a$$

is maximized among all feasible patterns of allocation $[c^\nu, a_c^\nu, x^\nu, z^\nu, b^\nu, a_p^\nu, a^\nu (\nu \in N)]$:

$$\sum_\nu c^\nu = \sum_\nu x^\nu, \quad a = \sum_\nu a^\nu, \quad (x^\nu, z^\nu, b^\nu, a_p^\nu) \in T^\nu \quad (\nu \in N),$$

where π^ν is the imputed price of the forests in country ν and ψ is the imputed price of the atmospheric concentrations of CO_2, respectively, to be given by

$$\psi = \frac{\tau(V)}{\delta+\mu}\, y$$

$$\pi^\nu = \frac{1}{\delta}\left[\tau^\nu(R^\nu) + \gamma^\nu \frac{\tau(V)}{\delta+\mu}\right] y^\nu \ (\nu \in N).$$

Then the imputed price ψ of the atmospheric concentrations of CO_2 is equal to carbon tax rate θ:

$$\psi = \theta.$$

Social optimum in the dynamic context may be defined for any arbitrarily given set of positive weights for the utilities of individual countries, $(\alpha^1, \ldots, \alpha^n)$ $[\alpha^\nu > 0]$. An allocation $[c^\nu, a_c^\nu, x^\nu, z^\nu, b^\nu, a_p^\nu, a^\nu$ $(\nu \in N)]$ is a social optimum if the imputed world utility U_* is maximized among all feasible patterns of allocation.

A social optimum in the dynamic context necessarily implies the existence of the uniform carbon tax scheme with the same rate $\theta = \frac{\tau(V)}{\delta + \mu} y$. However, the balance-of-payments requirements

$$pc^\nu = px^\nu$$

are generally not satisfied.

It is apparent that if a social optimum satisfies the balance-of-payments requirements, then it corresponds to the market equilibrium under the uniform carbon tax scheme. The existence of such a social optimum is guaranteed by Proposition 7 below, which may be proved in exactly the same manner as Proposition 3 in Uzawa (2003, Chapter 1).

Proposition 7. *There always exists a set of positive weights for the utilities of individual countries* $(\alpha^1, \ldots, \alpha^n)$ $[\alpha^\nu > 0]$ *such that the social optimum with respect to the imputed world utility*

$$U_* = \sum_\nu \alpha^\nu \phi^\nu(V) \varphi^\nu(R^\nu) u^\nu(c^\nu, a_c^\nu) + \sum_\nu \pi^\nu(z^\nu - b^\nu) - \psi a$$

satisfies the balance-of-payments requirements, that is,

$$pc^\nu = px^\nu.$$

Hence, the corresponding pattern of allocation $[c^\nu, a_c^\nu, x^\nu, z^\nu, b^\nu, a_p^\nu, a^\nu (\nu \in N)]$, *in conjunction with prices of goods* p *and the carbon tax scheme with the uniform rate* $\theta = \frac{\tau(V)}{\delta + \mu} y$, *constitutes a market equilibrium.*

8

Education as Social Common Capital

1. INTRODUCTION

Education, along with medical care, constitutes one of the most important components of social common capital and, as such, may require institutional arrangements substantially different from those for the standard economic activities that are generally pursued from the viewpoint of profit maximization and are subject to transactions on the market. Whereas medical care is provided for those who are not able to perform ordinary human functions because of impaired health or injuries, education is provided to help young people develop their human abilities, both innate and acquired, as fully as possible. Both activities play a crucial role in enabling every member of the society in question to maintain his or her human dignity and to enjoy basic human rights as fully as possible. If either medical care or education is subject to market transactions based merely on profit motives or falls under the bureaucratic control of state authorities, its effectiveness may be seriously impaired and the resulting distribution of real income may tend to become extremely unfair and unequal. Thus the economics of education and medical care may be better carefully analyzed within the theoretical framework of social common capital. In this chapter, we examine the role of education as social common capital within the analytical framework introduced in Chapter 2.

2. EDUCATION AS SOCIAL COMMON CAPITAL

We consider a society that consists of a finite number of individuals and two types of institutions: private firms that specialize in producing goods that are transacted on the market, on the one hand, and social institutions concerned with the provision of education as services of social common capital, on the other.

All social institutions discussed in this chapter are characterized by the property that all factors of production needed for the professional provision of education are either privately owned or managed as if privately owned. However, the social institutions in charge of education are managed strictly in accordance with professional discipline and expertise.

Subsidy payments are made for the provision of education, with the rate to be administratively determined by the government and announced prior to the opening of the market. The fees paid to social institutions for the provision of education exceed, by the subsidy rate, those charged for the attainment of education. Given the subsidy rate for the provision of education, the two levels of fees are determined so that the general level of education provided by all educational institutions in the society is precisely equal to the total level of education attained by all individuals of the society. One of the crucial roles of the government is to determine the subsidy rate for education in such a manner that the ensuing pattern of resource allocation and income distribution is optimum in a certain well-defined, socially acceptable sense.

Production of Goods by Private Firms

Individuals are generically denoted by $\nu = 1, \ldots, n$, and private firms by $\mu = 1, \ldots, m$, whereas social institutions in charge of education are denoted by $\sigma = 1, \ldots, s$. Goods produced by private firms are generically denoted by $j = 1, \ldots, J$. We consider the situation in which services provided by educational institutions are measured in a certain well-defined unit. There are two types of factors of production: labor and capital. Labor is assumed to be homogeneous and measured in terms of a certain well-defined unit. As a factor of production, labor is assumed to be variable; that is, labor may be transferred from one type of job to another, without incurring any significant cost or time. There are several kinds of capital goods; they are generically denoted by $f = 1, \ldots, F$. Capital goods are all assumed to be fixed factors of production so that they are specific and fixed components of the particular institutions to which they belong. Once capital goods are installed in a particular institution, they are not shifted to another; only through the process of investment activities may the endowments of capital goods in a particular institution be increased.

Static analysis of private firms or social institutions in charge of education presupposes that the endowments of fixed factors of production are given, as the result of the investment activities carried out by the institutions in the past. Dynamic analysis, on the other hand, concerns processes of the accumulation of fixed factors of production in private firms or social institutions in charge of education and the ensuing implications for the productive capacity in the future.

Quantities of fixed factors of production accumulated in each firm μ are expressed by a vector $K^\mu = (K_f^\mu)$, where K_f^μ denotes the quantity of factor of production f accumulated in firm μ. Quantities of goods produced by firm μ are represented by a vector $x^\mu = (x_j^\mu)$, where x_j^μ denotes the quantity of goods j produced by firm μ, net of the quantities of goods used by firm μ itself. The employment of labor employed by firm μ to carry out production activities is denoted by ℓ^μ.

Social Institutions in Charge of Education

The structure of social institutions in charge of education is similarly postulated. Quantities of capital goods accumulated in social institution σ are expressed by a vector $K^\sigma = (K_f^\sigma)$, where K_f^σ denotes the quantity of fixed factor of production f accumulated in social institution σ. It is assumed that $K^\sigma \geq 0$. The level of education provided by educational institution σ is expressed by a^σ. Labor employed by educational institution σ for the provision of education is denoted by ℓ^σ. We also denote by $x^\sigma = (x_j^\sigma)$ the vector of quantities of produced goods used by educational institution σ for the provision of education.

Principal Agency of the Society

The principal agency of the society in question is each individual who consumes goods produced by private firms and receives education provided by educational institutions. The vector of goods consumed by individual ν is denoted by $c^\nu = (c_j^\nu)$, where c_j^ν is the quantity of good j consumed by individual ν, whereas the level of education attained by individual ν is denoted by a^ν. The amount of labor of each individual ν is given by ℓ^ν. We assume that the labor of all individuals is inelastically supplied to the market.

We assume that both private firms and educational institutions are owned by individuals of the society. We denote by $s^{\nu\mu}$ and $s^{\nu\sigma}$, respectively, the shares of private firm μ and educational institution σ owned by individual ν, where the following conditions are satisfied:

$$s^{\nu\mu} \geqq 0, \quad \sum_{\nu} s^{\nu\mu} = 1; \qquad s^{\nu\sigma} \geqq 0, \quad \sum_{\nu} s^{\nu\sigma} = 1.$$

3. SPECIFICATIONS OF THE MODEL OF EDUCATION AS SOCIAL COMMON CAPITAL

Neoclassical Conditions for Utility Functions

As in previous chapters, we assume that the economic welfare of each individual ν is expressed by a preference ordering that is represented by the utility function

$$u^{\nu} = u^{\nu}(c^{\nu}),$$

where c^{ν} is the vector of goods consumed by individual ν.

We assume that for each individual ν, utility function $u^{\nu}(c^{\nu})$ satisfies the following neoclassical conditions:

(U1) $u^{\nu}(c^{\nu})$ is defined, positive, continuous, and continuously twice-differentiable for all $c^{\nu} \geqq 0$.

(U2) Marginal utilities of consumption are positive; that is,

$$u^{\nu}_{c^{\nu}}(c^{\nu}) > 0 \quad \text{for all } c^{\nu} \geqq 0.$$

(U3) Marginal rates of substitution between any pair of consumption goods are diminishing, or more specifically, $u^{\nu}(c^{\nu})$ is strictly quasi-concave with respect to c^{ν}.

(U4) $u^{\nu}(c^{\nu})$ is homogeneous of order 1 with respect to c^{ν}.

The linear homogeneity hypothesis (U4) implies the following Euler identity:

$$u^{\nu}(c^{\nu}) = u^{\nu}_{c^{\nu}}(c^{\nu})c^{\nu} \quad \text{for all } c^{\nu} \geqq 0.$$

Effects of Education

The effect of education is twofold: private and social. First, regarding the private effect of education, the ability of the labor of each individual as a factor of production is increased by the level of education he or she attains. Second, regarding the social effect of education, an increase in the general level of education enhances an increase in the level of social welfare, whatever the measure taken.

The private effect of education may be expressed by the hypothesis that the ability of labor of each individual ν as a factor of production is given by

$$\varphi^{\nu}(a^{\nu})\ell^{\nu},$$

where ℓ^{ν} is the amount of labor provided by individual ν and $\varphi^{\nu}(a^{\nu})$ expresses the extent to which the ability of labor of individual ν as a factor of production is affected by the level of education a^{ν} he or she attains.

The function $\varphi^{\nu}(a^{\nu})$ specifies the extent of the private effect of education, depending upon the specific level of education a^{ν} each individual ν attains and taking a functional relationship specific to individual ν. It may be referred to as the *impact index of education* for individual ν.

We may assume that for each individual ν, as the level of education a^{ν} he or she attains becomes higher, the impact index of education $\varphi^{\nu}(a^{\nu})$ is accordingly increased, but with diminishing marginal effects. These assumptions may be stated as follows:

$$\varphi^{\nu}(a^{\nu}) > 0, \quad \varphi^{\nu\prime}(a^{\nu}) > 0, \quad \varphi^{\nu\prime\prime}(a^{\nu}) < 0 \quad \text{for all } a^{\nu} \geqq 0.$$

In the analysis of education as social common capital, an important role is played by the *impact coefficient of education*. The impact coefficient of education $\tau^{\nu}(a^{\nu})$ for each individual ν is defined as the relative rate of the marginal increase in the impact index of education due to the marginal increase in the level of education; that is,

$$\tau^{\nu}(a^{\nu}) = \frac{\varphi^{\nu\prime}(a^{\nu})}{\varphi^{\nu}(a^{\nu})}.$$

For each individual ν, the impact coefficient of education $\tau^{\nu}(a^{\nu})$ is decreased as the level of education a^{ν} of individual ν is increased:

$$\tau^{\nu\prime}(a^{\nu}) = \frac{\varphi^{\nu\prime\prime}(a^{\nu})}{\varphi^{\nu}(a^{\nu})} - [\tau^{\nu}(a^{\nu})]^2 < 0.$$

The social effect of education may be expressed by the hypothesis that an increase in the general level of education induces an increase in the utility of every individual in the society; that is, the utility of each individual ν is given by

$$\phi^{\nu}(a)u^{\nu}(c^{\nu}),$$

where $\phi^{\nu}(a)$ is the function specifying the extent to which the utility of each individual ν is increased as the general level of education a is increased. In the analysis developed in this chapter, we take as the general level of education a the aggregate sum of the levels of education of all individuals in the society; that is,

$$a = \sum_{\nu} a^{\nu}.$$

The function $\phi^{\nu}(a)$ specifies the extent of the social effect of education, depending upon the general level of education a of the society but taking a functional relationship specific to each individual ν. It may be referred to as the *impact index of the general level of education* for individual ν.

We may assume that for each individual ν, as the general level of education a of the society becomes higher, the impact index of the general level of education $\phi^{\nu}(a)$ is accordingly increased, but with diminishing marginal effects. These assumptions may be stated as follows:

$$\phi^{\nu}(a) > 0, \quad \phi^{\nu\prime}(a) > 0, \quad \phi^{\nu\prime\prime}(a) < 0 \quad \text{for all } a > 0.$$

The *impact coefficient of the general level of education* for each individual ν, $\tau^{\nu}(a)$, is defined as the relative rate of the marginal increase in the impact index of general education $\phi^{\nu}(a)$ due to the marginal increase in the level of general education a; that is,

$$\tau^{\nu}(a) = \frac{\phi^{\nu\prime}(a)}{\phi^{\nu}(a)}.$$

For each individual ν, the impact coefficient of the general level of education $\tau^{\nu}(a)$ is decreased as the general level of education a is increased:

$$\tau^{\nu\prime}(a) = \frac{\phi^{\nu\prime\prime}(a)}{\phi^{\nu}(a)} - [\tau^{\nu}(a)]^2 < 0.$$

We assume that the impact coefficient of the general level of education $\tau^{\nu}(a)$ is identical for all individuals:

$$\tau^{\nu}(a) = \tau(a) \quad \text{for all individuals } \nu.$$

The Consumer Optimum

Markets for produced goods are perfectly competitive; prices of goods are denoted by $p = (p_j)$ $(p \geq 0)$, and the price charged for the use of educational services is denoted by θ $(\theta \geqq 0)$.

Each individual ν chooses the combination (c^ν, a^ν) of consumption c^ν and level of education a^ν that maximizes the utility of individual ν

$$u^\nu = \phi^\nu(a) u^\nu(c^\nu)$$

subject to the budget constraint

$$pc^\nu + \theta a^\nu = y^\nu = w\varphi^\nu(a^\nu)\ell^\nu + \widehat{y}^\nu, \tag{1}$$

where $w\varphi^\nu(a^\nu)\ell^\nu$ are wages of individual ν, $\widehat{y}^\nu$ is the portion of income y^ν of individual ν other than wages, $\phi^\nu(a)$ and $\phi^\nu(a^\nu)$ are, respectively, the impact indices of social and private effects of education, ℓ^ν is the amount of labor of individual ν, and w is the wage rate.

The optimum combination (c^ν, a^ν) of consumption c^ν and level of education a^ν is characterized by the following marginality conditions:

$$\alpha^\nu \phi^\nu(a) u^\nu_{c^\nu}(c^\nu) \leqq p \quad (\text{mod.}\, c^\nu) \tag{2}$$

$$w\tau^\nu(a^\nu)\varphi^\nu(a^\nu)\ell^\nu = \theta, \tag{3}$$

where $\alpha^\nu > 0$ is the inverse of marginal utility of income of individual ν and $\tau^\nu(a^\nu)$ is the impact coefficient of the private effect of education for individual ν.

Relation (2) expresses the familiar principle that the marginal utility of each good, when measured in units of market price, is exactly equal to the market price. Relation (3) means that the marginal private gains at the level of education a^ν are equal to the educational fee θ.

We derive a relation that will play a central role in our analysis of education as social common capital. By multiplying both sides of relation (2) by c^ν, we obtain

$$\alpha^\nu \phi^\nu(a) u^\nu_{c^\nu}(c^\nu) c^\nu = pc^\nu.$$

On the other hand, in view of the Euler identity for utility function $u^\nu(c^\nu)$ and budgetary constraint (1), we have

$$\alpha^\nu \phi^\nu(a) u^\nu(c^\nu) = pc^\nu. \tag{4}$$

Relation (4) means that at the consumer optimum, the level of utility of individual ν, when expressed in units of market price, is precisely equal to the consumption expenditures of individual ν.

Production Possibility Sets of Private Firms

The conditions concerning the production of goods for each private firm μ are expressed by the production possibility set T^μ that summarizes the technological possibilities and organizational arrangements for firm μ with the endowments of fixed factors of production of firm μ given at $K^\mu = (K^\mu_f)$. It is assumed that $K^\mu \geq 0$.

In view of the hypothesis concerning the heterogeneity of the ability of labor as a factor of production, we need to be careful about the role of labor in production processes of firm μ when the employment of labor by firm μ consists of labor of several individuals. Let us suppose that the employment of labor of firm μ consists of $\ell^{\nu\mu}$ $(\nu = 1, \ldots, n)$, where $\ell^{\nu\mu}$ denotes the amount of labor of individual ν employed by firm μ. As the amount of labor of individual ν is given by ℓ^ν, we have the following relation:

$$\ell^\nu = \sum_\mu \ell^{\nu\mu} + \sum_\sigma \ell^{\nu\sigma} \; (\nu = 1, \ldots, n), \tag{5}$$

where $\ell^{\nu\sigma}$ is the amount of labor of individual ν employed by social institution σ engaged in education.

The amounts of labor of individual ν employed by private firms and social institutions, $\ell^{\nu\mu}$ and $\ell^{\nu\sigma}$, are in ordinary circumstances either ℓ^ν or 0. However, to make the exposition as simple as possible, we express them as if they may take any amount not larger than ℓ^ν.

To define the total employment of labor of firm μ, we must take into account the private effect of education for the ability of labor as a factor of production. The employment of labor of individual ν by the amount $\ell^{\nu\mu}$ may be regarded as the employment of simple labor by the amount $\varphi^\nu(a^\nu)\ell^{\nu\mu}$, where $\varphi^\nu(a^\nu)$ is the impact index of education for individual ν that specifies the extent of the private effect of education depending on the level of education a^ν attained by each individual ν.

Hence, the total labor employment of firm μ, consisting of the employment of labor of individuals by $\ell^{\mu\nu}$ $(\nu = 1, \ldots n)$, may be converted to the employment of simple labor of the following amount:

$$\ell^\mu = \sum_\nu \varphi^\nu(a^\nu)\ell^{\nu\mu} \quad (\mu = 1, \ldots, m). \tag{6}$$

In each private firm μ, the minimum quantities of factors of production required to produce goods by x^μ with the employment of labor at the level ℓ^μ are specified by an F-dimensional vector-valued function:

$$f^\mu(x^\mu, \ell^\mu) = \left(f_f^\mu(x^\mu, \ell^\mu)\right).$$

We assume that marginal rates of substitution between production of goods and employment of labor are smooth and diminishing, there are always trade-offs between them, and the conditions of constant returns to scale prevail. That is, we assume

(T$^\mu$ 1) $f^\mu(x^\mu, \ell^\mu)$ are defined, positive, continuous, and continuously twice-differentiable for all $(x^\mu, \ell^\mu) \geqq 0$.

(T$^\mu$ 2) $f_{x^\mu}^\mu(x^\mu, \ell^\mu) > 0$, $f_{\ell^\mu}^\mu(x^\mu, \ell^\mu) \leqq 0$ for all $(x^\mu, \ell^\mu) \geqq 0$.

(T$^\mu$ 3) $f^\mu(x^\mu, \ell^\mu)$ are strictly quasi-convex with respect to (x^μ, ℓ^μ).

(T$^\mu$ 4) $f^\mu(x^\mu, \ell^\mu)$ are homogeneous of order 1 with respect to (x^μ, ℓ^μ).

From the constant-returns-to-scale conditions (T$^\mu$4), we have the Euler identity:

$$f^\mu(x^\mu, \ell^\mu) = f_{x^\mu}^\mu(x^\mu, \ell^\mu)x^\mu + f_{\ell^\mu}^\mu(x^\mu, \ell^\mu)\ell^\mu \quad \text{for all } (x^\mu, \ell^\mu) \geqq 0.$$

The production possibility set of each private firm μ, T^μ, is composed of all combinations (x^μ, ℓ^μ) of vectors of production x^μ and employment of labor ℓ^μ that are possible with the organizational arrangements, technological conditions, and given endowments of factors of production K^μ in firm μ. Hence, it may be expressed as

$$T^\mu = \left\{(x^\mu, \ell^\mu)\colon (x^\mu, \ell^\mu) \geqq 0,\ f^\mu(x^\mu, \ell^\mu) \leqq K^\mu\right\}.$$

Postulates (T$^\mu$1–T$^\mu$3) imply that the production possibility set T^μ is a closed, convex set of $J + 1$-dimensional vectors (x^μ, ℓ^μ).

The Producer Optimum for Private Firms

As in the case of the consumer optimum, prices of goods and wage rates in perfectly competitive markets are, respectively, denoted by $p = (p_j)$ and w.

Each private firm μ chooses the combination (x^μ, ℓ^μ) of vector of production x^μ and employment of labor ℓ^μ that maximizes net profit

$$px^\mu - w\ell^\mu$$

over $(x^\mu, \ell^\mu) \in T^\mu$.

Conditions ($T^\mu 1$–$T^\mu 3$) postulated above ensure that for any combination of prices p and wage rate w, the optimum combination (x^μ, ℓ^μ) of vector of production x^μ and employment of labor ℓ^μ always exists and is uniquely determined.

To see how the optimum levels of production and labor employment are determined, let us denote the vector of imputed rental prices of capital goods by $r^\mu = (r^\mu_f)$ $[r^\mu_f \geqq 0]$. Then the optimum conditions are

$$p \leqq r^\mu f^\mu_{x^\mu}(x^\mu, \ell^\mu) \quad (\text{mod.}\, x^\mu) \tag{7}$$

$$w \geqq r^\mu[-f^\mu_{\ell^\mu}(x^\mu, \ell^\mu)] \quad (\text{mod.}\, \ell^\mu) \tag{8}$$

$$f^\mu(x^\mu, \ell^\mu) \leqq K^\mu \quad (\text{mod.}\, r^\mu). \tag{9}$$

Condition (7) means that the choice of production technologies and the levels of production are adjusted so as to equate marginal factor costs with output prices.

Condition (8) means that the employment of labor is controlled so that the marginal gains due to the marginal increase in the employment of labor are equal to the wage rate w when $\ell^\mu > 0$, and no larger than w when $\ell^\mu = 0$.

Condition (9) means that the employment of fixed factors of production does not exceed the endowments and the conditions of full employment are satisfied whenever imputed rental price r^μ_f is positive.

In what follows, for the sake of expository brevity, marginality conditions are often assumed to be satisfied by equality.

The technologies are subject to constant returns to scale, ($T^\mu 4$), and thus, in view of the Euler identity, conditions (7)–(9) imply that

$$\begin{aligned} px^\mu - w\ell^\mu &= r^\mu[f^\mu_{x^\mu}(x^\mu, \ell^\mu)x^\mu + f^\mu_{\ell^\mu}(x^\mu, \ell^\mu)\ell^\mu] \\ &= r^\mu f^\mu(x^\mu, \ell^\mu) = r^\mu K^\mu. \end{aligned} \tag{10}$$

That is, for each private firm μ, the net evaluation of output is equal to the sum of the imputed rental payments to all fixed factors of production of private firm μ. The meaning of relation (10) may be better brought out if we rewrite it as

$$px^{\mu} = w\ell^{\mu} + r^{\mu} K^{\mu}.$$

That is, the value of output measured in market prices, px^{μ}, is equal to the sum of wages for the employment of labor, $w\ell^{\mu}$, and the payments, in terms of imputed rental prices, made to the fixed factors of production, $r^{\mu} K^{\mu}$. Thus, the validity of the Menger-Wieser principle of imputation is assured with respect to processes of production of private firms.

Production Possibility Sets of Educational Institutions

As with private firms, the conditions concerning the level of education provided by each educational institution σ are specified by the production possibility set T^{σ} that summarizes the technological possibilities and organizational arrangements of educational institution σ; the endowments of factors of production in educational institution σ are given at

$$K^{\sigma} = (K_f^{\sigma})\ [K^{\sigma} \geq 0].$$

In each educational institution σ, the minimum quantities of factors of production required to provide education at the level a^{σ} with the employment of labor by the amount ℓ^{σ} and the use of produced goods by the amounts $x^{\sigma} = (x_j^{\sigma})$ are specified by an F-dimensional vector-valued function:

$$f^{\sigma}(a^{\sigma}, \ell^{\sigma}, x^{\sigma}) = \left(f_f^{\sigma}(a^{\sigma}, \ell^{\sigma}, x^{\sigma})\right).$$

Exactly as in the case of private firms, we must be careful about the role of labor in the provision of education by educational institution σ when the employment of educational institution σ consists of labor of several individuals. Let us suppose that the employment of labor of educational institution σ consists of $\ell^{\nu\sigma}$ $(\nu = 1, \ldots, n)$, where $\ell^{\nu\sigma}$ denotes the employment of labor of individual ν by educational institution σ.

To define the total employment of labor by educational institution σ, we must take into account the private effect of education for the ability of labor as a factor of production. The employment of labor of individual ν by the amount $\ell^{\nu\sigma}$ may be regarded as the employment of simple labor by the amount $\varphi^{\nu}(a^{\nu})\ell^{\nu\sigma}$. Hence, the total labor employment of social institution σ may be regarded as the employment of simple labor of the amount

$$\ell^{\sigma} = \sum_{\nu} \varphi^{\nu}(a^{\nu})\ell^{\nu\sigma}. \tag{11}$$

We assume that, for each educational institution σ, marginal rates of substitution between any pair of the provision of education, the employment of labor, and the use of produced goods are smooth and diminishing, there are always trade-offs among them, and the conditions of constant returns to scale prevail. Thus we assume

(T$^{\sigma}$1) $f^{\sigma}(a^{\sigma}, \ell^{\sigma}, x^{\sigma})$ are defined, positive, continuous, and continuously twice-differentiable with respect to $(a^{\sigma}, \ell^{\sigma}, x^{\sigma})$ for all $(a^{\sigma}, \ell^{\sigma}, x^{\sigma}) \geqq 0$.

(T$^{\sigma}$2) $f^{\sigma}_{a^{\sigma}}(a^{\sigma}, \ell^{\sigma}, x^{\sigma}) > 0,\ f^{\sigma}_{\ell^{\sigma}}(a^{\sigma}, \ell^{\sigma}, x^{\sigma}) < 0,\ f^{\sigma}_{x^{\sigma}}(a^{\sigma}, \ell^{\sigma}, x^{\sigma}) < 0$ for all $(a^{\sigma}, \ell^{\sigma}, x^{\sigma}) \geqq 0$.

(T$^{\sigma}$3) $f^{\sigma}(a^{\sigma}, \ell^{\sigma}, x^{\sigma})$ are strictly quasi-convex with respect to $(a^{\sigma}, \ell^{\sigma}, x^{\sigma})$.

(T$^{\sigma}$4) $f^{\sigma}(a^{\sigma}, \ell^{\sigma}, x^{\sigma})$ are homogeneous of order 1 with respect to $(a^{\sigma}, \ell^{\sigma}, x^{\sigma})$.

From the constant-returns-to-scale conditions (T$^{\sigma}$4), we have the Euler identity

$$\begin{aligned} f^{\sigma}(a^{\sigma}, \ell^{\sigma}, x^{\sigma}) = {} & f^{\sigma}_{a^{\sigma}}(a^{\sigma}, \ell^{\sigma}, x^{\sigma})a^{\sigma} + f^{\sigma}_{\ell^{\sigma}}(a^{\sigma}, \ell^{\sigma}, x^{\sigma})\ell^{\sigma} \\ & + f^{\sigma}_{x^{\sigma}}(a^{\sigma}, \ell^{\sigma}, x^{\sigma})x^{\sigma} \quad \text{for all } (a^{\sigma}, \ell^{\sigma}, x^{\sigma}) \geqq 0. \end{aligned}$$

For each educational institution σ, the production possibility set T^{σ} is composed of all combinations $(a^{\sigma}, \ell^{\sigma}, x^{\sigma})$ of provision of education a^{σ}, employment of labor ℓ^{σ}, and use of produced goods x^{σ} that are possibly produced with the organizational arrangements, technological conditions, and given endowments of factors of production K^{σ} of educational institution σ. Hence, it may be expressed as

$$T^{\sigma} = \{(a^{\sigma}, \ell^{\sigma}, x^{\sigma})\colon\ (a^{\sigma}, \ell^{\sigma}, x^{\sigma}) \geqq 0,\ f^{\sigma}(a^{\sigma}, \ell^{\sigma}, x^{\sigma}) \leqq K^{\sigma}\}.$$

Postulates (T$^{\sigma}$1–T$^{\sigma}$3) imply that the production possibility set T^{σ} of educational institution σ is a closed, convex set of $1+1+J$-dimensional vectors $(a^{\sigma}, \ell^{\sigma}, x^{\sigma})$.

The Producer Optimum for Educational Institutions

As with private firms, the conditions of the producer optimum for social institutions in charge of education may be obtained. We denote by π the rate of fees paid for the provision of education.

Each educational institution σ chooses the combination $(a^\sigma, \ell^\sigma, x^\sigma)$ of provision of education a^σ, employment of labor ℓ^σ, and use of produced goods w^σ that maximizes net value

$$\pi a^\sigma - w\ell^\sigma - px^\sigma, (a^\sigma, \ell^\sigma, x^\sigma) \in T^\sigma.$$

Conditions ($T^\sigma 1$–$T^\sigma 3$) postulated for educational institution σ ensure that for any combination of fees paid for the provision of education π, wage rate w, and prices of produced goods p, the optimum combination $(a^\sigma, \ell^\sigma, x^\sigma)$ of provision of education a^σ, employment of labor ℓ^σ, and use of produced goods x^σ always exists and is uniquely determined.

The optimum combination $(a^\sigma, \ell^\sigma, x^\sigma)$ of provision of education a^σ, employment of labor ℓ^σ, and use of produced goods x^σ may be characterized by the marginality conditions, in exactly the same manner as for the case of private firms. We denote by $r^\sigma = (r_f^\sigma)$ $[r_f^\sigma \geqq 0]$ the vector of imputed rental prices of fixed factors of production of educational institution σ. Then the optimum conditions are

$$\pi \leqq r^\sigma f_{a^\sigma}^\sigma(a^\sigma, \ell^\sigma, x^\sigma) \quad (\text{mod.}\, a^\sigma) \tag{12}$$

$$w \geqq r^\sigma [-f_{\ell^\sigma}^\sigma(a^\sigma, \ell^\sigma, x^\sigma)] \quad (\text{mod.}\, \ell^\sigma) \tag{13}$$

$$p \geqq r^\sigma [-f_{x^\sigma}^\sigma(a^\sigma, \ell^\sigma, x^\sigma)] \quad (\text{mod.}\, x^\sigma) \tag{14}$$

$$f^\sigma(a^\sigma, \ell^\sigma, x^\sigma) \leqq K^\sigma \quad (\text{mod.}\, r^\sigma). \tag{15}$$

Condition (12) expresses the principle that the levels of educational services are adjusted so as to equate marginal factor costs with the fees for education π.

Condition (13) means that employment of labor ℓ^σ is adjusted so that the marginal gains due to the marginal increase in the employment of labor are equal to the price w when $\ell^\sigma > 0$ and are not larger than the price w when $\ell^\sigma = 0$.

Condition (14) means that the use of produced goods is adjusted so that the marginal gains due to the marginal increase in the use of produced goods are equal to price p_j when $x_j^\sigma > 0$ and are not larger than p_j when $x_j^\sigma = 0$.

Condition (15) means that the employments of fixed factors of production do not exceed the endowments and the conditions of full employment are satisfied whenever imputed rental price r_f^σ is positive.

We have assumed that the technologies are subject to constant returns to scale ($\mathrm{T}^\sigma 4$), and thus, in view of the Euler identity, conditions (12)–(15) imply that

$$\begin{aligned}\pi a^\sigma - w\ell^\sigma - px^\sigma &= r^\sigma\big[f_{a^\sigma}^\sigma(a^\sigma, \ell^\sigma, x^\sigma)a^\sigma + f_{\ell^\sigma}^\sigma(a^\sigma, \ell^\sigma, x^\sigma)\ell^\sigma \\ &\quad + f_{x^\sigma}^\sigma(a^\sigma, \ell^\sigma, x^\sigma)x^\sigma\big] \\ &= r^\sigma K^\sigma. \end{aligned} \tag{16}$$

That is, for each educational institution σ, the net evaluation of provision of education is equal to the sum of the imputed rental payments to all fixed factors of production in social institution σ. As in the case for private firms, the meaning of relation (16) may be better brought out if we rewrite it as

$$\pi a^\sigma = w\ell^\sigma + px^\sigma + r^\sigma K^\sigma.$$

The value of education provided by educational institution σ, πa^σ, is equal to the sum of wages $w\ell^\sigma$, payments for the use of produced goods px^σ, and payments, in terms of the imputed rental prices, made to fixed factors of production $r^\sigma K^\sigma$. The validity of the Menger-Wieser principle of imputation is also assured for the case of the provision of education by educational institutions.

4. EDUCATION AS SOCIAL COMMON CAPITAL AND MARKET MECHANISM

We first recapitulate the basic premises of the model of education as social common capital introduced in the previous sections. Markets for produced goods are perfectly competitive; prices of goods are denoted by vector p, the fees charged for educational services and paid for the provision of educational services are, respectively, denoted by θ and π, and the wage rate is denoted by w.

Neoclassical Conditions for Utility Functions

The economic welfare of each individual ν is expressed by a preference ordering that is represented by the utility function

$$u^\nu = \phi^\nu(a)u^\nu(c^\nu),$$

where c^ν is the vector of goods consumed by individual ν and $\phi^\nu(a)$ is the impact index of general education for individual ν, specifying the extent of the social effect of education, depending upon the general level of education a of the society:

$$a = \sum_\nu a^\nu,$$

where a^ν denotes the level of education of individual ν.

The impact coefficient of general education for individual ν, as defined by

$$\tau(a) = \frac{\phi^{\nu\prime}(a)}{\phi^\nu(a)},$$

is assumed to be identical for all individuals ν, where

$$\tau'(a) < 0.$$

The private effect of education may be expressed by the hypothesis that the ability of labor of each individual ν as a factor of production is given by

$$\varphi^\nu(a^\nu)\ell^\nu,$$

where $\varphi^\nu(a^\nu)$ is the impact index of education for individual ν.

The impact coefficient of education $\tau^\nu(a^\nu)$ for individual ν is given by

$$\tau^\nu(a^\nu) = \frac{\varphi^{\nu\prime}(a^\nu)}{\varphi^\nu(a^\nu)},$$

where

$$\tau^{\nu\prime}(a^\nu) < 0.$$

The Consumer Optimum

The consumer optimum is characterized by the following conditions:

$$pc^\nu + \theta a^\nu = y^\nu = w\varphi^\nu(a^\nu)\ell^\nu + \widehat{y}^\nu \tag{17}$$

$$\alpha^\nu \phi^\nu(a) u^\nu_{c^\nu}(c^\nu) \leqq p \quad (\text{mod.}\, c^\nu) \tag{18}$$

$$w\tau^\nu(a^\nu)\varphi^\nu(a^\nu)\ell^\nu = \theta \tag{19}$$

$$\alpha^\nu \phi^\nu(a) u^\nu(c^\nu) = pc^\nu, \tag{20}$$

where $w\varphi^{\nu}(a^{\nu})\ell^{\nu}$ denotes the wages of individual ν, $\widehat{y}^{\nu}$ is the portion of income y^{ν} of individual ν other than wages, $\alpha^{\nu} > 0$ is the inverse of marginal utility of income of individual ν, $\phi^{\nu}(a)$ and $\varphi^{\nu}(a^{\nu})$ are, respectively, the impact indices of social and private effects of education, $\tau^{\nu}(a^{\nu})$ is the impact coefficient of the private effect of education for individual ν, and ℓ^{ν} is the amount of labor of individual ν.

We denote by $\ell^{\nu\mu}$ and $\ell^{\nu\sigma}$ the amounts of labor of individual ν, respectively, employed by private firm μ and educational institution σ ($\mu = 1, \ldots m$; $\sigma = 1, \ldots s$), so that

$$\ell^{\nu} = \sum_{\mu} \ell^{\nu\mu} + \sum_{\sigma} \ell^{\nu\sigma} \quad (\nu = 1, \ldots, n), \tag{21}$$

where ℓ^{ν} is the total labor of individual ν.

Production Possibility Sets of Private Firms

The production possibility set of each private firm μ, T^{μ}, is given by

$$T^{\mu} = \{(x^{\mu}, \ell^{\mu})\colon (x^{\mu}, \ell^{\mu}) \geqq 0,\ \ f^{\mu}(x^{\mu}, \ell^{\mu}) \leqq K^{\mu}\},$$

where $f^{\mu}(x^{\mu}, \ell^{\mu})$ specifies the minimum quantities of factors of production that are required to produce goods by x^{μ} with the employment of labor at ℓ^{μ}.

The employment of labor at firm μ, ℓ^{μ}, when converted to simple labor, is given by

$$\ell^{\mu} = \sum_{\nu} \varphi^{\nu}(a^{\nu})\ell^{\nu\mu}, \tag{22}$$

where $\ell^{\nu\mu}$ denotes the employment of labor of individual ν by firm μ ($\nu = 1, \ldots n$).

The Producer Optimum for Private Firms

Each private firm μ chooses the combination (x^{μ}, ℓ^{μ}) of vectors of production x^{μ} and labor employment ℓ^{μ} that maximizes net profit

$$px^{\mu} - w\ell^{\mu}$$

over $(x^{\mu}, \ell^{\mu}) \in T^{\mu}$.

The producer optimum is characterized by the following marginality conditions:

$$p \leqq r^{\mu} f^{\mu}_{x^{\mu}}(x^{\mu}, \ell^{\mu}) \quad (\mathrm{mod.}\, x^{\mu}) \tag{23}$$

$$w \geqq r^{\mu} \left[- f^{\mu}_{\ell^{\mu}}(x^{\mu}, \ell^{\mu})\right] \quad (\mathrm{mod.}\, \ell^{\mu}) \tag{24}$$

$$f^{\mu}(x^{\mu}, \ell^{\mu}) \leqq K^{\mu} \quad (\mathrm{mod.}\, r^{\mu}). \tag{25}$$

The constant-returns-to-scale hypothesis implies the following identity:

$$px^{\mu} - w\ell^{\mu} = r^{\mu} K^{\mu}. \tag{26}$$

Production Possibility Sets for Educational Institutions

For each educational institution σ, the production possibility set T^{σ} is given by

$$T^{\sigma} = \{(a^{\sigma}, \ell^{\sigma}, x^{\sigma})\colon (a^{\sigma}, \ell^{\sigma}, x^{\sigma}) \geqq 0,\ f^{\sigma}(a^{\sigma}, \ell^{\sigma}, x^{\sigma}) \leqq K^{\sigma}\},$$

where the F-dimensional vector-valued function $f^{\sigma}(a^{\sigma}, \ell^{\sigma}, x^{\sigma})$ specifies the minimum quantities of factors of production required to provide education by the level a^{σ} with the employment of labor by ℓ^{σ} and the use of produced goods by x^{σ}, and K^{σ} denotes the endowments of fixed factors of production of social institution σ.

Total employment of labor of social institution σ, ℓ^{σ}, is given by

$$\ell^{\sigma} = \sum_{\nu} \varphi^{\nu}(a^{\nu}) \ell^{\nu\sigma}. \tag{27}$$

The Producer Optimum for Educational Institutions

Each educational institution σ chooses the combination $(a^{\sigma}, \ell^{\sigma}, x^{\sigma})$ of provision of educational services a^{σ}, employment of labor ℓ^{σ}, and use of produced goods that maximizes net value

$$\pi a^{\sigma} - w\ell^{\sigma} - px^{\sigma}$$

over $(a^{\sigma}, \ell^{\sigma}, x^{\sigma}) \in T^{\sigma}$.

The optimum conditions are

$$\pi \leqq r^{\sigma} f^{\sigma}_{a^{\sigma}}(a^{\sigma}, \ell^{\sigma}, x^{\sigma}) \quad (\mathrm{mod.}\, a^{\sigma}) \tag{28}$$

$$w \geqq r^{\sigma} [- f^{\sigma}_{\ell^{\sigma}}(a^{\sigma}, \ell^{\sigma}, x^{\sigma})] \quad (\mathrm{mod.}\, \ell^{\sigma}) \tag{29}$$

$$p \geqq r^\sigma [-f^\sigma_{x^\sigma}(a^\sigma, \ell^\sigma, x^\sigma)] \quad (\text{mod.}\, x^\sigma) \tag{30}$$

$$f^\sigma(a^\sigma, \ell^\sigma, x^\sigma) \leqq K^\sigma \quad (\text{mod.}\, r^\sigma). \tag{31}$$

The constant-returns-to-scale hypothesis implies the following identity:

$$\pi a^\sigma - w\ell^\sigma - px^\sigma = r^\sigma K^\sigma. \tag{32}$$

Market Equilibrium for the Model of Education as Social Common Capital

Market equilibrium for the model of education as social common capital is obtained if the following equilibrium conditions are satisfied:

(i) Each individual ν chooses the combination (c^ν, a^ν) of consumption c^ν and level of education a^ν that maximizes the utility of individual ν

$$u^\nu = \phi^\nu(a)u^\nu(c^\nu)$$

subject to the budget constraint

$$pc^\nu + \theta a^\nu = y^\nu = w\varphi^\nu(a^\nu)\ell^\nu + \widehat{y}^\nu,$$

where $w\varphi^\nu(a^\nu)\ell^\nu$ denotes the wages of individual ν, $\widehat{y}^\nu$ is the portion of income y^ν of individual ν other than wages, and a is the general level of education of the society:

$$a = \sum_\nu a^\nu. \tag{33}$$

The optimum level of education attained by individual ν, a^ν, is determined at the level at which

$$\tau^\nu(a^\nu)w\varphi^\nu(a^\nu)\ell^\nu = \theta.$$

(ii) Each private firm μ chooses the combination (x^μ, ℓ^μ) of vector of production x^μ and labor employment ℓ^μ that maximizes net profits

$$px^\mu - w\ell^\mu, \quad (x^\mu, \ell^\mu) \in T^\mu,$$

where

$$\ell^{\mu} = \sum_{\nu} \varphi^{\nu}(a^{\nu})\ell^{\nu\mu}.$$

(iii) Each educational institution σ chooses the combination $(a^{\sigma}, \ell^{\sigma}, x^{\sigma})$ of provision of education a^{σ}, employment of labor ℓ^{σ}, and use of produced goods that maximizes net value

$$\pi a^{\sigma} - w\ell^{\sigma} - px^{\sigma}, \quad (a^{\sigma}, \ell^{\sigma}, x^{\sigma}) \in T^{\sigma},$$

where

$$\ell^{\sigma} = \sum_{\sigma} \varphi^{\nu}(a^{\nu})\ell^{\nu\sigma}.$$

(iv) The general level a of education of the society is equal to the sum of the levels of education provided by all educational institutions σ; that is,

$$a = \sum_{\sigma} a^{\sigma}. \tag{34}$$

(v) At the wage rate w, total demand for the employment of labor is equal to total supply:

$$\sum_{\mu} \ell^{\mu} + \sum_{\sigma} \ell^{\sigma} = \sum_{\nu} \varphi^{\nu}(a^{\nu})\ell^{\nu}. \tag{35}$$

(vi) At the vector of prices for produced goods p, total demand for goods is equal to total supply:

$$\sum_{\nu} c^{\nu} + \sum_{\sigma} x^{\sigma} = \sum_{\mu} x^{\mu}. \tag{36}$$

(vii) Subsidy payments, at the rate τ ($\tau \geqq 0$), are made to social institutions in charge of education, so that

$$\pi - \theta = \tau. \tag{37}$$

In the following discussion, we suppose that for any given rate τ of subsidy payments to educational institutions, the state of the economy that satisfies all conditions for market equilibrium generally exists and is uniquely determined.

Concerning National Income Accounting

Income y^ν of each individual ν is given as the sum of wages and dividend payments of private firms and social institutions, subtracted by tax payments t^ν:

$$y^\nu = w\varphi^\nu(a^\nu)\ell^\nu + \sum_\mu s^{\nu\mu} r^\mu K^\mu + \sum_\sigma s^{\nu\sigma} r^\sigma K^\sigma - t^\nu, \tag{38}$$

where

$$s^{\nu\mu} \geqq 0, \quad \sum_\nu s^{\nu\mu} = 1, \quad s^{\nu\sigma} \geqq 0, \quad \sum_\nu s^{\nu\sigma} = 1.$$

Tax payments of individuals $\{t^\nu\}$ are arranged so that the sum of tax payments made by all individuals is equal to the sum of subsidy payments to all social institutions in charge of education, τa:

$$\sum_\nu t^\nu = \tau a, \quad \tau = \pi - \theta. \tag{39}$$

National income y is the sum of incomes of all individuals:

$$y = \sum_\nu y^\nu.$$

Hence,

$$\begin{aligned} y &= \sum_\nu w\varphi^\nu(a^\nu)\ell^\nu + \sum_\mu r^\mu K^\mu + \sum_\sigma \rho^\sigma V^\sigma - \sum_\nu t^\nu a \\ &= \sum_\nu w\varphi^\nu(a^\nu)\ell^\nu + \sum_\mu (px^\mu - w\ell^\mu) + \sum_\sigma (\pi a^\sigma - w\ell^\sigma - px^\sigma) - \tau a \\ &= \sum_\nu (pc^\nu + \theta a^\nu) + (\pi - \theta)a - \tau a \\ &= \sum_\nu (pc^\nu + \theta a^\nu). \end{aligned}$$

Thus we have established the familiar identity of two definitions of national income.

5. MARKET EQUILIBRIUM AND SOCIAL OPTIMUM

To explore welfare implications of market equilibrium under the subsidy payment scheme to the social institutions in charge of education with the rate τ, we would like to consider the social utility U given by

$$U = \sum_\nu \alpha^\nu u^\nu = \sum_\nu \alpha^\nu \phi^\nu(a) u^\nu(c^\nu),$$

where utility weight α^ν is the inverse of marginal utility of income y^ν of individual ν at the market equilibrium.

We consider the following maximum problem:

Maximum Problem for Social Optimum. Find the pattern of consumption and production of goods, employment of labor, and provision of education $c^\nu, a^\nu, x^\mu, \ell^\mu, a^\sigma, \ell^\sigma, x^\sigma, a$ that maximizes the social utility

$$U = \sum_\nu \alpha^\nu u^\nu = \sum_\nu \alpha^\nu \phi^\nu(a) u^\nu(c^\nu)$$

among all feasible patterns of allocation

$$\sum_\nu c^\nu + \sum_\sigma x^\sigma \leqq \sum_\mu x^\mu \tag{40}$$

$$\sum_\mu \ell^{\nu\mu} + \sum_\sigma \ell^{\nu\sigma} \leqq \ell^\nu \tag{41}$$

$$\ell^\mu = \sum_\nu \varphi^\nu(a^\nu) \ell^{\nu\mu} \tag{42}$$

$$\ell^\sigma = \sum_\nu \varphi^\nu(a^\nu) \ell^{\sigma\nu} \tag{43}$$

$$\sum_\nu a^\nu \leqq a \tag{44}$$

$$a \leqq \sum_\sigma a^\sigma \tag{45}$$

$$f^\mu(x^\mu, \ell^\mu) \leqq K^\mu \tag{46}$$

$$f^\sigma(a^\sigma, \ell^\sigma, x^\sigma) \leqq K^\sigma, \tag{47}$$

where utility weights α^ν are evaluated at the market equilibrium corresponding to the given subsidy rate τ.

The maximum problem for social optimum may be solved in terms of the Lagrange method. Let us define the Lagrangian form:

$$L(c^\nu, a^\nu, x^\mu, \ell^\mu, \ell^{\nu\mu}, a^\sigma, \ell^\sigma, \ell^{\nu\sigma}, x^\sigma, a; p, w^\nu, w^\mu, w^\sigma, \theta, \pi, r^\mu, r^\sigma)$$
$$= \sum_\nu \alpha^\nu \phi^\nu(a) u^\nu(c^\nu) + p\left(\sum_\mu x^\mu - \sum_\nu c^\nu - \sum_\sigma x^\sigma\right)$$
$$+ \sum_\nu w^\nu \left[\ell^\nu - \sum_\mu \ell^{\nu\mu} - \sum_\sigma \ell^{\nu\sigma}\right] + \sum_\mu w^\mu \left[\sum_\nu \varphi^\nu(a^\nu) \ell^{\nu\mu} - \ell^\mu\right]$$

$$+ \sum_{\sigma} w^{\sigma} \left[\sum_{\nu} \varphi^{\nu}(a^{\nu}) \ell^{\nu\sigma} - \ell^{\sigma} \right] + \theta \left(a - \sum_{\nu} a^{\nu} \right) + \pi \left(\sum_{\sigma} a^{\sigma} - a \right)$$
$$+ \sum_{\mu} r^{\mu} \left[K^{\mu} - f^{\mu}(x^{\mu}, \ell^{\mu}) \right] + \sum_{\sigma} r^{\sigma} \left[K^{\sigma} - f^{\sigma}(a^{\sigma}, \ell^{\sigma}, x^{\sigma}) \right]. \quad (48)$$

The Lagrange unknowns $p, w^{\nu}, w^{\mu}, w^{\sigma}, \theta, \pi, r^{\mu}$, and r^{σ} are, respectively, associated with constraints (40), (41), (42), (43), (44), (45), (46), and (47).

The optimum solution may be obtained by differentiating the Lagrangian form (47) partially with respect to unknown variables $c^{\nu}, a^{\nu}, x^{\mu}, \ell^{\mu}, \ell^{\nu\mu}, a^{\sigma}, \ell^{\sigma}, \ell^{\nu\sigma}, x^{\sigma}, a$, and putting them equal to 0:

$$\alpha^{\nu} \phi^{\nu}(a) u^{\nu}_{c^{\nu}}(c^{\nu}) \leqq p \qquad (\text{mod.}\, c^{\nu}) \quad (49)$$

$$w \tau^{\nu}(a^{\nu}) \varphi^{\nu}(a^{\nu}) \ell^{\nu} = \theta \quad (50)$$

$$p \leqq r^{\mu} f^{\mu}_{x^{\mu}}(x^{\mu}, \ell^{\mu}) \qquad (\text{mod.}\, x^{\mu}) \quad (51)$$

$$w \geqq r^{\mu}[-f^{\mu}_{\ell^{\mu}}(x^{\mu}, \ell^{\mu})] \qquad (\text{mod.}\, \ell^{\mu}) \quad (52)$$

$$\pi \leqq r^{\sigma} f^{\sigma}_{a^{\sigma}}(a^{\sigma}, \ell^{\sigma}, x^{\sigma}) \quad (\text{mod.}\, a^{\sigma}) \quad (53)$$

$$w \geqq r^{\sigma} [-f^{\sigma}_{\ell^{\sigma}}(a^{\sigma}, \ell^{\sigma}, x^{\sigma})] \quad (\text{mod.}\, \ell^{\sigma}) \quad (54)$$

$$p \geqq r^{\sigma} [-f^{\sigma}_{x^{\sigma}}(a^{\sigma}, \ell^{\sigma}, x^{\sigma})] \quad (\text{mod.}\, x^{\sigma}) \quad (55)$$

$$f^{\mu}(x^{\mu}, \ell^{\mu}) \leqq K^{\mu} \quad (\text{mod.}\, r^{\mu}) \quad (56)$$

$$f^{\sigma}(a^{\sigma}, \ell^{\sigma}, x^{\sigma}) \leqq K^{\sigma} \quad (\text{mod.}\, r^{\sigma}) \quad (57)$$

$$\pi - \theta = \tau(a) p c, \quad c = \sum_{\nu} c^{\nu}, \quad (58)$$

where

$$w^{\nu} = \varphi^{\nu}(a^{\nu}) w, \quad w^{\mu} = w^{\sigma} = w$$

and $\tau(a)$ is the impact coefficient of the general level of education.

Only equation (58) may need clarification. Partially differentiate the Lagrangian form (48) with respect to a to obtain

$$\frac{\partial L}{\partial a} = \tau(a)\sum_{\nu} \alpha^{\nu}\phi^{\nu}(a)\varphi^{\nu}(a^{\nu})u^{\nu}(c^{\nu}) + \theta - \pi,$$

where it may be noted that marginality condition (49) and the linear homogeneity hypothesis for utility functions $u^{\nu}(c^{\nu})$ imply

$$\sum_{\nu} \alpha^{\nu}\phi^{\nu}(a)\varphi^{\nu}(a^{\nu})u^{\nu}(c^{\nu}) = \sum_{\nu} pc^{\nu}.$$

Hence, $\frac{\partial L}{\partial a} = 0$ implies equation (56).

Applying the classic Kuhn-Tucker theorem on concave programming, the Euler-Lagrange equations (49)–(58) are necessary and sufficient conditions for the optimum solution of the maximum problem for social optimum.

It is apparent that the Euler-Lagrange equations (49)–(58) coincide precisely with the equilibrium conditions for market equilibrium with the subsidy payment to social institutions in charge of education at the rate τ given by

$$\tau = \tau(a)pc.$$

We have thus established the following proposition.

Proposition 1. *Consider the subsidy scheme to social institutions in charge of education at the rate τ given by*

$$\tau = \tau(a)pc, \quad c = \sum_{\nu} c^{\nu},$$

where $\tau(a)$ is the impact coefficient of general education and c is aggregate consumption.

Tax payments of individuals $\{t^{\nu}\}$ are arranged so that the balance-of-budget conditions are satisfied:

$$\sum_{\nu} t^{\nu} = \tau a.$$

Then market equilibrium obtained under such a subsidy scheme is a social optimum in the sense that a set of positive weights for the utilities of individuals $(\alpha^1, \ldots, \alpha^n)$ $[\alpha^{\nu} > 0]$ exists such that the social utility

$$U = \sum_{\nu} \alpha^{\nu}u^{\nu} = \sum_{\nu} \alpha^{\nu}\phi^{\nu}(a)u^{\nu}(c^{\nu})$$

is maximized among all feasible patterns of allocation $(c^\nu, a^\nu, x^\mu, \ell^\mu, a^\sigma, \ell^\sigma, x^\sigma, a)$.

The optimum level of social utility U is equal to consumption expenditures pc:

$$U = pc.$$

Social optimum may be defined with respect to social utility

$$U = \sum_\nu \alpha^\nu u^\nu = \sum_\nu \alpha^\nu \phi^\nu(a) u^\nu(c^\nu),$$

where $(\alpha^1, \ldots, \alpha^n)$ is an arbitrarily given set of positive weights for the utilities of individuals. A pattern of allocation $(c^\nu, a^\nu, x^\mu, \ell^\mu, a^\sigma, \ell^\sigma, x^\sigma, a)$ is social optimum if the social utility U thus defined is maximized among all feasible patterns of allocation.

Social optimum necessarily implies the existence of the subsidy scheme to social institutions in charge of education at the rate τ given by

$$\tau = \tau(a) pc.$$

However, the budgetary constraints for individuals

$$pc^\nu + \theta a^\nu = y^\nu$$

are not necessarily satisfied. It is apparent that the following proposition holds.

Proposition 2. *Suppose a pattern of allocation* $(c^\nu, a^\nu, x^\mu, \ell^\mu, a^\sigma, \ell^\sigma, x^\sigma, a)$ *is a social optimum; that is, a set of positive weights for the utilities of individuals* $(\alpha^1, \ldots, \alpha^n)$ *exists such that the given pattern of allocation* $(c^\nu, a^\nu, x^\mu, \ell^\mu, a^\sigma, \ell^\sigma, x^\sigma, a)$ *maximizes the social utility*

$$U = \sum_\nu \alpha^\nu u^\nu = \sum_\nu \alpha^\nu \phi^\nu(a) u^\nu(c^\nu)$$

among all feasible patterns of allocation.

Then, a system of individual taxes $\{t^\nu\}$ *satisfying the balance-of-budget conditions*

$$\sum_\nu t^\nu = \tau a, \quad \tau = \tau(a) pc$$

exists such that the given pattern of allocation $(c^\nu, a^\nu, x^\mu, \ell^\mu, a^\sigma, \ell^\sigma, x^\sigma, a)$ *corresponds precisely to the market equilibrium under the subsidy* *scheme to social institutions in charge of education at the rate τ given by $\tau = \tau(a)pc$.*

6. MARKET EQUILIBRIUM AND LINDAHL EQUILIBRIUM

Lindahl Conditions

Let us recall the postulates for the behavior of individuals at market equilibrium. At market equilibrium, conditions for the consumer optimum are obtained if each individual ν chooses the combination (c^ν, a^ν) of consumption c^ν and level of education a^ν that maximizes the utility of individual ν

$$u^\nu = \phi^\nu(a)u^\nu(c^\nu)$$

subject to the budget constraint

$$pc^\nu + \theta a^\nu = y^\nu,$$

where

$$y^\nu = w\varphi^\nu(a^\nu)\ell^\nu + \sum_\mu s^{\nu\mu} r^\mu K^\mu + \sum_\sigma s^{\nu\sigma} r^\sigma K^\sigma - t^\nu$$

and the following conditions are satisfied:

$$\sum_\nu t^\nu = \tau a, \quad \tau = \tau(a)y.$$

Let us first rewrite the budget constraint as follows:

$$pc^\nu - \tau a^\nu = \overline{y}^\nu,$$

where

$$\overline{y}^\nu = y^\nu - \tau a^\nu, \quad \tau = \tau(a)pc.$$

Lindahl conditions are satisfied if a system of individual subsidy rates $\{\tau^\nu\}$ exists such that

$$\sum_\nu \tau^\nu = \tau, \quad \tau = \tau(a)pc$$

and for each individual ν, (c^ν, a) is the optimum solution to the following virtual maximum problem:

Find $(\overline{c}^\nu, \overline{a}^{(\nu)})$ that maximizes

$$u^\nu = \varphi^\nu(\overline{a}^{(\nu)})u^\nu(\overline{c}^\nu)$$

subject to the virtual budget constraint

$$p\bar{c}^{\nu} - \tau^{\nu}\bar{a}^{(\nu)} = \bar{y}^{\nu}.$$

Because (c^{ν}, a) is the optimum solution to the virtual maximum problem for individual ν, the optimum conditions imply

$$\tau^{\nu} = \alpha^{\nu}\tau(a)\phi^{\nu}(a)u^{\nu}(c^{\nu}) = \tau(a)pc^{\nu},$$

where α^{ν} is the inverse of marginal utility of income of individual ν.

Hence, Lindahl conditions are satisfied if, and only if,

$$\tau^{\nu}a = \tau a^{\nu},$$

which implies

$$[\tau(a)pc^{\nu}]a = [\tau(a)pc]a^{\nu} \Leftrightarrow \frac{a^{\nu}}{a} = \frac{pc^{\nu}}{pc}.$$

Thus, we have established the following proposition.

Proposition 3. *Consider the subsidy scheme to social institutions in charge of education at the rate* τ *given by*

$$\tau = \tau(a)pc, \quad c = \sum_{\nu} c^{\nu},$$

where $\tau(a)$ *is the impact coefficient of the general level of education and* c *is aggregate consumption.*

Then market equilibrium under such a subsidy scheme is Lindahl equilibrium if, and only if, the following conditions are satisfied:

$$\frac{a^{\nu}}{a} = \frac{pc^{\nu}}{pc},$$

where a^{ν} *is the level of education attained by individual* ν *and* a *is the general level of education.*

7. ADJUSTMENT PROCESSES OF SUBSIDY RATES FOR EDUCATIONAL INSTITUTIONS

Market equilibrium under the subsidy scheme to social institutions in charge of education at the rate τ given by

$$\tau = \tau(a)pc$$

coincides with the social optimum with respect to the social utility

$$U = \sum_\nu \alpha^\nu u^\nu = \sum_\nu \alpha^\nu \phi^\nu(a) u^\nu(c^\nu),$$

where for each individual ν, utility weight α^ν is the inverse of marginal utility of income y^ν at market equilibrium.

The subsidy rate $\tau = \tau(a)pc$ is administratively determined and announced prior to the opening of the market when the level of general education a is not known. We would like to introduce adjustment processes concerning the subsidy rate τ that are stable. We first consider an alternative adjustment process concerning the general level of education a.

First we examine the relationships between the general level of education a and the ensuing level of the social utility U. Let us assume that the general level of education a is announced at the beginning of the adjustment process and consider the pattern of resource allocation at market equilibrium with the general level of education at the announced level a.

Market equilibrium under the subsidy scheme to social institutions in charge of education at the rate $\tau = \tau(a)y$ is obtained if the following equilibrium conditions are satisfied:

(i) Each individual ν chooses the combination (c^ν, a^ν) of consumption c^ν and level of education a^ν that maximizes the utility of individual ν

$$u^\nu = \phi^\nu(a) u^\nu(c^\nu)$$

subject to the budget constraint

$$pc^\nu + \theta a^\nu = y^\nu,$$

where y^ν is the income of individual ν in units of market price.

(ii) Each private firm μ chooses the combination (x^μ, ℓ^μ) of vector of production x^μ and employment of labor ℓ^μ that maximizes net profit

$$px^\mu - w\ell^\mu, \quad (x^\mu, \ell^\mu) \in T^\mu,$$

where

$$\ell^\mu = \sum_\nu \varphi^\nu(a^\nu)\ell^{\nu\mu}$$

and $\ell^{\nu\mu}$ is the amount of labor of individual ν employed by private firm μ.

(iii) Each educational institution σ chooses the combination $(a^\sigma, \ell^\sigma, x^\sigma)$ of provision of education a^σ, employment of labor ℓ^σ, and use of produced goods x^σ that maximizes net value

$$\pi a^\sigma - w\ell^\sigma - px^\sigma, \quad (a^\sigma, \ell^\sigma, x^\sigma) \in T^\sigma,$$

where

$$\ell^\sigma = \sum_\nu \varphi^\nu(a^\nu)\ell^{\nu\sigma}$$

and $\ell^{\nu\sigma}$ is the amount of labor of individual ν employed by educational institution σ.

(iv) At the prices for produced goods p, total demand for goods is equal to total supply:

$$\sum_\nu c^\nu + \sum_\sigma x^\sigma = \sum_\mu x^\mu.$$

(v) At the wage rate w, total demand for the employment of labor is equal to total supply:

$$\sum_\mu \ell^\mu + \sum_\sigma \ell^\sigma = \sum_\nu \varphi^\nu(a^\nu)\ell^\nu.$$

(vi) The general level of education a is equal to the sum of the levels of education provided by all educational institutions σ; that is,

$$a = \sum_\sigma a^\sigma.$$

(vii) The general level of education a is equal to the sum of the levels of education attained by all individuals of the society; that is,

$$a = \sum_\nu a^\nu.$$

It may be noted that the general level of education is given arbitrarily at level a and announced prior to the opening of the market, whereas the subsidy rate for educational institutions, τ, is simply given at the level given by

$$\pi - \theta = \tau,$$

where π and θ are, respectively, the fees for the provision and attainment of education that are determined on the market.

Market equilibrium thus obtained corresponds to the social optimum with respect to the social utility

$$U = \sum_{\nu} \alpha^{\nu} u^{\nu} = \sum_{\nu} \alpha^{\nu} \phi^{\nu}(a) u^{\nu}(c^{\nu}),$$

where α^{ν} is the inverse of marginal utility of income of individual ν at the market equilibrium, with the general level of education at the predetermined level a.

We would like to examine the effect of the marginal change in the general level of education a on the level of the social utility U. The level of the social utility U at market equilibrium is given as the value of the Lagrangian form L, as defined by (48), where a is not a variable but rather is regarded as a parameter.

By taking total differentials of the Lagrangian form L and by noting equilibrium conditions

$$\frac{\partial L}{\partial c^{\nu}} = 0, \quad \frac{\partial L}{\partial a^{\nu}} = 0, \quad \frac{\partial L}{\partial x^{\mu}} = 0, \quad \frac{\partial L}{\partial \ell^{\mu}} = 0,$$

$$\frac{\partial L}{\partial a^{\mu}} = 0, \quad \frac{\partial L}{\partial a^{\sigma}} = 0, \quad \frac{\partial L}{\partial \ell^{\sigma}} = 0, \quad \frac{\partial L}{\partial x^{\sigma}} = 0, \text{ etc.},$$

we obtain

$$dU = \frac{\partial L}{\partial a} da = [\tau(a)pc + \theta - \pi] da.$$

Hence,

$$\frac{dU}{da} = \tau(a)pc + \theta - \pi. \tag{59}$$

The Lagrangian unknown θ may be interpreted as the imputed price for the use of educational services and it is decreased as the general level of education a is increased. Similarly, the Lagrangian unknown π may be interpreted as the imputed price for the provision of education, and it is increased as the general level of education a is increased. Hence, the right-hand side of equation (59) is a decreasing function of a.

Hence, the adjustment process with respect to the general level of education a defined by the differential equation

$$\dot{a} = k[\tau(a)pc - \tau],$$

with a positive speed of adjustment k, is globally stable.

The subsidy rate τ at the market equilibrium with the general level of education a is also uniquely determined:

$$\pi - \theta = \tau.$$

An increase in the subsidy rate τ is always associated with an increase in the general level of education a. It is apparent that the following proposition holds.

Proposition 4. *Consider the adjustment process defined by the following differential equation:*

$$\text{(A)} \qquad \dot{\tau} = k[\tau(a)pc - \tau],$$

with a positive speed of adjustment k, where all variables refer to the state of the economy at the market equilibrium under the subsidy scheme with the rate τ:

$$\pi - \theta = \tau.$$

Then differential equation (A) *is globally stable; that is, for any initial condition a_0, the solution path to differential equation* (A) *converges to the stationary level a, where*

$$\tau = \tau(a)pc.$$

9

Medical Care as Social Common Capital

1. INTRODUCTION

When medical care is regarded as social common capital, every member of the society is entitled, as basic human rights, to receive the best available medical care that the society can provide, regardless of the economic, social, and regional circumstances, even though this does not necessarily imply that medical care is provided free of charge. The government is required to compose the overall plan that would result in the management of the medical care component of social common capital that is socially optimum. This plan consists of the regional distribution of various types of medical institutions and the schooling system to train physicians, nurses, technical experts, and other co-medical staff to meet the demand for medical care. The government is then required to devise institutional and financial arrangements under which the construction and maintenance of the necessary medical institutions are realized and the required number of medical professionals are trained without social or bureaucratic coercion. It should be emphasized that all medical institutions and schools basically are private and the management is supervised by qualified medical professionals.

The fees for medical care then are determined based on the principle of marginal social cost pricing, not through mere market mechanisms. It may be noted that the smaller the capacity of the medical component of social common capital, the higher the fees charged to various types of medical care services. Hence, in composing the overall plan for the medical care component of social common capital, we must explicitly take into account the relationships between the capacity of the medical care component of social common capital and the imputed prices of medical care services. The socially optimum plan for the medical care component of social common capital, then, is one in which the resulting system of imputed prices of various types of medical care services leads to the allocation of scarce resources, privately appropriated or otherwise, and the accompanying distribution of real income that are socially optimum, in a way that is discussed in detail in this chapter.

When, however, physicians provide medical care services to those whose health is impaired because of diseases or injuries, the very nature of medical care necessarily implies that the processes of diagnosis and curative treatment may occasionally involve the impairment, physical or mental, of patients, whereas the curative effects are not necessarily absolutely guaranteed. If an ordinary person were to perform his or her job this way, he or she would certainly be criminally prosecuted. Only qualified physicians and co-medical staff are immune from such prosecution, because in addition to being licensed to practice medical care and being trusted on a fiduciary basis with the management of the medical care component of social common capital, they must obey professional codes of conduct truthfully and take care of patients using the best scientific knowledge and the highest technical proficiency of the medical sciences available today. For such presuppositions to be fulfilled, it is not only necessary for arrangements to be institutionalized so the provision of medical care and the conduct of each physician are properly monitored in terms of peer review or some other means, but it is also necessary for an overall system of incentive mechanisms, in terms of social esteem and a compensatory scheme, to be established whereby it becomes in physicians' own self-interest to obey professional codes of conduct truthfully and to seek the best scientific knowledge and the highest technical proficiency available in medicine.

Under such utopian presuppositions, total expenditures for the construction and maintenance of the socially optimum medical care component of social common capital exceed, generally by a large amount, the total fees paid by the patients under the principle of marginal social cost pricing. The resulting pattern of resource allocation and real income distribution, however, is optimum from the social point of view. The magnitude of the deficits with respect to the management of the socially optimum medical care component of social common capital then may appropriately be regarded as an indicator to measure the relative importance of medical care from the social point of view.

2. MEDICAL CARE AS SOCIAL COMMON CAPITAL

The model of medical care as social common capital will be formulated within the analytical framework of the prototype model of social common capital introduced in Chapters 2 and 3, along the lines of the model of education as social common capital introduced in Chapter 8.

We consider a society that consists of a finite number of individuals and two types of institutions: private firms that specialize in producing goods that are transacted on the market, on the one hand, and social institutions concerned with the provision of medical care, on the other.

As in the previous chapters, social institutions in charge of medical care are characterized by the property that all factors of production that are necessary for the professional provision of medical care are either privately owned or managed as if privately owned. The medical institutions, however, are managed strictly in accordance with professional discipline and expertise concerning medical care, as exemplified by the Hippocratic oath. In describing the behavior of medical institutions, we occasionally use the term profits strictly in accordance with accounting sense. Similarly, when we use the term profit maximization, it is used in the sense that the optimum and efficient pattern of resource allocations in the provision of medical care is sought strictly in accordance with professional disciplines and ethics.

Subsidy payments are made for the provision of medical care, with the rate to be administratively determined by the government and announced prior to the opening of the market. The fees paid to medical institutions for the provision of medical care exceed, by the subsidy rate, those charged for medical care. Given the subsidy rate for the provision of medical care, the two levels of fees are determined so that the total level of medical care provided by all medical institutions is precisely equal to the general level of medical care for all individuals of the society. As in the case of the model of education as social common capital, one of the crucial roles of the government is to determine the subsidy rate for the provision of medical care in such a manner that the ensuing pattern of resource allocation and income distribution is optimum in a certain well-defined, socially acceptable sense.

Basic Premises of the Model

Individuals are generically denoted by $\nu = 1, \ldots, n$, and private firms by $\mu = 1, \ldots, m$, whereas medical institutions are denoted by $\sigma = 1, \ldots, s$. Goods produced by private firms are generically denoted by $j = 1, \ldots, J$. We consider the situation in which medical care is measured in a certain well-defined unit. There are two types of factors of production: variable and fixed. Variable factors of production in our model are various types of labor, each of which is assumed to be homogeneous and measured in terms of a certain well-defined unit. As a factor of production, labor is assumed to be variable; that is, labor may be transferred from one type of job to another without incurring any significant cost or time. There are several kinds of fixed factors of production; they are generically denoted by $f = 1, \ldots, F$. Physicians and co-medical staff are either part of fixed factors of production or professional labor. Fixed factors of production are specific and fixed components of the particular institutions to which they belong. Once fixed factors of production are installed in a particular institution, they are not shifted to another; only through the process of investment activities may the endowments of capital goods in a particular institution be increased.

Static analysis of private firms or social institutions in charge of medical care presupposes that the endowments of fixed factors of production are given, as the result of the investment activities carried out by the institutions in the past. Dynamic analysis, on the other hand, concerns processes of the accumulation of fixed factors of production in private firms or social institutions in charge of medical care and the ensuing implications for the productive capacity in the future. In this chapter, we primarily are concerned with the static analysis of medical care as social common capital.

Quantities of fixed factors of production accumulated in each firm μ are expressed by a vector $K^\mu = (K_f^\mu)$, where K_f^μ denotes the quantity of factor of production f accumulated in firm μ. Quantities of goods produced by firm μ are denoted by a vector $x^\mu = (x_j^\mu)$, where x_j^μ denotes the quantity of goods j produced by firm μ, net of the quantities of goods used by firm μ itself. The amount of labor employed by firm μ to carry out production activities is denoted by ℓ^μ.

The structure of social institutions in charge of medical care is similarly postulated. Quantities of capital goods accumulated in medical institution σ are expressed by a vector $K^\sigma = (K_f^\sigma)$, where K_f^σ denotes the quantity of fixed factor of production f accumulated in medical institution σ. It is assumed that $K^\sigma \geq 0$. The level of medical care provided by medical institution σ is expressed by a^σ. We assume that professional labor employed in medical institutions requires specific knowledge, skill, and expertise, to be licensed as medical practitioners. Labor employed by medical institution σ for the provision of medical care is denoted by ℓ^σ. We also denote by $x^\sigma = (x_j^\sigma)$ the vector of quantities of produced goods used by social institution σ for the provision of medical care.

The principal agency of the society in question is each individual who consumes goods produced by private firms and receives medical care provided by medical institutions. The vector of goods consumed by individual ν is denoted by $c^\nu = (c_j^\nu)$, where c_j^ν is the quantity of good j consumed by individual ν, whereas the level of medical care received by individual ν is denoted by a^ν. Labor of each individual ν is given by ℓ^ν, which consists of two components, ℓ_p^ν and ℓ_s^ν:

$$\ell^\nu = \ell_p^\nu + \ell_s^\nu.$$

The ℓ_p^ν refers to the amount of labor of the standard quality, whereas the ℓ_s^ν refers to those licensed as medical practitioners. It is generally the case that, for each individual ν, either $\ell_p^\nu = 0$ or $\ell_s^\nu = 0$. The labor of each individual ν is inelastically supplied to the market.

We assume that both private firms and medical institutions are owned by individuals of the society. We denote by $s^{\nu\mu}$ and $s^{\nu\sigma}$, respectively, the shares of private firm μ and medical institution σ owned by individual ν, where the following conditions are assumed:

$$s^{\nu\mu} \geqq 0, \quad \sum_\nu s^{\nu\mu} = 1; \qquad s^{\nu\sigma} \geqq 0, \quad \sum_\nu s^{\nu\sigma} = 1.$$

3. SPECIFICATIONS OF THE MEDICAL CARE MODEL OF SOCIAL COMMON CAPITAL

Uncertainty and Medical Care as Social Common Capital

We assume that the economic welfare of each individual ν is expressed by a preference ordering that is represented by the utility function

$$u^\nu = u^\nu(c^\nu, \omega^\nu),$$

where c^ν is the vector of goods consumed by individual ν and ω^ν is the state of well-being of individual ν.

The state of well-being of individual ν, ω^ν, is a complete list that characterizes all health and medical symptoms concerning individual ν. The set of all conceivable states of well-being of individual ν is denoted by Ω^ν, which is assumed to be identical for all individuals in the society. For each individual ν, the state of well-being is subject to probability distribution. The probability density function of states of well-being of individual ν is denoted by $p^\nu(\omega)$, where

$$p^\nu(\omega^\nu) \geqq 0 \ (\omega^\nu \in \Omega^\nu), \quad \int_{\Omega^\nu} p^\nu(\omega^\nu) d\omega^\nu = 1.$$

We assume that for each state of well-being $\omega^\nu(\omega^\nu \in \Omega^\nu)$, the utility function $u^\nu(c^\nu, \omega^\nu)$ satisfies the following neoclassical conditions:

($U^\varpi 1$) $u^\nu(c^\nu, \omega^\nu)$ is defined, positive, continuous, and continuously twice-differentiable for all $c^\nu \geqq 0$, $\omega^\nu \in \Omega^\nu$.

($U^\varpi 2$) Marginal utilities of consumption are positive; that is, $u^\nu_{c^\nu}(c^\nu, \omega^\nu) > 0 \quad \text{for all } c^\nu \geqq 0, \omega^\nu \in \Omega^\nu$.

($U^\varpi 3$) Marginal rates of substitution between any pair of consumption goods are diminishing, or more specifically, $u^\nu(c^\nu, \omega^\nu)$ is strictly quasi-concave with respect to c^ν for given $\omega^\nu \in \Omega^\nu$.

($U^\varpi 4$) $u^\nu(c^\nu, \omega^\nu)$ is homogeneous of order 1 with respect to c^ν; that is,

$$u^\nu(tc^\nu, t\omega^\nu) = tu^\nu(c^\nu, \omega^\nu) \quad \text{for all } t \geqq 0, c^\nu \geqq 0, \omega^\nu \in \Omega^\nu.$$

The linear homogeneity hypothesis ($U^\varpi 4$) implies the following Euler identity:

$$u^\nu(c^\nu, \omega^\nu) = u^\nu_{c^\nu}(c^\nu, \omega^\nu)c^\nu \quad \text{for all } c^\nu \geqq 0 \text{ for given } \omega^\nu \in \Omega^\nu.$$

Effects of Medical Care

The effect of medical care is twofold: private and social. First, regarding the private effect of medical care, the ability of labor of each individual as a factor of production is increased by the level of medical care he or she receives. At the same time, the level of medical care each individual receives has a decisive impact on the level of well-being of each individual. Second, regarding the social effect of medical care, an increase in the general level of medical care enhances an increase in the level of welfare of each individual in society.

The private effect of medical care may be expressed by the hypothesis that the ability of labor of each individual ν as a factor of production is given by

$$\varphi^\nu(a^\nu, \omega^\nu)\ell^\nu,$$

where ℓ^ν is the amount of labor provided by individual ν and $\varphi^\nu(a^\nu, \omega^\nu)$ expresses the extent to which the ability of labor of individual ν as a factor of production is affected by the level of medical care a^ν he or she receives, depending on the state of well-being ω^ν.

The function $\varphi^\nu(a^\nu, \omega^\nu)$ specifies the extent of the private effect of medical care, depending on the specific level of medical care a^ν each individual ν receives, and takes a functional relationship specific to each individual ν. It may be referred to as the *impact index of medical care* on individual ν's labor as a factor of production.

We may assume that for each individual ν, as the level of medical care a^ν he or she receives becomes higher, the impact index of medical care on the labor of individual ν as a factor of production, $\varphi^\nu(a^\nu, \omega^\nu)$, is accordingly increased, but with diminishing marginal effects. These assumptions may be stated as follows:

$$\varphi^\nu(a^\nu, \omega^\nu) > 0, \quad \varphi^{\nu\prime}(a^\nu, \omega^\nu) > 0, \quad \varphi^{\nu\prime\prime}(a^\nu, \omega^\nu) < 0$$

for all $a^\nu \geqq 0$ and $\omega^\nu \in \Omega^\nu$.

In the analysis of medical care as social common capital, an important role is played by the *impact coefficient of medical care* on the labor of individual ν as a factor of production, $\tau^\nu(a^\nu, \omega^\nu)$. It is defined as the relative rate of the marginal increase in the impact index of medical care on the labor of individual ν as a factor of production due to the marginal increase in the level of medical care, $\varphi^\nu(a^\nu, \omega^\nu)$; that is,

$$\tau^\nu(a^\nu, \omega^\nu) = \frac{\varphi^{\nu\prime}(a^\nu, \omega^\nu)}{\varphi^\nu(a^\nu, \omega^\nu)}.$$

In the following discussion, we assume that the impact coefficient $\tau^\nu(a^\nu, \omega^\nu)$ is independent of the state of well-being ω^ν; that is,

$$\tau^\nu(a^\nu, \omega^\nu) = \tau^\nu(a^\nu) \quad \text{for all } a^\nu \geqq 0 \text{ and } \omega^\nu \in \Omega^\nu.$$

For each individual ν, the impact coefficient of medical care $\tau^{\nu}(a^{\nu})$ is decreased as the level of education a^{ν} of individual ν is increased:

$$\tau^{\nu\prime}(a^{\nu}) = \frac{\varphi^{\nu\prime\prime}(a^{\nu})}{\varphi^{\nu}(a^{\nu})} - [\tau^{\nu}(a^{\nu})]^2 < 0.$$

As for the private effect of medical care, we must take into account another, decisively more important effect. That effect is concerned with the increase in the general level of well-being of each individual ν, as expressed by the hypothesis that the level of utility of individual ν is expressed in the following form:

$$u^{\nu}(\omega^{\nu}) = \overline{\varphi}^{\nu}(a^{\nu}, \omega^{\nu}) u^{\nu}(c^{\nu}, \omega^{\nu}),$$

where the function $\overline{\varphi}^{\nu}(a^{\nu}, \omega^{\nu})$ expresses the extent to which the utility of individual ν is affected by the level of medical care a^{ν} he or she receives when the state of well-being is ω^{ν}. It may be referred to as the impact index of medical care on the state of well-being of individual ν.

We may assume that for each individual ν, as the level of medical care a^{ν} he or she receives becomes higher, the impact index of medical care on individual ν's well-being, $\phi^{\nu}(a, \omega^{\nu})$, is accordingly increased, but with diminishing marginal effects. These assumptions may be stated as follows:

$$\phi^{\nu}(a, \omega^{\nu}) > 0, \quad \phi^{\nu\prime}(a, \omega^{\nu}) > 0, \quad \phi^{\nu\prime\prime}(a, \omega^{\nu}) < 0$$

for all $a^{\nu} \geqq 0$ and $\omega^{\nu} \in \Omega^{\nu}$.

The impact coefficient of medical care on individual ν's well-being, $\tau^{\nu}(a^{\nu}\omega^{\nu})$, is defined as the relative rate of the marginal increase in the impact index of medical care on individual ν's well-being due to the marginal increase in the level of medical care, $\overline{\varphi}^{\nu}(a^{\nu}, \omega^{\nu})$; that is,

$$\overline{\tau}^{\nu}(a^{\nu}, \omega^{\nu}) = \frac{\overline{\varphi}^{\nu\prime}(a^{\nu}, \omega^{\nu})}{\overline{\varphi}^{\nu}(a^{\nu}, \omega^{\nu})}.$$

We assume that the impact coefficient $\tau^{\nu}(a^{\nu}, \omega^{\nu})$ is independent of the state of well-being ω^{ν}; that is,

$$\overline{\tau}^{\nu}(a^{\nu}, \omega^{\nu}) = \overline{\tau}^{\nu}(a^{\nu}) \quad \text{for all } a^{\nu} \geqq 0 \quad \text{and } \omega^{\nu} \in \Omega^{\nu}.$$

We also assume that, for each individual ν, the two impact coefficients of medical care, $\tau^{\nu}(a^{\nu})$ and $\overline{\tau}^{\nu}(a^{\nu})$, are identical:

$$\overline{\tau}^{\nu}(a^{\nu}) = \tau^{\nu}(a^{\nu}) \quad \text{for all } a^{\nu} \geqq 0.$$

Hence, we may, without loss of generality, assume that two indices of the private effect of medical care $\varphi^\nu(a^\nu, \omega^\nu)$ and $\overline{\varphi}^\nu(a^\nu, \omega^\nu)$ are identical:

$$\overline{\varphi}^\nu(a^\nu, \omega^\nu) = \varphi^\nu(a^\nu, \omega^\nu) \quad \text{for all } a^\nu \geqq 0 \text{ and } \omega^\nu \in \Omega.$$

The social effect of medical care may be expressed by the hypothesis that an increase in the general level of medical care induces an increase in the utility of every individual in the society; that is, the utility of each individual ν, $u^\nu(\omega^\nu)$, is given by

$$u^\nu(\omega) = \phi^\nu(a, \omega)\varphi^\nu(a^\nu, \omega^\nu)u^\nu(c^\nu, \omega^\nu),$$

where $\phi^\nu(a, \omega)$ is the function specifying the extent to which the utility of each individual ν is increased as the general level of medical care a is increased. In the analysis developed in this chapter, we take as an approximation of the first order the aggregate sum of the levels of medical care received by all individuals in the society as the general level of medical care $a(\omega)[\omega = (\omega^1, \ldots, \omega^n) \in \Omega = \Omega^1 \times \cdots \times \Omega^n]$; that is,

$$a(\omega) = \sum_\nu a^\nu(\omega^\nu).$$

The function $\phi^\nu(a, \omega)$ specifies the extent of the social effect of medical care, depending on the general level of medical care a of the society when the state of well-being of individual ν is ω, taking a functional relationship specific to each individual ν. It may be referred to as the *impact index of the general level of medical care* for individual ν.

We may assume that, for each individual ν, as the general level of medical care a of the society becomes higher, the impact index of the general level of medical care $\phi^\nu(a, \omega)$ is accordingly increased, but with diminishing marginal effects. These assumptions may be stated as follows:

$$\phi^\nu(a, \omega) > 0, \quad \phi^{\nu\prime}(a, \omega) > 0, \quad \phi^{\nu\prime\prime}(a, \omega) < 0 \quad \text{for all } a > 0 \text{ and } \omega \in \Omega.$$

The *impact coefficient of the general level of medical care* for each individual ν, $\tau^\nu(a, \omega)$, is defined as the relative rate of the marginal increase in the impact index of the general level of medical care $\phi^\nu(a, \omega)$ due to the marginal increase in the general level of medical care a; that is,

$$\tau^\nu(a, \omega) = \frac{\phi^{\nu\prime}(a, \omega)}{\phi^\nu(a, \omega)}.$$

We assume that the impact coefficient of medical care $\tau^\nu(a, \omega^\nu)$ is independent of the state of well-being ω^ν; that is,

$$\tau^\nu(a, \omega) = \tau^\nu(a) \quad (\omega \in \Omega).$$

For each individual ν, the impact coefficient of the general level of medical care $\tau^\nu(a)$ is decreased as the general level of medical care a is increased:

$$\tau^{\nu\prime}(a) = \frac{\phi^{\nu\prime\prime}(a)}{\phi^\nu(a)} - [\tau^\nu(a)]^2 < 0.$$

We assume that the impact coefficient of the general level of medical care $\tau^\nu(a)$ is identical for all individuals:

$$\tau^\nu(a) = \tau(a) \quad \text{for all individuals } \nu.$$

The Optimum Levels of Medical Care for Individuals

We assume that markets for produced goods are perfectly competitive; prices of goods are denoted by $p = (p_j)$ $(p \geq 0)$ and the fees charged for medical care are denoted by θ $(\theta > 0)$.

Each individual ν would choose the combination (c^ν, a^ν) of consumption c^ν and level of medical care a^ν that maximizes the mathematical expectations of individual ν's utility $u^\nu(\omega)$:

$$\mathrm{E}[u^\nu(\omega)] = \int_\Omega u^\nu(\omega) p^\nu(\omega^\nu) d\omega,$$

where the utility of each individual ν, $u^\nu(\omega^\nu)$, is a stochastic variable given by

$$u^\nu(\omega^\nu) = \phi^\nu(a, \omega)\varphi^\nu(a^\nu, \omega^\nu)u^\nu(c^\nu, \omega^\nu),$$

subject to the budget constraint

$$pc^\nu + \theta \mathrm{E}[u^\nu(\omega^\nu)] = \mathrm{E}[y^\nu(\omega^\nu)],$$

where y^ν is the income of individual ν,

$$y^\nu(\omega^\nu) = w^\nu(\omega^\nu) + \widehat{y}^\nu;$$

$w^\nu(\omega^\nu)$ denotes the imputed wages of individual ν, to be given by

$$w^\nu(\omega^\nu) = \varphi^\nu(a^\nu, \omega^\nu)\big(w_p \ell_p^\nu + w_s \ell_s^\nu\big);$$

w_p and w_s are, respectively, the wage rates of standard labor and professional labor; $\phi^\nu(a, \omega)$ and $\varphi^\nu(a^\nu, \omega^\nu)$ are, respectively, the impact indices of social and private effects of medical care for individual ν; and $\widehat{y}^\nu$ is the portion of income of individual ν other than wages.

It may be noted that the budget constraint above presupposes the existence of a fair medical insurance scheme.

The optimum combination (c^ν, a^ν) of consumption c^ν and level of medical care a^ν is characterized by the following marginality conditions:

$$\alpha^\nu \mathrm{E}\big[u^\nu_{c^\nu}(\omega^\nu)\big] \leqq p \quad (\mathrm{mod.}\ c^\nu)$$

$$\tau^\nu(a^\nu)\mathrm{E}[u^\nu(\omega) + w^\nu(\omega^\nu)] = \theta,$$

where $\alpha^\nu > 0$ is the inverse of marginal utility of income of individual ν and $\tau^\nu(a^\nu)$ is the impact coefficient of the private effect of medical care for individual ν.

Hence, the analysis of the consumer optimum concerning the choice of the level of medical care may be carried out under the presupposition that there is only one state of well-being for each individual ν, so that the reference to the state of well-being may be dispensed with entirely in our discussion of the model of medical care as social common capital. At the risk of repetition, the basic premises of the model are spelled out in detail.

The Consumer Optimum in the Certainty Equivalence Model of Medical Care

We assume that for each individual ν, the utility function $u^\nu(c^\nu)$ satisfies the following neoclassical conditions:

(U1) $u^\nu(c^\nu)$ is defined, positive, continuous, and continuously twice-differentiable for all $c^\nu \geqq 0$.

(U2) Marginal utilities of consumption are positive; that is,

$$u^\nu_{c^\nu}(c^\nu) > 0 \quad \text{for all } c^\nu \geqq 0.$$

(U3) Marginal rates of substitution between any pair of consumption goods are diminishing, or more specifically, $u^\nu(c^\nu)$ is strictly quasi-concave with respect to c^ν.

(U4) $u^\nu(c^\nu)$ is homogeneous of order 1 with respect to c^ν; that is,

$$u^\nu(tc^\nu) = tu^\nu(c^\nu) \quad \text{for all } t \geqq 0,\ c^\nu \geqq 0.$$

The linear homogeneity hypothesis (U4) implies the following Euler identity:

$$u^\nu(c^\nu) = u^\nu_{c^\nu}(c^\nu)c^\nu \quad \text{for all } c^\nu \geqq 0.$$

Effects of Medical Care

The effect of medical care is twofold: private and social. First, regarding the private effect of medical care, the ability of labor of each individual as a factor of production is increased by the level of medical care he or she receives. At the same time, the level of medical care each individual receives has a decisive impact on the level of well-being of each individual. Second, regarding the social effect of medical services, an increase in the general level of medical services enhances an increase in the level of the social welfare, whatever measure is taken.

The private effect of medical care may be expressed by the hypothesis that the ability of labor of each individual ν as a factor of production is given by

$$\varphi^\nu(a^\nu)\ell^\nu,$$

where ℓ^ν is the amount of labor provided by individual ν and $\varphi^\nu(a^\nu)$ is the impact index of medical care on the labor of individual ν as a factor of production. The impact index function $\varphi^\nu(a^\nu)$ satisfies the following assumptions:

$$\varphi^\nu(a^\nu) > 0, \quad \varphi^{\nu\prime}(a^\nu) > 0, \quad \varphi^{\nu\prime\prime}(a^\nu) < 0 \quad \text{for all } a^\nu \geqq 0.$$

The *impact coefficient of medical care* on the labor of individual ν as a factor of production $\tau^\nu(a^\nu)$ is defined by

$$\tau^\nu(a^\nu) = \frac{\varphi^{\nu\prime}(a^\nu)}{\varphi^\nu(a^\nu)},$$

where

$$\tau^{\nu\prime}(a^\nu) = \frac{\varphi^{\nu\prime\prime}(a^\nu)}{\varphi^\nu(a^\nu)} - [\tau^\nu(a^\nu)]^2 < 0.$$

As for the second private effect of medical care, the increase in the general level of well-being of each individual ν is expressed by the hypothesis that the level of utility of individual ν is expressed in the following form:

$$u^\nu = \overline{\varphi}^\nu(a^\nu)u^\nu(c^\nu),$$

where the function $\overline{\varphi}^{\nu}(a^{\nu})$ is the impact index of medical care on the state of well-being of individual ν. The function $\overline{\varphi}^{\nu}(a^{\nu})$ satisfies the following assumptions:

$$\overline{\varphi}^{\nu}(a^{\nu}) > 0, \quad \overline{\varphi}^{\nu\prime}(a^{\nu}) > 0, \quad \overline{\varphi}^{\nu\prime\prime}(a^{\nu}) < 0 \quad \text{for all } a^{\nu} \geqq 0.$$

The impact coefficient of medical care on individual ν's well-being, $\overline{\tau}^{\nu}(a^{\nu})$, is defined by

$$\overline{\tau}^{\nu}(a^{\nu}) = \frac{\overline{\varphi}^{\nu\prime}(a^{\nu})}{\overline{\varphi}^{\nu}(a^{\nu})}.$$

We assume that for each individual ν, the two impact coefficients of medical services, $\tau^{\nu}(a^{\nu})$ and $\overline{\tau}^{\nu}(a^{\nu})$, are identical:

$$\overline{\tau}^{\nu}(a^{\nu}) = \tau^{\nu}(a^{\nu}) \quad \text{for all } a^{\nu} \geqq 0.$$

Hence, we may also assume that two indices of the private effect of medical care $\varphi^{\nu}(a^{\nu})$ and $\overline{\varphi}^{\nu}(a^{\nu})$ are identical:

$$\overline{\varphi}^{\nu}(a^{\nu}) = \varphi^{\nu}(a^{\nu}) \quad \text{for all } a^{\nu} \geqq 0.$$

The social effect of medical services may be expressed by the hypothesis that an increase in the general level of medical care induces an increase in the utility of every individual in the society; that is, the utility of each individual ν is given by

$$u^{\nu} = \phi^{\nu}(a)\varphi^{\nu}(a^{\nu})u^{\nu}(c^{\nu}),$$

where $\phi^{\nu}(a)$ is the impact index of the general level of medical care for individual ν and $a = \sum_{\nu} a^{\nu}$.

The function $\phi^{\nu}(a)$ specifies the extent of the social effect of medical care, depending upon the general level of medical care of the society a, but by taking a functional relationship specific to each individual ν. It may be referred to as the impact index of the general level of medical care for individual ν. It is assumed that

$$\phi^{\nu}(a) > 0, \quad \phi^{\nu\prime}(a) > 0, \quad \phi^{\nu\prime\prime}(a) < 0 \quad \text{for all } a > 0.$$

The impact coefficient of the general level of medical care for each individual ν, $\tau^{\nu}(a)$, is defined by

$$\tau^{\nu}(a) = \frac{\phi^{\nu\prime}(a)}{\phi^{\nu}(a)}.$$

We assume that the impact coefficient of the general level of medical care $\tau^\nu(a)$ is identical for all individuals; that is,

$$\tau^\nu(a) = \tau(a) \quad \text{for all } \nu.$$

The Consumer Optimum

We assume that markets for produced goods are perfectly competitive; prices of goods are denoted by $p = (p_j)$ ($p \geq 0$), and the fees charged for medical care are denoted by θ ($\theta > 0$).

Each individual ν chooses the combination (c^ν, a^ν) of consumption c^ν and level of medical care a^ν that maximizes the utility of individual ν

$$u^\nu = \phi^\nu(a)\varphi^\nu(a^\nu)u^\nu(c^\nu)$$

subject to the budget constraint

$$pc^\nu + \theta a^\nu = y^\nu, \tag{1}$$

where y^ν is the income of individual ν,

$$y^\nu = w^\nu + \widehat{y}^\nu;$$

w^ν is the imputed wages of individual ν, to be given by

$$w^\nu = w_p\varphi^\nu(a^\nu)\ell_p^\nu + w_s\varphi^\nu(a^\nu)\ell_s^\nu;$$

w_p and w_s are, respectively, the wage rates for standard labor and professional labor; $\phi^\nu(a)$ and $\varphi^\nu(a^\nu)$ are, respectively, the impact indices of social and private effects of medical care for individual ν; and $\widehat{y}^\nu$ is the portion of income of individual ν other than wages.

The optimum combination (c^ν, a^ν) of consumption c^ν and level of medical care a^ν is characterized by the following marginality conditions:

$$\alpha^\nu\phi^\nu(a)\varphi^\nu(a^\nu)u_{c^\nu}^\nu(c^\nu) \leqq p \quad (\text{mod. } c^\nu) \tag{2}$$

$$\tau^\nu(a^\nu)[\alpha^\nu\phi^\nu(a)\varphi^\nu(a^\nu)u^\nu(c^\nu) + w^\nu] = \theta, \tag{3}$$

where $\alpha^\nu > 0$ is the inverse of marginal utility of income of individual ν and $\tau^\nu(a^\nu)$ is the impact coefficient of the private effect of medical care for individual ν.

Condition (2) expresses the familiar principle that the marginal utility of each good, when measured in units of market price, is exactly equal to the market price.

Condition (3) means that the level of medical care individual ν wishes to receive is determined so that the medical fee θ is equal to the sum of the marginal increase in individual ν's utility enhanced by the marginal increase in the level of medical care individual ν receives plus the marginal increase in the wages enhanced by the marginal increase in the level of medical care individual ν receives.

In view of the linear homogeneity condition for utility function $u^\nu(c^\nu)$, condition (3) implies

$$\alpha^\nu \phi^\nu(a)\varphi^\nu(a^\nu)u^\nu(c^\nu) = pc^\nu, \tag{4}$$

which may be substituted into (3), noting budget constraint (4), to obtain the following relations:

$$\tau^\nu(a^\nu)[pc^\nu + w^\nu] = \theta. \tag{5}$$

Let us denote the employment of labor of individual ν at private firms μ and medical institutions σ, respectively, by $\ell^{\nu\mu}$ and $\ell^{\nu\sigma}$. Then we have the following relations:

$$\ell_p^\nu = \sum_\mu \ell^{\nu\mu}, \quad \ell_s^\nu = \sum_\sigma \ell^{\nu\sigma} \quad (\nu = 1, \ldots, n). \tag{6}$$

The employment of labor of individual ν at private firms $\ell^{\nu\mu}$ are in ordinary circumstances either ℓ_p^ν or 0. However, for the sake of expository brevity, we express them as if they may take any amount no larger than ℓ_p^ν. The same applies to employment at medical institutions.

Production Possibility Sets of Private Firms

The conditions concerning the production of goods for each private firm μ are expressed by the production possibility set T^μ that summarizes the technological possibilities and organizational arrangements for firm μ with the endowments of fixed factors of production available in firm μ given at $K^\mu = (K_f^\mu)$.

In view of the hypothesis concerning the heterogeneity of the ability of standard labor as a factor of production, we must pay special attention to the composition of labor in production processes of firm μ in which the employment of labor by firm μ consists of standard labor of several individuals. Let us suppose that the employment of labor of firm μ consists of $\ell^{\nu\mu}$ $(\nu = 1, \ldots, n)$, where $\ell^{\nu\mu}$ denotes the amount of standard labor of individual ν employed by firm μ.

To define total employment of labor of firm μ, we must take into account the private effect of medical care on the ability of labor as a factor of production. The employment of labor of individual ν by the amount $\ell^{\nu\mu}$ may be regarded as the employment of standard labor by the amount $\varphi^{\nu}(a^{\nu})\ell^{\nu\mu}$, where $\varphi^{\nu}(a^{\nu})$ is the impact index of the private effect of medical care for individual ν that specifies the extent of the private effect of medical care, depending upon the level of medical care a^{ν} received by each individual ν.

Hence, labor employment of firm μ, consisting of the employment of labor of individuals by $\ell^{\nu\mu}$ $(\nu = 1, \ldots n)$, may be converted to the employment of simple labor of the following amount:

$$\ell^{\mu} = \sum_{\nu} \varphi^{\nu}(a^{\nu})\ell^{\nu\mu} \quad (\mu = 1, \ldots, m). \tag{7}$$

In each private firm μ, the minimum quantities of factors of production that are required to produce goods by x^{μ} with the employment of labor at the level ℓ^{μ} are specified by an F-dimensional vector-valued function:

$$f^{\mu}(x^{\mu}, \ell^{\mu}) = \left(f^{\mu}_{f}(x^{\mu}, \ell^{\mu})\right).$$

We assume that marginal rates of substitution between any pair of the production of goods and the employment of labor are smooth and diminishing, there are always trade-offs among them, and the conditions of constant returns to scale prevail. That is, we assume:

($\mathrm{T}^{\mu}1$) $f^{\mu}(x^{\mu}, \ell^{\mu})$ are defined, positive, continuous, and continuously twice-differentiable for all $(x^{\mu}, \ell^{\mu}) \geqq 0$.

($\mathrm{T}^{\mu}2$) $f^{\mu}_{x^{\mu}}(x^{\mu}, \ell^{\mu}) > 0, \quad f^{\mu}_{\ell^{\mu}}(x^{\mu}, \ell^{\mu}) \leqq 0$ for all $(x^{\mu}, \ell^{\mu}) \geqq 0$.

($\mathrm{T}^{\mu}3$) $f^{\mu}(x^{\mu}, \ell^{\mu})$ are strictly quasi-convex with respect to (x^{μ}, ℓ^{μ}) for all $(x^{\mu}, \ell^{\mu}) \geqq 0$.

($\mathrm{T}^{\mu}4$) $f^{\mu}(x^{\mu}, \ell^{\mu})$ are homogeneous of order 1 with respect to (x^{μ}, ℓ^{μ}).

From the constant returns to scale conditions ($\mathrm{T}^{\mu}4$), we have the Euler identity

$$f^{\mu}(x^{\mu}, \ell^{\mu}) = f^{\mu}_{x^{\mu}}(x^{\mu}, \ell^{\mu})x^{\mu} + f^{\mu}_{\ell^{\mu}}(x^{\mu}, \ell^{\mu})\ell^{\mu} \quad \text{for all } (x^{\mu}, \ell^{\mu}) \geqq 0.$$

The production possibility set of each private firm μ, T^μ, is composed of all combinations (x^μ, ℓ^μ) of production x^μ and employment of labor ℓ^μ that are possible with the organizational arrangements, technological conditions, and given endowments of factors of production K^μ in firm μ. Hence, it may be expressed as

$$T^\mu = \{(x^\mu, \ell^\mu): (x^\mu, \ell^\mu) \geqq 0,\ f^\mu(x^\mu, \ell^\mu) \leqq K^\mu\}.$$

Postulates (T^μ1–T^μ3) imply that the production possibility set T^μ is a closed, convex set of $J + 1$-dimensional vectors (x^μ, ℓ^μ).

The Producer Optimum for Private Firms

As in the case of the consumer optimum, prices of goods and the wage rate of standard labor in perfectly competitive markets are, respectively, denoted by $p = (p_j)$ and w_p.

Each private firm μ chooses the combination (x^μ, ℓ^μ) of vectors of production x^μ and employment of labor ℓ^μ that maximizes net profit

$$px^\mu - w_p \ell^\mu$$

over $(x^\mu, \ell^\mu) \in T^\mu$.

Conditions (T^μ1–T^μ3) postulated above ensure that for any combination of prices p and wage rate w_p, the optimum combination (x^μ, ℓ^μ) of vector of production x^μ and employment of labor ℓ^μ always exists and is uniquely determined.

To see how the optimum levels of production and labor employment are determined, let us denote the vector of imputed rental prices of capital goods by $r^\mu = (r_f^\mu)$ $[r_f^\mu \geqq 0]$. Then the optimum conditions are

$$p \leqq r^\mu f_{x^\mu}^\mu(x^\mu, \ell^\mu) \quad (\text{mod. } x^\mu) \tag{8}$$

$$w_p \geqq r^\mu[-f_{\ell^\mu}^\mu(x^\mu, \ell^\mu)] \quad (\text{mod. } \ell^\mu) \tag{9}$$

$$f^\mu(x^\mu, \ell^\mu) \leqq K^\mu \quad (\text{mod. } r^\mu). \tag{10}$$

Condition (8) expresses the familiar principle that the choice of production technologies and the levels of production are adjusted so as to equate marginal factor costs with output prices.

Condition (9) means that the employment of labor is controlled so that the marginal gains due to the marginal increase in the employment of labor are equal to the wage rate w_p when $\ell^\mu > 0$, and are no larger than w_p when $\ell^\mu = 0$.

Condition (10) means that the employment of fixed factors of production does not exceed the endowments and the conditions of full employment are satisfied whenever imputed rental price r_f^μ is positive.

The technologies are subject to constant returns to scale, ($T^\mu 4$), and thus, in view of the Euler identity, conditions (8)–(10) imply that

$$\begin{aligned} px^\mu - w_p\ell^\mu &= r^\mu\left[f^\mu_{x^\mu}(x^\mu, \ell^\mu)x^\mu + f^\mu_{\ell^\mu}(x^\mu, \ell^\mu)\ell^\mu\right] \\ &= r^\mu f^\mu(x^\mu, \ell^\mu) = r^\mu K^\mu. \end{aligned} \tag{11}$$

That is, for each private firm μ, the net evaluation of output is equal to the sum of the imputed rental payments to all fixed factors of production of private firm μ. The meaning of relation (11) may be better brought out if we rewrite it as

$$px^\mu = w_p\ell^\mu + r^\mu K^\mu.$$

The value of output measured in market prices, px^μ, is equal to the sum of wages for the employment of labor, $w_p\ell^\mu$, and the payments, in terms of imputed rental prices, made to the fixed factors of production, $r^\mu K^\mu$. Thus, the validity of the Menger-Wieser principle of imputation is assured with respect to processes of production of private firms.

Production Possibility Sets for Medical Institutions

As with private firms, the conditions concerning the level of medical care provided by each medical institution σ are specified by the production possibility set T^σ that summarizes the technological possibilities and organizational arrangements of medical institution σ; the endowments of factors of production in medical institution σ are given as $K^\sigma = (K_f^\sigma)$.

In each medical institution σ, the minimum quantities of factors of production required to provide medical care at the level a^σ with the employment of professional labor by the amount ℓ^σ and the use of produced goods by the amounts $x^\sigma = (x_j^\sigma)$ are specified by an F-dimensional vector-valued function:

$$f^\sigma(a^\sigma, \ell^\sigma, x^\sigma) = \left(f_f^\sigma(a^\sigma, \ell^\sigma, x^\sigma)\right).$$

Exactly as in the case of private firms, we must be careful about the role of labor in the provision of medical care by medical institution

σ when the labor employment of medical institution σ consists of the professional labor of several individuals. Let us suppose that the employment of professional labor by medical institution σ consists of $\ell^{\nu\sigma}$ ($\nu = 1, \ldots, n$), where $\ell^{\nu\sigma}$ denotes the employment of professional labor of individual ν by medical institution σ.

To define the total employment of professional labor by medical institution σ, we must take into account the private effect of medical care on the ability of professional labor as a factor of production. The employment of professional labor of individual ν by the amount $\ell^{\nu\sigma}$ may be regarded as the employment of standard labor by the amount $\varphi^{\nu}(a^{\nu})\ell^{\nu\sigma}$. Hence, the total labor employment of medical institution σ may be regarded as the employment of professional labor by the following amount:

$$\ell^{\sigma} = \sum_{\nu} \varphi^{\nu}(a^{\nu})\ell^{\nu\sigma}. \tag{12}$$

We assume that for each medical institution σ, marginal rates of substitution among the provision of medical care, the employment of professional labor, and the use of produced goods are smooth and diminishing, there are always trade-offs among them, and the conditions of constant returns to scale prevail. Thus we assume:

(T$^{\sigma}$1) $f^{\sigma}(a^{\sigma}, \ell^{\sigma}, x^{\sigma})$ are defined, positive, continuous, and continuously twice-differentiable with respect to $(a^{\sigma}, \ell^{\sigma}, x^{\sigma})$.

(T$^{\sigma}$2) $f^{\sigma}_{a^{\sigma}}(a^{\sigma}, \ell^{\sigma}, x^{\sigma}) > 0, \ \ f^{\sigma}_{\ell^{\sigma}}(a^{\sigma}, \ell^{\sigma}, x^{\sigma}) < 0, \ \ f^{\sigma}_{x^{\sigma}}(a^{\sigma}, \ell^{\sigma}, x^{\sigma}) < 0.$

(T$^{\sigma}$3) $f^{\sigma}(a^{\sigma}, \ell^{\sigma}, x^{\sigma})$ are strictly quasi-convex with respect to $(a^{\sigma}, \ell^{\sigma}, x^{\sigma})$.

(T$^{\sigma}$4) $f^{\sigma}(a^{\sigma}, \ell^{\sigma}, x^{\sigma})$ are homogeneous of order 1 with respect to $(a^{\sigma}, \ell^{\sigma}, x^{\sigma})$.

From the constant-returns-to-scale conditions (T$^{\sigma}$4), we have the Euler identity:

$$\begin{aligned} f^{\sigma}(a^{\sigma}, \ell^{\sigma}, x^{\sigma}) = {} & f^{\sigma}_{a^{\sigma}}(a^{\sigma}, \ell^{\sigma}, x^{\sigma})a^{\sigma} + f^{\sigma}_{\ell^{\sigma}}(a^{\sigma}, \ell^{\sigma}, x^{\sigma})\ell^{\sigma} \\ & + f^{\sigma}_{x^{\sigma}}(a^{\sigma}, \ell^{\sigma}, x^{\sigma})x^{\sigma} \quad \text{for all } (a^{\sigma}, \ell^{\sigma}, x^{\sigma}) \geqq 0. \end{aligned}$$

For each medical institution σ, the production possibility set T^{σ} is composed of all combinations $(a^{\sigma}, \ell^{\sigma}, x^{\sigma})$ of provision of medical care a^{σ}, employment of professional labor ℓ^{σ}, and use of produced goods x^{σ}

that are possibly produced with the organizational arrangements, technological conditions, and given endowments of factors of production K^σ of medical institution σ. Hence, it may be expressed as

$$T^\sigma = \{(a^\sigma, \ell^\sigma, x^\sigma): (a^\sigma, \ell^\sigma, x^\sigma) \geqq 0,\ f^\sigma(a^\sigma, \ell^\sigma, x^\sigma) \leqq K^\sigma\}.$$

Postulates (T^σ1–T^σ3) imply that the production possibility set T^σ of social institution σ is a closed, convex set of $I + 1 + J$-dimensional vectors $(a^\sigma, \ell^\sigma, x^\sigma)$.

The Producer Optimum for Medical Institutions

As with private firms, conditions of the producer optimum for medical institutions may be obtained. We denote by $\pi = (\pi_i)$ the vector of fees paid for the provision of medical care.

Each social institution σ chooses the optimum and efficient combination $(a^\sigma, \ell^\sigma, x^\sigma)$ of provision of medical care a^σ, employment of professional staff ℓ^σ, and use of produced goods x^σ; that is, the net value

$$\pi a^\sigma - w_s \ell^\sigma - p x^\sigma$$

is maximized over $(a^\sigma, \ell^\sigma, x^\sigma) \in T^\sigma$.

Conditions (T^σ1–T^σ3) postulated for medical institution σ ensure that for any combination of fees paid for medical care π, wage rate of professional staff w_s, and prices of produced goods p, the optimum combination $(a^\sigma, \ell^\sigma, x^\sigma)$ of provision of medical care a^σ, employment of professional labor ℓ^σ, and use of produced goods x^σ always exists and is uniquely determined.

The optimum combination $(a^\sigma, \ell^\sigma, x^\sigma)$ of provision of medical care a^σ, employment of professional labor ℓ^σ, and use of produced goods x^σ may be characterized by the marginality conditions, in exactly the same manner as in the case of private firms. We denote by $r^\sigma = (r^\sigma_f)$ $[r^\sigma_f \geqq 0]$ the vector of imputed rental prices of fixed factors of production of medical institution σ. Then the optimum conditions are

$$\pi \leqq r^\sigma f^\sigma_{a^\sigma}(a^\sigma, \ell^\sigma, x^\sigma) \quad (\text{mod. } a^\sigma) \tag{13}$$

$$w_s \geqq r^\sigma\left[-f^\sigma_{\ell^\sigma}(a^\sigma, \ell^\sigma, x^\sigma)\right] \quad (\text{mod. } \ell^\sigma) \tag{14}$$

$$p \geqq r^\sigma\left[-f^\sigma_{x^\sigma}(a^\sigma, \ell^\sigma, x^\sigma)\right] \quad (\text{mod. } x^\sigma) \tag{15}$$

$$f^\sigma(a^\sigma, \ell^\sigma, x^\sigma) \leqq K^\sigma \quad (\text{mod. } r^\sigma). \tag{16}$$

Condition (13) expresses the principle that the choice of technologies and the levels of medical care are adjusted so as to equate marginal factor costs with the fees for medical care, π.

Condition (14) means that employment of professional staff ℓ^σ is adjusted so that the marginal gains due to the marginal increase in the employment of professional staff are equal to wage rate w when $\ell^\sigma > 0$ and are no larger than w when $\ell^\sigma = 0$.

Condition (15) means that the use of produced goods is adjusted so that the marginal gains due to the marginal increase in the use of produced goods are equal to price p_j when $x_j^\sigma > 0$ and are not larger than p_j when $x_j^\sigma = 0$.

Condition (16) means that the employments of fixed factors of production do not exceed the endowments and the conditions of full employment are satisfied whenever imputed rental price r_f^σ is positive.

We have assumed that the technologies are subject to constant returns to scale ($\mathrm{T}^\sigma 4$), and thus, in view of the Euler identity, conditions (13)–(16) imply that

$$\begin{aligned}\pi a^\sigma - w_s \ell^\sigma - p x^\sigma &= r^\sigma \left[f_{a^\sigma}^\sigma (a^\sigma, \ell^\sigma, x^\sigma) a^\sigma + f_{\ell^\sigma}^\sigma (a^\sigma, \ell^\sigma, x^\sigma) \ell^\sigma \right. \\ &\quad \left. + f_{x^\sigma}^\sigma (a^\sigma, \ell^\sigma, x^\sigma) x^\sigma \right] \\ &= r^\sigma K^\sigma .\end{aligned}$$

Hence,

$$\pi a^\sigma - w_s \ell^\sigma - p x^\sigma = r^\sigma K^\sigma . \tag{17}$$

That is, for each medical institution σ, the net evaluation of provision of medical care is equal to the sum of the imputed rental payments to all fixed factors of production in medical institution σ. As in the case of private firms, the meaning of relation (17) may be better expressed as

$$\pi a^\sigma = w_s \ell^\sigma + p x^\sigma + r^\sigma K^\sigma .$$

The value of medical care provided by medical institution σ, πa^σ, is equal to the sum of wages of professional labor $w_s \ell^\sigma$, payments for the use of produced goods $p x^\sigma$, and payments, in terms of the imputed rental prices, made to fixed factors of production $r^\sigma K^\sigma$. The validity of the Menger-Wieser principle of imputation is also assured for the case of the provision of medicine by medical institutions.

4. MEDICAL CARE AS SOCIAL COMMON CAPITAL AND MARKET EQUILIBRIUM

The basic premises of the model of medical care as social common capital introduced in the previous sections may be recapitulated. Markets for produced goods are perfectly competitive; prices of goods are denoted by vector p, the fees charged for medical care and paid for the provision of medical services are, respectively, denoted by θ and π, and wage rates for standard labor and professional labor are denoted, respectively, by w_p and w_s.

The Consumer Optimum

The welfare of each individual ν is expressed by a preference ordering that is represented by the utility function

$$u^\nu = \phi^\nu(a)\varphi^\nu(a^\nu)u^\nu(c^\nu),$$

where $\phi^\nu(a)$ and $\varphi^\nu(a^\nu)$ are, respectively, the impact indices of social and private effects of medical services and a^ν, a are, respectively, private and general levels of medical care are:

$$a = \sum_\nu a^\nu.$$

Each individual ν chooses the combination (c^ν, a^ν) of consumption c^ν and level of medical care a^ν that maximizes the utility of individual ν

$$u^\nu = \phi^\nu(a)\varphi^\nu(a^\nu)u^\nu(c^\nu)$$

subject to the budget constraint

$$pc^\nu + \theta a^\nu = y^\nu, \tag{18}$$

where y^ν is the income of individual ν,

$$y^\nu = w^\nu + \widehat{y}^\nu;$$

w^ν is the imputed wages of individual ν, to be given by

$$w^\nu = w_p\varphi^\nu(a^\nu)\ell_p^\nu + w_s\varphi^\nu(a^\nu)\ell_s^\nu;$$

w_p and w_s are, respectively, the wage rates for standard labor and professional labor; $\phi^\nu(a)$ and $\varphi^\nu(a^\nu)$ are, respectively, the impact indices of social and private effects of medical care for individual ν; and $\widehat{y}^\nu$ is the portion of income of individual ν other than wages.

The optimum combination (c^ν, a^ν) of consumption c^ν and level of medical care a^ν is characterized by the following marginality conditions:

$$\alpha^\nu \phi^\nu(a)\varphi^\nu(a^\nu)u^\nu_{c^\nu}(c^\nu) \leqq p \quad (\text{mod. } c^\nu) \tag{19}$$

$$\tau^\nu(a^\nu)[pc^\nu + w^\nu] = \theta \tag{20}$$

$$\alpha^\nu \phi^\nu(a)\varphi^\nu(a^\nu)u^\nu(c^\nu) = pc^\nu \tag{21}$$

$$\ell^\nu_p = \sum_\mu \ell^{\nu\mu}, \quad \ell^\nu_s = \sum_\sigma \ell^{\nu\sigma} \quad (\nu = 1, \ldots, n). \tag{22}$$

The Producer Optimum for Private Firms

The production possibility set of each private firm μ, T^μ, is given by

$$T^\mu = \{(x^\mu, \ell^\mu) : (x^\mu, \ell^\mu) \geqq 0,\ f^\mu(x^\mu, \ell^\mu) \leqq K^\mu\},$$

where $f^\mu(x^\mu, \ell^\mu)$ specifies the minimum quantities of factors of production that are required to produce goods by x^μ with the employment of labor at ℓ^μ.

The employment of labor at firm μ, ℓ^μ, when converted to standard labor, is given by

$$\ell^\mu = \sum_\nu \varphi^\nu(a^\nu)\ell^{\nu\mu}, \tag{23}$$

where $\ell^{\nu\mu}$ denotes the employment of labor of individual ν by firm μ $(\nu = 1, \ldots\ n)$.

Each private firm μ chooses the combination (x^μ, ℓ^μ) of vectors of production x^μ and labor employment ℓ^μ that maximizes net profit

$$px^\mu - w_p\ell^\mu$$

over $(x^\mu, \ell^\mu) \in T^\mu$.

The producer optimum is characterized by the following marginality conditions:

$$p \leqq r^\mu f^\mu_{x^\mu}(x^\mu, \ell^\mu) \quad (\text{mod. } x^\mu) \tag{24}$$

$$w_p \geqq r^\mu[-f^\mu_{\ell^\mu}(x^\mu, \ell^\mu)] \quad (\text{mod. } \ell^\mu) \tag{25}$$

$$f^\mu(x^\mu, \ell^\mu) \leqq K^\mu \quad (\text{mod. } r^\mu) \tag{26}$$

$$px^\mu - w\ell^\mu = r^\mu K^\mu. \tag{27}$$

The Producer Optimum for Medical Institutions

For each medical institution σ, the production possibility set T^σ is given by

$$T^\sigma = \{(a^\sigma, \ell^\sigma, x^\sigma): (a^\sigma, \ell^\sigma, x^\sigma) \geqq 0,\ f^\sigma(a^\sigma, \ell^\sigma, x^\sigma) \leqq K^\sigma\},$$

where the function $f^\sigma(a^\sigma, \ell^\sigma, x^\sigma)$ specifies the minimum quantities of factors of production required to provide education by the level a^σ with the employment of professional labor by ℓ^σ and the use of produced goods by x^σ, and K^σ denotes the endowments of fixed factors of production of medical institution σ.

Total employment of professional staff at social institution σ, ℓ^σ, is given by

$$\ell^\sigma = \sum_\nu \varphi^\nu(a^\nu)\ell^{\nu\sigma}. \tag{28}$$

Each social institution σ chooses the most efficient combination $(a^\sigma, \ell^\sigma, x^\sigma)$ of provision of medical care a^σ, employment of professional labor ℓ^σ, and use of produced goods x^σ; that is, the net value

$$\pi a^\sigma - w\ell^\sigma - px^\sigma$$

is maximized over $(a^\sigma, \ell^\sigma, x^\sigma) \in T^\sigma$.

The optimum conditions are

$$\pi \leqq r^\sigma f^\sigma_{a^\sigma}(a^\sigma, \ell^\sigma, x^\sigma) \quad (\text{mod. } a^\sigma) \tag{29}$$

$$w_s \geqq r^\sigma[-f^\sigma_{\ell^\sigma}(a^\sigma, \ell^\sigma, x^\sigma)] \quad (\text{mod. } \ell^\sigma) \tag{30}$$

$$p \geqq r^\sigma[-f^\sigma_{x^\sigma}(a^\sigma, \ell^\sigma, x^\sigma)] \quad (\text{mod. } x^\sigma) \tag{31}$$

$$f^\sigma(a^\sigma, \ell^\sigma, x^\sigma) \leqq K^\sigma \quad (\text{mod. } r^\sigma) \tag{32}$$

$$\pi a^\sigma - w_s\ell^\sigma - px^\sigma = r^\sigma K^\sigma. \tag{33}$$

Market Equilibrium for the Medical Care Model of Social Common Capital

Market equilibrium for the model of medical care as social common capital is obtained if the following equilibrium conditions are satisfied:

(i) Each individual ν chooses the combination (c^ν, a^ν) of consumption c^ν and level of medical care a^ν in such a manner that the utility of individual ν

$$u^\nu = \phi^\nu(a)\varphi^\nu(a^\nu)u^\nu(c^\nu)$$

is maximized subject to the budget constraint

$$pc^\nu + \theta a^\nu = y^\nu = w\varphi^\nu(a^\nu)\ell^\nu + \widehat{y}^\nu,$$

where $w\varphi^\nu(a^\nu)\ell^\nu$ denotes the wages of individual ν, $\widehat{y}^\nu$ is the portion of income of individual ν other than wages, $\phi^\nu(a)$ and $\varphi^\nu(a^\nu)$ are, respectively, the impact indices of social and private effects of medical care for individual ν, and a^ν and a are, respectively, private and general levels of medical care.

(ii) The general level a of medical care of the society is equal to the sum of the levels of medical care provided by all medical institutions; that is,

$$a = \sum_\sigma a^\sigma.$$

(iii) Each private firm μ chooses the combination (x^μ, ℓ^μ) of vector of production x^μ and labor employment ℓ^μ that maximize net profits

$$px^\mu - w_p\ell^\mu, \quad (x^\mu, \ell^\mu) \in T^\mu,$$

where

$$\ell^\mu = \sum_\nu \varphi^\nu(a^\nu)\ell^{\nu\mu}.$$

(iv) Each medical institution σ chooses the optimum and efficient combination $(a^\sigma, \ell^\sigma, x^\sigma)$ of provision of medical care a^σ, employment of professional labor ℓ^σ, and use of produced goods x^σ; that is, the net value

$$\pi a^\sigma - w_s\ell^\sigma - px^\sigma, \quad (a^\sigma, \ell^\sigma, x^\sigma) \in T^\sigma$$

is maximized, where

$$\ell^\sigma = \sum_\sigma \varphi^\nu(a^\nu)\ell^{\nu\sigma}.$$

(v) At the wage rate of the standard labor w_p, total demand for the employment of standard labor is equal to total supply:

$$\sum_\nu \ell_p^\nu = \sum_\mu \ell^{\nu\mu}.$$

(vi) At the wage rate of professional staff w_s, total demand for the employment of professional labor is equal to total supply:

$$\sum_\nu \ell_s^\nu = \sum_\sigma \ell^{\nu\sigma}.$$

(vii) At the vector of prices for produced goods p, total demand for goods is equal to total supply:

$$\sum_\nu c^\nu + \sum_\sigma x^\sigma = \sum_\mu x^\mu.$$

(viii) Subsidiary payments, at the rate τ ($\tau \geqq 0$), are made to social institutions in charge of medical care so that

$$\pi - \theta = \tau.$$

In the following discussion, we suppose that for any given rate τ of subsidy payments to medical institutions, the state of the economy that satisfies all conditions for market equilibrium generally exists and is uniquely determined.

Concerning National Income Accounting

Income y^ν of each individual ν is given as the sum of wages and dividend payments of private firms and medical institutions, subtracted by tax payments t^ν:

$$y^\nu = w\varphi^\nu(a^\nu)\ell^\nu + \sum_\mu s^{\nu\mu} r^\mu K^\mu + \sum_\sigma s^{\nu\sigma} r^\sigma K^\sigma - t^\nu,$$

where

$$s^{\nu\mu} \geqq 0, \quad \sum_\nu s^{\nu\mu} = 1, \quad s^{\nu\sigma} \geqq 0, \quad \sum_\nu s^{\nu\sigma} = 1.$$

Tax payments of individuals $\{t^\nu\}$ are arranged so that the sum of tax payments made by all individuals are equal to the sum of subsidy payments to all social institutions in charge of medical care, τa:

$$\sum_\nu t^\nu = \tau a, \quad \tau = \pi - \theta$$

$$y = \sum_\nu y^\nu.$$

Hence,

$$
\begin{aligned}
y &= \sum_{\nu} w\varphi^{\nu}(a^{\nu})\ell^{\nu} + \sum_{\mu} r^{\mu} K^{\mu} + \sum_{\sigma} \rho^{\sigma} V^{\sigma} - \sum_{\nu} t^{\nu} \\
&= \sum_{\nu} w\varphi^{\nu}(a^{\nu})\ell^{\nu} + \sum_{\mu} (px^{\mu} - w_p\ell^{\mu} - \theta a^{\mu}) \\
&\quad + \sum_{\sigma} (\pi a^{\sigma} - w_p\ell^{\sigma} - px^{\sigma}) - \tau a \\
&= \sum_{\nu} (pc^{\nu} + \theta a^{\nu}) + (\pi - \theta)a - \tau a \\
&= \sum_{\nu} (pc^{\nu} + \theta a^{\nu}).
\end{aligned}
$$

Thus we have established the familiar identity of two definitions of national income.

5. MARKET EQUILIBRIUM AND SOCIAL OPTIMUM

To explore the welfare implications of market equilibrium under the subsidy payment scheme to the social institutions in charge of medical care with the rate τ, we consider the social utility U given by

$$U = \sum_{\nu} \alpha^{\nu} u^{\nu} = \sum_{\nu} \alpha^{\nu} \phi^{\nu}(a)\varphi^{\nu}(a^{\nu})u^{\nu}(c^{\nu}),$$

where utility weight α^{ν} is the inverse of marginal utility of income y^{ν} of individual ν at the market equilibrium.

We consider the following maximum problem:

Maximum Problem for Social Optimum. Find the pattern of consumption and production of goods, employment of labor, and provision and use of medical care $c^{\nu}, a^{\nu}, x^{\mu}, \ell^{\mu}, a^{\sigma}, \ell^{\sigma}, x^{\sigma}, a$ that maximizes the social utility

$$U = \sum_{\nu} \alpha^{\nu} u^{\nu} = \sum_{\nu} \alpha^{\nu} \phi^{\nu}(a)\varphi^{\nu}(a^{\nu})u^{\nu}(c^{\nu})$$

among all feasible patterns of allocation

$$\sum_{\nu} c^{\nu} + \sum_{\sigma} x^{\sigma} \leqq \sum_{\mu} x^{\mu} \tag{34}$$

$$\sum_{\mu} \ell^{\nu\mu} \leqq \ell_p^{\nu} \tag{35}$$

$$\sum_{\sigma} \ell^{\nu\sigma} \leqq \ell_s^{\nu} \tag{36}$$

$$\ell^{\mu} = \sum_{\nu} \varphi^{\nu}(a^{\nu}) \ell^{\nu\mu} \tag{37}$$

$$\ell^{\sigma} = \sum_{\nu} \varphi^{\nu}(a^{\nu}) \ell^{\nu\sigma} \tag{38}$$

$$\sum_{\nu} a^{\nu} \leqq a \tag{39}$$

$$a \leqq \sum_{\sigma} a^{\sigma} \tag{40}$$

$$f^{\mu}(x^{\mu}, \ell^{\mu}) \leqq K^{\mu} \tag{41}$$

$$f^{\sigma}(a^{\sigma}, \ell^{\sigma}, x^{\sigma}) \leqq K^{\sigma}, \tag{42}$$

where utility weights α^{ν} are evaluated at the market equilibrium corresponding to the given subsidy rate τ.

The maximum problem for social optimum may be solved in terms of the Lagrange method. Let us define the Lagrangian form

$$\begin{aligned}
&L(c^{\nu}, a^{\nu}, x^{\mu}, \ell^{\mu}, \ell^{\nu\mu}, a^{\sigma}, \ell^{\sigma}, \ell^{\nu\sigma}, x^{\sigma}, a; p, w_p^{\nu}, w_s^{\nu}, w^{\mu}, w^{\sigma}, \theta, \pi, r^{\mu}, r^{\sigma}) \\
&= \sum_{\nu} \alpha^{\nu} \phi^{\nu}(a) \varphi^{\nu}(a^{\nu}) u^{\nu}(c^{\nu}) + p \left(\sum_{\mu} x^{\mu} - \sum_{\nu} c^{\nu} - \sum_{\sigma} x^{\sigma} \right) \\
&\quad + \sum_{\nu} w_p^{\nu} \left[\ell_p^{\nu} - \sum_{\mu} \ell^{\nu\mu} \right] + \sum_{\nu} w_s^{\nu} \left[\ell_s^{\nu} - \sum_{\sigma} \ell^{\nu\sigma} \right] \\
&\quad + \sum_{\mu} w^{\mu} \left[\sum_{\nu} \varphi^{\nu}(a^{\nu}) \ell^{\nu\mu} - \ell^{\mu} \right] + \sum_{\sigma} w^{\sigma} \left[\sum_{\nu} \varphi^{\nu}(a^{\nu}) \ell^{\nu\sigma} - \ell^{\sigma} \right] \\
&\quad + \theta \left(a - \sum_{\nu} a^{\nu} \right) + \pi \left(\sum_{\sigma} a^{\sigma} - a \right) + \sum_{\mu} r^{\mu} [K^{\mu} - f^{\mu}(x^{\mu}, \ell^{\mu})] \\
&\quad + \sum_{\sigma} r^{\sigma} [K^{\sigma} - f^{\sigma}(a^{\sigma}, \ell^{\sigma}, x^{\sigma})].
\end{aligned} \tag{43}$$

The Lagrange unknowns $p, w_p^{\nu}, w_s^{\nu}, w^{\mu}, w^{\sigma}, \theta, \pi, r^{\mu}$, and r^{σ} are associated, respectively, with constraints (34), (35), (36), (37), (38), (39), (40), (41), and (42).

The optimum solution may be obtained by partially differentiating the Lagrangian form (43) with respect to unknown variables $c^\nu, a^\nu, x^\mu, \ell^\mu, \ell^{\nu\mu}, a^\sigma, \ell^\sigma, \ell^{\nu\sigma}, x^\sigma, a, p, w_p^\nu, w_s^\nu, w^\mu, w^\sigma, \theta, \pi, r^\mu, r^\sigma$ and putting them equal to 0:

$$\alpha^\nu \phi^\nu(a)\varphi^\nu(a^\nu)u^\nu_{c^\nu}(c^\nu) \leqq p \quad (\text{mod. } c^\nu) \tag{44}$$

$$\tau^\nu(a^\nu)[pc^\nu + w^\nu] = \theta \tag{45}$$

$$p \leqq r^\mu f^\mu_{x^\mu}(x^\mu, \ell^\mu) \quad (\text{mod. } x^\mu) \tag{46}$$

$$w_p \geqq r^\mu \left[-f^\mu_{\ell^\mu}(x^\mu, \ell^\mu)\right] \quad (\text{mod. } \ell^\mu) \tag{47}$$

$$f^\mu(x^\mu, \ell^\mu) \leqq K^\mu \quad (\text{mod. } r^\mu) \tag{48}$$

$$\pi \leqq r^\sigma f^\sigma_{a^\sigma}(a^\sigma, \ell^\sigma, x^\sigma) \quad (\text{mod. } a^\sigma) \tag{49}$$

$$w_s \geqq r^\sigma\left[-f^\sigma_{\ell^\sigma}(a^\sigma, \ell^\sigma, x^\sigma)\right] \quad (\text{mod. } \ell^\sigma) \tag{50}$$

$$p \geqq r^\sigma\left[-f^\sigma_{x^\sigma}(a^\sigma, \ell^\sigma, x^\sigma)\right] \quad (\text{mod. } x^\sigma) \tag{51}$$

$$f^\sigma(a^\sigma, \ell^\sigma, x^\sigma) \leqq K^\sigma \quad (\text{mod. } r^\sigma) \tag{52}$$

$$\pi - \theta = \tau(a)pc, \tag{53}$$

where

$$w_p^\nu = \varphi^\nu(a^\nu)w_p, \quad w_p^\nu = w_p$$

$$w_s^\nu = \varphi^\nu(a^\nu)w_s, \quad w_s^\nu = w_s,$$

w^ν denotes the wages of individual ν

$$w^\nu = w_p\varphi^\nu(a^\nu)\ell_p^\nu + w_s\varphi^\nu(a^\nu)\ell_s^\nu,$$

c is aggregate consumption

$$c = \sum_\nu c^\nu,$$

and $\tau(a)$ is the impact coefficient of the general level of medical care.

Only equation (53) may need clarification. Partially differentiate the Lagrangian form (43) with respect to a to obtain

$$\frac{\partial L}{\partial a} = \tau(a) \sum_{\nu} \alpha^{\nu} \phi^{\nu}(a) \varphi^{\nu}(a^{\nu}) u^{\nu}(c^{\nu}) + \theta - \pi.$$

Note that marginality condition (44) and the linear homogeneity hypothesis for utility functions $u^{\nu}(c^{\nu})$ imply

$$\sum_{\nu} \alpha^{\nu} \phi^{\nu}(a) \varphi^{\nu}(a^{\nu}) u^{\nu}(c^{\nu}) = \sum_{\nu} pc^{\nu}.$$

Hence, $\frac{\partial L}{\partial a} = 0$ implies equation (53).

Applying the classic Kuhn-Tucker theorem on concave programming, the Euler-Lagrange equations (44)–(53) are necessary and sufficient conditions for the optimum solution of the maximum problem for social optimum.

It is apparent that the Euler-Lagrange equations coincide precisely with the equilibrium conditions for market equilibrium with the subsidy payment to social institutions in charge of medical care at the rate τ given by

$$\tau = \tau(a) pc.$$

We have thus established the following proposition.

Proposition 1. *Consider the subsidy scheme to social institutions in charge of medical care at the rate* τ *given by*

$$\tau = \tau(a) pc,$$

where $\tau(a)$ *is the impact coefficient of the general level of medical care and* c *is aggregate consumption* $[c = \sum_{\nu} c^{\nu}]$. *Tax payments for individuals* $\{t^{\nu}\}$ *are arranged so that the balance-of-budget conditions are satisfied:*

$$\sum_{\nu} t^{\nu} = \tau a.$$

Then market equilibrium obtained under such a subsidy scheme is a social optimum in the sense that a set of positive weights for the utilities of individuals $(\alpha^1, \ldots, \alpha^n)$ *exists such that the social utility*

$$U = \sum_{\nu} \alpha^{\nu} u^{\nu} = \sum_{\nu} \alpha^{\nu} \phi^{\nu}(a) \varphi^{\nu}(a^{\nu}) u^{\nu}(c^{\nu})$$

is maximized among all feasible allocation $(c^{\nu}, a^{\nu}, x^{\mu}, \ell^{\mu}, a^{\sigma}, \ell^{\sigma}, x^{\sigma}, a)$.

The optimum level of social utility U is equal to the value of aggregate consumption:

$$U = pc.$$

Social optimum is defined with respect to social utility

$$U = \sum_{\nu} \alpha^{\nu} u^{\nu} = \sum_{\nu} \alpha^{\nu} \phi^{\nu}(a) \varphi^{\nu}(a^{\nu}) u^{\nu}(c^{\nu}),$$

where $(\alpha^1, \ldots, \alpha^n)$ is an arbitrarily given set of positive weights for the utilities of individuals. A pattern of allocation $(c^{\nu}, a^{\nu}, x^{\mu}, \ell^{\mu}, a^{\sigma}, \ell^{\sigma}, x^{\sigma}, a)$ is a social optimum if the social utility U thus defined is maximized among all feasible patterns of allocation.

Social optimum necessarily implies the existence of the subsidy scheme to medical institutions at the rate τ given by

$$\tau = \tau(a) pc.$$

However, the budgetary constraints for individuals

$$pc^{\nu} + \theta a^{\nu} = y^{\nu}$$

are not necessarily satisfied. It is apparent that the following proposition holds.

Proposition 2. *Suppose a pattern of allocation $(c^{\nu}, a^{\nu}, x^{\mu}, \ell^{\mu}, a^{\sigma}, \ell^{\sigma}, x^{\sigma}, a)$ is a social optimum; that is, a set of positive weights for the utilities of individuals $(\alpha^1, \ldots, \alpha^n)$ exists such that the given pattern of allocation $(c^{\nu}, a^{\nu}, x^{\mu}, \ell^{\mu}, a^{\sigma}, \ell^{\sigma}, x^{\sigma}, a)$ maximizes the social utility*

$$U = \sum_{\nu} \alpha^{\nu} u^{\nu} = \sum_{\nu} \alpha^{\nu} \phi^{\nu}(a) \varphi^{\nu}(a^{\nu}) u^{\nu}(c^{\nu})$$

among all feasible patterns of allocation.

Then, a system of individual taxes $\{t^{\nu}\}$ satisfying the balance-of-budget conditions:

$$\sum_{\nu} t^{\nu} = \tau a, \quad \tau = \tau(a) pc,$$

exists such that the given pattern of allocation $(c^{\nu}, a^{\nu}, x^{\mu}, \ell^{\mu}, a^{\sigma}, \ell^{\sigma}, x^{\sigma}, a)$ corresponds precisely to the market equilibrium under the subsidy scheme to social institutions in charge of medical care at the rate τ given by $\tau = \tau(a) pc$.

6. MARKET EQUILIBRIUM AND LINDAHL EQUILIBRIUM

Lindahl Conditions

Let us recall the postulates for the behavior of individuals at market equilibrium. At market equilibrium, conditions for the consumer optimum are obtained if each individual ν chooses the combination (c^ν, a^ν) of consumption c^ν and medical care a^ν in such a manner that the utility of individual ν

$$u^\nu = \phi^\nu(a)\varphi^\nu(a^\nu)u^\nu(c^\nu)$$

is maximized subject to the budget constraint

$$pc^\nu + \theta a^\nu = y^\nu,$$

where income y^ν of each individual ν is given as the sum of wages and dividend payments of private firms and social institutions, subtracted by tax payments t^ν:

$$y^\nu = w_p\varphi^\nu(a^\nu)\ell_p^\nu + w_s\varphi^\nu(a^\nu)\ell_s^\nu + \sum_\mu s^{\nu\mu}r^\mu K^\mu + \sum_\sigma s^{\nu\sigma}r^\sigma K^\sigma - t^\nu,$$

where the following conditions are satisfied:

$$\sum_\nu t^\nu = \tau a,$$

where it is assumed that only one kind of medical care exists.

Let us first rewrite the budget constraint as follows:

$$pc^\nu + \theta a^\nu - \tau a^\nu = \overline{y}^\nu,$$

where

$$\overline{y}^\nu = y^\nu - \tau a^\nu, \quad \tau = \tau(a)pc.$$

Lindahl conditions are satisfied if a system of individual subsidy rates $\{\tau^\nu\}$ exists such that

$$\sum_\nu \tau^\nu = \tau, \quad \tau = \tau(a)pc,$$

and for each individual ν, (c^ν, a^ν, a) is the optimum solution to the following virtual maximum problem:

Find $(\overline{c}^\nu, \overline{a}^\nu, \overline{a}^{(\nu)})$ that maximizes

$$u^\nu = \phi^\nu(\overline{a}^{(\nu)})\varphi^\nu(\overline{a}^\nu)u^\nu(\overline{c}^\nu)$$

subject to the virtual budget constraint

$$p\bar{c}^{\nu} + \theta\bar{a}^{\nu} - \tau^{\nu}\bar{a}^{(\nu)} = \bar{y}^{\nu}.$$

Because (c^{ν}, a^{ν}, a) is the optimum solution of the virtual maximum problem for individual ν, the optimum conditions imply

$$\tau^{\nu} = \alpha^{\nu}\tau(a)\phi^{\nu}(a)\varphi^{\nu}(a^{\nu})u^{\nu}(c^{\nu}) = \tau(a)pc^{\nu},$$

where α^{ν} is the inverse of marginal utility of income of individual ν.

Hence, Lindahl conditions are satisfied if, and only if,

$$\tau^{\nu}a = \tau a^{\nu},$$

which implies

$$[\tau(a)pc^{\nu}]a = [\tau(a)pc]a^{\nu} \Leftrightarrow \frac{a^{\nu}}{a} = \frac{pc^{\nu}}{pc}.$$

Thus, we have established the following proposition.

Proposition 3. *Consider the case in which only one kind of medical care exists and the subsidy scheme to social institutions in charge of medical services at the rate τ is given by*

$$\tau = \tau(a)pc, \quad c = \sum_{\nu} c^{\nu},$$

where $\tau(a)$ is the impact coefficient of the general level of medical care.

Then market equilibrium under such a subsidy scheme is Lindahl equilibrium if, and only if, the following conditions are satisfied:

$$\frac{a^{\nu}}{a} = \frac{pc^{\nu}}{pc},$$

where a^{ν} is the level of medical services received by individual ν and a is the general level of medical services.

7. ADJUSTMENT PROCESSES OF SUBSIDY RATES FOR MEDICAL INSTITUTIONS

Market equilibrium under the subsidy scheme to social institutions in charge of medical care at the rate $\tau = \tau(a)pc$ coincides with the social optimum with respect to the social utility

$$U = \sum_{\nu} \alpha^{\nu}u^{\nu} = \sum_{\nu} \alpha^{\nu}\phi^{\nu}(a)\varphi^{\nu}(a^{\nu})u^{\nu}(c^{\nu}),$$

where, for each individual ν, utility weight α^ν is the inverse of marginal utility of income y^ν at market equilibrium.

The subsidy rate $\tau = \tau(a)pc$ is administratively determined and announced prior to the opening of the market when the general level of medical care a is not known. We introduce adjustment processes concerning the subsidy rate τ that are stable. We first consider an alternative adjustment process with respect to the general level of medical care a.

We examine the relationships between the general level of medical care a and the ensuing level of the social utility U.

Let us assume that the general level of medical care a is announced at the beginning of the adjustment process and consider the pattern of resource allocation at market equilibrium with the general level of medical care at the announced level a.

Market equilibrium with the subsidy scheme to medical institutions at the rate τ is obtained if the following equilibrium conditions are satisfied:

(i) Each individual ν chooses the combination (c^ν, a^ν) of consumption c^ν and level of medical care a^ν in such a manner that the utility of individual ν

$$u^\nu = \phi^\nu(a)\varphi^\nu(a^\nu)u^\nu(c^\nu)$$

is maximized subject to the budget constraint

$$pc^\nu + \theta a^\nu = y^\nu,$$

where y^ν is the income of each individual ν in units of market price.

(ii) Each private firm μ chooses the combination (x^μ, ℓ^μ) of vector of production x^μ and the employment of labor ℓ^μ that maximizes net profits

$$px^\mu - w_p\ell^\mu, \quad (x^\mu, \ell^\mu) \in T^\mu,$$

where

$$\ell^\mu = \sum_\nu \varphi^\nu(a^\nu)\ell^{\nu\mu}$$

and $\ell^{\nu\mu}$ is the amount of standard labor of individual ν employed by private firm μ.

(iii) Each social institution σ chooses the combination $(a^\sigma, \ell^\sigma, x^\sigma)$ of provision of medical care a^σ, employment of professional staff ℓ^σ, and use of produced goods x^σ that maximizes net value

$$\pi a^\sigma - w_s \ell^\sigma - p x^\sigma, \quad (a^\sigma, \ell^\sigma, x^\sigma) \in T^\sigma,$$

where

$$\ell^\sigma = \sum_\nu \varphi^\nu(a^\nu) \ell^{\nu\sigma}$$

and $\ell^{\nu\sigma}$ is the amount of medical labor of individual ν employed by social institution σ.

(iv) At the prices for produced goods p, total demand for goods is equal to total supply:

$$\sum_\nu c^\nu + \sum_\sigma x^\sigma = \sum_\mu x^\mu.$$

(v) At the wage rates w_p and w_s, total demand for the employment of labor of two types is equal to total supply:

$$\ell^\mu = \sum_\nu \varphi^\nu(a^\nu) \ell^{\nu\mu}, \quad \ell^\sigma = \sum_\nu \varphi^\nu(a^\nu) \ell^{\nu\sigma}.$$

(vi) The general level of medical care a is equal to the sum of the levels of medical services provided by all medical institutions σ; that is,

$$a = \sum_\sigma a^\sigma.$$

(vii) The general level of medical care a is equal to the sum of the levels of medical care received by all individuals of the society; that is,

$$a = \sum_\nu a^\nu.$$

It may be noted that the general level of medical care is given at an arbitrarily given level a and announced prior to the opening of the market, whereas the subsidy rate for medical institutions, τ, is simply given at the level:

$$\tau = \pi - \theta,$$

where π and θ are, respectively, the fees for the provision and use of medical care that are determined on the market.

Market equilibrium thus obtained corresponds to the social optimum with respect to the social utility

$$U = \sum_{\nu} \alpha^{\nu} u^{\nu} = \sum_{\nu} \alpha^{\nu} \phi^{\nu}(a) \varphi^{\nu}(a^{\nu}) u^{\nu}(c^{\nu}),$$

where for each individual ν, utility weight α^{ν} is the inverse of marginal utility of income of individual ν at the market equilibrium and the general level of medical care at the predetermined level a.

We next examine the effect of the marginal change in the general level of medical care a on the level of the social utility U. The level of the social utility U at market equilibrium is given as the value of the Lagrangian form (43), where a is not a variable but rather is regarded as a parameter.

By taking total differentials of both sides of the Lagrangian form L and by noting Euler-Lagrange conditions

$$\frac{\partial L}{\partial c^{\nu}} = 0, \quad \frac{\partial L}{\partial a^{\nu}} = 0, \quad \frac{\partial L}{\partial x^{\mu}} = 0, \quad \frac{\partial L}{\partial \ell^{\mu}} = 0,$$

$$\frac{\partial L}{\partial a^{\mu}} = 0, \quad \frac{\partial L}{\partial a^{\sigma}} = 0, \quad \frac{\partial L}{\partial \ell^{\sigma}} = 0, \quad \frac{\partial L}{\partial x^{\sigma}} = 0,$$

we obtain

$$dU1 = [\tau(a)pc + \theta - \pi] d\theta.$$

Hence, we have

$$\frac{dU}{da} = \tau(a)pc - (\pi - \theta). \tag{54}$$

The Lagrangian unknown θ may be interpreted as the imputed price of medical care, and it is decreased as the general level of medical care a becomes higher. Similarly, the Lagrangian unknown π may be interpreted as the imputed price for the provision of medical care, and it is increased as the general level of medical care a becomes higher. Hence, the right-hand side of equation (54) is a decreasing function of a.

Hence, the adjustment process with respect to the general level of medical care a defined by the differential equation

$$\dot{a} = k[\tau(a)pc - \tau],$$

with a positive constant k as the speed of adjustment, is globally stable.

The subsidy rate τ at the market equilibrium with the general level of medical care a is also uniquely determined:

$$\pi - \theta = \tau.$$

An increase in the subsidy rate τ is always associated with an increase in the general level of medical care a. The following proposition may be established.

Proposition 4. *Consider the adjustment process defined by the following differential equation:*

$$\text{(A)} \qquad \dot{\tau} = k[\tau(a)pc - \tau],$$

where the speed of adjustment k is a positive constant and all variables refer to the state of the economy at the market equilibrium under the subsidy scheme with the rate τ*:*

$$\pi - \theta = \tau.$$

Then differential equation (A) is globally stable; that is, for any initial subsidy rate τ_o*, the solution path to differential equation (A) converges to the stationary state, where*

$$\tau = \tau(a)pc.$$

Main Results Recapitulated

1. FISHERIES, FORESTRY, AND AGRICULTURE IN THE THEORY OF THE COMMONS

When we examine the interaction of economic activities with the natural environment, one of the more crucial issues concerns the organizational characteristics of the social institutions that manage the natural environment, in conjunction with their behavioral and financial criteria, which would realize the patterns of repletion and depletion of the natural environment and the levels of economic activities that are dynamically optimum from the social point of view. The dynamically optimum time-paths generally converge to the long-run stationary state at which the processes of economic activities are sustained at levels that are at the optimum balance vis-á-vis the natural environment. The problem we face now concerns the organizational and institutional arrangements for sustainable economic development.

Such an organizational framework may be provided by the institutional arrangements of the commons, as has been demonstrated in terms of a large number of historical, traditional, and contemporary commons in McCay and Acheson (1987) and Berkes (1989), for example. The commons discussed in these references refer to a variety of natural resources extending from fisheries, forestry, and grazing grounds, to irrigation and subterranean water systems. The processes of industrialization, however, together with the accompanying changes in economic, social, and cultural conditions prevailing in modern society, have made these commons untenable from both economic and social points of view, and the survival of the majority of the traditional commons has become extremely difficult.

In Chapter 1, we focus our attention on examining the role of the commons in the intertemporal processes of resource allocation, with respect to both the natural environment and privately owned property resources, and on analyzing the dynamic implications of the institutional arrangements of the commons for the sustainability of economic development.

We are primarily concerned with the phenomenon of externalities, both static and dynamic, that is generally observed with respect to the allocative processes in the commons. Static externalities occur when, with the stock of the natural environment kept constant, the schedules of marginal products of both private means of production and natural resources extracted from the environment for individual members of the commons are affected by the levels of economic activities carried out by other members of the commons. On the other hand, dynamic externalities concern the effect on the future schedules of the marginal products for individual members of the commons due to the repletion or depletion of the stock of the commons as the result of economic activities carried out by members of the commons today.

We examine those institutional arrangements regarding the use of the natural resources extracted from the stock of the commons that may result in the intertemporal allocation of scarce resources in the commons as a whole that is dynamically optimum in terms of the intertemporal preference criterion prevailing in the society. The analysis in Chapter 1 has been carried out with respect to three kinds of the commons – the fisheries, forestry, and agricultural commons – which represent most familiar cases of historical and traditional commons and are relatively easily examined in terms of the analytical apparatuses developed by the recent literature as described in Clark (1990) and elaborated by Uzawa (1992b, 1998, 2003).

2. THE PROTOTYPE MODEL OF SOCIAL COMMON CAPITAL

Chapter 2 introduces the prototype model of social common capital, in which we consider a particular type of social common capital – social infrastructure such as highways, ports, and public transportation systems.

Services of social common capital are subject to the phenomenon of congestion, resulting in the divergence between private and social costs. Therefore, to obtain efficient and equitable allocation of scarce resources, it becomes necessary to levy taxes on the use of services of social common capital. The prices charged for the use of services of social common capital exceed, by the tax rates, the prices paid to social institutions in charge of social common capital for the provision of services of social common capital. In the first part of Chapter 2, we examine the conditions for social common capital taxes to ensure market equilibrium that is social optimum.

We consider a society, either a nation or a specific region. The society consists of a finite number of individuals and two types of institutions – private firms specialized in producing goods that are transacted on the market, on the one hand, and social institutions that are concerned with the provision of services of social common capital, on the other.

In the prototype model of social common capital introduced in Chapter 2, we assume that the effect induced by the phenomenon of congestion with respect to the use of social common capital is Harrod-neutral in the sense originally introduced in Uzawa (1961) so that the utility function of each individual ν and the factor-requirement function of each private firm μ are, respectively, expressed in the following manner:

$$u^\nu = u^\nu(c^\nu, \varphi^\nu(a)a^\nu), \quad f^\mu(x^\mu, \ell^\mu, \varphi^\mu(a)a^\mu),$$

where a is the total amount of services of social common capital used by all members of the society; that is,

$$a = \sum_\nu a^\nu + \sum_\mu a^\mu,$$

where a^ν and a^μ are the amounts of services of social common capital used, respectively, by individual ν and private firm μ; c^ν is the vector of goods consumed by individual ν; and x^μ and ℓ^μ are, respectively, the vectors of goods produced and the employment of labor by private firm μ. The functions $\varphi^\nu(a)$ and $\varphi^\mu(a)$ are referred to as the impact indices.

The phenomenon of congestion may be expressed by the condition that as the total use of services of social common capital a is increased, the effect of congestion is intensified, but with diminishing marginal effects. The impact coefficients of social common capital, $\tau^{\nu}(a)$, $\tau^{\mu}(a)$, are the relative rates of the marginal change in the impact indices due to the marginal increase in the use of social common capital:

$$\tau^{\nu}(a) = -\frac{\varphi^{\nu\prime}(a)}{\varphi^{\nu}(a)}, \quad \tau^{\mu}(a) = -\frac{\varphi^{\mu\prime}(a)}{\varphi^{\mu}(a)},$$

where we assume that these impact coefficients of social common capital are identical:

$$\tau^{\nu}(a) = \tau^{\mu}(a) = \tau(a).$$

We have shown that, under certain qualifying constraints concerning preference relations of individuals and production possibility sets of both private firms and social institutions in charge of social common capital, the ensuing market equilibrium is a social optimum if, and only if, social common capital taxes are levied with the tax rate τ for the use of services of social common capital given by

$$\tau = \tau(a)a.$$

The concept of social optimality is primarily concerned with the efficiency aspect of resource allocation. Concerning the equity aspect of resource allocation and income distribution, the concept of Lindahl equilibrium that was introduced by Lindahl (1919) to examine the equity problems in the theory of public goods plays a crucial role in the theory of social common capital as well. In the second part of Chapter 2, we have shown that in the prototype model of social common capital, the market equilibrium under the social common capital tax with the tax rate $\tau = \tau(a)a$ is always a Lindahl equilibrium.

In the prototype model of social common capital introduced in Chapter 2, the exact magnitude of the optimum social common capital rate $\tau = \tau(a)a$ is not easily calculated. An adjustment process for the social common capital tax rate τ is introduced in terms of the following differential equation:

$$\dot{\tau} = k[\tau(a)a - \tau],$$

with initial condition τ_0, where k is an arbitrarily given positive number.

Then, we have proved that this adjustment process is always globally stable; that is, for any initial condition τ_0, the solution path τ to the differential equation converges to the market equilibrium with social common capital tax rate $\tau(a)a$.

3. SUSTAINABILITY AND SOCIAL COMMON CAPITAL

Chapter 3 examines the problems of the accumulation of social common capital primarily from the viewpoint of the intergenerational distribution of utility and explores the conditions under which processes of the accumulation of social common capital over time are sustainable. The conceptual framework of the economic analysis of social common capital developed in Chapter 2 is extended to deal with the problems of the irreversibility of processes of the accumulation of social common capital owing to the Penrose effect.

The analysis focuses on the examination of the system of imputed prices associated with the time-path of consumption and capital accumulation that is dynamically optimum with respect to the intertemporal preference relation prevailing in society, where the presence of the Penrose effect implies the diminishing marginal rates of investment in both private capital and social common capital. The sustainable time-path of consumption and investment is characterized by the stationarity of the imputed prices associated with the given intertemporal preference ordering, where the efficiency of resource allocation from a short-run point of view may be guaranteed. In other words, a time-path of consumption and investment is sustainable if all future generations would face the same imputed prices of various kinds of social common capital as those faced by the current generation. The existence of the sustainable time-path of consumption and capital accumulation starting with an arbitrarily given stock of capital, both private and social common capital, is ensured when the processes of capital accumulation are subject to the Penrose effect that exhibits the law of diminishing marginal rates of investment.

In the analysis of dynamic optimality, a crucial role is played by the imputed price of social common capital such as forests, oceans, the atmosphere, and social infrastructure. The imputed price of a particular kind of social common capital expresses the extent to which the marginal increase of the stock of the capital today contributes to the marginal increase of the welfare of the future generations of the society. The concept of sustainability introduced in Chapter 3 may be defined in terms of imputed price. Dynamic processes involving the accumulation of social common capital are sustainable when, at each time, intertemporal allocation of scarce resources is arranged so that the imputed prices of the various kinds of social common capital are to remain stationary at all future times.

In the prototype model of social common capital, the optimum conditions for the dynamically optimum time-path of consumption and accumulation of private capital and social common capital coincide precisely with those for market equilibrium with the social common capital tax at the rate $\tau = \tau(a)a$:

$$\theta - \pi = \tau\theta, \quad \tau = \tau(a)a,$$

where $\tau(a)$ is the impact coefficient of social common capital, with perfect foresight concerning the schedules of marginal efficiency of investment both in private capital and social common capital.

On the other hand, the conditions for the sustainable time-path of consumption and accumulation of social common capital coincides precisely with the optimum conditions for market equilibrium with the social common capital tax at the rate $\tau = \tau(a)a$:

$$\theta - \pi = \tau\theta, \quad \tau = \tau(a)a,$$

with stationary expectations concerning the schedules of marginal efficiency of investment both in private capital and social common capital.

4. A COMMONS MODEL OF SOCIAL COMMON CAPITAL

In Chapter 1, we formulate simple dynamic models of the fisheries and forestry commons to examine critically the theory of "the tragedy of the commons," originally put forward by Hardin. However, the analysis primarily is confined to the cases in which the commons are evaluated in terms of the pecuniary gains accrued to the members of the communities that communally own or control the commons, where the role of the commons as social common capital is only tangentially noted. When the natural environment is regarded as social common capital, there are two crucial properties that must be explicitly incorporated in any dynamic analysis of social common capital. The first property concerns the externalities, both static and dynamic, with respect to the use of the natural environment as a factor of production. The second property is concerned with the role of the natural environment as an important component of the living environment, significantly affecting the quality of human life.

The commons model of social common capital introduced in Chapter 4 consists of a finite number of commons. Each commons is composed of individuals and two types of institutions – private firms that are specialized in producing goods that are transacted on the market and social institutions that are concerned with the provision of services of social common capital. The discussion is carried out in terms of the representative individual, the private firm, and the social institution of each commons, to be generically denoted by ν.

For each commons ν, the economic welfare is represented by the utility function

$$u^\nu = u^\nu\big(c^\nu, \varphi^\nu(a)a_c^\nu\big),$$

where a is the total amount of services of social common capital used by all members of the society:

$$a = \sum_\nu a^\nu, \quad a^\nu = a_c^\nu + a_p^\nu \quad (\nu \in N).$$

For each commons ν, a^ν denotes the amounts of services of social common capital used by commons ν, whereas a_c^ν and a_p^ν are the amounts of services of social common capital, respectively, used by the representative individual and the private firm of commons ν, and $\varphi^\nu(a)$ is the impact index function of social common capital in commons ν.

Social common capital taxes with the rate τ are levied on the use of services of social common capital. Market equilibrium is obtained if we find the vector of prices of produced goods p, the prices charged for the use of services of social common capital θ, and the prices paid for the provision of services of social common capital π such that demand and supply are equal for all goods and the total provision of services of social common capital is equal to the total use of services of social common capital. The prices charged for the use of services of social common capital θ are higher, by the tax rates $\tau\theta$, than the prices paid for the provision of services of social common capital π; that is,

$$\theta - \pi = \tau\theta, \quad \tau = \tau(a)a.$$

Then market equilibrium obtained under such a social common capital tax scheme is a social optimum in the sense that a set of positive weights for the utilities of the commons $(\alpha^1, \dots, \alpha^n)$ exists such that the social utility

$$U = \sum_{\nu \in N} \alpha^\nu u^\nu(c^\nu, \varphi^\nu(a) a_c^\nu)$$

is maximized among all feasible patterns of allocation.

The Cooperative Game for the Commons Model of Social Common Capital

The commons model of social common capital introduced in Chapter 4 is regarded as a cooperative game, and the conditions under which the core of the cooperative game is nonempty are examined.

The players of the cooperative game for the commons model of social common capital are the commons in the society. Each commons may choose as a strategy a combination of the vector of goods consumed, the vector of goods produced, and the amount of services of social common capital used by the commons. The payoff for each commons is simply the utility of the representative individual of the commons.

A coalition for the social common capital game is any group of the commons, and the value of each coalition is the maximum of the sum of the utilities of the commons in the coalition on the assumption that those commons not belonging to the coalition form their own coalition and try to maximize the sum of their utilities.

The core of the cooperative game for the commons model of social common capital consists of those allotments of the value of the game among the commons that no coalition can block. On the assumption that the standard neoclassical conditions for utility functions and production possibility sets are satisfied, we examine the conditions under which the core of the social common capital game is nonempty.

Two coalitions, S and $N - S$, are in equilibrium if the total amount a_{N-S} of services of social common capital used by the commons belonging to the complementary coalition $N - S$ that the commons belonging to coalition S take as given is exactly equal to the total amount a_{N-S} of services of social common capital actually used by the commons belonging to coalition $N - S$, and vice versa.

Let $G = (N, v(S))$ be the cooperative game associated with the commons model of social common capital game. Then the core of cooperative game $G = (N, v(S))$ is nonempty if the following condition is satisfied:

$$\frac{a_S(S)}{a(S)} = \frac{a_S(N)}{a(N)} \quad \text{for all } S \subset N.$$

For any coalition S, $(S \subset N)$, the value $v(S)$ of the cooperative game associated with $G(N, v(S))$ is defined as the sum of the utilities of the commons belonging to coalition S when coalition S and its complementary $N - S$ are balanced. Then, the core of the cooperative game associated with the commons model of social common capital $G(N, v(S))$ is always nonempty.

5. ENERGY AND RECYCLING OF RESIDUAL WASTES

In Chapter 5, a model of social common capital is introduced in which the energy use and recycling of residual waste are explicitly taken into consideration and the optimal arrangements concerning the pricing of energy and recycling of residual wastes are examined in terms of the prototype model of social common capital introduced in Chapter 2.

In the model of social common capital introduced in Chapter 5, we consider a particular type of social institution that is specialized in reprocessing disposed residual wastes and converting them to raw materials to be used as inputs for the production processes of energy-producing firms.

Services of social common capital are subject to the phenomenon of congestion, resulting in the divergence between private and social costs. Therefore, to obtain efficient allocation of scarce resources, it becomes necessary to levy taxes on the disposal of residual wastes and to pay subsidy payments for the reprocessing of disposed residual wastes. Subsidy payments are made to the social institutions specialized in the recycling of disposed residual wastes based on the imputed price of the disposed residual wastes, whereas members of the society are charged taxes for the disposal of residual wastes at exactly the same rate as the subsidy payments made to social institutions in charge of the recycling of residual wastes.

There are two types of private firms: those specialized in producing goods that are transacted on the market, on the one hand, and those that are engaged in the production of energy, on the other. The residual wastes that are disposed of in the processes of consumption and production activities by members of the society are partly recycled by social institutions in charge of social common capital and converted into the raw materials to be used for energy production.

Social common capital taxes are charged for the disposal of residual wastes, with the rates to be administratively determined by the government and announced prior to the opening of the market. Social institutions in charge of social common capital recycle the residual wastes disposed of by members of the society and convert them to the raw materials that are used in the processes of energy production. Subsidy payments are made to social institutions for the recycling of residual wastes, at the rates exactly equal to the tax rates charged on the disposal of residual wastes. The raw materials produced by social institutions in charge of the recycling of residual wastes are sold, on a competitive market, to private firms engaged in the production of energy.

The extent to which the quality of the environment is diminished by the accumulation of residual wastes may be expressed by the postulate that utility level u^ν of each individual ν is a decreasing function of the accumulation of residual wastes W:

$$u^\nu = \phi^\nu(W)u^\nu(c^\nu, b^\nu, a^\nu),$$

where c^ν is the vector of goods consumed, b^ν is the amount of energy used, and a^ν denotes the amount of residual wastes disposed of by individual ν.

The impact coefficient of the disposal of residual wastes, $\tau^\nu(W)$, is given by

$$\tau^\nu(W) = -\frac{\phi^{\nu\prime}(W)}{\phi^\nu(W)}.$$

As in the case of the prototype model of social common capital, we assume that the impact coefficients $\tau^\nu(W)$ are identical for all individuals:

$$\tau^\nu(W) = \tau(W) \quad \text{for all } \nu.$$

We consider the social common capital tax scheme with the rate θ for the disposal of residual wastes in the energy-recycling model of social common capital:

$$\theta = \frac{\tau(W)y}{\delta},$$

where $\tau(W)$ is the impact coefficient of the disposal of residual wastes, y is the national income at the market equilibrium, and δ is the social rate of discount. Then market equilibrium obtained under such a social common capital tax scheme is a social optimum with respect to the given net level of the total disposal of residual wastes a; that is, the social utility

$$U = \sum_{\nu} \alpha^{\nu} \phi^{\nu}(W) u^{\nu}(c^{\nu}, b^{\nu}, a^{\nu})$$

is maximized among all feasible patterns of allocation, where utility weight α^{ν} is the inverse of marginal utility of income of individual ν at the market equilibrium and a is the given net level of the total disposal of residual wastes at the market equilibrium.

We consider the adjustment process with respect to the social common capital tax rate θ defined by the following differential equation:

$$\dot{\theta} = k\left[\frac{\tau(W)y}{\delta} - \theta\right], \tag{A}$$

with initial condition θ_0, where k is an arbitrarily given positive speed of adjustment.

The adjustment process defined by differential equation (A) is globally stable; that is, for any initial condition θ_0, the solution path θ to differential equation (A) converges to the optimum tax rate $\frac{\tau(W)y}{\delta}$.

6. AGRICULTURE AND SOCIAL COMMON CAPITAL

In Chapter 6, we formulate an agrarian model of social common capital and examine the conditions for the sustainable development of social common capital and privately owned scarce resources.

We consider a society that consists of two sectors: the agricultural sector and the industrial sector. The agricultural sector consists of a finite number of villages, each located around a forest and composed of a finite number of farmers engaged in the maintenance of the forest and agricultural activities. The forest of each village is regarded as social common capital and managed as common property resources. The resources of the forest are used by farmers in the village for agricultural activities, primarily for the production of food and other necessities. The forests of the agricultural sector also play an important role in the maintenance of a decent and cultural environment. The industrial sector consists of a finite number of private firms, each engaged in the production of industrial goods that are either consumed by individuals of the society or used by the agricultural and industrial sectors in the processes of production activities.

Subsidy payments are made by the central government to the villages for the maintenance and preservation of the forests of the villages. Social common capital taxes are levied by each village to the farmers in the village for the use of natural resources from the forest of the village. Social common capital subsidy and tax rates are administratively determined by either the central government or the villages and are announced prior to the opening of the market.

Subsidy payments at the rate τ are made by the central government to the villages for the reforestation of the forests, whereas in each village σ, social common capital taxes at the rate θ^σ are charged to the depletion of resources in the forest of village σ, where θ^σ is equal to the imputed price of resources in the forest of village σ, as given by

$$\theta^\sigma = \psi^\sigma + \theta^\sigma \tau^\sigma \left(\frac{a^\sigma}{V^\sigma}\right) \frac{a^\sigma}{V^\sigma},$$

and ψ^σ is the imputed price of the stock of natural capital in the forest of village σ, as given by

$$\psi^\sigma = \frac{1}{\delta}\left[\tau + \psi^\sigma \gamma^{\sigma\prime}(V^\sigma) + \theta^\sigma \tau^\sigma \left(\frac{a^\sigma}{V^\sigma}\right)\left(\frac{a^\sigma}{V^\sigma}\right)^2\right].$$

Then market equilibrium obtained under such a social common capital tax scheme is a social optimum in the sense that a set of positive weights for the utilities of individuals $(\alpha^1, \ldots, \alpha^n)$ $[\alpha^\nu > 0]$ exists such that the imputed social utility U^* given by

$$U^* = \sum_\nu \alpha^\nu \phi^\nu(V) u^\nu(c^\nu, b^\nu) + \psi^\sigma[\gamma^\sigma(V^\sigma) + z^\sigma - a^\sigma]$$

is maximized among all feasible patterns of allocation.

The rate of change in the stock of natural capital in the forest of each village σ, V^σ, is given by

$$\dot{V}^\sigma = \gamma^\sigma(V^\sigma) + z^\sigma - a^\sigma,$$

where $\gamma^\sigma(V^\sigma)$ is the ecological rate of increase in the stock of natural capital, z^σ is the investment in the stock of natural capital, and a^σ is the stock of natural capital depleted by the agricultural activities of the farmers in village σ.

Then market equilibrium obtained under such a social common capital subsidy and tax scheme induces a sustainable time-path of patterns of resource allocation if, and only if,

$$\tau = \tau(V)y,$$

where $\tau(V)$ is the impact coefficient of the welfare effect of forests and V is the total stock of natural capital in the forests of the villages.

Suppose a pattern of allocation is a social optimum; that is, a set of positive weights for the utilities of individuals $(\alpha^1, \ldots, \alpha^n)$ exists such that the given pattern of allocation maximizes the imputed social utility

$$U^* = \sum_\nu \alpha^\nu \phi^\nu(V) u^\nu(c^\nu, b^\nu) + \psi^\sigma[\gamma^\sigma(V^\sigma) + z^\sigma - a^\sigma]$$

among all feasible patterns of allocation.

Then, a system of income transfer among individuals of the society $\{t^\nu\}$ exists such that

$$\sum_\nu t^\nu = 0,$$

and the given pattern of allocation corresponds precisely to the market equilibrium under the social common capital tax scheme with the rate τ given by

$$\tau = \tau(V)y,$$

where $\tau(V)$ is the impact coefficient of the welfare effect of forests and V is the total stock of natural capital in the forests of the villages.

Market equilibrium obtained under such a social common capital tax scheme is a Lindahl equilibrium if, and only if, income of individual ν, y^ν, is proportional to the virtual ownership of the forests of the villages,

$$\frac{y^\nu}{y} = \frac{V^\nu}{V},$$

where, for each individual ν, V^ν is the virtual ownership of the forests of the villages in the agricultural sector of the economy,

$$V^\nu = \sum_\sigma s^{\nu\sigma} V^\sigma,$$

where $\{s^{\nu\sigma}\}$ are the shares of forests in the villages owned by individual ν,

$$s^{\nu\sigma} \geqq 0, \quad \sum_\nu s^{\nu\sigma} = 1.$$

An adjustment process with respect to the social common capital subsidy rate τ is defined by the differential equation

$$\text{(A)} \qquad \dot{\tau} = k[\tau(V)y - \tau],$$

where the speed of adjustment k is a positive constant and all variables refer to the state of the economy at the market equilibrium with the social common capital subsidy rate τ.

Then differential equation (A) is globally stable; that is, for any initial condition τ_0, the solution path to differential equation (A) converges to the stationary state.

7. GLOBAL WARMING AND SUSTAINABLE DEVELOPMENT

In Chapter 7, we are primarily concerned with the economic analysis of global warming within the theoretical framework of dynamic analysis of global warming, as introduced in Uzawa (1991b, 2003). In the first part of Chapter 7, we consider the case in which the oceans are the only reservoir of carbon dioxide on the earth, whereas in the second part, we explicitly take into consideration the role of the terrestrial forests in moderating processes of global warming by absorbing the atmospheric accumulation of CO_2, on the one hand, and in affecting the level of the welfare of people in the society by providing a decent and cultural environment, on the other.

The change in the atmospheric level of CO_2, V, is given by

$$\dot{V} = a - \mu V,$$

where a is the annual rate of increase in the atmospheric level of CO_2 owing to anthropogenic activities and μ is the amount of atmospheric CO_2 annually absorbed by the oceans. The rate of anthropogenic change in the atmospheric level of CO_2, a, is determined by the combustion of fossil fuels and is closely related to the levels of production and consumption activities conducted during the year observed.

The utility function for each country ν is expressed in the following manner:

$$u^\nu = \varphi^\nu(V)u^\nu\left(c^\nu, a_c^\nu\right),$$

where c^ν is the vector of goods consumed in country ν, a_c^ν is the amount of CO_2 emissions released during the processes of consumption, and V is the atmospheric concentration of CO_2.

The impact coefficient of global warming for country ν is the relative rate of the marginal change in the impact index due to the marginal increase in the atmospheric accumulation of CO_2:

$$\tau^\nu(V) = -\frac{\phi^{\nu\prime}(V)}{\phi^\nu(V)}.$$

We assume that the impact coefficients of global warming $\tau^\nu(V)$ are identical for all countries ν:

$$\tau^\nu(V) = \tau(V).$$

Deferential equilibrium is obtained if, when each country chooses the levels of consumption production activities today, it takes into account the negative impact on the future levels of its own utilities brought about by the CO_2 emissions of that country today.

Consider the situation in which a combination (x^ν, a^ν) of production vector and CO_2 emissions is chosen in country ν. Deferential equilibrium is obtained if this marginal decrease in country ν's future utility due to the marginal increase in CO_2 emissions today in country ν is taken into consideration in determining the levels of consumption, production, and CO_2 emissions today. Deferential equilibrium corresponds precisely to the standard market equilibrium under the system of carbon taxes, where in each country ν, the carbon taxes are levied with the rate θ^ν that is proportional to the national income y^ν

of each country ν:

$$\theta^{\nu} = \frac{\tau(V)}{\delta + \mu} y^{\nu},$$

where δ is the rate of utility discount.

The sustainable time-path of development with respect to global warming is obtained if, and only if, deferential equilibrium is obtained at each moment in time.

We next consider the uniform carbon tax scheme, where the rate θ is given by

$$\theta = \frac{\tau(V)}{\delta + \mu} y, \quad y = \sum_{\nu} y^{\nu}.$$

The process of the atmospheric accumulation of CO_2 with the uniform carbon tax rate $\theta = \frac{\tau(V)}{\delta + \mu} y$ is dynamically stable. That is, solution paths for the dynamic equation

$$\dot{V} = a - \mu V,$$

where a is the level of total emissions of CO_2 at time t, always converge to the stationary level V_* to be given by the stationarity condition

$$a_* = \mu V_*,$$

where a_* is the total CO_2 emissions at the market equilibrium under the uniform carbon tax scheme with the atmospheric concentrations of CO_2 at the level V_*.

Global Warming and Forests

Terrestrial forests are regarded as social common capital and are managed by social institutions with an organizational structure similar to that of private enterprise, except for the manner in which prices of the forests themselves and products from the forests are determined. The amount of atmospheric CO_2 absorbed by the terrestrial forest per hectare in each country ν is a certain constant on the average to be denoted by $\gamma^{\nu} > 0$. Then the basic dynamic equation concerning the change in the atmospheric concentrations of carbon dioxide V may be given by

$$\dot{V} = a - \mu V - \sum_{\nu} \gamma^{\nu} R^{\nu},$$

where a denotes the total CO_2 emissions in the world, μ is the rate at which atmospheric carbon dioxide is absorbed by the oceans, and R^ν is the acreage of terrestrial forests of country ν.

We denote by z^ν the acreages of terrestrial forests annually reforested and by b^ν the acreages of terrestrial forests in country ν annually lost as a result of economic activities. Then the acreage of terrestrial forests R^ν in each country ν is subject to the following dynamic equations:

$$\dot{R}^\nu = z^\nu - b^\nu.$$

The utility function for each country ν is expressed in the following manner:

$$u^\nu\left(c^\nu, a_c^\nu, R^\nu, V\right) = \phi^\nu(V)\varphi^\nu(R^\nu)u^\nu\left(c^\nu, a_c^\nu\right),$$

where c^ν is the vector of goods consumed in country ν, a_c^ν is the amount of CO_2 emitted by the consumers in country ν, R^ν is the acreage of terrestrial forests in country ν, and V is the atmospheric concentration of CO_2 accumulated in the atmosphere. The impact coefficients of global warming $\tau^\nu(V)$ are assumed to be identical for all countries ν:

$$\tau^\nu(V) = \tau(V).$$

Deferential equilibrium corresponds precisely to the standard market equilibrium under the following system of proportional carbon taxes for the emission of CO_2 and tax subsidy measures for the reforestation and depletion of resources of the forests:

(i) In each country ν, the carbon taxes are levied with the tax rate θ^ν to be given by

$$\theta^\nu = \frac{\tau(V)}{\delta + \mu} y^\nu.$$

(ii) In each country ν, tax subsidy arrangements are made for the reforestation and depletion of resources of forests with the rate π^ν that is proportional to the national income y^ν, to be given by

$$\pi^\nu = \frac{1}{\delta}\left[\tau^\nu(R^\nu) + \gamma^\nu \frac{\tau(V)}{\delta + \mu}\right] y^\nu,$$

where $\tau^\nu(R^\nu)$ is the impact coefficient of forests of country ν.

Consider the uniform carbon tax scheme with the same rate θ everywhere in the world, where the rate θ is given by

$$\theta = \frac{\tau(V)}{\delta + \mu} y, \quad y = \sum_\nu y^\nu.$$

Then the market equilibrium obtained under such a uniform carbon tax scheme is a social optimum in the sense that there exists a set of positive weights for the utilities of individual countries $(\alpha^1, \ldots, \alpha^n)$ such that the net level of world utility defined by

$$U_* = \sum_\nu \alpha^\nu \phi^\nu(V) \varphi^\nu(R^\nu) u^\nu(c^\nu, a_c^\nu) + \sum_\nu \pi^\nu (z^\nu - b^\nu) - \psi a$$

is maximized among all feasible patterns of allocation, where π^ν is the imputed price of forests in country ν and ψ is the imputed price of the atmospheric concentrations of CO_2, respectively, to be given by

$$\pi^\nu = \frac{1}{\delta}\left[\tau^\nu(R^\nu) + \gamma^\nu \frac{\tau(V)}{\delta + \mu}\right] y^\nu$$

$$\psi = \frac{\tau(V)}{\delta + \mu} y.$$

Then the imputed price ψ of the atmospheric concentration of CO_2 is equal to carbon tax rate θ:

$$\psi = \theta.$$

8. EDUCATION AS SOCIAL COMMON CAPITAL

In Chapter 8, we examine the role of education as social common capital within the analytical framework as introduced in Chapter 2. In describing the behavior of educational institutions, we occasionally use the term profit maximization, in the sense that the efficient and optimum pattern of resource allocation in the provision of education is sought, strictly in accordance with professional discipline and ethics.

The effect of education is twofold: private and social. First, regarding the private effect of education, the ability of the labor of each individual as a factor of production is increased by the level of education he or she attains. Second, regarding the social effect of education, an increase in the general level of education enhances an increase in the level of social welfare, whatever the measure taken.

The private effect of education may be expressed by the hypothesis that the ability of labor of each individual ν as a factor of production is given by

$$\varphi^{\nu}(a^{\nu})\ell^{\nu},$$

where ℓ^{ν} is the amount of labor provided by individual ν and $\varphi^{\nu}(a^{\nu})$ expresses the extent to which the ability of labor of individual ν as a factor of production is affected by the level of education a^{ν} he or she attains.

The impact coefficient of education $\tau^{\nu}(a^{\nu})$ for each individual ν is the relative rate of the marginal increase in the impact index of education due to the marginal increase in the level of education:

$$\tau^{\nu}(a^{\nu}) = \frac{\varphi^{\nu\prime}(a^{\nu})}{\varphi^{\nu}(a^{\nu})}.$$

The social effect of education may be expressed by the hypothesis that an increase in the general level of education induces an increase in the utility of every individual in the society; that is, the utility of each individual ν is given by

$$\phi^{\nu}(a)u^{\nu}(c^{\nu}),$$

where the general level of education a is the aggregate sum of the levels of education of all individuals in the society:

$$a = \sum_{\nu} a^{\nu}.$$

The function $\phi^{\nu}(a)$ specifies the extent of the social effect of education, depending upon the general level of education a of the society, to be referred to as the impact index of the general level of education for individual ν. The impact coefficient of the general level of education $\tau^{\nu}(a)$ is assumed to be identical for all individuals:

$$\tau^{\nu}(a) = \tau(a).$$

Consider the subsidy scheme to social institutions in charge of education at the rate τ given by

$$\tau = \tau(a)pc, \quad c = \sum_{\nu} c^{\nu},$$

where $\tau(a)$ is the impact coefficient of general education and c is aggregate consumption. Tax payments $\{t^\nu\}$ of individuals are arranged so that the balance-of-budget conditions are satisfied:

$$\sum_\nu t^\nu = \tau a.$$

Then market equilibrium obtained under such a subsidy scheme is a social optimum in the sense that a set of positive weights for the utilities of individuals $(\alpha^1, \ldots, \alpha^n)$ exists such that the social utility

$$U = \sum_\nu \alpha^\nu \phi^\nu(a)\varphi^\nu(a^\nu)u^\nu(c^\nu)$$

is maximized among all feasible allocations.

On the other hand, if a pattern of allocation is a social optimum, then a system of individual tax rates $\{t^\nu\}$ satisfying the balance-of-budget conditions

$$\sum_\nu t^\nu = \tau a, \quad \tau = \tau(a)pc$$

exists such that the given pattern of allocation corresponds precisely to the market equilibrium under the subsidy scheme to social institutions in charge of education at the rate τ given by $\tau = \tau(a)pc$.

We consider the subsidy scheme to social institutions in charge of education at the rate τ given by

$$\tau = \tau(a)pc, \quad c = \sum_\nu c^\nu,$$

where $\tau(a)$ is the impact coefficient of the general level of education and c is aggregate consumption. Then market equilibrium under such a subsidy scheme is Lindahl equilibrium if, and only if, the following conditions are satisfied:

$$\frac{a^\nu}{a} = \frac{pc^\nu}{pc},$$

where a^ν is the level of education attained by individual ν and a is the general level of education.

An adjustment process is defined by the following differential equation:

$$\text{(A)} \qquad \dot{\tau} = k[\tau(a)pc - \tau],$$

with a positive speed of adjustment k as a positive constant, where all variables refer to the state of the economy at the market equilibrium under the subsidy scheme with the rate τ:

$$\pi - \theta = \tau.$$

The differential equation (A) is globally stable; that is, for any initial condition a_0, the solution path to differential equation (A) converges to the stationary level a, where

$$\tau = \tau(a)pc.$$

9. MEDICAL CARE AS SOCIAL COMMON CAPITAL

When medical care is regarded as social common capital, every member of the society is entitled, as a basic, human right, to receive the best available medical care that the society can provide, regardless of the economic, social, and regional circumstances, even though this does not necessarily imply that medical care is provided free of charge. The government then is required to compose the overall plan that would result in the management of the medical care component of social common capital that is socially optimum. This plan includes the regional distribution of various types of medical institutions and the schooling system to train physicians, nurses, technical experts, and other co-medical staff to meet the demand for medical care. The government is then required to devise institutional and financial arrangements under which the construction and maintenance of the necessary medical institutions are realized and the required number of medical professionals are trained without social or bureaucratic coercion. It should be emphasized that all medical institutions and schools basically are private and subject to strict professional discipline and their management is supervised by qualified medical professionals.

The fees for medical care then are determined based on the principle of marginal social cost pricing. It may be noted that the smaller the capacity of the medical component of social common capital, the higher the fees charged to various types of medical care services. Hence, in composing the overall plan for the medical care component of social common capital, we must explicitly take into account the relationships between the capacity of the medical care component of social common capital and the imputed prices of medical care services. The socially optimum plan for the medical care component of social common capital then is one in which the resulting system of imputed prices of various types of medical care services leads to the allocation of scarce resources, privately appropriated or otherwise, and the accompanying distribution of real income that are socially optimum.

Under such utopian presuppositions, total expenditures for the construction and maintenance of the socially optimum medical care component of social common capital then exceed, generally by a large amount, the total fees paid by the patients under the principle of marginal social cost pricing. The resulting pattern of resource allocation and real income distribution, however, is optimum from the social point of view. The magnitude of the deficits with respect to the management of the socially optimum medical care component of social common capital then may appropriately be regarded as an index to measure the relative importance of medical care from the social point of view.

The effect of medical care is twofold: private and social. First, regarding the private effect of medical care, the ability of labor of each individual as a factor of production is increased by the level of medical care he or she receives. At the same time, the level of medical care each individual receives has a decisive impact on the level of well-being of each individual. Second, regarding the social effect of medical services, an increase in the general level of medical services enhances an increase in the level of the social welfare, whatever measure is taken.

The private effect of medical care may be expressed by the hypothesis that the ability of labor of each individual ν as a factor of production is given by

$$\varphi^{\nu}(a^{\nu})\ell^{\nu},$$

where ℓ^{ν} is the amount of labor provided by individual ν and $\varphi^{\nu}(a^{\nu})$ is the impact index of medical care on the labor of individual ν as a factor of production.

As for the second private effect of medical care, the increase in the general level of well-being of each individual ν is expressed by the hypothesis that the level of utility of individual ν is expressed in the following form:

$$u^\nu = \phi^\nu(a)u^\nu(c^\nu),$$

where $\phi^\nu(a)$ is the impact index of the general level of medical care for individual ν.

We assume that the impact coefficient of the general level of medical care $\tau^\nu(a)$ is identical for all individuals; that is,

$$\tau^\nu(a) = \tau(a) \quad \text{for all } \nu.$$

Consider the subsidy scheme to social institutions in charge of medical care at the rate τ given by

$$\tau = \tau(a)pc,$$

where $\tau(a)$ is the impact coefficient of the general level of medical care and c is aggregate consumption $[c = \sum_\nu c^\nu]$. Tax payments for individuals $\{t^\nu\}$ are arranged so that the balance-of-budget conditions are satisfied:

$$\sum_\nu t^\nu = \tau a.$$

Then market equilibrium obtained under such a subsidy scheme is a social optimum in the sense that a set of positive weights for the utilities of individuals $(\alpha^1, \ldots, \alpha^n)$ exists such that the social utility

$$U = \sum_\nu \alpha^\nu \phi^\nu(a)\varphi^\nu(a^\nu)u^\nu(c^\nu)$$

is maximized among all feasible allocations.

We consider the case in which only one kind of medical care exists and the subsidy scheme to social institutions in charge of medical services at the rate τ given by

$$\tau = \tau(a)pc, \quad c = \sum_\nu c^\nu,$$

where $\tau(a)$ is the impact coefficient of the general level of medical care.

Then market equilibrium under such a subsidy scheme is Lindahl equilibrium if, and only if, the following conditions are satisfied:

$$\frac{a^\nu}{a} = \frac{pc^\nu}{pc},$$

where a^ν is the level of medical services received by individual ν and a is the general level of medical services.

We consider the adjustment process defined by the following differential equation:

$$\text{(A)} \qquad \dot{\tau} = k[\tau(a)pc - \tau],$$

where the speed of adjustment k is a positive constant, and all variables refer to the state of the economy at the market equilibrium under the subsidy scheme with the rate τ:

$$\pi - \theta = \tau.$$

Then differential equation (A) is globally stable; that is, for any initial subsidy rate τ_0, the solution path to differential equation (A) converges to the stationary state, where

$$\tau = \tau(a)pc.$$

References

Aghion, P., and Howitt, P. (1992). "A Model of Growth through Creative Destruction," *Econometrica*, **60**, 323–352.

Arrow, K. J. (1962a). "Optimal Capital Adjustment" in K. J. Arrow, S. Karlin, and H. Scarf (eds.), *Studies in Applied Probability and Management Science*, Stanford: Stanford University Press.

Arrow, K. J. (1962b). "The Economic Implications of Learning by Doing," *Review of Economic Studies*, **29**, 155–173.

Arrow, K. J. (1965). "Criteria for Social Investment," *Water Resources Research*, **1**, 1–8.

Arrow, K. J. (1968). "Optimal Capital Policy with Irreversible Investment," in J. N. Wolfe (ed.), *Value, Capital and Growth: Papers in Honour of Sir John Hicks*, Edinburgh: Edinburgh University Press.

Arrow, K. J. (2000). "Observation on Social Capital," in P. Dasgupta and I. Serageldin (eds.), *Social Capital: A Multi-Faceted Perspective*, Washington, DC: World Bank.

Arrow, K. J., Hurwicz, L., and Uzawa, H. (1958). *Studies in Linear and Non-linear Programming*, Stanford: Stanford University Press.

Arrow, K. J., and Kurz, M. (1970). *Public Investment, Rate of Return, and Optimal Fiscal Policy*, Baltimore: Johns Hopkins University Press.

Aumann, R. J. (1989). *Lectures on Game Theory*, Boulder, CO: Westview Press.

Barrett, S. (1994). "The Self-Enforcing International Environmental Agreements," *Oxford Economic Papers*, **46**, 878–894.

Berkes, F. (ed.) (1989). *Common Property Resources: Ecology and Community-Based Sustainable Development*, London: Balhaven Press.

Bondareva, O. N. (1962). "The Theory of Core in an *n*-Person Game," *Bulletin of Leningrad University*, Mathematics, Mechanics, and Astronomy Series, **13**, 141–142.

Bondareva, O. N. (1963). "Some Applications of Linear Programming Methods to the Theory of Cooperative Games," *Problemy Kybernikiti*, **10**, 119–139.

Bovenberg, A. L, and Smulders, E. (1995). "Environmental Quality and Pollution-Argumenting Technological Change in a Two-Sector Endogenous Growth Model," *Journal of Public Economics*, **57**, 369–391.

Bradford, D. F. (1975). "Constraints on Government Investment Opportunities and the Choice of Discount Rate," *American Economic Review*, **65**, 887–899.

Bromley, D. W. (1991). *Environment and Economy: Property Rights and Public Policy*, Oxford: David Blackwell.

Bromley, D. W. (ed.) (1995). *The Handbook of Environmental Economics*, Cambridge, MA: Blackwell.

Cass, D. (1965). "Optimum Economic Growth in an Aggregative Model of Capital Accumulation," *Review of Economic Studies*, **32**, 233–240.

Clark, C. W. (1973). "The Economics of Over-Exploitation," *Science*, **181**, 630–634.

Clark, C. W. (1990). *Mathematical Bioeconomics: The Optimal Management of Renewable Resources*, Second Edition, New York: John Wiley.

Clark, C. W., and Munro, G. R. (1975). "The Economics of Fishing and Modern Capital Theory," *Journal of Environmental Economics and Management*, **2**, 92–106.

Coase, R. H. (1960). "The Problem of Social Cost," *Journal of Law and Economics*, **3**, 1–44.

Cornes, R., and Sandler, T. (1983). "On Commons and Tragedies," *American Economic Review*, **73**, 787–792.

Cropper, M., and Portney, P. (1992). *Discounting Human Lives*, Washington, DC: Resources for the Future.

Crutchfield, J. A., and Zellner, A. (1962). *Economic Aspect of the Pacific Halibut Fishery*, US Government Printing Office, Washington, D.C.

Daly, H. E. (1977). *Steady State Economics: Economics of Biophysical Equilibrium and Moral Growth*, San Francisco: W. H. Freeman.

Daly, H. E. (1999). *Steady State Economics: Second Edition with New Essays*, Washington DC: Island Press.

d'Arge, R. C. (1971a). "Ethical and Economic System for Managing the Global Commons," in D. B. Botkin, F. Margriet, J. E. Caswell, J. E. Estes, and A. A. Orio (eds.), *Changing the World Environment*, New York: Academic Press.

d'Arge, R. C. (1971b). "Essays on Economic Growth and Environmental Quality," *Swedish Journal of Economics*, **11**, 25–41.

Dasgupta, P. (1982a). "Resource Depletion, R&D, and the Social Rate of Discount," in R. C. Lind, K. J. Arrow, and G. R. Corey (eds.), *Discounting for Time and Risk in Energy Policy*, Baltimore: Johns Hopkins University Press, 275–324.

Dasgupta, P. (1982b). *The Control of Resources*, Oxford, UK: Blackwell.

Dasgupta, P. (1993). *An Inquiry into Well-Being and Destitution*, Oxford, UK: Clarendon Press.

Dasgupta, P., and Heal, G. M. (1974). "The Optimal Depletion of Exhaustible Resources," *Review of Economic Studies*, **51**, 3–27.

Dasgupta, P., and Heal, G. M. (1979). *Economic Theory and Exhaustible Resources,* Cambridge, UK: Cambridge University Press.

Dasgupta, P., and Serageldin, I. (eds.). (2000). *Social Capital: A Multi-Faceted Perspective*, Washington, DC: World Bank.

Demsetz, H. (1967). "Toward a Theory of Property Rights," *American Economic Review*, **62**, 347–359.

Dyson, F., and Marland, G. (1979). "Technical Fixes for the Climatic Effects of CO_2," in W. P. Elliot and L. Machta (eds.), *Workshop on the Global Effects of Carbon Dioxide from Fossil Fuels*, Washington, DC: United States Department of Energy, 111–118.

Epstein, L. G. (1987). "A Simple Dynamic General Equilibrium Model," *Journal of Economic Theory*, **41**, 68–95.

Epstein, L. E., and Haynes, J. A. (1983). "The Rate of Time Preference and Dynamic Economic Analysis," *Journal of Political Economy*, **91**, 611–681.

Fabre-Sender, F. (1969). "Biens collectifs et biens équalité variable," *CEPREMAP*.

Foley, D. (1967). "Resource Allocation and the Public Sector," *Yale Economic Essays*, **7**, 43–98.

Foley, D. (1970). "Lindahl Solution and the Core of an Economy with Public Goods," *Econometrica*, **38**, 66–72.

Forster, B. A. (1973). "Optimal Capital Accumulation in a Polluted Environment," *Southern Economic Journal*, **39**, 544–547.

Furubotn, E. H., and Pejovich, S. (1972). "Property Rights and Economic Theory: A Survey of Recent Literature," *Journal of Economic Literature*, **10**, 1137–1162.

Godwin, R. K., and Shepard, W. B. (1979). "Forcing Squares, Triangles, and Ellipses into a Circular Paradigm: The Use of the Commons Dilemma in Examining the Allocation of Common Resources," *Western Political Quarterly*, **32**, 265–277.

Goldman, S. M., and Uzawa, H. (1964). "On the Separability in Demand Analysis," *Econometrica*, **32**, 387–399.

Gordon, H. S. (1954). "The Economic Theory of a Common Property Resources: The Fishery," *Journal of Political Economy*, **62**, 124–142.

Gradus, R., and Smulders, E. (1993). "The Trade-Off between Environmental Care and Long-Term Growth: Pollution in Three Prototype Growth Models," *Journal of Economics*, **58**, 25–51.

Grossman, G., and Helpman, E. (1991). *Innovation and Growth in the Global Economy,* Cambridge, MA: The MIT Press.

Hardin, G. (1968). "The Tragedy of the Commons," *Science*, **162**, 1243–1248.

Hirschman, A. O. (1958). *The Strategy of Economic Development*, New Haven: Yale University Press.

Hotelling, H. (1931). "The Economics of Exhaustible Resources," *Journal of Political Economy*, **39**, 137–175.

Howarth, R. B. (1991a). "Intergenerational Competitive Equilibria under Technological Uncertainty and an Exhaustible Resources Constraint," *Journal of Environmental Economics and Management*, **21**, 225–243.

Howarth, R. B. (1991b). "Intertemporal Equilibria and Exhaustible Resources: An Overlapping Generations Approach," *Ecological Economics*, **4**, 237–252.

Howarth, R. B., and Monahan, P. A. (1992). *Economics, Ethics, and Climate Policy*, Lawrence Berkeley Library, LBL-33230.

Howarth, R. B., and Norgaard, R. B. (1990). "Intergenerational Resource Rights, Efficiency, and Social Optimally," *Land Economics*, **66**, 1–11.

Howarth, R. B., and Norgaard, R. B. (1992). "Environmental Valuation under Sustainable Development," *American Economic Review*, **82**, 473–477.

Howarth, R. B., and Norgaard, R. B. (1995). "Intergenerational Choices under Global Environmental Changes," in D. B. Bromley (ed.), *The Handbook of Environmental Economics*, Oxford, UK: Blackwell, 112–138.

Huan, C-H., and Cai, D. (1994). "Constant Returns Endogenous Growth with Pollution Control," *Environmental and Resource Economics*, **4**, 383–400.

IPCC (1991a). *Scientific Assessment of Climate Change – Report of Working Group I*, Cambridge, UK: Cambridge University Press.

IPCC (1991b). *Impact Assessment of Climate Change – Report of Working Group II*, Cambridge, UK: Cambridge University Press.

IPCC (1992). *Supplementary Report to the IPCC Scientific Assessment,* edited by J. T. Houghton, B. A. Callander, and S. K. Varney, Cambridge, UK: Cambridge University Press.

IPCC (1996a). *Climate Change 1995: The Science of Climate,* Cambridge, UK: Cambridge University Press.

IPCC (1996b). *Climate Change 1995: Impacts, Adaptations and Mitigation of Climate Change: Scientific-Technical Analysis*, Cambridge, UK: Cambridge University Press.

IPCC (2000). *Land Use, Land-Use Change, and Forestry*, Cambridge, UK: Cambridge University Press.

IPCC (2001a). *Climate Change 2001: The Scientific Basis,* Cambridge, UK: Cambridge University Press.

IPCC (2001b). *Climate Change 2001: Impacts, Adaptations and Vulnerability*, Cambridge, UK: Cambridge University Press.

IPCC (2002). *Climate Change 2001: Synthesis Report*, Cambridge, UK: Cambridge University Press.

Johansen, L. (1963). "Some Notes on the Lindahl Theory of Determination of Public Expenditures," *International Economic Review*, **4**, 346–358.

Johansson, P.-O., and Löfgren, K.-G. (1985). *The Economics of Forestry and Natural Resources*, Oxford: Basil Blackwell.

John Paul II (1991). Encyclical Letter *Centesimus Annus*, Vatican City: Libreria Editorice Vaticana.

Kaneko, M. (1977). "The Ratio Equilibrium and a Voting Game in a Public Goods Economy," *Journal of Economic Theory*, **16**, 123–136.

Kannai, Y. (1992). "The Core and Balancedness," in R. J. Aumann and S. Hart (eds.), *Handbook of Game Theory I*, Amsterdam: Elsevier Science, 355–395.

Keeler, E., Spence, M., and Zeckhauser, R. (1971). "The Optimal Control of Pollution," *Journal of Economic Theory*, **4**, 19–34.

Keeling, C. D. (1968). "Carbon Dioxide in Surface Ocean Waters, 4: Global Distribution," *Journal of Geophysical Research*, **73**, 4543–4553.

Keeling, C. D. (1983). "The Global Carbon Cycle: What We Know from Atmospheric, Bio-Spheric, and Oceanic Observations," *Proceedings of Carbon Dioxide Research, Science and Consensus*, United States Department of Energy, Washington, DC, II, 3–62.

Koopmans, T. C. (1965). "On the Concept of Optimum Economic Growth," *Semaine d'Etude sur le Role de l'Analyse Econometrique dans la Formation de Plans de Development*, Pontificae Academemiae Scientiarium Seprita Varia, 225–287.

Krautkraemer, J. A. (1985). "Optimal Growth, Resource Amenities, and the Preservation of Natural Environments," *Review of Economic Studies*, **52**, 153–170.

Kurz, M. (1994). "Game Theory and Public Economics," in R. J. Aumann and S. Hart (eds.), *Handbook Game Theory II*, Amsterdam: Elsevier Science, 1153–1192.

Leo XIII (1891). Encyclical Letter *Rerum Novarum, Leonis XIII P. M. Acta, XI*, Romae 1892.

Lind, R. C. (1982a). "A Primer on Major Issues Relating to the Discount Rate for Evaluating National Energy Options," in R. C. Lind, K. J. Arrow, and G. R. Corey (eds.), *Discounting for Time and Risk in Energy Policy*, Baltimore: Johns Hopkins University Press, 275–324.

Lind, R. C. (1982b). "Intergenerational Equity, Discounting, and the Role of Cost-Benefit Analysis in Evaluating Global Climate Policy," *Energy Policy*, **23**, 379–389.

Lind, R. C., and Arrow, K. J. (1970). "Uncertainty and the Evaluation of Public Investment Decision," *American Economic Review*, **60**, 364–378.

Lindahl, E. (1919). Positive Lösung, die Gerechtigkeit der Besteurung, Lund. Translated in R. A. Musgrave and A. T. Peacock (eds.), *Classics in the Theory of Public Finance*, 1958.

Lloyd, W. F. (1833). "On the Checks to Population," reprinted in G. Hardin and J. Baden (eds.), *Managing the Commons*, San Francisco: W. H. Freeman, 1977, 8–15.

Lucas, R. E., Jr., and Stokey, N. L. (1984). "Optimal Growth with Many Consumers," *Journal of Economic Theory*, **32**, 139–171.

Mäler, K.-G. (1974). *Environmental Economics: A Theoretical Inquiry*, Baltimore: The Johns Hopkins University Press.

Mäler, K.-G., and Uzawa, H. (1994). "Tradable Emission Permits, Pareto Optimality, and Lindahl Equilibrium," The Beijer Institute Discussion Paper Series.

Malinvaud, E. (1971). "A Planning Approach to the Public Goods Problem," *Swedish Journal of Economics* **11**, 96–112.

Marland, G. (1988). *The Prospect of Solving the* CO_2 *Problem through Global Reforestation*, United States Department of Energy, Washington, DC.

Mas-Colell, A. (1980). *The Theory of General Economic Equilibrium: A Differentiable Approach*, New York: Cambridge University Press.

McCay, B. J., and Acheson, J. M. (eds.). (1987). *The Question of the Commons: The Culture and Economy of Communal Resources*, Tucson: The University of Arizona Press.

Mill, J. S. (1848). *Principles of Political Economy with Some of Their Applications to Social Philosophy,* New York, D. Appleton [5th edition, 1899].

Milleron, J.-C. (1972). "The Theory of Value with Public Goods: A Survey Article," *Journal of Economic Theory*, **5**, 419–477.

Musu, I. (1990). "A Note on Optimal Accumulation and the Control of Environmental Quality," *Revista Internationale di Scienze Economiche et Commerciali,* **37**, 193–202.

Musu, I. (1994). "On Sustainable Endogenous Growth," ENI Enrico Mattei Working Paper Series.

Myers, N. (1988). "Tropical Forests and Climate," referred to in United States Environmental Protection Agency, *Policy Options for Stabilizing Global Climate*, Washington, DC, 1989.

Norgaard, R. B. (1990a). "Economic Indicators of Resource Scarcity: A Critical Essay," *Journal of Environmental Economics and Management*, **19**, 19–25.

Norgaard, R. B. (1990b). *Sustainability and the Economics of Assuring Assets for Future Generations*, WPS 832, Washington, DC: World Bank.

Norton, B. G. (1989). "Intergenerational Equity and Environmental Decisions: A Model Using Rawls's Veil of Ignorance," *Ecological Economics*, **1**, 137–159.

Ostrom, E. (1992). *Governing the Commons*, Cambridge, UK: Cambridge University Press.

Ostrom, E., Gardner, R., and Walker, J. (1994). *Rules, Games and Common-Pool Resources*, Ann Arbor: University of Michigan Press.

Page, T. (1991). "On the Problem of Achieving Efficiency and Equity Intergenerationally," *Land Economics*, **73**, 580–596.
Page, T. (1997). "Sustainability and the Problem of Valuation," in R. Costanza (ed.), *Ecological Economics: The Science and Management of Sustainability*, New York: Columbia University Press, 58–74.
Penrose, T. E. (1959). *The Theory of the Growth of the Firm*. Oxford, UK: Blackwell.
Pezzey, J. (1992). "Sustainability: An Interdisciplinary Guide," *Environmental Values*, **1**, 321–362.
Pigou, A. C. (1925). *The Economics of Welfare*, London: Macmillan.
Putnam, R. (2000). *Bowling Alone: The Collapse and Revival of American Community*, New York: Simon and Schuster.
Ramanathan, V., Cicerone, R. J., Singh, H. B., and Kiehl, J. T. (1985). "Trace Gas Trends and Their Potential Role in Climate Change," *Journal of Geophysical Research*, **90**, 5547–5566.
Ramsey, F. P. (1928). "A Mathematical Theory of Saving," *Economic Journal*, **38**, 543–559.
Rawls, J. (1971). *A Theory of Justice*, Cambridge, MA: Harvard University Press.
Rebelo, S. T. (1993). "Transitional Dynamics and Economic Growth in the Neoclassical Model," *American Economic Review*, **83**, 903–931.
Roberts, D. J. (1974). "The Lindahl Solution for Economies with Public Goods," *Journal of Public Economics*, **3**, 23–42.
Roemer, P. M. (1986). "The Rate of Time Preference and Dynamic Economic Analysis," *Journal of Political Economy*, **91**, 611–681.
Samuelson, P. A. (1954). "The Pure Theory of Public Expenditures," *Review of Economics and Statistics*, **36**, 387–389.
Schaefer, M. B. (1957). "Some Considerations of Population Dynamics and Economics in Relation to the Management of Commercial Marine Fisheries," *Journal of the Fisheries Research Board of Canada*, **14**, 669–681.
Scott, A. D. (1955). "The Fishery: The Objectives of Sole Ownership," *Journal of Political Economy*, **63**, 116–124.
Sen, A. K. (1973). *On Economic Inequality*, Oxford, UK: Clarendon Press.
Sen, A. K. (1982). "Approaches to the Choice of Discount Rate for Social Benefit-Cost Analysis," in R. C. Lind, K. J. Arrow, and G. R. Corey (eds.), *Discounting for Time and Risk in Energy Policy*, Baltimore: Johns Hopkins University Press, 325–353.
Shapley, L. S. (1967). "On Balanced Sets and Cores," *Navel Research Logistics Quarterly*, **14**, 453–460.
Smith, A. (1776). *An Inquiry into the Nature and Causes of the Wealth of Nations* [The Modern Library Edition, New York: Random House, 1937].

Smith, M. E. (1984). "The Tragedy of the Commons," paper presented at the Annual Meeting of the Society for Applied Anthropology, Toronto.

Smulders, S. (1995). "Entropy, Environment, and Endogenous Economic Growth," *Journal of International Tax and Public Finance*, **2**, 317–338.

Smulders, S., and Gradus, R. (1996). "Pollution Abatement and Long-Term Growth," *European Journal of Political Economy*, **12**, 505–532.

Solow, R. M. (1974a). "Intergenerational Equity and Exhaustible Resources," *Review of Economic Studies*, **41**, 29–45.

Solow, R. M. (1974b). "The Economics of Resources, or the Resources of Economics," *American Economic Review*, **64**, 1–14.

Solow, R. M. (2000). "Note on Social Capital and Economic Performance," in Dasgupta, P., and Serageldin, I. (eds.), *Social Capital: A Multi-Faceted Perspective*, Washington, DC: World Bank.

Srinivasan, T. N. (1965). "Optimum Saving in a Two-Sector Growth Model," *Econometrica*, **32**, 358–373.

Stiglitz, J. E. (1982). "The Rate of Discount for Cost-Benefit Analysis and the Theory of Second Best," in R. C. Lind, K. J. Arrow, and G. R. Corey (eds.), *Discounting for Time and Risk in Energy Policy*, Baltimore: Johns Hopkins University Press, 151–204.

Stockfish, J. A. (1982). "Measuring the Social Rate of Return on Private Investment," in R. C. Lind, K. J. Arrow, and G. R. Corey (eds.), *Discounting for Time and Risk in Energy Policy*, Baltimore: Johns Hopkins University Press, 257–271.

Tahvonen, O. (1991). "On the Dynamics of Renewable Resource Harvesting and Population Control," *Environmental and Resource Economics*, **1**, 97–117.

Tahvonen, O., and Kuuluvainen, J. (1993). "Economic Growth, Pollution, and Renewable Resources," *Journal of Environmental Economics and Management*, **24**, 101–118.

Takahashi, T., Broeker, W. S., Werner, S. R., and Bainbridge, A. E. (1980). "Carbonate Chemistry of the Surface Waters of the World Oceans," in E. Goldberg, Y. Horibe, and K. Saruhashi (eds.), *Isotope Marine Chemistry*, Tokyo: Uchida Rokkakubo, 291–326.

Throsby, D. (2001). *Economics and Culture*, Cambridge, UK: Cambridge University Press.

Uzawa, H. (1961). "Neutral Inventions and the Stability of Growth Equilibrium," *The Review of Economic Studies*, **28**, 117–24.

Uzawa, H. (1962). "On a Two-Sector Model of Economic Growth," *Review of Economic Studies*, **14**, 40–7.

Uzawa, H. (1963). "On a Two-Sector Model of Economic Growth, II," *Review of Economic Studies*, **19**, 105–18.

Uzawa, H. (1964). "Optimal Growth in a Two-Sector Model of Capital Accumulation," *Review of Economic Studies*, **31**, 1–24.

Uzawa, H. (1968). "The Penrose Effect and Optimum Growth," *Economic Studies Quarterly*, **19**, 1–14.

Uzawa, H. (1969). "Time Preference and the Penrose Effect in a Two-Class Model of Economic Growth," *Journal of Political Economy*, **77**, 628–652.

Uzawa, H. (1974a). "Sur la théorie économique de capital collectif social," *Cahier du Séminaire d'Économetrie*, 103–22. Translated in *Preference, Production, and Capital: Selected Papers of Hirofumi Uzawa*, New York: Cambridge University Press, 1988, 340–362.

Uzawa, H. (1974b). "The Optimum Management of Social Overhead Capital," in J. Rothenberg and I. G. Heggie (eds.), *The Management of Water Quality and the Environment*, London: Macmillan, 3–17.

Uzawa, H. (1974c). *Social Costs of the Automobile* (in Japanese), Tokyo, Iwanami Shoten.

Uzawa, H. (1975). "Optimum Investment in Social Overhead Capital," in E. S. Mills (ed.), *Economic Analysis of Environmental Problems*, New York: Columbia University Press, 9–26.

Uzawa, H. (1982). "Social Stability and Collective Public Consumption," in R. C. O. Matthews and G. B. Stafford (eds.), *The Grants Economy and Public Consumption*, London: Macmillan, 23–37.

Uzawa, H. (1989). *A History of Economic Thought* (in Japanese), Tokyo: Iwanami Shoten.

Uzawa, H. (1991a). "*Rerum Novarum* Inverted: Abuses of Capitalism and Illusions of Socialism," *Rivista di Politica Economica*, **81**, 19–31.

Uzawa, H. (1991b). "Global Warming Initiatives: The Pacific Rim," in R. Dornbusch and J. M. Poterba (eds.), *Global Warming: Economic Policy Responses*, Cambridge, MA: MIT Press, 275–324.

Uzawa, H. (1992a). "Imputed Prices of Greenhouse Gases and Land Forests," *Renewable Energy* **3**, 499–511.

Uzawa, H. (1992b). "The Tragedy of Commons and the Theory of Social Overhead Capital," The Beijer Institute Discussion Paper Series.

Uzawa, H. (1992c). "Institutions, Development, and Environment," in Pontifical Council for Justice and Peace (ed.), *Social and Ethical Aspects of Economics: A Colloquium in the Vatican*, Vatican City, 129–43.

Uzawa, H. (1993). "Equity and Evaluation of Environmental Degradation," in D. Ghai and D. Westendorff (eds.), *Monitoring Social Development in the 1990s: Data Constraint, Concerns, and Priorities*, Avebury, UK: Aldershot.

Uzawa, H. (1996). "An Endogenous Rate of Time Preference, the Penrose Effect, and Dynamic Optimality of Environmental Quality," *Proceedings of the National Academy of Sciences of the United States of America*, **93**, 5770–5776.

Uzawa, H. (1997). "Lindahl Equilibrium and the Core of an Economy Involving Public Goods," The Beijer Institute Discussion Paper Series.

Uzawa, H. (1998). "Toward a General Theory of Social Overhead Capital," in G. Chichilnsky (ed.), *Markets, Information, and Uncertainty*, New York: Cambridge University Press, 253–304.

Uzawa, H. (1999). "Global Warming as a Cooperative Game," *Environmental Economics and Policy Studies*, **2**, 1–37.

Uzawa, H. (2003). *Economic Theory and Global Warming*, New York: Cambridge University Press.

Veblen, T. B. (1899). *The Theory of Leisure Class*, New York: Macmillan.

Veblen, T. B. (1904). *The Theory of Business Enterprise*, New York: Charles Scribners' Sons.

Wallace, L. (1993). "Discounting Our Descendants," *Finance and Development*, **30**, 2.

Weitzman, M. L. (1993). "On the Environmental Discount Rate," *Journal of Environmental Economics and Management*, **26**, 200–209.

Wicksell, K. (1901). *Föreläsningar i Nationalekonomi*, Häfte 1, Gleerups, Lund. Translated as *Lectures on Political Economy, Vol. I: General Theory*, edited by L. Robbins, London: George Routhledge, 1934.

Williamson, O. E. (1985), *The Economic Institutions of Capitalism: Firms, Markets, and Relational Contacting*, New York: Free Press.

World Resources Institute. (1991). *World Resources 1990–91*, New York: Oxford University Press.

World Resources Institute. (1996). *World Resources 1996–97*, New York: Oxford University Press.

Index